"Quick Picks"
—American Library Association/YALSA

"A Book for the Teen Age"
—New York Public Library

"Read, America!" Selection

"Commendable. This practical, do-it-for-yourself book encourages young people to see the importance of values in everyday life and challenges readers to cultivate their own positive character traits and to be open to new ones as well."
—*Youth Today*

# What Do You Stand For?

## A Kid's Guide to Building Character

Barbara A. Lewis

Edited by Pamela Espeland

free spirit
PUBLiSHiNG®

Works
for kids®

**Library of Congress Cataloging-in-Publication Data**
Lewis, Barbara A., 1943-
    What do you stand for? : a kid's guide to building character / by Barbara A. Lewis.
        p.   cm.
    Includes bibliographical references and index.
    Summary: Text, anecdotes, and activities direct the reader to explore and practice honesty, kindness, empathy, integrity, tolerance, and more.
    ISBN 1-57542-029-5
    1. Personality development—Juvenile literature. 2. Character—Juvenile literature. [1. Values. 2. Conduct of life.]
    I. Title.
    BF723.P4L49   1998
    170'.83—dc21
                            97-13952
                            CIP
                            AC

At the time of this book's publication, all facts and figures cited are the most current available; all telephone numbers, addresses, and Web site URLs are accurate and active; all publications, organizations, Web sites, and other resources exist as described in this book; and all have been verified as of June 2003. The author and Free Spirit Publishing make no warranty or guarantee concerning the information and materials given out by organizations or content found at Web sites, and we are not responsible for any changes that occur after this book's publication. If you find an error or believe that a resource listed here is not as described, please contact Free Spirit Publishing. Parents, teachers, and other adults: We strongly urge you to monitor children's use of the Internet.

The four reasons to be more tolerant on pages 144–145 are from *Respecting Our Differences: A Guide to Getting Along in a Changing World* by Lynn Duvall (Minneapolis: Free Spirit Publishing Inc., 1994). Used with permission of the publisher. The "Be a mediator" activity on page 178 and the "Steps for Mediation" on page 180 are reprinted with the permission of Educators for Social Responsibility © 1997 Educators for Social Responsibility, Cambridge, MA. Several of the "success stories that started out as failures" listed on pages 184–185 are from Dr. Milton E. Larson, "Humbling Cases for Career Counselors," *Phi Delta Kappan*, February 1973, vol. LIV, No. 6, p. 374. The goal-setting strategies and tips on pages 195–197 are adapted from *The Gifted Kids' Survival Guide: A Teen Handbook* by Judy Galbraith and Jim Delisle (Minneapolis: Free Spirit Publishing Inc., 1996). Used with permission of the publisher. The "ASSERT Formula" on page 218 is adapted from *Fighting Invisible Tigers: A Stress Management Guide for Teens* by Earl Hipp (Minneapolis: Free Spirit Publishing Inc., 1995), page 96. Used with permission of the publisher.

Photo credits: p. 19—Jerry Bryan; p. 20—Don Orcutt; p. 69—Cindy Reinitz; p. 93—Kylee Thomas, Columbus North Log Yearbook; p. 163—Mike McCleary, *Bismarck Tribune*.

Cover design by Circus Design
Book interior design by Julie Odland Smith
Illustrations by Jeff Tolbert
Index prepared by Eileen Quam and Theresa Wolner

20 19 18 17 16 15 14 13 12 11 10 9
Printed in the United States of America

**Free Spirit Publishing Inc.**
217 Fifth Avenue North, Suite 200
Minneapolis, MN 55401-1299
(612) 338-2068
help4kids@freespirit.com
*www.freespirit.com*

*To Pooker,*
*who has both demonstrated good character*
*and who is one.*

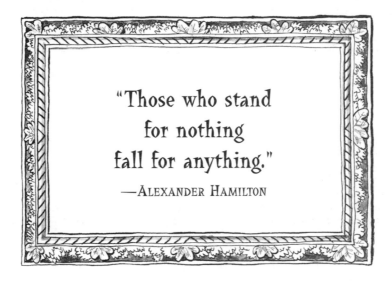

"Those who stand
for nothing
fall for anything."
—ALEXANDER HAMILTON

# Acknowledgments

First and foremost, my appreciation and love to Judy Galbraith, my intrepid, gifted publisher, and to all the staff at Free Spirit. It takes a whole publishing company to give birth to a book. And special thanks to Pamela Espeland, my diligent editor, safety net, and friend who blew the breath of life into this book.

I will always be indebted to Kristie Fink, Supervisor of Character Education, Utah State Office of Education, for editorial help and for living what character education means, and to the resourceful librarians who helped research books: Carolyn Campbell and Janelle Mattheus (Salt Lake County Library System), and Mary White and Pam Sadler (Salt Lake City Library System).

Thanks to the many people who helped me find stories and who also shared expertise: Renata Hron (Hitachi Foundation), Jackie Scott, Marc Chambers, Carol Reid, Donna Friedman, Carol Burnett, Indiana Chamber of Commerce, Bud Ellis, Tom Green, Emily Martinez, Pamela Bloom, U.S. Fencing Association, Trish Wade (musical theory), Vivian Meiers, Neva J. Pratico, Gloria Jones, A Pledge & A Promise Environmental Awards—Busch Theme Parks.

Gratitude to many individuals, organizations, offices, and agencies who shared information and contacts: U.S. Department of Justice, American Bar Association, and the Law Related Education group, Tom Oertel, University of Utah Law Library, Tracy Godwin (Teen Court), U.S. Patent & Trademark Office, U.S. Department of Health, U.S. Office of Management and Budget, U.S. Department of Health and Human Services, Red Cross, Care, NASA.

Thanks, too, to the many professional educators who helped with expertise and support: Character Education Partnership, Corporation for National Service, and Maryland Student Service Alliance.

# Contents

# List of Reproducible Pages

# Introduction

> "It's not our weaknesses that frighten us.
> It's our strengths."
> *Nelson Mandela*

**A**re you perfect? Don't worry; nobody is. In fact, it's likely that no two people could agree on what it means to be perfect.

Even though you're not perfect, you're still a unique and wonderful individual with many strong, positive character traits. And you may have other traits you haven't fully developed or even discovered yet.

If you could see how truly terrific you are, you might catch your breath. Like a dog who buries a bone so no other animals can find it, you might be hiding the true, marvelous you for fear of losing it, or fear of what other people might think or say. You might be afraid that you can't live up to the strengths you know (or suspect) you have, or the traits that other people want or expect you to have.

Positive character traits are something you can and should develop. There is a core group of character traits that every member of the human family needs to have. People don't always agree on which six or ten core traits these are. But most experts include traits like *love* or *caring, respect for life, honesty* or *trustworthiness, responsibility, justice,* and *fairness*. Worldwide, some people define character traits in terms of values and also include ideas like *freedom* and *unity*. You'll find many more positive character traits besides these in this book.

You can choose whether you want to eat chocolate or pistachio ice cream, whether you want to play the lute or lacrosse, and whether you want to be an electrician, brain surgeon, or lion tamer. You can choose whether to be friendly, happy, or grumpy (and either attract friends or drive them away). But in most cultures, you can't choose whether or not you want to be honest. You can't choose whether or not you value human life.

Whether or not you push your brakes at a stop light isn't optional, either.

Why? Because history has shown that societies tend to self-destruct when their people don't possess a core group of positive character traits. In the words of General Douglas MacArthur, "History fails to record a single precedent in which nations subject to moral decay have not passed into political and economic decline. There has been either a spiritual awakening to overcome the moral lapse, or a progressive deterioration leading to ultimate national disaster."

To put this more simply: Every nation that decays morally, without changing, faces disaster. Positive character traits are good for a nation, good for a family, and good for *you*.

If you suspect that you might have some weak or negative character traits, you probably do, but that's normal. Your weaknesses might actually be sleeping strengths. And negative traits, like bad habits, can be changed.

Developing positive character traits isn't something you do in a vacuum or totally on your own. Your traits are linked to your conscience, moral convictions, beliefs, personal experiences, upbringing, rights, and responsibilities; to your culture and its laws and expectations; and to your relationships with yourself, others, and the world. Many of your traits will probably coincide with the beliefs and practices of other people you admire and appreciate—people you see as role models. Developing positive character traits means that you respect yourself, others, and the world. You find value in your experiences so that life itself becomes your teacher.

The goal of this book is to help you understand yourself better, to figure out what you stand for— and what you won't stand for. Then you can be more confident and accepting of yourself and others. You can share your talents, abilities, skills, and interests.

In doing so, you can be a stronger, more complete and happier person.

# How to Use This Book

The ancient Greek philosophers recognized four main virtues: *temperance, justice, courage,* and *wisdom.* Socrates, Plato, and Aristotle believed that the virtues were connected, and you couldn't have one without having them all. Christian philosophers in the Middle Ages added *faith, hope,* and *charity.* The list of positive traits continues to grow—you could probably name several yourself—but most can be grouped into general categories. That's how this book is organized.

If you can't find a character trait you're looking for in the Contents, turn to the Index at the back, and you'll probably find it (or a related trait) there. For example, you won't find a chapter on "Assertiveness," but you will find that trait in the chapter on "Respect."

Each chapter begins with a quotation to help you start thinking about a particular character trait or group of traits. Background information, definitions, explanations of related terms, and other lore and knowledge about the trait help you to understand more about it.

Each chapter describes several dilemmas to use for journaling, writing essays, discussion, debate, role-playing, and/or reflection. The dilemmas usually don't have one right answer. Instead, they make you think. Sometimes they show a positive character trait "out of balance" with another positive trait that might have a higher principle. For example, can you think of a time when caring for others might come before telling the truth? Or when forgiveness might come before justice? Sometimes you might need to ask an adult how to help you weigh two traits and the consequences of putting one ahead of the other. Being human can be challenging! As you choose dilemmas to consider with your friends, family, club, faith community, or classmates, keep these basic guidelines in mind:

✔ As much as possible, clarify the facts and issues first.

✔ If you're exploring these dilemmas with others, do it in a safe, trusting atmosphere where all ideas are accepted.

✔ Piggyback on each other's ideas. Share insights, inspirations, and expertise.

✔ When you lead a discussion of a dilemma, be sure not to take sides or try to control or influence what other people think and say.

✔ It's okay to disagree, but without criticism, name-calling, insults, or offensive language. Those are not allowed.

✔ Remember that there often isn't only one right answer.

Each chapter suggests activities in various categories including language arts, science, technology, math, social studies, history, family studies, social action or service to others, the arts, popular culture, sports, and/or games. The activities help you to develop a character trait by connecting it with something you're learning in school; your interests; your learning styles; and/or your life at home, with your friends, in your neighborhood, and in your community. Some chapters include checklists, quizzes, and questionnaires that help you to think about, question, and clarify your own feelings and beliefs.

Each chapter (except "Getting to Know You") ends with an inspiring true story of someone who exemplifies that trait. You'll read about young people of different ages and ethnic origins, with varying beliefs, interests, and talents. Some of them did spectacular things, like Merrick Johnston, the youngest person to climb Mt. McKinley (see pages 77–78), or Winfred Rembert Jr., who risked his life to save his brother (see page 141). Some had less dramatic but equally important experiences, like Jana Benally, who told the truth (see pages 124–125).

Throughout, you'll find descriptions of other books, organizations, and Web sites to read, contact, and explore to learn more about the traits.

You might try Benjamin Franklin's tactic of concentrating on one trait per week (or day, or month). Or dip into the book anywhere to read a quote, consider a dilemma, or find an activity to try. Or dig deeply into a particular chapter. Jump around, or read straight through. How you use this book is up to you.

"We are not human beings having a spiritual experience. We are spiritual beings having a human experience."
*Pierre Teilhard de Chardin*

# Getting to Know You

## Self-knowledge, self-awareness, self-acceptance, self-esteem, self-actualization

> "To do good things in the world, first you must know who you are and what gives meaning in your life."
> *Paula P. Brownlee*

**W**ho are you? What do you want to become? What should you become? If you saw an ear of corn for the first time, you might describe it as a rough-textured, oblong, greenish-yellow thing that doesn't really have any special qualities. To discover the delicious corn inside, you'd have to peel away the husk.

As you peel away the outer layers of husk that surround you, you'll discover talents, abilities, and interests that make you different from everyone else. When you combine your talents, abilities, and interests and develop the character traits to help you express them, you'll discover a basic secret of happiness.

The image you see when you look in the mirror is the image you reflect to others. Maybe you see yourself as a husk, covering up the juicy kernels inside. How you see yourself—what you think of yourself—can either attract other people to you or push them away. This is one reason why a positive self-image is important to you. If you look in the mirror today and see a husk, it's not the end of the world. You can develop a positive self-image and the confidence to be yourself and let it show.

Accepting and liking who and what you are is an essential part of being "good-looking." To get to know yourself, you first have to peel away your outer layers and discover what's inside. When you do this, you'll find that:

- ☀ you have your own *values, opinions,* and *beliefs*
- ☀ you have strong *feelings* and probably some *fears* and *anxieties*
- ☀ you *think* and *learn* in special ways
- ☀ your *personality* is different from everyone else's
- ☀ you have special *interests,* unique *talents,* and secret *dreams* and *desires.*

On pages 7–11, you'll find a series of inventories (checklists) you can use to get to know yourself better. If you think you already have a good idea of who you are, you might want to skip these for now. Or you might want to complete them anyway (you may be surprised by the results). Or complete them now, then repeat them in a month or a year as you continue to develop the character traits you need. Taken together, these inventories will create a fascinating self-portrait of the person you are and the person you're becoming or would like to become. (You'll find a Self-Portrait form to fill out on pages 12–13.)

Following are suggestions for interpreting the inventories and ideas for using what they tell you about yourself. Complete the inventories *before* you read these. Then come back to them and see if you agree with the interpretations.

# Interpreting the Inventories

As you read these interpretations and suggestions, keep in mind that labels can limit you. These inventories are meant to help you understand yourself better, not to label you. No one is one way all of the time.

## Character Traits (see page 7)

Do you have most of the character traits you need? Or did you discover several that you think you should develop? Do you see yourself any differently now than you did before you completed this inventory?

Make a list of the character traits you'd like to have or strengthen (anything you checked in the second column). Decide which trait to work on first. Look it up in the Contents or Index and turn to that part of the book. In a day, a week, or a month, go back to your list and choose another trait to work on. Or you can work on several traits at a time.

## Fears (see page 8)

You can learn a lot about yourself by looking at what scares you. Psychologists believe that our fears can influence or even control our character and behavior. Our fears can discourage us from developing or strengthening positive character traits.

Sometimes people make up excuses for their fears instead of facing them. Sigmund Freud, the founder

of psychoanalysis, called this "using defense mechanisms." Carl Jung, the founder of analytical psychology, suggested that we dream about the things we're afraid to face when we're awake. (Maybe that's why we have nightmares.) Identifying your fears can be a key to unlocking your secret diary of self-knowledge.

Take a look at each item on the list for which you checked "a little afraid" or "afraid." Try to figure out why it scares you. Did something happen to make you afraid? Has someone told you that you should be afraid? Decide if this is something you'd like to be less afraid of—or not afraid of. What can you do to reduce or eliminate your fear?

Your fears can grow into strengths if you face them, tackle them, and wrestle them to the ground. The very act of admitting and naming your fears can help you to control them better.

IMPORTANT: If you checked "terrified" for any item(s) on the list, talk to a parent, teacher, school counselor, spiritual leader, or other trusted adult. Explain your fears and ask for help.

---

## CHECK IT OUT

*Don't Pop Your Cork on Mondays! The Children's Anti-Stress Book* by Adolph Moser, Ed.D. (Kansas City, MO: Landmark Editions, Inc., 1988). An informative, entertaining book that explores the causes and effects of stress and offers practical ideas for managing and preventing it. Written for younger kids ages 6–9, but full of good information and worth reading at any age.

*Fighting Invisible Tigers: A Stress Management Guide for Teens* by Earl Hipp (Minneapolis: Free Spirit Publishing, 1995). A wealth of practical advice on managing stress, being assertive, building supportive relationships, taking risks, making decisions, staying healthy, dealing with fears—even growing a funny bone. Ages 11 & up. A *Leader's Guide* is also available.

---

## Interests (see page 9)

In all four lists, the same letter represents the same category. Here are the categories:

a = music, art
b = writing
c = entertainment
d = computers, technology

e = animals (care or research)

f = public service (medicine, counseling, job service, etc.)

g = teaching

h = child care

i = environment, the outdoors, forestry, farming

j = mechanical, technical, electrical, engineering

k = cooking

l = business (starting one or being involved in one)

m = law enforcement

n = athletics

o = building, construction

Look back at how you scored this inventory. Your first choices (anything you marked with a 1) indicate your strongest areas of interest. If two or more of your first choices have the same letter, that indicates an especially strong interest in that category. You might want to study that area more. If the same letter shows up four times (as choice 1, 2, 3, or 4), that also indicates a strong interest—something you may want to pursue in greater depth.

What about the letters that don't show up anywhere in your score? These indicate areas you have less or no interest in. Maybe you really don't care about them, or maybe you haven't had much experience in these areas. Are there any you might want to explore?

---

## CHECK IT OUT

If you have a computer with Internet access, you already know that the World Wide Web (WWW) is an incredibly rich source of information on virtually any topic you can think of. Do a Web search for any of the words in the 15 categories of the Interests Inventory, and you'll probably find thousands of hits and hotlinks. Just for fun, pick a word in a category that doesn't interest you. Visit a few sites and you might change your mind. TIP: If you don't have access to the Internet at home or at school, ask at your local library about *free* community Internet access.

---

## Relationships (see page 10)

For once, a low score is good! If you scored below 30, you probably have good relationships with other people. If you scored between 31–40, you might want to work on developing better relationships with some of the people in your life. If you scored between 41–60, you could meet with a favorite teacher, a school counselor or social worker, or another adult you trust and ask for help in developing better relationships. Why ask an adult instead of a close friend your own age? Because sometimes friends don't keep confidences, and sometimes they don't have the skills to really help you.

Don't worry if you scored high on this inventory. You might have been having a bad day when you completed it. Or you might have better relationships with some people than you think. Either way, it's possible to bring your score down. Look back at the Character Traits Inventory and the list of traits you'd like to develop or strengthen. Then dip into those sections of this book and enjoy the activities. The character traits you have can affect your relationships with others—and vice versa.

## Learning Styles (see page 11)

Look back at the number of the description you checked.

✔ If you checked 1, you might learn best by brainstorming, speaking, working in teams, gathering information, and listening.

✔ If you checked 2, you might learn best by analyzing, classifying, theorizing, organizing, observing, testing theories, and listening.

✔ If you checked 3, you might learn best by manipulating, experimenting, doing hands-on activities, tinkering, setting goals, and making lists.

✔ If you checked 4, you might learn best by leading, collaborating, influencing, adapting, taking risks, and modifying.

There are no right or wrong responses to this inventory. Everyone learns differently. If you said to yourself "Wait a minute—I fit more than one of these descriptions," you probably do. Your response indicates a tendency toward a certain learning style, and it can help you to understand why you learn more easily at some times than others. You can use this information to be more successful in school. *Example:* Suppose you're having a tough time in math. You checked 3 on the inventory, and now you know that you might learn best by doing hands-on activities. Ask your teacher if you can use manipulatives (things you hold and touch) to learn math concepts.

---

## CHECK IT OUT

*Learning Styles: Personal Exploration and Practical Applications: An Inquiry Guide for Students* by Kathleen A. Butler, Ph.D. (Columbia, CT: Learner's Dimension, 1995). This hands-on workbook invites you to explore your special abilities and qualities as a person, learner, and thinker. Exercises, checklists, and questionnaires encourage you to find new ways of looking at yourself, understand more about how you learn and think, make the most of your learning abilities, and broaden the ways you relate to others. Ages 13 & up. A *Teacher's Guide* is also available.

---

### Self-Portrait (see pages 12–13)

You can interpret this however you want. If you're honest in your answers *and* your interpretation, you'll have a good idea of who you are, here and now. You might want to complete a new Self-Portrait from time to time as you develop and strengthen your character traits.

# Character Dilemmas

*For journaling or writing essays, discussion, debate, role-playing, reflection*

**Suppose that . . .**

**1** You're very interested in expressing yourself or fulfilling yourself. Could this interest ever get out of control? If so, then how?

**2** You think you might be "addicted" to one of your interests. Could you ever become too involved in something you enjoy? If so, then how? Would this be good or bad?

**3** You have many strong, positive character traits. Could your good character traits ever become too extreme or get out of control? If so, then how?

**4** You're very self-confident about your traits and abilities. Can you ever have too much self-confidence? Why or why not? Justify your answer.

**5** You've been granted the power to choose the character traits you want and develop them instantly. Are there certain traits that might help you if you want to be a police officer, mayor, teacher, parent, friend, athlete, husband or wife, doctor, engineer, etc.? Explain your ideas.

**6** You have a high or low opinion of yourself. How might what you think of yourself influence what you do in life? Give examples.

# Character Traits Inventory

To interpret this inventory, see page 4.

*Read each pair of sentences. Check the ONE from each pair that describes you. Or check BOTH sentences if you believe that you already have a particular trait or quality but would like to develop it further.*

1. ___ I have positive attitudes.     ___ I'd like to have better attitudes.
2. ___ I'm kind and I care about helping others.     ___ I need to be kinder and more caring.
3. ___ I accept responsibility for the choices I make.     ___ I want to learn how to accept responsibility for my choices.
4. ___ I'm a good citizen and an involved member of my community.     ___ I want to be a better citizen and more involved in my community
5. ___ I keep my body clean.     ___ I need to work on my personal hygiene.
6. ___ I have clean habits and a clean mind.     ___ I'd like to have more positive habits, thoughts, and influences.
7. ___ I communicate well with others.     ___ I'd like to be a better communicator.
8. ___ I work to conserve things and resources, and I'm thrifty.     ___ I need to conserve and save better than I do.
9. ___ I have the courage to do and become what I want to be.     ___ I'd like to be more courageous.
10. ___ I have empathy (deep understanding) for others.     ___ I need to be more empathetic.
11. ___ I have endurance and patience, even in tough times.     ___ I need more endurance and patience.
12. ___ I'm able to forgive others and myself.     ___ I want to learn how to forgive more easily.
13. ___ I'm physically, mentally, and emotionally healthy.     ___ I want to be more physically, mentally, and emotionally healthy.
14. ___ I'm honest and trustworthy.     ___ I need to be more honest and trustworthy.
15. ___ I'm a risk taker, and I have good imagination skills.     ___ I'd like to take positive risks more easily or improve my imagination skills.
16. ___ I have integrity. I "walk as I talk."     ___ I want to develop my integrity.
17. ___ I'm tolerant and fair with others.     ___ I need to be more tolerant and fair.
18. ___ I'm a good leader.     ___ I'd like to be a better leader.
19. ___ I'm a good follower.     ___ I need to be a better follower.
20. ___ I know when to be loyal and/or obedient.     ___ I'd like to be more loyal and/or obedient.
21. ___ I'm a calm and peaceful person.     ___ I need to become more calm and/or peaceful.
22. ___ I'm a good problem solver.     ___ I want to be a better problem solver.
23. ___ I have direction and purpose in my life.     ___ I'd like to have more direction or purpose in my life.
24. ___ I'm friendly and have healthy, positive relationships with others.     ___ I'd like to be more friendly and to have better relationships with others.
25. ___ I treat others with respect and courtesy.     ___ I need to be more respectful and courteous.
26. ___ I'm responsible and hard-working.     ___ I want to develop my sense of responsibility and my work ethic.
27. ___ I practice safety measures in my life.     ___ I'd like to be more cautious and safety-conscious.
28. ___ I'm self-disciplined.     ___ I want to be more self-disciplined.
29. ___ I have wisdom.     ___ I want to develop my wisdom.

# Fears Inventory

*Read through the list of things people fear. Put a check mark in the column that best describes how you feel about each one. Use the blank lines at the end to write any fears you have that aren't listed here.*

To interpret this inventory, see page 4.

| | Not afraid | A little afraid | Afraid | Terrified |
|---|---|---|---|---|
| insects/spiders | ❏ | ❏ | ❏ | ❏ |
| animals (mice, rats, dogs, etc.) | ❏ | ❏ | ❏ | ❏ |
| snakes/reptiles | ❏ | ❏ | ❏ | ❏ |
| doctors/dentists | ❏ | ❏ | ❏ | ❏ |
| sickness | ❏ | ❏ | ❏ | ❏ |
| choking/suffocating | ❏ | ❏ | ❏ | ❏ |
| injury | ❏ | ❏ | ❏ | ❏ |
| blood | ❏ | ❏ | ❏ | ❏ |
| death | ❏ | ❏ | ❏ | ❏ |
| violence | ❏ | ❏ | ❏ | ❏ |
| automobile accidents | ❏ | ❏ | ❏ | ❏ |
| flying in planes | ❏ | ❏ | ❏ | ❏ |
| water | ❏ | ❏ | ❏ | ❏ |
| heights | ❏ | ❏ | ❏ | ❏ |
| the dark | ❏ | ❏ | ❏ | ❏ |
| being in a small area | ❏ | ❏ | ❏ | ❏ |
| being alone | ❏ | ❏ | ❏ | ❏ |
| being in groups | ❏ | ❏ | ❏ | ❏ |
| nightmares/ghosts | ❏ | ❏ | ❏ | ❏ |
| amusement park rides (*example:* the roller coaster) | ❏ | ❏ | ❏ | ❏ |
| severe weather/disasters (storms, fires, floods, earthquakes, tornadoes, hurricanes, etc.) | ❏ | ❏ | ❏ | ❏ |
| God (or Higher Being/Higher Power) | ❏ | ❏ | ❏ | ❏ |
| your teachers/principal/boss | ❏ | ❏ | ❏ | ❏ |
| your parent(s)/guardian(s) | ❏ | ❏ | ❏ | ❏ |
| girls (if you're a boy)/boys (if you're a girl) | ❏ | ❏ | ❏ | ❏ |
| bullies | ❏ | ❏ | ❏ | ❏ |
| disagreements | ❏ | ❏ | ❏ | ❏ |
| making mistakes/failing | ❏ | ❏ | ❏ | ❏ |
| talking to other people | ❏ | ❏ | ❏ | ❏ |
| being criticized/teased/embarrassed | ❏ | ❏ | ❏ | ❏ |
| your own talents/abilities | ❏ | ❏ | ❏ | ❏ |
| responsibility/being in charge | ❏ | ❏ | ❏ | ❏ |
| performing (speaking, singing, etc.) | ❏ | ❏ | ❏ | ❏ |
| growing up | ❏ | ❏ | ❏ | ❏ |
| _____ | ❏ | ❏ | ❏ | ❏ |
| _____ | ❏ | ❏ | ❏ | ❏ |
| _____ | ❏ | ❏ | ❏ | ❏ |

# Interests Inventory

*For each "Would you rather . . ." list, put a 1 by the thing you like to do most, a 2 by your second choice, a 3 by your third choice, and a 4 by your fourth choice.*

**I.  Would you rather . . .**

___ a.  paint a landscape?
___ b.  write in your journal?
___ c.  be in a play?
___ d.  surf the Internet?
___ e.  take care of your neighbor's dog?
___ f.  bandage someone's cut?
___ g.  make math flash cards for a younger kid?
___ h.  rock a baby?
___ i.  plant flowers?
___ j.  repair a light switch?
___ k.  bake cookies?
___ l.  organize your friends in a walk-a-thon?
___ m.  patrol your school halls to stop kids from running?
___ n.  play catch?
___ o.  help put a roof on a house?

**II.  Would you rather . . .**

___ a.  hear a symphony?
___ b.  tell a story?
___ c.  demonstrate how to do a new dance?
___ d.  work on a computer?
___ e.  go to the zoo?
___ f.  listen to someone's heartbeat?
___ g.  give a report on the weather?
___ h.  teach a younger kid how to play ball?
___ i.  learn how to raise chickens?
___ j.  put a new wheel on a bike?
___ k.  make a cake for a friend?
___ l.  make bumper stickers and sell them?
___ m.  help with a neighborhood watch?
___ n.  go swimming?
___ o.  build a playhouse for the kids in your neighborhood?

**III.  Would you rather . . .**

___ a.  decorate a mural?
___ b.  read a book?
___ c.  be on the program for a school assembly?
___ d.  take apart a telephone?
___ e.  find homes for abandoned animals?
___ f.  help people find jobs?
___ g.  give an inspiring speech?
___ h.  comfort a sick child?
___ i.  be a guide for hikers?
___ j.  work with hand tools (squares, saws, rules, plumb lines)?
___ k.  plan a menu?
___ l.  start a landscaping business with your friends?
___ m.  start a Youth Crime Watch at your school?
___ n.  compete in sports?
___ o.  paint, plaster, or hang wallpaper?

**IV.  Would you rather . . .**

___ a.  play a musical instrument?
___ b.  write a poem or limerick?
___ c.  make people laugh with your jokes?
___ d.  put together a kid's toy wagon?
___ e.  watch a video on the habits of gorillas?
___ f.  counsel people who are troubled?
___ g.  research a topic you'd like to learn more about?
___ h.  play games with children?
___ i.  landscape a barren hill?
___ j.  follow directions to put a machine together?
___ k.  learn about how to season foods?
___ l.  start a recycling program at your school?
___ m.  patrol a neighborhood to keep it safe?
___ n.  watch football on TV?
___ o.  build cupboards?

**SCORING:** Each response begins with a letter of the alphabet. For each response you marked with a 1, 2, 3, or 4, write its letter here. (*Example:* 1: a, a, b, c.)

*Your scores:*

1: ____, ____, ____, ____

2: ____, ____, ____, ____

3: ____, ____, ____, ____

4: ____, ____, ____, ____

# Relationships Inventory

*For each statement in this inventory, check the box that comes closest to describing how you feel about your relationships.*

|  | Most of the time | Some of the time | Seldom or never |
|---|:---:|:---:|:---:|
| 1. Most of my friends seem to like me. | ❏ | ❏ | ❏ |
| 2. My parents respect my opinions. | ❏ | ❏ | ❏ |
| 3. My friends seem to have a good time with me. | ❏ | ❏ | ❏ |
| 4. My brother(s), sister(s) or parents seem to enjoy my company. | ❏ | ❏ | ❏ |
| 5. My peers admire me or look up to me. | ❏ | ❏ | ❏ |
| 6. I enjoy hanging out with my friends. | ❏ | ❏ | ❏ |
| 7. I like my teachers. | ❏ | ❏ | ❏ |
| 8. I feel accepted by my parents. | ❏ | ❏ | ❏ |
| 9. My family doesn't get on my nerves. | ❏ | ❏ | ❏ |
| 10. I'm able to talk with my parent(s) or guardian(s). | ❏ | ❏ | ❏ |
| 11. I don't feel left out of activities with friends. | ❏ | ❏ | ❏ |
| 12. I'm satisfied with the friend(s) I have. | ❏ | ❏ | ❏ |
| 13. My family and I share responsibilities. | ❏ | ❏ | ❏ |
| 14. I'm confident when I am around people my own age. | ❏ | ❏ | ❏ |
| 15. I can share my opinions with my peers. | ❏ | ❏ | ❏ |
| 16. I don't look down on others. | ❏ | ❏ | ❏ |
| 17. I like to talk with older people. | ❏ | ❏ | ❏ |
| 18. I can talk easily with younger children. | ❏ | ❏ | ❏ |
| 19. My parent(s) or guardian(s) seem to understand me. | ❏ | ❏ | ❏ |
| 20. I'm on friendly terms with most people I know in my neighborhood and community. | ❏ | ❏ | ❏ |

**SCORING:** Give yourself 1 point for every check mark in the "Most of the time" column, 2 points for every check mark in the "Some of the time" column, and 3 points for every check mark in the "Seldom or never" column.

Number of "Most of the time" responses: _____ x 1 = _____

Number of "Some of the time" responses: _____ x 2 = _____

Number of "Seldom or never" responses: _____ x 3 = _____

**TOTAL** _____

# Learning Styles Inventory

*Read the following descriptions.*
*Check the ONE that sounds most like you.*

___ **1.** I like to know *why* things happen. I like to consider many different ideas. I have a good imagination, and I usually come up with good ideas. I like to find solutions to problems and issues. I like practical solutions. I don't like to set schedules; I'm very flexible.

___ **2.** I like to think about concepts. I enjoy listening to guest speakers. I love theories about *what* makes things work. I like to work hard and prefer following definite steps to find solutions. I enjoy studying principles and details, and I like columns and figures.

___ **3.** I like to know *how* things work. I enjoy lectures and abstract ideas. I like to experiment, solve problems, and make decisions. I enjoy technical tasks more than "people problems." I like to tinker, and I like schedules.

___ **4.** I like to talk about "what if" situations. I enjoy real, concrete experiences. I like to apply what I learn. I rely on my gut feelings more than on logic. I love taking risks, and I enjoy helping other people to be creative. I bring action to ideas.

To interpret this inventory, see page 6.

# Self-Portrait

*Take a good look at yourself. What do you see? After you complete this verbal self-portrait, you should have a more clear and complete view of the person you are at this point in time. Answer each question as honestly as you can; add more paper if you run out of space.*

1. What do I look like?

2. What do I like to think about?

3. What do I like about myself?

4. What are my best character traits?
   (Look back at the Character Traits Inventory on page 7.)

5. What traits would I like to develop or strengthen?

6. What scares me the most?
   (Look back at the Fears Inventory on page 8.)

7. What am I most interested in?
   (Look back at the Interests Inventory on page 9.)

To interpret this inventory, see page 6.

# Self-Portrait continued

**8.** How well do I get along with others?
(Look back at the Relationships Inventory on page 10.)

**9.** How do I learn best?
(Look back at the Learning Styles Inventory on page 11.)

**10.** What are my best-developed talents?

**11.** What talents would I like to develop?

**12.** What is my secret dream or goal?

**13.** What do I wish/hope I'll be doing 10 years from now?

**14.** What steps do I need to take to get there?

# Positive Attitudes

**Optimism, acceptance, resiliency, cheerfulness, enthusiasm, alertness, humor, being a good sport, humility, gratitude, faith, hope**

> "Everything can be taken from a man but one thing: the last of human freedoms—to choose one's own attitude in any given set of circumstances, to choose one's own way."
> *Viktor Frankl*

An illness left Helen Keller blind, deaf, and mute at 21 months of age. Although she lived in a world of silence and darkness, she became a voice of hope and a light. It wasn't easy for her. She struggled in her mind to find a connection to others, a door to the world. When she did, she held the door for others, making it possible for many people to believe in themselves.

When Malcolm X was in prison from 1946–1952, he could have vegetated. Instead, he spent those years educating himself. He copied every word from the dictionary, learned about the Black Muslims, and became a convert. Upon his release from prison, he drew national attention for his writings and powerful speeches.

Joe Paterno, a coach of the Penn State University football team, once said after losing a game that losing was probably good for the team, since that was how they learned what they were doing wrong.

Today, "having an attitude" usually means a *bad* attitude (as in "He's got an attitude!" or "Don't give me any attitude!"). This chapter focuses on developing *positive* attitudes—as shown by the three examples you just read.

Your attitude is your point of view, your outlook on life, your state or frame of mind. It determines the choices you make and how you feel about the people, things, and events around you. If your attitude tells you "Algebra is boring," that's how it will seem to you, and you probably won't do your best in that class. Similarly, raking leaves can either be torture or fun. Why not have fun?

When you have positive attitudes, you can choose how to react to each situation you encounter. You can't choose everything that happens to you, but you can choose what you think, feel, and do. This gives you enormous personal power—to control yourself from the inside out, to direct your own future.

Who's got an attitude?

# 12 Ways to Be More Positive

*1.   You can choose to be optimistic.* You've probably heard a pessimist described as someone who sees a glass of water as half empty, while an optimist sees it as half full. The pessimist focuses on the negative (the missing water), while the optimist sees the positive (the water that's there). Who has a better outlook? Who's likely to be happier, more confident and sure?

*2.   You can choose to accept things as they are.* This doesn't mean that you wilt and give up. It means that you don't struggle, whine, and bang your head against a brick wall when things don't go right—behaviors that make you a helpless victim. (It's what eats *you* that puts the pounds of weight on your spirit.) Instead, you get on with your life. You move forward.

> "You accept things as they are, not as you wish they were in this moment. . . . The past is history, the future is a mystery, and this moment is a gift. That is why this moment is called the *present.*"
> *Deepak Chopra, M.D.*

*3.   You can choose to be resilient.* Have you ever watched a tree swaying in a storm? A tree that stands rigidly will never win a battle against the wind. Trees that bend with the wind are those that survive. Like a tree, you can bend and sway as life batters and blasts you—then bounce back again, supported by your strong, deep roots. When you're resilient, you can survive almost anything—being hurt, frustrated, or let down; losing friends, making mistakes, and much more. Remember the image of a tree in the storm. You can learn a lot from nature.

Developing positive attitudes doesn't mean that you'll never experience pain, suffering, or disappointment. You will.[1] But having good attitudes will help you to turn your problems into teachers so you can learn from them and grow.

Developing positive attitudes doesn't mean you should ignore problems. If someone steals your bike, you won't say "So what?" Instead, you'll contact the police and report your stolen bike. You'll do everything you can to get it back. But if you can't get it back, you'll accept the fact that it's gone. And you won't let that drag you down.

Flip a coin in the air. What do you get? Either heads or tails. Problems always have a flip side, too. If you fail a test, you can flip the coin and learn to study harder or find a tutor. If you lose a friend, you can flip the coin, repair the friendship, or find a new friend. If you don't like your looks, you can flip the coin and develop a fantastic personality.

*4.   You can choose to be cheerful.* Have you spent time around cheerful people? If you have, then you know that they energize you. They're like human battery chargers. You can be one, too. Start by refusing to say gloomy things. Bite your tongue. Count to 10. Pull up the corners of your mouth. When you send out positive words, thoughts, and feelings, positive people (and things) are attracted to you.

*5.   You can choose to be enthusiastic.* Greet each new day with excitement. Approach tasks and chores with zest. Enthusiasm is catching! The more upbeat you are, the more people around you will feel and act the same.

*6.   You can choose to be more alert.* If you're more alert to potential problems, you can be better prepared for them and even dodge some. *Example:* A friend invites you to a party at her house on Saturday. But you remember overhearing her tell someone else that her parents are going out of town for the weekend. Parties without parents can spell trouble. You say "No, thanks!"

Of course, you can also be alert to positive experiences. You hear an announcement about a team tryout or new club. You write down the time and place and plan to go.

*7.   You can choose to have a sense of humor.* When you do something silly (everyone does), don't miss the opportunity to laugh at yourself. It's one of life's great joys. I've done lots of loony things, and I've provided myself (and others) with many happy hours of entertainment. Once I was invited to give a talk to some senior citizens at a rest home. Without checking the address carefully, I mistakenly charged into the Board of Realtors and announced to their startled faces that I was there to teach them a lesson on honesty!

---

[1] See "Endurance," pages 86–93.

If you laugh a lot, you'll be healthier. Laughter releases good chemicals in your body that stimulate you and can help you to grow.

**8. *You can choose to be a good sport.*** This attitude can win you friends even if you don't win the game or competition. Being a good sport means losing gracefully—smiling, shaking hands with the winner, not blaming other people or circumstances for your loss. As 16-year-old Alissa Harman explained, "I ran in the race even though I knew I wouldn't win." Being a good sport also means not pounding your chest Tarzan-style or gloating when you're victorious. In other words . . .

**9. *You can choose to be humble.*** People who toot their own horns seldom attract an audience. If you're genuinely interested in others, they'll see your good qualities even if you don't advertise them. They won't feel that you're trying to one-up them. They can relax around you and be themselves.

**10. *You can choose to be grateful.*** Think about it: You probably have a lot to be grateful for. Gratitude puts a smile on your face. It makes you feel good about your life. And other people feel good about being around you.

**11. *You can choose to have faith.*** For some people, this means believing in God or another Higher Being/Higher Power. Others put their faith in their country, in other people, in things, or in themselves. Having faith means believing that things will work out for you—and that you can work things out for yourself. If you expect to fail, you probably will. If you expect to achieve, you're much more likely to reach your goal.

> "When the legends die, the dreams die. When the dreams die, there is no greatness."
> *Ute Indian Nation saying*

**12. *You can choose to have hope.*** Without hope, life has no meaning or point. We expect nothing, plan nothing, and don't set goals for ourselves (why bother?). Hope may be your most important positive attitude—the basis for all the others. What do you hope for? What are your dreams? What are your ambitions? Your purpose in life? If you're willing to consider these questions, you're already a hopeful person.

> "'Hope' is the thing with feathers—
> That perches on the soul—
> And sings the tune without the words—
> And never stops—at all—"
> *Emily Dickinson*

# Character Dilemmas

*For journaling or writing essays, discussion, debate, role-playing, reflection*

**Suppose that . . .**

**1** You learn that a friend stuffed the ballot box to win an election in your school. What should your attitude be? Acceptance? Rejection? Silence? What attitude would help you and your friend the most?

**2** You learn that a family member has an incurable disease. What are some of the many attitudes you might have toward this? Might your attitudes change over time? Which attitudes would help you and your family the most?

**3** Your two best friends make the basketball team, and you're the last person cut. Because your friends practice every night after school, they're always together. Whenever you see them at lunch, they talk basketball, which makes you feel even more excluded. Before you know it, you're out of the loop. How might you react? What kind of attitude could you develop that would help you feel better about yourself? What attitude could you take to help your friends be more thoughtful and accepting of you?

**4** A manager of a finance department in a bank discovers that an employee has dipped into the cash register to help pay for his daughter's college tuition. What position should the manager take? How might the manager's attitude affect the outcome?

**5** You're applying for a job, and the interviewer asks you to describe your qualifications and abilities. How might you be both humble and self-confident while talking about yourself?

**6** You find yourself in one (or more) of the following situations. Imagine what might happen if you approach it with a negative attitude. Then imagine what might happen if you approach it with a positive attitude.

a.  You're about to miss the best party of the summer because your parents have gone out of town and you have to watch your younger brother.

b.  Someone your best friend has always wanted to date asks you out.

c.  You have to give up karate or gymnastics lessons because your parents need the money to help your older brother at college.

d.  You oversleep and arrive late for school. Meanwhile, you miss an important test.

e.  You make dinner for your family, and your mom comes home and gets mad at you for messing up the kitchen.

f.  Your coach tells you that you'll never amount to anything.

# Activities

**ROLE-PLAY** these situations to show how people might demonstrate positive and negative attitudes:

▲  an employer firing an employee
▲  a tennis coach instructing a student
▲  a mother correcting a child who screams when he doesn't get his own way
▲  an older brother trying to get a younger sibling to stay out of his room
▲  a student pointing out that a teacher has made a mistake on a test
▲  a friend trying to stop another friend from lying.

**COLLECT QUOTES** about attitudes. Surf the Internet or visit the library. Do keyword searches for any of the words listed at the start of this chapter (optimism, acceptance, resiliency, cheerfulness, enthusiasm, alertness, humor, being a good sport, humility, gratitude, faith, hope). Or look them up in books of quotations. Create your own book with the quotations you find. Make copies as gifts for friends and family members.

## CHECK IT OUT

*Attitude in a Jar*™ *for Kids* by Deborah Stein. Inside this colorful jar are 365 "attitude slips" printed with positive messages. ("You are the only one who can grade your life, so give yourself an A+." "Laughter softens life's rough edges.") A great way to start the day at home or at school. All ages. Inquire or order by fax: (612) 397-8119.

**IMAGINE HOW DIFFERENT ATTITUDES** might affect the outcome of an environmental project. Suppose there's a stream nearby that once was rich in salmon. Recently the salmon population has been decreasing because the water is being diverted for farmland irrigation. You want to save the salmon. What attitude(s) should you take when approaching the various people involved? How might you best communicate your concerns and help others to see your point of view? Make a flow chart to show how different attitudes might bring about different results. *Example:*

> You accuse community leaders of poor judgment and planning
>
> ↓
>
> The leaders (in defense) blame the farmers
>
> ↓
>
> The farmers accuse the leaders of not having enough knowledge or experience

**CREATE BAR GRAPHS** about job attitudes. Follow these steps:

**1.** Brainstorm a list of positive attitudes (or use the one at the start of this chapter). Choose 6–8 you want to focus on.

**2.** Find out the names, addresses, and telephone numbers of 5 or 6 business leaders in your community. Write each one a letter explaining that you're collecting information about positive attitudes in the workplace. Say that you'd like to call them and interview them about their opinions.

**3.** In a week or so, follow up with a phone call to set a specific time for your interview.

**4.** When you call to do an interview, read aloud your list of positive attitudes. Ask the business leader to choose the 3 attitudes he or she thinks are most important for executives to have, and the 3 attitudes he or she thinks are most important for employees to have. Ask the person to rank the attitudes in order for each. *Example:* One business leader assigns these rankings:

| The Most Important Attitudes for Executives | The Most Important Attitudes for Employees |
| --- | --- |
| 1. Optimism<br>2. Alertness<br>3. Humor | 1. Enthusiasm<br>2. Being a good sport<br>3. Humor |

**5.** Tabulate the results of your interviews. Create bar graphs to show the results.

> *Variations:* Survey coaches about players' and fans' attitudes, hospital and health clinic administrators about doctors' and patients' attitudes, or come up with your own variation.

**LEARN ABOUT ATTITUDES** toward your country. Choose several leaders from other countries and research what they have said and written about your country. (Start by finding a book of short biographies of famous people.) What attitudes have your country's leaders communicated to them? Give a speech to share what you learn. Or present your information in a puppet show. Have the puppets explain their attitudes toward your country.

**MAKE A PUZZLE OR MATCH-UP CARD GAME** that connects descriptions of attitudes (positive and negative) with examples of each. *Examples:* One pair of pieces (or cards) might say "Cheerful" and "Laughing when a truck splatters you with mud." Another might say "Grumpy" and "Complaining to your parents because there's no milk in the refrigerator." Present your puzzle or game to younger children in your school, club, community center, or place of worship, or to a local hospital or shelter.

*Variation:* Create a simpler puzzle or game by pairing words with faces showing expressions. *Examples:* "Cheerful" and a smiling face; "Grumpy" and a scowling face.

**PRACTICE HAVING POSITIVE ATTITUDES** on someone who doesn't like you or doesn't treat you very well. This might be a student, a teacher, a sibling or someone else you see often. Whenever you're with the person, try to have a positive attitude (optimism, acceptance, cheerfulness, humor, humility, etc.). Make a chart or keep a journal to note any progress in how the person acts toward you and how you feel about him or her.

**CREATE SYMBOLS OR SIGN LANGUAGE** to show different attitudes. The "happy face" is a universal symbol of cheerfulness. Come up with your own creative and unusual symbols or hand signals. Be prepared to explain what your symbols mean and why they make sense.

## CHECK IT OUT

*The Illustrated Book of Signs & Symbols* by Miranda Bruce-Mitford (New York: DK Publishing, Inc., 1996). A fully illustrated visual guide to thousands of signs and symbols from around the world. Ages 12 & up.

**STUDY POPULAR SONGS** to find out what attitudes they reveal. Are they mostly positive or mostly negative?

> *Variation:* Listen to different kinds of music and pay attention to how each kind affects your attitude. Try popular, country, classical, R&B, Gregorian chant, jazz, oldies, techno, rap, etc. Which type of music seems to inspire positive attitudes in you? What about negative attitudes?

**PLAY "ATTITUDES CHARADES."** Brainstorm a list of positive and negative attitudes. Take turns acting them out. As in the game Charades, you can't talk or mouth the words. You can only show them by your facial expressions and body language. Some will be easy to act out (happy, fearful, humorous); others will be more difficult (humble, suspicious, accepting).

**READ STORIES ABOUT POSITIVE ATTITUDES.** Look for these books:

*Are You There, God? It's Me, Margaret* by Judy Blume (New York: Bantam Doubleday Dell

Books for Young Readers, 1991). Eleven-year-old Margaret is the daughter of a Catholic mother and a Jewish father. As she waits for and notices signs that she's growing up, she also struggles with choosing which religion she will embrace. Ages 10–13.

 *Once I Was A Plum Tree* by Johanna Hurwitz (New York: William Morrow and Co., 1992). When Gerry meets Edgar and learns that his family fled Germany before World War II, she becomes interested in her own Jewish heritage. Ages 10–13.

# Character in *ACTION*

## Ricardo Dence: Having an Attitude

When Ricardo Dence was in fourth grade, he challenged a teacher who had given him a detention slip. He ran to her desk, grabbed all the detention lists, and tossed them out to the other students. Then he spent the rest of the day warming the chair in the principal's office.

And that's where he spent most of his fifth and sixth grade years, too. Ricardo's grades were mostly D's and F's. He was a chubby guy, weighing 180 pounds and standing 5'5" tall. Kids called him "fatso" and "dense" (a mean pun on his name).

When Ricardo was in sixth grade, a friend taught him how to fight, and from then on, whenever anyone challenged Ricardo, he attacked them physically. Kids stopped poking fun at him, and he gained respect as a fighter. "I felt proud," Ricardo says, "but I wasn't too happy with myself. And I hated beating up on people."

Not long after, Ricardo met a woman at his church named June Shoup. She was a college professor and widow with curly brown hair and glasses, and she became Ricardo's friend and mentor. She "adopted" Ricardo, took him to Disneyland and Magic Mountain, and insisted that he start improving his attitudes. "If you don't," she warned, "I won't be your friend anymore." Ricardo decided that he would try to change.

June began teaching Ricardo that "the pen is mightier than the sword"—that writing was better than fighting. This was no easy task, because Ricardo had a writing disability. He had a terrible time trying to string sentences together. June offered to proofread his work and help him strengthen his writing skills. His grades began to rise.

In the summer before he started eighth grade, Ricardo went to a Christian camp. "It was a big turning point for me," he explains. "I decided that from then on I would change my attitudes and help people instead of fighting them."

Ricardo Dence

With the help of his friend June, Ricardo wrote a formal letter to his school principal, asking for permission to start his own service club at the school. The shocked principal gave him permission. When Ricardo went on to Fallbrook Union High School, he joined another club and got knee-deep into community service.

While at Fallbrook, Ricardo planted trees, tutored minority students in math, and helped to feed homeless people twice a month. He went to Mexico twice and helped to build shelters and an outhouse for disadvantaged people. He fund-raised for food for needy families and helped out once a week at a Youth Crisis Hotline.

He even found time for sports. "I was never that great at any sport," Richard admits with a smile. "In swimming, I never won one race in the entire time. In fact, I came in last. I wrestled and won one match." But his accepting attitude toward others got him elected sophomore vice president, and he started earning B's on his report card.

"Now my goal is to help a minimum of two other people, like June helped me," Richard says. "Then they can help out two more people. It helps the world, like a ripple effect. You need to never get discouraged and just strive forward. No matter how hard it gets. The best attitude is striving forward."

Ricardo, dressed as a clown, playing with children

# Caring

**Giving, service, sharing, love, helpfulness, kindness, generosity, unselfishness, sacrifice**

> "Someone's got to go out there and love people and show it."
> *Diana, Princess of Wales*

**B**enjamin Franklin developed the stove now called the Franklin Stove, and it's still being manufactured today. At the time, he was offered a patent for his invention, which would have earned him a lot of money and given him a monopoly on it. But Franklin refused the patent. Instead, he published a pamphlet describing how to build the stove so blacksmiths or other clever people could make one themselves.

Reaching out to others makes life meaningful. What's really great about this is the more you give, the more you receive. Philosopher Deepak Chopra says that when you serve others, you gain more in return. If you give good things, then good things will flow your way.

You might be thinking "Wrong! I gave ten dollars to a friend, and I'm still waiting to get it back!" It's important to understand that when you give and share, you won't always be paid in kind (or on time). But over the long run, you'll attract love, respect, and generosity from others *in general*. You'll become a magnet for positive thoughts and actions.

When you truly care for others, there are no strings attached. You don't expect to receive anything in return for your gifts or services. You don't give or serve grudgingly; you do it with a free and open heart, and without keeping score. You don't let the fear of rejection hold you back. Sometimes caring takes courage.[1]

Real caring is unconditional. You don't stop to think whether someone deserves it. And when you really love someone, you don't worry about what's in it for you. You don't love your dad so he'll raise your allowance, or your little brother so he'll keep his hands off of your comic book collection.

Mother Teresa spent her life loving needy people in poverty-stricken countries. She saved many infants by tirelessly rubbing and stroking their weak, undernourished limbs. Human touch releases chemicals in the body which help it to thrive and grow. (How about giving your little brother a hug?)

There are many ways you can care about, share with, and serve others:

♥ *With your actions.* You might make your mother's bed, rake leaves off the front lawn, tutor a younger child in reading, open a door for a senior citizen, or sit with someone unpopular at lunch. Spend an hour listening to a lonely person. Be helpful and kind to someone who needs a hand.

♥ *With your words.* Say kind things to and about other people. Offer advice when it's wanted and sympathy when it's needed. Sometimes the kindest words are those that aren't spoken. Don't spread gossip, rumors, or cruel stories, even if they're true.

---

[1] See "Courage," pages 71–78.

**With your thoughts.** Positive thoughts and prayers can be very powerful. You can do an act of kindness for another person merely by thinking good thoughts about him or her. This is harder than it may seem at first. It's easier to tell your hand to share a candy bar with a friend than it is to tell yourself "Even though he shoots baskets better than I do, he's cool and I like him." Other people will feel the positive thoughts you send their way.

**With material gifts.** Try giving mittens to the homeless, donating trees to your community, buying a shirt for your brother or chocolates for a friend. Don't limit your gifts to special occasions (charity drives, birthdays, holidays). Give when you're in the mood and when you're not. Do it just because.

Look around you, and you'll notice many opportunities to give and serve. Think about your family, other relatives, friends, people in your neighborhood, pets and animals, the environment, your community, and the world. How can you use your skills, smarts, and experiences to improve the lives of others? What can you do for your school, club, community center, place of worship, or local government? How can you help another person (or group of people) to develop, grow, and become independent?

Sometimes service involves sacrifice—giving up something you value to benefit someone else. This might be your time, your talents, your energy and muscles, your money, or even your blood.

> "If every American donated five hours a week, it would equal the labor of 20 million full-time volunteers."
> *Whoopi Goldberg*

There's a story about a little boy whose older sister was seriously injured in a car accident. She had a rare blood type—which her little brother's matched—and she needed a donor immediately. The doctor approached the boy and asked if he would donate some of his blood to his sister. The boy turned ghostly white, but he hesitated for only a moment before nodding his head in agreement. After giving blood, he looked up at his mom and asked with wide, moist eyes, "How much longer do I get to live?"

If everyone pitched in, where would all the problems go?

When you shift your attention away from your problems and focus on helping others, your own problems don't seem as serious or daunting. If you use your unique talents and abilities to work for the good of others, you'll find greater joy, inspiration, and satisfaction in your own life.

TIP: Before you can love others, you first must love yourself.

> "I have found the paradox that if I love until it hurts, then there is no hurt, but only more love."
> *Mother Teresa*

# Character Dilemmas

*For journaling or writing essays, discussion, debate, role-playing, reflection*

**Suppose that . . .**

**1** Your little sister never hangs up her clothes. So you decide to help by hanging them up for her. You're doing a service . . . but are you really helping your sister? Why or why not? Give other examples of times when service to others might not be helpful.

**2** Your high school requires students to perform 200 hours of community service in order to graduate. What are the pros and cons of this requirement? How might it affect students' attitudes toward service?

**3** You're a parent of a child who doesn't know how to share (or just doesn't want to). How might you encourage your child to develop this trait? What learning experiences might you create for him or her?

**4** You live in a world where service is always rewarded. If you help someone, you immediately receive thanks, kindness, and money in return. How might this affect you and others?

**5** You've been asked to head a national committee to evaluate the welfare system in your country. Currently your country has thousands of second-, third-, and even fourth-generation welfare recipients; some people who receive welfare have children, grandchildren, and great-grandchildren who also receive it. As committee chair, you can decide to change the welfare system or leave it the way it is. What will you do and why?

# Activities

READ AND DISCUSS THIS POEM by Edwin Markham:

> He drew a circle that shut me out—
> Heretic, rebel, a thing to flout.
> But Love and I had the wit to win:
> We drew a circle that took him in!

What does this poem mean to you and your friends? Can you think of examples from your own life that seem to fit the poem? Is there anyone you know who might benefit from being drawn into your circle?

WRITE IN YOUR JOURNAL[2] about a time when someone was kind to you or did a service for you. How did you feel? Have you ever received a service that made you feel uncomfortable or embarrassed? Why did you feel that way? What can you learn from that experience?

READ A BIOGRAPHY about a famous philanthropist—someone who has dedicated his or her life to improving the lives of others. Make a poster illustrating the person's achievements. Write a report or make a speech about him or her.

LEARN ABOUT THE WELFARE SYSTEM in your country. Contact your city or state government to find out

how much welfare costs your city or state. Make a line graph showing how welfare costs have increased or decreased over the past 10 years. You might want to make separate graphs showing the costs for children (ages 5–18), adults (19–65), and seniors (66 and over). Find out if the number of people receiving welfare benefits has increased, decreased, or stayed the same.

---

## CHECK IT OUT

To learn more about the welfare system in the United States, contact:

**U.S. Department of Health and Human Services**
200 Independence Avenue, SW
Washington, DC 20201
1-877-696-6775
*www.dhhs.gov*

---

RESEARCH HOW OTHER COUNTRIES have cared for their citizens through history. You might take a look at Egypt, Greece, African nations, China, Russia (or the former Soviet Union), or Canada. Or find out how the United States has cared for Native American peoples. Make a chart comparing the countries or cultures you choose to research.

PLAN AND DO A SERVICE PROJECT. Follow these steps:[3]

**1. *Research your project.*** Choose an issue or need that concerns you, then come up with a project related to that issue or need.

**2. *Form a team.*** If you don't want to go it alone, or if the project seems too complicated to do by yourself, invite others to join you.

**3. *Find a sponsor.*** Ask a responsible adult (teacher, parent, neighbor, scout leader, etc.) to act as your sponsor. This can give your project credibility with other adults whose help and/or permission you might need.

**4. *Make a plan.*** Decide when and where to meet. Decide how you will get to the meeting place and service location. Define your goal; what do you hope to achieve? Set a schedule for your project. Estimate your

---

[2] See "Endurance," pages 88, 89, and 92, for journaling resources.

[3] Adapted from *The Kid's Guide to Service Projects* by Barbara A. Lewis (Minneapolis: Free Spirit Publishing, 1995), pages 8–12. Used with permission of the publisher.

costs. Think hard about your project; is it realistic? Too complicated? Too simple? How could you improve it?

**5. *Consider the recipient.*** Always make sure that the people you plan to serve really want your help. What's the best way to do this? Ask them!

**6. *Decide where you'll perform your service.*** Will you go to the people you plan to serve, or will they come to you? If you go to them, be sure to visit the location ahead of time and find out if it has what you need. If they come to you, make sure that your location has what you need.

**7. *Get any permissions you need to proceed.*** Depending on your project, you might have to ask permission from your principal, teacher(s), school district personnel, youth leader, parents, etc.

**8. *Advertise.*** Let other people know about your project. Make a flyer, create a public service announcement, or send out a press release.

**9. *Fund-raise.*** Do you need start-up money for your service project? Will you need to buy equipment or supplies? If your project will cost anything beyond pocket money, you'll need to fund-raise.

**10. *When your project has ended, evaluate it.*** Reflect on your experience. Discuss it with your team, family, teachers, friends, and neighbors. Talk it over with the people you served. What did you learn? What did you accomplish? Would you do the project again? How could you improve it?

---

## CHECK IT OUT

Four national programs that promote youth service are:

**Corporation for National and Community Service**
1201 New York Avenue, NW
Washington, DC 20525
(202) 606-5000
*www.cns.gov*

**National Youth Leadership Council**
1667 Snelling Avenue, N.
St. Paul, MN 55108
(651) 631-3672
*www.nylc.org*

---

**Youth as Resources**
Center for Youth as Resources
1000 Connecticut Avenue, NW, 12th Floor
Washington, DC 20036
(202) 261-4131
*www.yar.org*

**Youth Service America**
1101 15th Street, NW, Suite 200
Washington, DC 20005
(202) 296-2992
*www.ysa.org*

---

**DO A "SECRET SERVICE."** Choose someone you'd like to do something nice for or give something to. Leave a treat on a porch, in a locker, on a desk. Write an anonymous note telling the person why you admire him or her.

> *Variation:* Do the "Twelve Days of Christmas Surprise" for someone lonely or in need. Secretly leave a treat or perform a service for the person 12 days in a row. (You don't have to wait until Christmas.)

---

## CHECK IT OUT

For inspiration when planning your "secret service," read:

*Kids' Random Acts of Kindness* by the editors of Conari Press (Emeryville, CA: Conari Press, 1994). Kids from around the world tell their own stories of sudden, impetuous acts of kindness.

---

**WRITE YOUR OWN "RANDOM ACTS" BOOK.** Collect stories from friends, classmates, family members, and neighbors. Illustrate your book with drawings or photographs. Make several copies to hand out.

**BRAINSTORM A LIST OF POSSIBLE NEEDS** for family members (parents, brothers, sisters, grandparents, etc.). You could also brainstorm lists of needs for teachers, custodians, lunchroom aides, your school, the PTA, seniors, people with special needs, animals, etc. Review your lists and choose a project to do based on a need.

**START A KINDNESS "CHAIN REACTION."** Place a "Kindness Box" in your school, home, or club. Put a stack of paper and a marker beside the box. Above the box, include a sheet of simple instructions. They might say "Write about an anonymous act of kindness you've done or seen someone do." Each week, take the papers out of the box and display them in a chain on a wall. Or decorate a bulletin board with care messages or quotations about caring.

**WRITE A SKIT** about acts of kindness and ways to serve others. Present it to celebrate a favorite holiday or any time during the year. You might perform your skit for children in a hospital or shelter.

**MAKE "I CARE" KITS.** Collect personal items such as combs, toothbrushes, soaps, deodorants, etc. for a traveler's aid service. Or collect clothing, mittens, and shoes for a homeless shelter. Or collect pens, pencils, crayons, paper, and lap games for children in hospitals. Or make a Newcomer's Kit for new kids who come into your school. (This kit might include a map of the school, a school schedule, information about clubs and activities, a bus schedule, or anything else you can think of.)

**COLLECT SONGS ABOUT CARING.** Do this with a group of friends—you'll have more fun and find more songs. Perform some of your songs for your school, your community center, or children at a hospital or shelter.

**BE A CARING TEAM PLAYER.** Brainstorm ways to support team members when they make mistakes, have poor skills, or insult each other. How can you show care and concern for members of your own team, other teams, your coach, and yourself?

**PLAY A "LET ME HELP YOU" GAME.** Create an obstacle course that isn't too difficult. Pair off into partners. One partner wears a blindfold; the other is the helper. Start by having the blindfolded players try to navigate the obstacle course without help. They may refuse—or they may try and laugh, trip, or fall. Next, have the helpers guide the blindfolded players through the course. Switch places so all players have the chance to experience how good it feels to give and receive help.

*Variations:*

**1.** The helper gives verbal instructions but doesn't touch the blindfolded person.
**2.** The helper says nothing, but guides the blindfolded person with his or her hands.
**3.** The helper uses a combination of words and touches to guide the blindfolded person.

**READ STORIES ABOUT CARING.** Look for these books:

*Dicey's Song* by Cynthia Voigt (New York: Atheneum, 1982). Dicey struggles with school, a job, and responsibility for her brothers and sisters as she adjusts to living with her grandmother. Ages 11–12.

*The Gift of the Magi* by O. Henry (Wheaton, IL: Victor Books, 1996). A husband and wife give up their most valued possessions to purchase Christmas presents for each other. Ages 10 & up. (You can also find this story in many anthologies.)

*The Giving Tree* by Shel Silverstein (New York: HarperCollins Children's Books, 1964). A tree becomes an important part of a young boy's life. As they both age, the tree keeps giving happiness to the boy until she has none left for herself. All ages.

*Monkey Island* by Paula Fox (New York: Dell Publishing Co., Inc., 1993). Clay's father has left, and one day his mother doesn't come home. After a few days, 11-year-old Clay runs away and begins living on the streets, where he finds new friends to help him get by. Ages 11 & up.

*Sarah Bishop* by Scott O'Dell (New York: Scholastic, Inc., 1991). During the Revolutionary War, Sarah is befriended by an Indian couple and a young Quaker. When Sarah's reclusive lifestyle leads to charges of witchcraft, she is defended by the Quaker. Ages 11–15.

# Character in *ACTION*

## Claudia Rodriguez: Someone Who Cares

Claudia's mom first saw the advertisement in a Spanish language newspaper in Framingham, Massachusetts. The advertisement told of an AmeriCorps-sponsored workshop to train 100 teenagers in leadership skills and community service. Claudia sent in her application and was one of the teenagers chosen to go to Fort Devens, Massachusetts, in the summer when she was 16.

During the leadership training, Claudia worked with a team of 10 kids from New Mexico, Puerto Rico, Utah, and Texas. Together they surveyed, planned, and set up a meeting for minority business owners to find out how crime and safety affected them. After surveying more than 150 people, Claudia and her friends provided information to businesses about alarm systems and other safety measures.

At the end of her AmeriCorps training, Claudia was one of only two teens chosen to attend a Summer of Safety National Forum. She received more training there and returned home drenched in enthusiasm.

That's when her mom told her about a problem at the day-care center where she worked. All day long, Mrs. Rodriguez explained, kids from a nearby housing project would press their noses against the windows of the center, knocking and begging to use the playground. But the playground was always locked, and only children whose parents paid for day care were allowed to use it.

"That's when it hit me," Claudia remembers. "I had really developed my leadership skills and a desire to serve by helping those small businesses. So I went to a teacher at Framingham High School and made a proposal for an after-school Esperanza program for those children living in the low-income housing project." Claudia received lots of support from about 20 other teens in a service club at the high school.

Claudia Rodriguez (far right) on Cultural Day

The project wasn't easy. First, Claudia struggled to find a place to house the program. The Framingham Housing Authority finally agreed to donate a facility next door to the day-care center.

Claudia immediately organized her friends to collect donations of crayons, paper, scissors, and supplies from teachers and day-care centers. Then she made a flyer and distributed it around the housing project.

Only a handful of kids showed up on the first day, but by the end of the year, 30 or more children attended the program each Monday night for one hour. Claudia oversaw all the activities, which included arts, crafts, board games, and tutoring for the kids.

Kids like J.J., a nine-year-old hyperactive child with freckles peppered over his cheeks. "He was the kind of kid I wanted to hug," Claudia explains, "but he would never hug me back, even though I could tell he wanted affection. One day, we wrote him a get-well letter because he had been sick for two weeks. When he returned, he handed me a cake with a rose on top, and I almost cried."

When Claudia graduated from high school, another girl from the service club took over the program, and it's still running.

"Everything is a cycle," Claudia says. "The adults in the training program cared for me and had hope in me as a teenager. They believed I could do something. I tried to carry this to my community. I helped the kids. When these children grow up, they will have a sense of caring for others, because they have been cared for. I hope they will pass it on.

"I realize that if you care for someone and give them confidence, you never know what treasures are inside them and what they hold."

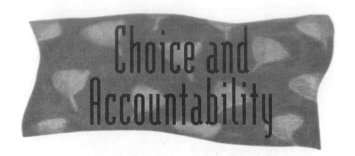

# Choice and Accountability

**Making decisions, accepting consequences,
being responsible for your choices**

> "We are free up to the point of choice,
> then the choice controls the chooser."
> *Mary Crowley*

## Choice

A 22-year-old man lit a firecracker in a fireworks store in Scottown, Ohio, that killed several people, including two children. His friends dared him to do it. He took the dare, and it was meant to be a joke. The joke ran amok as rockets whizzed and firecrackers exploded in a violent chain reaction. The man was charged with involuntary manslaughter, and he learned the hard way that you'd better think about consequences before making a choice.

You may think you have the right to choose many things: what you wear to school, what you eat, who your friends are. You can choose between right and wrong, to do your homework or not, to tell the truth or lie. But you can't control the consequences of your choices, and sometimes those consequences can limit you. *Examples:*

3, You can choose what you want to eat. But what if your parents don't agree with you that potato chips and onion rings belong to the vegetable food group? Unless you buy your own food, your choices are limited. And even if you do buy your own food, you can't control the consequences of eating only junk food—the harm it eventually does to your body and your health.

3, You can choose your friends. But what if the ones you choose don't choose you? Or what if the ones you choose are kids who get into trouble all the time? Are you willing to go along with them and suffer the consequences?

3, You can choose to wear a loincloth and scuba mask to school, but you might not be allowed to stay there. In fact, you'll probably be invited to spend a session with the school psychologist.

3, You can choose between right and wrong. But what if you don't know the difference? What if the adults in your life have never taught you? Or what if their definitions of right and wrong conflict with what most people in your society or culture believe? Or what if you know that it's wrong to steal, but your family is starving and if you don't steal food, they might die? (You're right; this can get very complicated and confusing.)

3 You can choose not to do your homework. But you can't control whether and for how long your parents will ground you when you bring home a bad report card.

3 You can choose to tell a lie. But the consequences of your lie—losing your parents' trust, losing a friend, ruining your reputation—are out of your control.

Ideally, any choice you make should be both *conscious* and *informed.*

- A *conscious* choice is one you're aware of. You think it through ahead of time. You're mindful and alert when you make your decision. You realize that it might have both positive and negative consequences.

- An *informed* choice is based on information and facts you've gathered in advance. You find out as much about your choice as you can. You look at it from all sides. You try to predict the consequences.

*Example:* Your teacher has just assigned you a paper due tomorrow. The problem is, today is your grandmother's birthday, and your whole family is taking her out to dinner tonight. You have to choose between writing your paper or celebrating your grandmother's birthday. The choice is up to you. What will you do?

1. **Think it through.** If you choose to stay home and write your paper, your paper will get done but your grandmother will be disappointed. If you choose to go out to dinner, your grandmother will be happy but you'll get a zero grade on your paper. Neither choice is perfect.

2. **Gather information.** Before you leave school, talk to your teacher about your dilemma. Can you turn in your paper a day late? If not, how much will one zero hurt your final grade? Talk to your parents about your dilemma. Ask what they think you should do. Can you call your grandmother

and explain the problem? Can you can arrange to see her later in the week and celebrate her birthday at that time?

3. **Weigh your choices and the possible consequences, then make your decision.** It might not be perfect, but it will be the best it can be under the circumstances. It will be conscious and informed.

Sometimes we make choices that aren't really choices at all. They're habits. *Example:* You walk to school the same way every day. This may be the fastest and most efficient route, but it's not a conscious choice. What if you decided to walk another way instead? Maybe you wouldn't have to cross so many busy streets, or maybe you'd pass a friend's house on the way and could walk with him or her.

The worst choices are the ones you make by default. Instead of making a conscious, informed choice, you simply allow something to happen. *Example:* You want school lunches to be better. On the day your school votes for a new menu, you forget to vote. So do a lot of other students, so the vote doesn't pass and school lunches stay the same. By not choosing, you have made a choice, and the results weren't what you wanted.

> "Use wisely your power of choice."
> *Og Mandino*

# Accountability

When you're accountable, you take responsibility for the choices you make. Maybe they weren't the best choices; maybe you made mistakes. Perhaps you didn't find out as much about your choices ahead of time as you could have, or perhaps there were too many factors you couldn't control. Still, they were *your* choices.

Have you ever heard someone say "You made me do that" or "It's your fault that I didn't finish"? When you're accountable, you don't blame other people for your actions. You know that you can't control what others say and do—only what *you* say and do. You don't lie or make excuses for your behavior ("I'm sorry I was late. My brother kept me up last night and I overslept." "I didn't do my homework because I had to wash the dishes"). Instead, you make conscious and informed choices. *Examples:*

▲ "If I stay up late and watch another video, I'll oversleep tomorrow. Then I'll be late to school and I'll probably get a detention. Plus I'll be tired all day. It's not worth it. I'll watch the video on Friday night instead."

▲ "Since it's my turn to wash the dishes, I'm not going to have enough time to talk to my friends on the phone and do my homework besides. If I talk on the phone, I won't get my homework done. I guess I'll have to sacrifice some of my phone time tonight."

Besides choosing and being accountable for your actions, you also choose and are accountable for your *thoughts, feelings, reactions,* and *attitudes.*[1] For example, you can choose to think that one race of people is superior to another—and you might choose to feel superior to other people as a result. But what if you're asked to be accountable for these choices? Are they informed choices? Are they based on facts? Or have you simply accepted something you've heard or read? If you choose to believe everything you hear and read, you might make a poor choice that leads to other poor choices in the future.

Or let's say that the school bully dumps his lunch tray in your lap. You might choose to punch him in the stomach and get into a fight. You might choose to do nothing and hold a grudge. Or you might choose to walk away, report him to a teacher, and let the teacher do something about it. You can't control what the bully does, but you can control how you react. Your reaction is a choice.

## How Can You Make Better Choices?

Your life is and will be full of choices and decisions. What can you do to make sure that your choices are the best they can be?

☀ Be conscious and informed whenever you make a choice.

☀ Try to determine if your choice is more likely to help someone or hurt someone. Try to make choices that help other people, yourself, or the world.

☀ Talk over your choice with people you trust—people who care about you and want what's best for you. Make sure to talk to at least one adult.

☀ After making a choice, review what you did and what happened as a result. Did it help someone? Did it make something better? Would you make a different choice next time?

☀ Learn from your choice. Remember what you did and what the consequences were. Use this knowledge to keep making good choices in the future.

## What If You Make a Poor Choice?

◆ Admit it. Be honest and accountable. ("I stole a CD from the music store.")

◆ Accept the consequences. ("I have a court hearing now and must do 15 hours of community service. Plus I have a police record.")

◆ Do what you can to make up for your poor choice and turn it into something positive. ("I'll pay the store for the CD. I'll teach and warn other kids not to steal. I won't steal anymore or get into worse trouble so my criminal record can be erased when I'm 19.")

◆ Learn from your choice. ("I'll be more careful with my money. I'll be patient and wait until I earn enough money to get the things I want—or I'll do without them.")

◆ Ask someone you trust to monitor your progress and give you support and encouragement. ("I'll talk to my parents about what happened and what I've decided to do about it. I'll ask for their help and advice.")

◆ Make a personal commitment to make better choices in the future.

> "Your life is the sum result of all the choices you make, both consciously and unconsciously. If you can control the process of choosing, you can take control of all aspects of your life. You can find the freedom that comes from being in charge of yourself."
> *Robert F. Bennett*

---

[1] See "Positive Attitudes," pages 14–20.

# Character Dilemmas

*For journaling or writing essays, discussion, debate, role-playing, reflection*

**Suppose that ...**

**1** Your wealthy aunt offers to pay for a year's worth of any kind of lessons you want to take. Money is no object. How will you decide what lessons to take—or whether to take any lessons at all? How will you make the best possible choice?

**2** You're planning your course schedule for the upcoming school year. There are two courses you really want and need to take. Unfortunately, they're both being taught during third hour. How will you choose which course to take?

**3** You've been saving your money for a new mountain bike. You know exactly what kind you want and how much it costs. For the past year, you've done extra chores, baby-sat, brown-bagged your school lunch, rented videos instead of going to movies, and saved more than half of your weekly allowance. You're almost ready to buy your bike when something terrible happens: A fire destroys the home of one of your classmates, and the family loses everything. The student council announces a donation drive to help the family get back on their feet. How will you choose what to do?

**4** You learn that a piece of land next to your school is up for grabs. The city hasn't decided what to do with it. Some people want to use it for a park. Others want to build stores and businesses there. Still others think it's the perfect site for a new housing development. A committee has been formed to consider the various issues involved and make recommendations, and you've been chosen to represent the students in your school. How will you choose what to recommend? Can you predict the consequences of your choice?

**5** Two weeks ago, a friend of yours ran away from home. Yesterday, you saw him at the mall. He told you that he was living with someone he met at the bus station. Then he explained why he ran away from home: his parents were abusive, and he wasn't going to take it anymore. He swore you to secrecy. How will you choose what to do next?

**6** There's a student at your school who's always being bullied and teased. One day, you overhear a group of popular kids planning a mean practical joke to play on him. You're friends with one of the popular kids, and you'd really like to be part of that group. What are your choices? What will you do?

# Activities

**MAKE A LIST** of the most important choices you need to make today, this week, this year. Think about how you can make the best choices. Jot down some possible consequences. Try to do this daily or weekly. In a month, review your list and notes. Has this made a positive difference in your life? Has it helped you to make better choices?

**MAKE A TIMELINE** of the most important choices you'll face during your lifetime. Show the ages at which you think you'll be making those choices. What can you do to plan ahead? If you want, you can illustrate your timeline.

**WRITE IN YOUR JOURNAL**[2] about a time when you made a poor choice. Describe the consequences of your choice. What have you learned as a result of your choice and the consequences? Write about a time when you made a good choice.

**ROLE-PLAY** with a friend how you might talk to another friend who's considering joining a gang. Or how you might role play talking with someone who's using drugs or alcohol, or who's planning to run away from home.

**LEARN ABOUT POOR CHOICES** in the history of science. *Example:* Around 150 A.D., Ptolemy theorized that the earth was the center of the universe. He chose to keep believing this in spite of other theories and evidence. Other scientists chose to believe Ptolemy's theory, too, and this halted the advance of knowledge in this area for many years. Try to find more examples of times when people have made poor choices and stuck with them in spite of evidence to

---

[2] See "Endurance," pages 88, 89, and 92, for journaling resources.

the contrary. *Example:* Sigmund Freud searched for a substance that would enhance the workings of the brain. He found and used cocaine and called it a "magical drug." His enthusiasm for cocaine led to widespread use before its harmful side effects were discovered. Find out more about the consequences of this choice—for Freud personally and for others.

**FIND OUT WHAT HAPPENS** to people who choose not to pay their income taxes. If your state has an income tax, contact your state tax commission. Try to find answers to these questions: Approximately how many people who live in your state don't pay their income taxes? About how much money does your state spend each year trying to recover lost revenues? What happens to nonpayers who get caught? If your state doesn't have an income tax, contact the Internal Revenue Service (IRS) and ask about federal taxes.

**INTERVIEW THE OWNER** of a successful small business in your town or city. Ask questions like:

**?**   "What kinds of choices have you faced over the years?"

**?**   "What's the best choice you've ever made? The poorest choice?"

**?**   "Were you able to predict the consequences of your choices? Were there any big surprises?"

**?**   "If you could go back in time and change just one of your choices, which one would it be? How would your choice be different? How would the consequences be different?"

**WRITE TO 10 FAMOUS PEOPLE** and ask this question: "What's the hardest choice you've ever had to make?" If you do this as a class, compile the responses you receive into a book. Donate it to your school library.

## CHECK IT OUT

*The Kid's Address Book: Over 3,000 Addresses of Celebrities, Athletes, Entertainers, and More . . . Just for Kids!* by Michael Levine (New York: Perigree Books, 1997; updated often). Over 2,800 addresses (and many email addresses) for famous people. Also by Michael Levine: *The Address Book: Direct Access to Over 4,000 Celebrities, Corporate Execs, and Other VIPs* (New York: Perigree Books, 1997; updated often).

**START A "CHOICES AND CONSEQUENCES"** discussion group. Talk about the following choices. Try to come up with at least three possible consequences for each choice. Or, if you prefer, consider real choices you're facing at this time in your life.

▲   going to college vs. not going to college

▲   eating healthful food vs. eating a regular diet of junk food

▲   getting regular exercise vs. being a couch potato

▲   joining an after-school club vs. hanging out with friends

▲   doing a random act of kindness vs. not making the effort

▲   coming home before curfew vs. staying out past curfew

▲   doing your homework vs. not doing your homework

▲   standing up for a friend who's being bullied vs. ignoring the situation

▲   doing your chores vs. not doing your chores

▲   making friends with someone who's not very popular vs. not making friends with the person.

**WRITE A SERIES OF 5-MINUTE SKITS** about choices, consequences, and being accountable. Present your skits to younger kids at your school. Depending on how well they're received, you might perform them for children in a hospital or shelter.

**CREATE A COMIC BOOK** about choices, consequences, and being accountable. You might invent a character and show scenes from his or her life. Or you might use examples from your own life or the life of someone you know. Follow the look and style of one of your favorite comic books.

## CHECK IT OUT

*Understanding Comics: The Invisible Art* by Scott McCloud (New York: HarperPerennial, 1994). Explores the history and symbolism of comics, the energy of line and color, and the hidden worlds of comics storytelling. Ages 13 & up.

**RESEARCH THE LIFE OF A FAMOUS COMPOSER,** past or present. What kinds of major choices did he or she have to make? How did these choices affect the composer's life and work? What can you learn from his or her example?

**READ THE AUTOBIOGRAPHY OF AN ATHLETE** in the news. Or learn about the athlete's life by reading articles in magazines, in newspapers, or online, or by watching televised interviews. What kinds of choices has the athlete made during his or her life and career? From what you can tell, is the athlete accountable for his or her choices, or does he or she blame other people, events, and circumstances for the hard times and problems in his or her life?

**PLAY A "STICK TO THE TRUTH" GAME.** Sit in a circle. Pass a stick around. The person who holds the stick shares a story about a time when he or she made a good or poor choice, and what the consequences were. People who don't have anything to share can pass the stick to the next person. TIP: Go around the circle at least twice. People who "pass" the first time might have something to say the second time.

**READ STORIES ABOUT CHOICE** and accountability. Look for these books:

*Choosing Sides* by Ilene Cooper (New York: Morrow Junior Books, 1990). Jonathan doesn't want to be called a quitter, but his coach is turning middle school basketball into a forgettable experience. Ages 10–13.

*Here at the Scenic-Vu Motel* by Thelma Hatch Wyss (New York: HarperCollins Childrens Books, 1989). Seven teens board at the Scenic-Vu Motel because they live too far from Pineville to make the commute to the high school every day. High school senior Jake finds himself responsible for the group. Ages 13 & up.

*Shiloh* by Phyllis Naylor (New York: Atheneum, 1991). Young Marty discovers a puppy near the Shiloh schoolhouse and soon learns that the dog's owner mistreats him and his other animals. As the dog does not belong to him, Marty struggles to decide what he should do. Ages 10–13.

*So Far from the Bamboo Grove* by Yoko Kawashima Watkins (New York: Puffin, 1987). Eight-year-old Yoko escapes from Korea to Japan with her family at the end of World War II. Ages 10–14.

*Trouble's Child* by Mildred Pitts Walter (New York: Lothrop, Lee & Shepard Books, 1985). Martha dreams of leaving her island home off the Louisiana coast. She longs to attend high school to learn more than the ways of her grandmother and perhaps broaden the lives of the superstitious villagers. Ages 12 & up.

# Character in *ACTION*
## Jed Michael: Living With Your Choices

Jed's science teacher looked at him sternly and asked "Did you tie Mandy's hair in knots?" Jed hung his head and said "Yep." He grinned fiendishly.

"Jed, is that you talking in the back of the room?" his math teacher asked. Although several other students were also talking, Jed pulled his long, corn-colored hair over his face and answered "Uh-huh."

"Which of you students threw food in the cafeteria today?" the principal wanted to know. Jed rolled his eyes, raised his hand, and said "I did." No one else said a word. For telling the truth, Jed was only allowed to eat a sliced carrot and one slice of yellow American cheese on bread, with milk, for the rest of the school year. "I don't think I deserved the punishment, but it worked," Jed admits. "I stopped throwing food!"

Telling the truth doesn't always get you out of trouble, especially if you're guilty. Jed didn't always make the best choices, but he always accepted the consequences for what he did.

Many of his choices were good. For example, he spoke out at public meetings to keep out radioactive dumping near his house in Cincinnatus, New York.

But school was a different matter. "I was a pain in the neck, for sure," Jed confesses.

When you're a pain in the neck, sometimes you get blamed for things you didn't do. "I got blamed for vandalizing a mural in the hallway," Jed remembers. "I was standing outside the classroom as a punishment for speaking out of turn, and I deserved that. But I *didn't* vandalize the mural. I also got accused of stealing a carton of orange juice from the breakfast program—something else I didn't do."

Although Jed was able to prove that the hand smears on the mural were larger than his, and that the orange juice was part of his school breakfast, the school authorities expelled him anyway. For a while, Jed had a tutor for a couple of hours each day. Then

Jed Michael

his parents were able to arrange for him to attend an alternative high school.

"It's a great school," he explains. "Everyone respects people for who they are instead of what they do." At his new school, Jed chose to help other people instead of getting into trouble. He started earning a good reputation, and many people sought him out.

"There was a guy who was pumped up on drugs and having problems. He wanted to kill himself. I pointed out to him that suicide wouldn't leave him with any choices at all. It wouldn't accomplish anything. After we talked, the guy went back to his parents' house, and then he went into rehab. He's doing okay now."

A girl Jed knew came to him with boyfriend problems. There were two guys who liked her, and they were fighting over her. "I told her to get them both together and talk it out. I was a mediator. Now all three of them are friends."

Then there was a kid nobody liked. "He had a grating personality. Kids were making fun of him and accusing him of being gay. I told him to tell the truth and people would respect him more."

Not every story Jed tells has a happy ending. "A close friend of mine fell into a wrong crowd and started dealing drugs. He's in prison now. He's smart enough to realize that dealing drugs is a dumb thing to do, but he made the wrong choice and now he's paying for it."

Jed knows firsthand the difference between good choices and poor choices. "If I do something wrong, I accept the consequences. That's just the way I am. But now I have the chance to graduate a year early, because I've worked hard at this school and made the right choices.

"Honesty works. It could be its own system of government, if everyone followed it. You can settle almost any dispute with honesty. You can get ahead by being honest. And you don't have to worry about getting caught if you tell the truth."

# Citizenship

**Activism, participation, community service,
love of freedom, patriotism**

> "I grew up with the idea that democracy is
> not something you believe in, or a place
> you hang your hat, but it's something you
> do. You participate. If you stop doing it,
> democracy crumbles and falls apart."
>
> *Abbie Hoffman*

Fourteen-year-old Angela Pratico stood before Vermont lawmakers in 1992 and told them that children should have certain rights—including the right to good health care, the right to a good education, and the right to be safe and free from exploitation. She also testified in the Senate chambers in Washington, D.C., about children's rights.

In Harford County, Maryland, more than 16,000 children in kindergarten through high school accompanied their parents to the polls to cast their votes in the 1996 presidential election. The results were published so everyone could see how the students (some of whom would be old enough to vote in the next election) felt about the candidates and the issues.

A group of students in Lauren Mullen's fifth grade class at Jackson Elementary School in Salt Lake City, Utah, borrowed voter registration books from the local election office and registered 40 residents who lived near the school. At least 15 were from their own families.

These young people were demonstrating good citizenship. But what do those words really mean? If you claimed to be a good citizen because you take care of yourself, don't throw erasers at other kids in school, and pick up trash in the halls, you'd

be right. Taking care of yourself and following school rules are important things for a good citizen to do.

You can also look at citizenship in the broader sense. *Citizenship usually refers to your membership in, responsibility toward, or contribution to your community, and your conduct within your community and nation.* This means that you follow family rules and don't stay out beyond your curfew. It also means that you participate in making rules for walking down the halls at school, and you don't throw food in the lunchroom. It means that you vote when you're old enough. It means that you speak out for what you believe in at your community council meeting, and you might even campaign for someone running for office. It can also mean that you volunteer at your local hospital, carrying flowers to patients.[1] Or it might mean that you work with your local animal shelter to find homes for abandoned pets.

> "This country has more problems
> than it should tolerate and more
> solutions than it uses."
>
> *Ralph Nader*

In a representative democracy, "citizenship" is an action word. It means that you do something to help out. United States Supreme Court Justice Sandra Day O'Connor has said that the 50 states are laboratories for citizens to develop new ideas.

---

[1] See "Caring," pages 21–27.

"Hello? I'm calling about a pet who needs a home . . ."

And there isn't one right way to practice citizenship. You might pass a petition calling for free pizza at lunch for all school kids. Or you might write a letter to Congress asking lawmakers to stop giving food stamps to low-income families. Either would be an important action, for democracy allows for a stewpot of ideas.

> "One has the right to be wrong
> in a democracy."
> *Claude Pepper*

In a democracy, "freedom" doesn't mean "freedom from responsibility." You can't wait for the government to clean up all the litter in the parks, fix all the potholes in the streets, tutor all the children at homeless shelters, or repair your grandmother's lawn sprinkler. An army of energetic citizens like you could accomplish that and more. If you wait for government officials to solve every problem, it will take a millennium to do and cost you too much in taxes. And you'll lose the chance to help design the solutions.

Here are four ways you can be a good citizen, starting today:

**1.** Be a caring, contributing, respectful person who obeys laws and rules.

**2.** Be an active participant in your family, school, and community. Help people. Fix things. Work to improve conditions for everyone and everything.

**3.** Get involved in your government. Campaign for causes and candidates. Lobby for or against ordinances or laws. Vote in all local, state, and national elections (when you're old enough).

**4.** Speak out against social injustice. Work for equality, fairness, safety, and opportunity for all people.

Good citizens are often patriotic. If you're an American who sometimes get a lump in your throat when you say the Pledge of Allegiance or sing the National Anthem, if you feel pride when you watch the U.S. athletes competing in the Olympics, if you feel a tug at your heart when you watch the Fourth of July parades or fireworks, you're patriotic. Although you might not agree with everything that happens in the United States, you love your country, defend its values, and work for improvements.

# Character Dilemmas

*For journaling or writing essays, discussion, debate, role-playing, reflection*

**Suppose that . . .**

**1** Julius loves animals. One day, he discovers that his next-door neighbor beats his dog and doesn't feed or water him enough. That night, Julius sneaks over the fence between their houses and unties the dog, setting him free. The dog runs away. Was this the act of a good citizen? Why or why not? What's the problem here? Are human rights and animal rights the same? Different? What might you tell Julius to do?

**2** You're watching CNN one morning when you hear that the voting age might be lowered to 16. This would mean that high school students could vote in local, state, and national elections. Do you think this is a good idea? Why or why not? What will you do?

**3** You've just learned that from now on, *all* government officials will be elected by the citizens. Supreme Court justices, cabinet members, agency heads, and others who used to be appointed will have to run for office. How do you think this might change the country and its policies?

**4** A new law is passed, and citizens are no longer allowed to speak out against the policies of public officials.[2] How might this change your life? The lives of your friends? Your parents and teachers? How might it change the country as a whole? What will you do about this new law? What are the advantages—and disadvantages—of being able to speak out?

**5** You and your friends decide to boycott a product. (To *boycott* a product means to refuse to buy or use it.) A few years ago, kids across the country banded together and boycotted a certain fast-food chain that used styrofoam to package its hamburgers. Do you think it's a good idea to boycott a product? What are the dangers of doing this? Of not doing this?

**6** You come to school one morning to find graffiti all over the walls. Someone has also sprayed graffiti on nearby billboards, overpasses, and road signs. No one knows who did it. Whose responsibility is it to clean up and paint over the graffiti? Why? Is there anything you can do to protect your school and community against graffiti in the future?

# Activities

**WRITE IN YOUR JOURNAL**[3] about what it means to you to be a citizen of your country. Study its important documents (the U.S. Constitution, the Bill of Rights) and write about how these concepts and principles affect you.

**PREPARE AND GIVE A SPEECH.**[4] Research and write a speech on the importance of rights for children and youth (for food, shelter, safety, medical care, education, etc.). Arrange to give your speech at your community council, school, club, religious organization, or other group. Find out who agrees with your views. Build a team. You might be able to speak out about kids' rights at many places around your community.

**WRITE A RAP OR SONG** about the rights and needs of children and youth, senior citizens, people with disabilities, or another topic that interests you. Make a cassette recording, take it to a local radio station, and ask them to play it. This is called a public service announcement (PSA), and radios provide free time for citizens to publicize issues that are important to them. TIPS: Be clever and concise. Most PSAs are only 10, 20, or 30 seconds long.

**HELP YOUR SCHOOL GET UP-TO-DATE** on technology. Find out what's currently available: Does your school have computers? Where are they located? Who uses them? Is access available to everyone? If not, why not? Does your school have the software students need most? What about Internet access? Work with the technology specialist in your school or district to prepare a "Most Wanted" list of technology tools and figure out ways to get them.

**LEARN ABOUT CITIZENSHIP IN HISTORY.** Research the policies of Alexander Hamilton and Thomas Jefferson during the 1780s and 1790s. How did their opinions of citizen involvement affect the United States? HINTS: Hamilton wanted a strong central government; Jefferson supported putting power in the hands of the people. How different might citizen involvement in the U.S. be today if the nation had followed only Hamilton's ideas? Only Jefferson's ideas? Compare their differences on a chart.

**CAMPAIGN FOR SOMEONE** who's running for office in your school. Or call the campaign headquarters of someone who's running for office in your city or state and ask how you can help. Maybe you can pass out door tags and other literature or answer phones.

*Variation:* Hold a mock city, state, or national election in your school. Invite students to speak for or represent the views of various candidates running for office. Or ask the real candidates to come to your school and speak. After the election, tabulate the votes to see who won.

**GET OUT THE VOTE.** Contact your local League of Women Voters or voter registration office. Ask what you can do to help people register to vote. You might volunteer to:

✔ telephone residents and explain how to register

✔ work at the polling place during elections

---

[2] This freedom is guaranteed by the Bill of Rights, but if you defame people or tell lies about them, you can be sued for slander.
[3] See "Endurance," pages 88, 89, and 92, for journaling resources.
[4] See "Communication," pages 50–60.

✔ go door-to-door to register residents (with an adult chaperon)

✔ hand out absentee ballots for seniors, people with disabilities, or people who will be out of town during the elections

✔ work to provide a voter pick-up or transportation service for seniors or other people with special needs who might not be able to travel to the polling place.

## CHECK IT OUT

**Kids Voting USA**
398 South Mill Avenue, Suite 304
Tempe, AZ 85281
(480) 921-3727
*www.kidsvotingusa.org*
This nonprofit, nonpartisan organization makes it possible for kids to visit official polling sites on election days and cast their own ballots on the same issues and candidates the adults are voting for. Studies are showing that the program also increases *adult* voter turnout. Find out if your state is a member.

**PLAY A VOTING GAME.** Make a list of issues that your classmates could vote for. *Examples:*

**?** Should our school have vending machines?

**?** Should our school have coeducational sports teams?

**?** Should school run year-round?

**?** Should the voting age be lowered to 16?

**?** Should students have the power to interview and hire teachers?

Place three glass jars around the room labeled "Yes," "No," and "Not Sure." Give each student a marble. Read the first issue and ask everyone to think quietly for one minute, then place his or her marble in one of the three labeled jars. Watch how the votes add up. Do students seem to vote independently, or do they wait to see how their friends vote? Read the second issue, and so on. Notice how 1) by voting or *not* voting, you can swing an election, and 2) not all issues have definite right or wrong choices.

*Variations:* Allow students who voted "Yes" or "No" to debate the issue further. Allow those who voted "Not Sure" to take their marbles out of that jar and vote "Yes" or "No" instead. Notice how 1) people might not vote if they lack information, and 2) by giving people information, you can influence the way they vote.

**STUDY THE BUDGET.** Contact your local government office (city or county) and ask for printed information about last year's projected budget, revenues, and expenditures. Study this information. Was there a shortfall (did your local government spend more than they received in revenues)? Was there a surplus (did they spend less than they received)? Analyze the budget. Write up your findings and ideas, and present them in a speech at your community or city council and before your local government budget committee.

**BE A BUDDY** for students at your school who have special needs or disabilities. Organize a group of friends so someone is always available to spend time with special needs students during recess, between classes, at assemblies, etc.

*Variations:*
1. Find out if there are places in your school where kids with special needs can't go (for example, because of no wheelchair access). You might try fund-raising for better access. Or contact your school district to seek help.
2. Find out if any bills (measures being considered for laws) are before your city government or state legislature that affect people with special needs. Support or oppose the bill with letters, phone calls, and/or emails to legislators. Or go to the government offices or state house and lobby (talk with) the legislators in person to tell them how you feel.

**LEARN ABOUT ACTIVISM** in your community. See what organizations and groups are out there and find out what they do. *Examples:* Does your community have neighborhood associations and block clubs? Environmental action groups? Co-ops? Homeless shelters? Service organizations? Coalitions? Mentoring programs? Literacy groups? Volunteer cleanup crews? Food banks? Organizations that promote peaceful conflict resolution? How can you find out?

## CHECK IT OUT

*The American Promise Videos*
An inspiring series about grassroots democracy and activism in America today, produced for public television. More than 40 stories filmed in 21 states and the District of Columbia profile volunteers and visionaries who are making America work. Check to see if your school or library has a copy. To order, call 1-800-358-3000.

*The American Promise: Adventures in Grass-Roots Democracy* by James C. Crimmins (San Francisco: KQED Books and Video, 1996). The companion book to the television series includes tales of community and democracy. Ages 13 & up.

**The American Promise**
*www.pbs.org/ap*
The Web site for the series includes a Community Action Guide featuring stories, local heroes, and community resources; a Teacher's Tune-In Guide with teacher tools, class activities, and discussion topics; and QuickTime movies from the series.

BE AN ACTIVIST. Follow these steps:[5]

*1. Choose a problem.* Look around your neighborhood, school, or community for something that needs fixing, improving, or changing.

*2. Do your research.* Find out everything you can about your problem. Read about it. Talk to your friends, teachers, and neighbors. Contact experts and city or state officials.

*3. Brainstorm many possible solutions to your problem.* Choose your best solution(s).

*4. Build a strong support team.* Find people who agree with your ideas and ask them to join you.

*5. Identify your opposition.* Find people who *don't* agree with your ideas. Talk with them. Include them. They might decide to help you instead of oppose you. And you might discover places where you can compromise and improve your chances of success.

*6. Advertise.* TV, radio, and newspaper reporters love stories about young people taking social action. TV and radio stations offer free airtime for good causes. Don't forget community newspapers and church bulletins.

*7. Raise money for your cause.* Even if you only collect a small amount, this shows you're serious about wanting to solve the problem.

*8. Carry out your solution.* Make a list of all the steps you need to take. Give speeches, write letters, pass petitions. Get it done!

---

[5] Adapted from *The Kid's Guide to Social Action* by Barbara A. Lewis (Minneapolis: Free Spirit Publishing, 1991), pages 12–13. Used with permission of the publisher.

*9. Evaluate your progress.* Reflect on what you've done so far. Is your plan working or not? Should you ask for more help? Should you try something different?

*10. Don't give up.* Even if some people tell you why your solution won't work, keep trying until you find something that *does* work. Don't stop until you're ready to stop.

## CHECK IT OUT

The Internet is a rich resource for all kinds of activists. Log on and you'll discover thousands of sites and resources; go to a single site and find links to hundreds more. Here are some great places to start exploring:

**Institute for Global Communications**
*www.igc.org*
Home to PeaceNet, EcoNet, ConflictNet, and LaborNet, each a gateway to articles, headlines, features, and links.

**Voices of Youth**
*www.unicef.org/voy*
Developed as part of UNICEF's 50th Anniversary celebration, this site invites kids around the world to take part in an electronic discussion about the future. Includes links for global activism and children's rights.

**WebActive**
*www.webactive.com*
A weekly online publication that helps activists to find other organizations and individuals with similar values and interests.

**Who Cares Online**
*www.judeok.es.kr/tgc/politica/whocares/home.htm*
The home page for *Who Cares: A Journal of Service and Action,* a national quarterly journal devoted to community service and social activism, with a special focus on young activists.

---

DON'T BE BORED; JOIN A BOARD. School boards across the country exist to serve kids in the school system— but where are the kids? Are there students on your school board and, if so, do they have a vote? Some districts across the country allow students to sit on boards in an advisory capacity, but usually they aren't allowed to vote (yet). If this is something that interests you, contact your principal, your school district, and your school board (in that order). If you don't get any encouragement, contact a state legislator and ask him or her to sponsor a bill that would pave the way for students to participate on local school boards.

> *Variations:* Contact your city, community, or state house to find out about other boards in your area that might welcome kids. What about an animal rights council? An environmental action group? Or some other citizens' group?

**JOIN YOUR MAYOR'S YOUTH COUNCIL.** Does your town or city have a mayor's youth council or another type of community youth council? If it does, find out how to get involved. If it doesn't, contact your mayor and ask if he or she will start one. Write a proposal on why you think a youth council is important and what its goals might be. *Examples:* to make city officials aware of kids' views on issues that affect them; to reduce gang activity; to promote public awareness of kids' rights and needs.

**TAKE THE ACTIVISM INVENTORY** on page 41. Instructions for interpreting the inventory are printed upside down at the bottom of this page. Don't read them until you've finished taking and scoring the inventory.

**ILLUSTRATE THE BILL OF RIGHTS.** Find a copy of the Bill of Rights. (Look in an encyclopedia, a large dictionary, or a American History textbook.) Draw a cartoon to illustrate each right. Color your cartoons and gather them into a book. Share your book with younger students, then donate it to your school library.

**START A SPORTS PROGRAM.** Do schools and parks in your community offer a good selection of team and individual sports? Do you wish someone would start a lacrosse team or an interdistrict marbles tournament? Use your citizenship skills to write a proposal to your city athletic or recreation organization, school, or district. Find an enthusiastic adult to sponsor your idea, then collect a group of people to help you develop the program.

**READ STORIES ABOUT CITIZENSHIP.** Look for these books:

*Blatherskite* by Marian Potter (New York: Morrow, 1980). Maureen McCracken is a regular "talking machine," according to her brother. In the midst of the Great Depression, she does what she can to make the best of things and entertain her family, but all she hears are complaints. Ages 9–12.

*The Day They Came to Arrest the Book* by Nat Hentoff (New York: Bantam Doubleday Dell, 1983). High school students and teachers become part of a heated debate over the censorship of *Huckleberry Finn.* Ages 13 & up.

*The Last Safe Place on Earth* by Richard Peck (New York: Bantam Doubleday Dell, 1996). Todd's world starts to come apart after his sister is confronted by a member of a fundamentalist sect and he begins to notice signs of censorship in his community. Ages 12 & up.

*The Well: David's Story* by Mildred Taylor (New York: Dial, 1995). In the early 1900s, David's rural Mississippi family shares their well water with black and white neighbors. Ages 8–12.

*White Lilacs* by Carolyn Meyer (San Diego, CA: Harcourt, Brace, and Co., 1993). Rose Lee's community is threatened when the whites decide to forcibly relocate black families to make room for a new park. Ages 8–12.

"Seventy-five percent of us think that school should start at 9:00 and end at 3:00."

Interpreting your Activism Inventory score: 25–30 points = Super Citizen; 15–24 points = Average Participating Citizen; 10–14 points = What Are You Waiting For?

# Activism Inventory

*Read each statement, then check the box that describes how often you do what it says.*

See "Take the activism inventory" on page 40.

|  |  | Often | Sometimes | Never |
|---|---|:---:|:---:|:---:|
| 1. | Help an older person carry groceries or cross the street. | ❑ | ❑ | ❑ |
| 2. | Vote in a school election. | ❑ | ❑ | ❑ |
| 3. | Run for a school office or volunteer to serve on a school committee. | ❑ | ❑ | ❑ |
| 4. | Do volunteer work in your community. *Examples:* rake leaves, shovel snow, help to serve food at a center for homeless people, read to seniors, tutor a younger student. | ❑ | ❑ | ❑ |
| 5. | Do a voluntary service for your family. *Examples:* clean the house, do yard work, baby-sit for free. | ❑ | ❑ | ❑ |
| 6. | Give a speech, make a phone call, or write a letter to someone in your school, community, or state to support or oppose an issue. | ❑ | ❑ | ❑ |
| 7. | Put your hand over your heart, listen respectfully, or sing along when the National Anthem is playing. | ❑ | ❑ | ❑ |
| 8. | Read the newspaper or watch the news on TV. | ❑ | ❑ | ❑ |
| 9. | Pass a student petition at your school, club, community, or faith community. | ❑ | ❑ | ❑ |
| 10. | Encourage your parents or other adults to vote in an election. | ❑ | ❑ | ❑ |

**SCORING:** Give yourself 3 points for every "Often," 2 points for every "Sometimes," and 0 points for every "Never."

Number of "Often" responses: _____ x 3 = _____

Number of "Sometimes" responses: _____ x 2 = _____

Number of "Never" responses: \_\_0\_\_ = \_\_0\_\_

**TOTAL** _____

# Character in *ACTION*

## William Kane Marin: A Voice for Youth

**W**hen William Kane Marin (Bill) was in ninth grade, he decided that the youth of his town should have a voice with the mayor and the city council. So he wrote a letter to Terry Frizzel, mayor of Riverside, California. The mayor didn't answer.

Not long after Bill mailed his letter, Los Angeles erupted in fire and violence in the 1992 riots. Bill wrote a second letter to Mayor Frizzel. This time he expressed his concern over Riverside's problems and the riots that had happened only 60 miles away. He also included a proposal for the mayor to consider.

"I thought they should start a 15-member youth council to advise the mayor and city council on the problems facing youth," Bill explains. "And there should be activities available for young people. I didn't expect to hear anything from the mayor, but she actually wrote back. She said she was starting a task force of business and government people, and she wanted to get youth involved."

Bill called some of his friends, and together they wrote and passed a petition at local malls, collecting names of people who agreed that a youth council would be a good idea. After 19 months of lobbying, the city council approved the plan. The mayor appointed Bill to chair the Youth Council Support Campaign Team, where he worked to improve conditions in the city.

Many kids in Riverside thought that violence was a problem, so Bill helped to organize a Youth Violence Forum. Police and other law-enforcement people spoke in the forum, and a reformed criminal told how he had turned his life around.

In high school, Bill served on the Riverside County Juvenile Justice Commission. He remembers the first time he visited Twin Pines Ranch, a juvenile detention center for troubled boys in the mountains near Riverside. "I was a little nervous," Bill admits. "I'd been in public schools my whole life and had friends who didn't get into trouble. The boys from the center came in and sat down. They were dressed in military clothes and wore combat boots, and they all had shaved heads. I was there for two purposes: to try to understand why they had committed crimes, and to make sure the place was adequate—that they were treated safely. It was a good facility.

"There was one kid who was about 17 years old. I think he was in there for drug abuse. He told me he had a wife and a child, and that he was taking parenting classes and wanted to be with them. He was completing high school there and taking some trade

William Kane Marin holding the Young American Medal for Service, which he received at the Department of Justice during a special ceremony hosted by U.S. Attorney General Janet Reno

classes. He said he really regretted what he had done. I understood where he was coming from."

Bill visited four juvenile detention centers during his junior and senior years at Notre Dame High School. "I had always cared about social issues. One place I visited had both boys and girls, and a staff person told me that about 60 percent of the kids had been sexually abused. When I hear statistics like that and talk with kids in trouble, I realize the horrible things some of them have been through. Instead of instantly judging them for doing stupid things, you start asking yourself what's happened in their lives."

Bill also served as a member of the Mayor's Alliance for Youth, volunteered in the Community Relations Division of the City Manager's Office, and was appointed one of three Youth Commissioners for the City of Riverside. "It's very easy to get involved in government if you're persistent," he says. "I believe that we all have a responsibility to take action when it's needed. People fail to realize that the government belongs to us. You shouldn't just sit and steam about the problems around your city. Get involved. That will determine whether our society succeeds or not."

## Cleanliness

**Clean body, mind, and habits;
personal hygiene, neatness**

> "What America needs is dirtier fingernails
> and cleaner minds."
> *Will Rogers*

Once I had a student with a smile that could melt an iceberg and big brown eyes that made you want to hug him. The problem was, you could smell him before you could see him. One day I took him aside and talked with him very candidly. I learned that he didn't have soap in his house or a washing machine. It was a great lesson for both of us. Somehow he found a way to get clean, while I saw a new side of tolerance.

## Keeping Your Body Neat and Clean

In some cultures, body odor is okay, but in Western cultures, it isn't. If you don't have washing facilities or adequate clothing, you should ask your teacher, your religious leader, or another trusted adult what to do. You'll probably find someone who can help you.

Try not to form opinions about people's character based on the way they look or smell, how long (or short) their hair is, or what they wear. As the old saying goes, "Don't judge a book by its cover." Whether you like it or not, however, other people might judge *your* character by your cleanliness and neatness, and often those people are adults.

If you dress sloppily, have uncombed hair that looks like a wildlife refuge, don't brush your teeth, or wear pants that are so full of holes they look as if you use them for target practice, your teacher might misjudge you and might even give you a lower grade. You might not get chosen for special activities and privileges. Your parents might try to restrict your freedom. If you're applying for a job, forget that. It's not fair, but it's a fact of life.

"But wait!" you might say. "I'm just expressing my individuality!" And you might be right. But remember that most people you meet won't be able to see into your heart. They're not perfect, either. So find a way to express your individuality that doesn't jeopardize your reputation, grades, opportunities, parents' respect, and job prospects. Your life will be a lot easier.

"I'd like to apply for a job."

# Clean Environment, Clean Mind

Keeping your body tidy isn't all there is to cleanliness. This trait can also include vacuuming up the dust bunnies under your bed, recycling the stack of newspapers in your garage, cleaning up the broken glass and discarded aluminum cans along your street, or washing the pesticides off your apple before you eat it. Cleanliness can include avoiding cigarettes for the sake of your breath and your health.[1]

What about the words that come out of your mouth and the thoughts that crowd your head? If you stuff your body with garbage and gutter water, you won't last long. Don't stuff your mind with trash, either. You might have a friend who watches X-rated videos. If that's all he watches, he'll gradually become desensitized to the things he's hearing and seeing. He might even start to think that some of them are okay.

Before you drive too far into the muck (where you might get stuck), stop and ask yourself:

**?**   "Would I want my little sister or brother to do this?"

**?**   "If I were a parent, would I want my children to do this?"

**?**   "Would I want my parents and teachers to know that I do this?"

If you can't answer yes, throw your gears into reverse and back out fast.

Bad influences can lead to questionable behaviors that become bad habits, and habits are hard to break. So choose your movies, videos, and TV programs carefully. Listen to uplifting music. Read thought-provoking, inspiring books. Hang out with people who enjoy safe, wholesome activities.

"But wait!" you might say. "I'll miss all the fun!" It's true: Things that aren't good for you can taste good, feel good, and be exciting. (Who would want to do them if they were nasty, painful, and boring?) It

"I'd love to hire you. Can you start tomorrow?"

takes courage to make positive choices. But whenever you make one, you weaken your bad habits and strengthen your good habits. Healthy habits can keep you from making poor choices. Just as what you eat shows up on your body, what you take into your mind shows up on your face. Most people don't like to be around mean-looking, violent, crude people.

Your family and friends will like you better if you keep your mind and body clean. You'll attract people with similar attitudes and goals. You'll be more successful because your positive thoughts will attract positive people and experiences.[2] Remember that garbage attracts flies and flowers attract butterflies.

# Character Dilemmas

*For journaling or writing essays, discussion, debate, role-playing, reflection*

**Suppose that . . .**

**1** You know someone who has body odor or uses bad language. Is it your responsibility to talk to him or her? Why or why not? Is it anyone's responsibility? Whose? Would it make any difference to you if you knew about the person's living conditions? If you decided to speak up about this sensitive issue, what would you say to the person?

---

[1] See "Health," pages 103–114.

[2] See "Positive Attitudes," pages 14–20.

**2** You have to choose between being clean or being thoughtful and kind. Which would you rather be and why? Which is more important in developing friendships?

**3** You have a friend who often watches X-rated shows on cable TV. Do you think there's a relationship between what a person sees and hears and what a person says and does? Explain your thoughts.

**4** Your community has scheduled an open hearing about a rock band scheduled to appear at a local club. The band is known for songs that promote violence and drug use. Should you attend the hearing? Should the band be allowed to perform? The First Amendment to the U.S. Constitution guarantees the right to free speech. Do you think that performers are protected by this amendment? Explain your answer.

**5** You often imagine yourself doing things you know you shouldn't do. For some reason, scary ideas just keep popping into your head. What can you do about this? Why should you do something about this? Or do you think it's no big deal and you shouldn't do anything? Explain your answer.

# Activities

**WRITE A SONG OR JINGLE** about cleanliness. Balance humor with helpful suggestions. Perform your song or jingle for younger students at your school or community center. For inspiration, visit the children's music section at your local library and listen to songs by Raffi, especially "Brush Your Teeth" from *Singable Songs for the Very Young*.

**READ AND DISCUSS THIS VERSE** from Alexander Pope's *Essay on Man*. You might want to start by "translating" it, since Pope wrote during the 18th century and his use of language is different from ours today:

> Vice is a monster of so frightful mien,
> As to be hated needs but to be seen;
> Yet seen too oft, familiar with her face,
> We first endure, then pity, then embrace.

**RESEARCH THE HISTORY OF CLEANLINESS.** Which ancient civilizations had running water? What did people in the past use for soap? How often did they change their clothing? Was personal hygiene as important to them as it is to us today? What did they use to cover up or mask unpleasant odors? Report on your findings.

> *Variation:* Learn about inventors who have created cleaning products and devices. *Examples:* The drive-through car wash; the Jacuzzi; liquid dishwashing soap; the vacuum cleaner. Make a timeline of inventions.

## CHECK IT OUT

*Panati's Extraordinary Origins* by Charles Panati (New York: HarperCollins, 1989). The fascinating origins of hundreds of things we take for granted, including antiperspirants, the carpet sweeper, the clothes washer and dryer, shampoo, soap, S.O.S. pads, the vacuum cleaner, and *much* more. Ages 12 & up.

**The Soap and Detergent Association**
*www.sdahq.org*
Explore this site to learn about the history, chemistry, human safety, environmental safety, and effective use of personal cleaning products, laundry products, dishwashing products, and household cleaning products.

**RESEARCH DISEASES AND EPIDEMICS** that were related to poor sanitary conditions. *Example:* Bubonic plague was spread by the bites of fleas from infected rats. If you're online, search the Internet for information on diseases and epidemics. (Some words to search for: epidemics, pestilence, infestations, plagues, Black Death, cholera.) Prepare a brief report on your findings to present to your class.

**LEARN ABOUT THE COSTS** of cleanliness. Interview 1) men, 2) women, and 3) teenagers or children. Ask how much money they spend on cleaning products during a typical month. *Examples:* toothpaste, soap, shampoo, detergent, dish soap, house/room cleaning supplies, car cleaning supplies, etc. If the people you interview can't come up with exact amounts, estimates are okay. (Parents will probably pay for most of their kids' cleaning supplies.) Make charts or graphs showing how much each group spends per month and which products they use most.

*Variation:* Calculate how much money an average family of four might spend on cleaning products during a typical month.

**FIND WAYS TO SAVE MONEY** on cleaning products. Is there a less expensive brand of dishwashing soap than the one your family normally uses? Can you use a less expensive soap (without fragrances, deodorants, and fancy packaging)? Can you buy cleaning products in bulk at a local warehouse store?

*Variation:* Research environmentally friendly cleaning products. Look for stores that recycle containers. See if your family will commit to making a switch to environmentally friendly products. Are these products more or less expensive than regular commercial products? Is the actual dollar cost the only consideration? *Example:* Maybe an environmentally friendly laundry detergent costs more per ounce than a popular national brand, but it takes less to do a load of laundry.

**INVENT A CLEANING PRODUCT** from simple products or recycled objects. *Examples:* Combine vinegar, water, and a little dish soap to make a window cleaner. Or design a toothbrush that brushes and sprays your teeth.

**KEEP TRACK** of your personal cleaning habits. Write on a calendar how often you brush your teeth, wash your hair, shower or bathe, change your socks, clean your room, change your bedsheets, clean your locker or desk, etc. (Add your own ideas.) Which things do you do most often? Least often? Where do you need improvement? Is there anything you do *too* often?

# CHECK IT OUT

**BeingGirl**
*www.beinggirl.com*
A site run by Tampax, with personal hygiene information for girls and young women.

**Colgate Kid's World**
*kids-world.colgatepalmolive.com*
Visit Dr. Rabbit's No Cavities Clubhouse, play "Tell the Tooth," get a message from the Tooth Fairy, and more while learning how to take care of your teeth.

**COLLECT CLEANING PRODUCTS** to donate to a traveler's aid organization, homeless shelter, or "free store" in your town or city. When you travel, gather hotel shampoo and soaps. Ask manufacturers and local retailers to donate products and samples.

**BE A CLEANUP HELPER.** Find people in your neighborhood or community who are ill or disabled. Offer to sweep, dust, or clean house for them. Make this a club or classroom project.

*Variation:* Get more involved in cleanup around your own home. Are you doing your share of the family chores? What else could you do to make your home cleaner and more pleasant for everyone?

**HAVE A CLEANUP CONTEST** in your community or school. Make "Great Balls of Foil" (an idea from the Reynolds Metals company) by collecting all the discarded foil you can find and creating a ball. Give prizes for the biggest and heaviest balls, then recycle them.

*Variations:* Pick up litter, pop bottles, cans, etc. to recycle. Donate any money you earn from recycling to a charitable organization.

**FIND OUT WHAT YOUR SCHOOL IS DOING** to promote personal hygiene and clean minds. For centuries, many schools had this saying by the Roman poet Juvenal as their educational goal: *Mens sana in corpora sano*—"A sound mind in a sound body." How is your school building "sound minds"?

**ANALYZE ADVERTISEMENTS.** Videotape ads for cleaning products you see on TV; clip ads from magazines and newspapers. Which ones seem most interesting? Most truthful? Which ones seem to exaggerate?

*Variations:* Videotape a day's worth of a single TV channel. Fast-forward to the commercials. Keep track of how many commercials you see for cleaning products. Or make a poster montage of ads for cleaning products cut from magazines. As you watch commercials and gather advertisements, you'll probably notice that a lot of companies have Web sites. Visit them to see what they have to say about their products. You'll also find some interesting facts and helpful cleaning tips.

**INTERVIEW ELDERS** in your family or community (your grandparents, neighbors, etc.) to find out how cleaning products and practices have changed over the years. Ask if they ever used homemade cleaning products and, if so, what they were.

# Character in *ACTION*

## Sarah Shirkey: Staying Clean

**S**eventeen-year-old Sarah Shirkey stepped out of the shower and dressed quickly. This was an exciting morning and she didn't want to be late.

Starting today, Sarah would spend a week at Michigan Tech University. Sarah had been selected to take part in a special program called "Minorities in Engineering." She would meet other students from as far away as Belgium, and she would be able to speak Spanish with some of them. She would also get to have hands-on experiences in chemistry, metallurgy—even visit a classroom in a mine.

She ran a brush through her wash-and-wear, shoulder-length brown hair, leaving it still damp, and tied her shoes. "I've always liked to be clean and organized," Sarah explains, "but I don't fuss over my hair or try to impress people. Being clean is the most important."

Sarah Shirkey

As Sarah headed for the back door, she paused to rewrite her mother's grocery list so it was neat. This was kind of a joke between them. Her mom had told Sarah that when she was a little girl and they went to the grocery store, Sarah would rearrange the cans and boxes on the shelves.

Sarah isn't perfect, however. Her mom reports that she doesn't do much housework, and Sarah confesses that, although her room is clean, it's sometimes cluttered.

Sarah's friends at Addison High School think highly of her. She's a varsity cheerleader and class secretary, and she's been a homecoming princess and prom queen. Because she's a good student, she's made the honor roll for each report card period and is a member of the National Honor Society.

Sarah feels that it's just as important to keep her body clean on the inside as on the outside. "I don't do drugs, drink alcohol, or smoke anything. I never have. I try to live a clean life. I joined SADD (Students Against Driving Drunk) to try to make an impression on people before it's too late.

"Breath that smells like cigarette smoke is a big turnoff. I won't let anyone smoke in my car, and I keep my ashtray full of papers or candy so no one can use it. I'm not rude about it. I have friends who smoke. But if I'm in a smoky room, I'll get up and leave." She laughs. "One of my friend's parents used to smoke. My friend put on a painter's mask and wore it around her house until her parents got the idea and finally quite smoking.

"I remember one day when a couple of my friends asked me to walk with them down the dirt road past my house. They stopped under a big maple tree and pulled out a joint. I knew they were potheads, but they were still my friends. They knew I had never tried drugs before and didn't want to. One of them said 'Here, try this. It'll make you feel good.' I refused. They kept pressuring me and actually tried to push it into my mouth. I just turned and said 'I'm sorry. I don't want to join in your fun. I'll see you later.' And then I walked back home."

Moral cleanliness is also important to Sarah. She doesn't use profanity or make crude remarks. And she's decided to wait until marriage to have sex. "I signed a pledge called 'True Love Waits.' Thousands of kids all over the country have signed these pledges."

Plus Sarah is committed to keeping the environment clean. Her science class conducted a watershed project to test the waters in their area. "I tested the water quality in a nearby creek ten times in just nine weeks and presented my results to six schools and also in the community.

"I think the next generation is going to have so much to worry about that they shouldn't have to worry about the environment, too. We should try to take good care of it so they can focus on their future and not our past.

"Our bodies are gifts, and our environment is a priceless heirloom. Those are two things I would definitely avoid trashing."

## CHECK IT OUT

**SADD (Students Against Driving Drunk)**
National SADD
PO Box 800
Marlborough, MA 01752
1-877-723-3462
*www.saddonline.com*
Consider signing the SADD "Contract for Life" with your parents. To request a copy, contact SADD.

Sarah at school

# Communication

**Effective speaking and listening,
public speaking**

"**S**ticks and stones will break my bones, but words will never hurt me." Do you believe that old saying? Probably not, because you know that words can sometimes hurt more than a broken arm. The words we speak show how we feel about each other, and unkind words hurt both the person who hears them *and* the person who says them.

On the other hand, kind words encourage others *and* build up the people who say them. If you become a good communicator, you'll win more friends. You'll impress your teachers and parents, and you'll even have a better chance of getting a job in an interview. It makes sense to learn to communicate clearly and effectively.

If you throw a stick into the ocean, the stick comes back to you. If you toss a boomerang into the air, the boomerang comes back to you. Words are like that. What you throw out eventually comes back to you. It's true that sometimes people won't answer your kind words with kindness. But over the long run, if you communicate kindness, you'll attract kind words in return.

We communicate in many ways. The illustration on the next page shows some. Can you name others?

In general, any movements you make with your body, any sounds that come out of your mouth, the expression you wear, and sometimes the things you think or feel, can send a message to someone.

# 12 Ways to Be a Good Communicator

**1.** Speak clearly. Look at the person you're speaking to.

**2.** Really *listen* to what the other person says, and respond accordingly. Look at the person when he or she is speaking.

**3.** Maintain eye contact at a mutually comfortable level—somewhere between staring and avoiding each other's eyes. Try to pick up on cues that tell you what's comfortable for the other person.

**4.** Do your best to understand what the other person is saying. If there's something you don't understand, ask about it.

**5.** Be alert to body language and verbal cues— yours and the other person's. Look alert and interested. Watch for signs that the other person is losing interest, wants to change the subject, or needs to end the conversation.

**6.** Give feedback when it's asked for. Ask for feedback, too.

**7.** Give examples to support what you're saying.

**8.** Give your opinion if it's asked for.

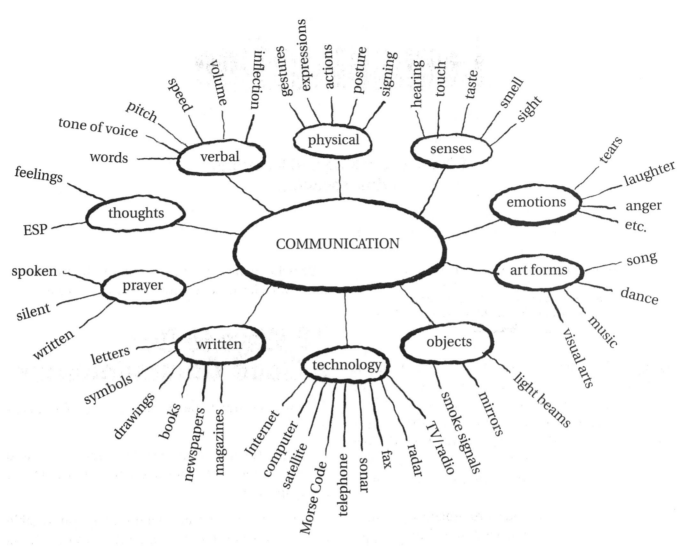

**9.** Take turns speaking.

**10.** Match the level and language of the person you're speaking to. For example, you'll speak differently to young child than to an adult. (Use simpler words and sentences, not baby talk.)

**11.** Listen for requests. (These won't always come in the form of questions or direct statements.)

**12.** Use your intuition. Sometimes words aren't necessary and you can communicate with feelings, expressions, and gestures.

And here are a few don'ts to keep in mind: Don't be nosy. Don't gossip or pry. Don't interrupt. Don't change the subject. Don't contradict or correct what the other person is saying. Don't brag. Don't fall asleep!

# 12 Ways to Break Through a Communications Roadblock

**1.** Express anger, disappointment, or frustration in "I-messages" ("I don't like it when someone lies about me"), not "you-messages" ("You've been lying about me").

**2.** Focus on the *problem* ("I don't like it when my locker is messed up"), not the *person* ("I knew it wouldn't work to share a locker with you").

**3.** Remember that a cornered animal will bite and scratch. Always give the other person a way out ("I'm sure you didn't mean to hurt my feelings"). Don't back him or her into a corner ("I know you did that on purpose!").

**4.** Listen without being defensive. Everyone makes mistakes—even you.

**5.** Don't allow yourself to be a victim. Don't take the blame for something you didn't do. Stick up for yourself without attacking the other person.

**6.** Say you're sorry if you need to.

**7.** Look for the good in the other person, even when this is hard to do. Make it clear that you care about him or her. ("You're my friend, and I really want to help.")

**8.** Look for common ground—something you can agree on.

**9.** Try to stay calm no matter what.

**10.** Brainstorm solutions together. Try to reach an agreement on what's best to do. Carry out your agreement.

**11.** If your best efforts don't succeed, get a third party involved. Find a peer mediator or an adult to help you talk through your problem.

**12.** If spoken communication isn't going anywhere, try writing a letter. But wait at least a day before mailing it. You might change your mind about what you want to say.

# Public Speaking

Does the mere thought of giving a speech make you break out in hives? Or are you someone who loves to grab the microphone? Even if you hate public speaking, it's hard to avoid it. (You might not have to address the whole school at an assembly, but you'll probably have to give an oral report in class.) Here are some hints to help you give great speeches.

***Plan it out and write it down.***

🔊 Open with a snappy beginning to grab your audience's attention. ("Selena helped to put a robber behind bars. And she's just 10 years old.")

🔊 Develop the body of your speech with facts. ("During the past year alone, more than 40 crimes have been stopped or solved with help from kids.")

🔊 Include quotes and statistics. ("In the words of police chief Bob Darien, 'Kids are making a difference in our community.'")

🔊 Include anecdotes and examples. ("When Jason saw a stranger trying to open his neighbor's window, he called 911 right away.")

🔊 Summarize your main idea(s). ("You don't have to be a grown-up to fight crime. All you have to be is alert and willing to speak out and get involved.")

🔊 Give your opinion, if it's appropriate. ("I'm glad our community has so many young crimefighters. I know I feel safer!")

🔊 Close with a snappy ending. ("If we all work together—adults and kids—we can cut down on crime in our community.")

***Memorize ideas, not whole sentences.*** This will help your speech to sound more natural and less canned. You'll also save yourself a brain cramp from trying to remember the exact words you want to say.

| If your written speech says this: | Jot down and remember this: |
|---|---|
| "Sanitation was a big problem for the ancient Romans. Although they didn't know about bacteria yet, experience had taught them that poor disposal of human wastes led to disease." | Romans: sanitation<br><br>Bacteria<br><br>Human wastes/disease |

***Practice giving your speech.*** Practice by yourself at first. Give your speech to the wall; give it to your dog. (Neither will criticize you.) When you feel more secure, practice with a family member or friend.

***Don't worry about "wixing your mords."*** Just smile and repeat yourself. Even the best speakers sometimes twist their words around.

"If you vote for me, I promise to work for better school lunches."

**Look at your audience when you speak.** Keep your chin up. Look confident and relaxed. Smile. Then any mistakes you make won't matter.

**Know how to handle interruptions.** If you're distracted by noise, or by people coming into or leaving the room, stop speaking. Wait until it gets quiet again before you continue.

**Speak LSC (Loudly, Slowly, Clearly).** Use your playground voice. The larger the room, the longer it takes for sound to travel from your mouth to your audience's ears. If you have a microphone, speak right into it.

**Leave time for questions and answers.** This is especially important if you're speaking to a group such as the PTA or community council.

**Add interest wherever you can.** Tell a story, a joke, a surprising (or shocking) statistic. Use charts, graphs, slides, overheads, and/or a video. (Make sure that any visuals are large enough for your whole audience to see.)

**Prepare a one-page flyer about your speech.** List the major points of your speech and, if you want, include a phone number where you can be reached for more details. Hand it out before or after you give your speech.

## CHECK IT OUT

*What! I Have to Give a Speech?* by Thomas J. Murphy and Kenneth Snyder (Bloomington, IN: Grayson Bernard Publishing, 1995). How to organize a speech, use humor, control nerves, and gain confidence and professionalism. Ages 12–14.

*Great Speeches of the 20th Century.* History comes to life in original recordings of famous speeches by presidents, civil rights leaders, astronauts, and more. Available on CD or cassette. Check your library or record store or contact:
**Rhino Records**
1-800-432-0020
*www.rhino.com*

**Toastmasters International**
PO Box 9052
Mission Viejo, CA 92690
1-800-993-7732
*www.toastmasters.org*
Founded in 1924, dedicated to helping people speak more effectively, this international organization has more than 8,000 clubs around the world. Contact your local Toastmasters club to see if it's willing to conduct a Youth Leadership program for you and your friends. The program lasts for eight sessions, and you'll need at least ten participants ages 13–16. Regular Toastmasters clubs are open to people ages 18 & up.

# Character Dilemmas
*For journaling or writing essays, discussion, debate, role-playing, reflection*

**Suppose that . . .**

**1** You're trying to communicate with a teacher about a problem, but he cuts you off and won't listen. What might you do to improve communication with him?

**2** Your parents ground you for a whole week for something you did. You think the punishment is unfair, but they won't listen to your explanation. What might you do?

**3** You overhear your parents arguing. Should you get involved and try to help them communicate better, or should you stay out of it? What if you overhear your siblings arguing? Your friends? Strangers?

**4** You're the mayor of your city, and newspaper reporters keep misquoting you. People are starting to think you're dishonest. How could you approach the reporters about the problem and improve your relationship with them? In what ways can a public official best communicate with the people he or she serves?

**5** You're a parent whose daughter won't listen to you. Whenever you try to talk with her or correct her behavior, she stomps off to her room and slams the door. What might you do to improve communication with your daughter? How can you discipline her *and* keep the lines of communication open? Does it matter what age she is? What if she's a preschooler? A fourth grader? A high school student?

**6** You're on a peacekeeping committee for the United Nations. Two third-world countries are constantly fighting. One country has recently started building nuclear weapons. How might you bring about peaceful negotiations between the two warring nations?

# Activities

**WRITE AND RECORD** a jingle, rap, or public service announcement (PSA) about something you care about and want to communicate to others. Do it just for fun, or play it over your school intercom. Some radio stations will play PSAs free of charge.

**WRITE IN YOUR JOURNAL**[1] about a time when poor communication hurt your feelings (or someone else's). Jot down ideas for a solution. Then ask the person to sit down and talk with you. Practice the skills described in this chapter.

**WRITE AN ARTICLE** for your school newspaper.

> *Variation:* If your school doesn't have a newspaper, see if you can start one to improve communication at your school. You'll need a teacher to serve as your sponsor and advisor, a place to work and store supplies, money to fund the newspaper, and reporters to write for it.

**SEND A FAX** to someone you know. If you don't know how to use a fax machine, ask for help. Your school, library, post office, or local copy center will probably have a fax machine you can use. You might be charged a fee.

**LEARN ANOTHER ALPHABET.** You might choose Morse Code (combinations of short and long signals transmitted by electricity or light), Braille (a system of raised dots used by people who are blind or visually impaired), or the Manual Alphabet (hand motions used by people who are deaf or hearing impaired). If you and a friend learn it together, you can practice sending messages to each other. You'll find all three alphabets on pages 55–56.

> *Variation:* If you learn Braille or the Manual Alphabet, find a school or class for children in your community who are blind or deaf and donate your time as a tutor or helper. Get permission and support from your parents, and ask the school's or teacher's permission.

**RESEARCH ANIMAL AND PLANT COMMUNICATION.** What have experts learned about how animals communicate? Do they use sounds? Movements? Do plants communicate? Can we communicate with them? Write a report on a topic that interests you.

> *Variations:* Try to communicate with a pet. Using repetition and rewards, train your dog to fetch, your cat to sit in your lap, etc. Or try communicating with a plant. Talk to it, play music for it, etc., and see what happens.

**RESEARCH SPACE COMMUNICATION.** Have any messages been received from outer space? Have they been interpreted? Write a report about your findings. You might start by finding out about the SETI Institute. (SETI stands for Search for Extraterrestrial Intelligence.)

---

## CHECK IT OUT

**SETI Institute**
2035 Landings Drive
Mountain View, CA 94043
(650) 961-6633
*www.seti-inst.edu*
The SETI Institute is a nonprofit research organization with more than two dozen projects funded by government agencies, private foundations, and individual donors. Write, call, or visit the Web site to learn about ongoing projects, education programs, and related science and education sites.

---

[1] See "Endurance," pages 88, 89, and 92, for journaling resources.

See "Learn another alphabet" on page 54.

# The MORSE CODE Alphabet

A: • —
B: — • • •
C: — • — •
D: — • •
E: •
F: • • — •
G: — — •
H: • • • •
I: • •

J: • — — —
K: — • —
L: • — • •
M: — —
N: — •
O: — — —
P: • — — •
Q: — — • —
R: • — •

S: • • •
T: —
U: • • —
V: • • • —
W: • — —
X: — • • —
Y: — • — —
Z: — — • •

# The BRAILLE Alphabet

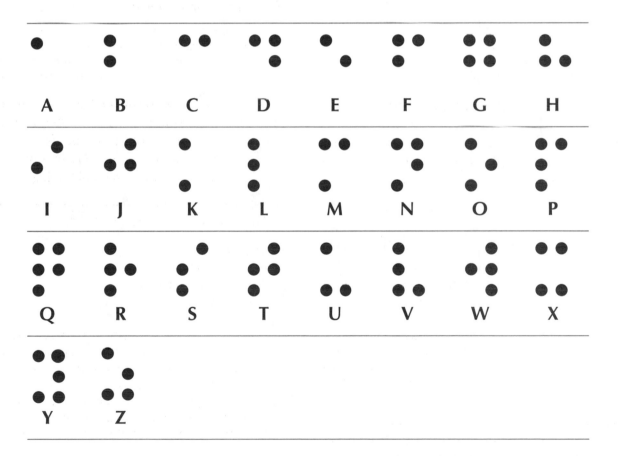

# The MANUAL Alphabet

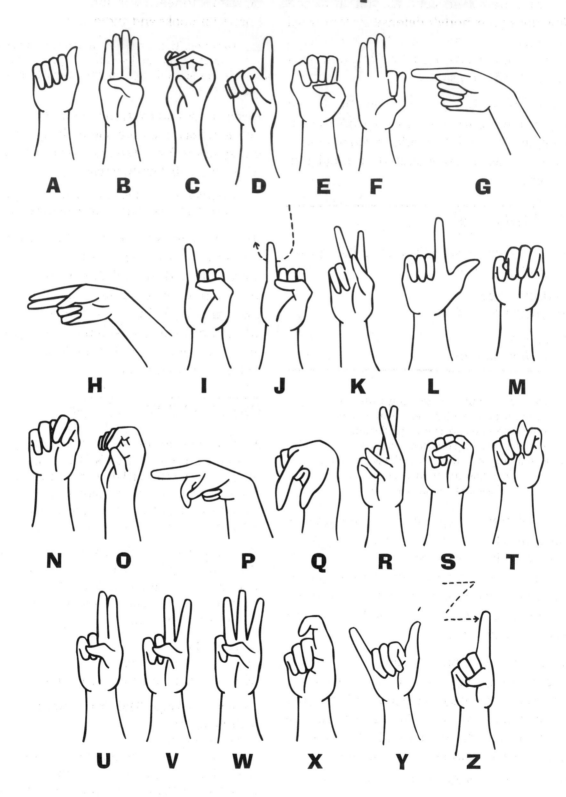

**LEARN HOW THE PARTS OF YOUR BODY** communicate. How does your brain send signals to your arms and legs? How does your body's defense system warn you of danger? How does one cell communicate with another—and what does it "say"? Draw a chart to illustrate your findings.

**JOIN AN INTERNET USENET NEWSGROUP** on a topic that interests you, then communicate with people across the country and around the world. If you're not yet hooked up at home or at school, start a campaign to make it happen.

## CHECK IT OUT

Learn about newsgroups, search for specific types of newsgroups, and more at:

**Google's Usenet News**
*www.groups.google.com*

**Yahoo's Groups**
*dir.groups.yahoo.com/dir*

> "A world community can exist only with world communication, which means something more than extensive shortwave facilities scattered about the globe. It means common understanding, a common tradition, common ideas, and common ideals."
> *Robert M. Hutchins*

**CALCULATE HOW LONG** it might take to communicate with someone 1) in the same town or city, 2) in another state, 3) in another country, 4) on another planet in the solar system, 5) in another galaxy. Decide what method of communication you'd use (letter, phone, cell phone, fax, email, Web page, satellite, light beam, etc.).

**GATHER INFORMATION ABOUT CELL PHONES.** Call local companies that sell connections and phones. Try to determine what percentage of the population in your city has cell phones. Find out what age group(s) use cell phones the most. Are most users male or female? At what time(s) of the day are most calls made?

*Variation:* Gather information about pagers.

**FIND OUT HOW MANY MAJOR LANGUAGES** are spoken in the world today. Make a pie chart showing the percentages of the world's population that speak each language.

**LEARN A FOREIGN LANGUAGE.** Pick one that interests you and start to learn common phrases. Check your library for books and audiocassettes.

*Variation:* There may be someone in your class or school who can help you learn the language. If so, find out if there's something you can teach him or her. Swap lessons.

**INVENT A NEW LANGUAGE.** You might try designing symbols for ideas (such as ancient pictographs) or different symbols for letters. Share your new language with your club, family, or class.

*Variation:* Learn about Esperanto, a language invented by Dr. Ludwig L. Zamenhof in the late 1800s.

**BECOME A PUBLISHED WRITER.** Do you write stories, articles, essays, poems, plays, or. . .? Have you always wanted to publish your writing? What are you waiting for? Find out what to do, then follow through. Get help and support from peers and adults. Enter contests, submit your work to publishers—and don't forget that the Internet offers many publishing opportunities.

## CHECK IT OUT

*Market Guide for Young Writers* by Kathy Henderson (Cincinnati, OH: Writer's Digest Books, updated often). Over 140 market and contest listings especially for young writers, plus profiles of successful young writers, answers to questions young writers ask most, and more. Ages 8–18.

*To Be a Writer: A Guide for Young People Who Want to Write and Publish* by Barbara Seuling (New York: Twenty-First Century Books, 1997). Read up on honing your writing skills and learn how to have work published. Ages 8–13.

**Merlyn's Pen**
*www.merlynspen.com*
Advice, articles, interviews, and links.

**Writes of Passage: The Online Source for Teenagers**
*www.writes.org*
This interactive literary journal for writers ages 12–19 features poems and short stories by teens across the country and advice from established authors. The site is being used by hundreds of high school English classes. A Teachers' Guide is available.

**BE A PEER MEDIATOR.** Help others improve their communication skills by resolving conflicts peacefully. Here are the basic rules of peer mediation:[2]

1. Everyone has an equal chance to express his or her point of view.

2. No interrupting.

3. No bad language.

4. No physical fighting.

5. At the end of the session, everyone signs an agreement stating their conclusions and compromises.

> *Variation:* If your school doesn't have a peer mediation program in place, write a proposal to your principal to start one.

**DESIGN A PLAN** to help the nations of the world learn to communicate and understand each other better. You might research NATO, the United Nations, and other international organizations to learn what has already been done.

**TRY TO COMMUNICATE** without using words. Sit across from a friend. Relax and close your eyes. Concentrate on each other. Each of you should think of *one* thing—a hobby, interest, family member, food you like or dislike, etc. Try to guess what each other is thinking. See how accurate you can be.

**INTERPRET ART.** Find a book of famous paintings. Pick two or three you like. Try to determine what the artists were trying to communicate through their paintings. Then read about the artists and the paintings to see if you were right.

**CHOREOGRAPH A DANCE** that communicates anger, joy, fear, surprise, wonder, or any emotion(s) you choose. Perform it for your club, class, or school.

**PLAY CHARADES.** Act out song titles, words, movie titles, books, names, etc. *Example:* You might act out "Silent Night" by first putting a finger to your lips (the "shhhh!" sign) and then placing your hands on either side of your head, tilting your head, and shutting your eyes.

**READ STORIES ABOUT COMMUNICATION.** Look for these books:

- *Operation Siberian Crane* by Judi Friedman (New York: Dillon Press, 1992). Describes the efforts of Soviet and American scientists to save the Siberian Crane. Ages 11 & up.

- *Racing the Sun* by Paul Pitts (New York: Avon Books, 1988). Twelve-year-old Brandon has lived in the suburbs all his life. When his grandfather comes to live with the family, Brandon discovers the importance and difficulty of staying true to his Navajo heritage. Ages 11–13.

- *A Solitary Blue* by Cynthia Voigt (New York: Scholastic, 1993). Jeff is raised by his father after his mother deserts the family. When his mother returns, Jeff must deal with the conflict between his parents. Ages 11–14.

- *The Twelfth of June* by Marilyn Gould (Newport Beach, CA: Allied Crafts Press, 1994). Thirteen-year-old Janis wonders how her cerebral palsy will affect her future and her relationship with her friend Barney. Ages 10–14.

- *Wild Magic* by Tamora Pierce (Thorndike, ME: Thorndike Press, 1993). Thirteen-year-old Daine is enlisted to help battle the fierce immortals threatening the kingdom of Tortall. Ages 10–14.

---

[2] See "Peacefulness," pages 178 and 180, for more about being a mediator.

# Character in *ACTION*

## Jackson Elementary: Getting the Message Out

Jogette rushed her words and spoke in a breathless voice: "And I was just out on my front lawn eating a Popsicle when this big old car drove by and began shooting. I hit the dirt. Those guys shot fifteen shots over my head, and then I crawled into the house to warn my mom."

Richard chimed in: "And someone broke into my house and stole my Nintendo and all my games. And then they stole our car."

"And my mom was shot at when she was shopping at the 7–Eleven," Moleni added.

Precious pulled her dark hair into a ponytail and said: "Well, someone broke into my house and pulled a gun on my dad. I ran out the back door and went to my neighbor's house and called the police."

"You're like a hero or something," Moleni grinned.

Another child told the group that he had been abused by a family member.

All told, 18 children shared their stories with each other. Then they surveyed the school and found out that approximately one-sixth of the students or their family members had been shot at, and almost one-fourth of the kids had been chased or threatened with knives or other weapons.

Although most of Salt Lake City is tame, the area around Jackson Elementary School was troubled. Railroad tracks, a homeless shelter, a liquor store, and many abandoned buildings and houses attracted transients who brought crimes with them. Gang membership had also increased.

The students brainstormed and decided that they needed a massive communications campaign to try to reduce crime in the area. Here's how they got their message across:

The Jackson Elementary kids and their teacher, Barbara Lewis (far left)

🔊 They talked with their parents and sponsored an anti-crime night with the community, working with the McGruff House program to get Safe Houses in their neighborhoods. Parents were asked to take charge of a Neighborhood Watch program.

🔊 They gave speeches at assemblies, in schools, at the Utah State Education Association, and nationally at a Youth Crime Watch convention.

🔊 They measured off a drug-free zone 1,000 feet around their school, then worked with the Utah Council for the Prevention of Crime to install warning signs aimed at drug dealers and users.

🔊 They spoke with the mayor and wrote a proclamation for an anti-crime month.

🔊 They put a Crime Clue Box in the school, where kids and parents could drop anonymous tips on crimes. The tips led to identifying a person who had written graffiti on the school, foiling an attempted kidnapping, and stopping a gang fight.

🔊 They spoke to legislators, testifying and lobbying for stiffer penalties for 1) drive-by shootings, 2) possession of weapons near schools, and 3) graffiti. They testified and lobbied for an anti-child-abuse law. All four bills sailed through and became laws.

🔊 They wrote public service announcements (PSAs) about child abuse. One of them—"You always lose if you choose to abuse," featuring one of the students and Utah's Attorney General—was seen on TV.

🔊 They wrote a small city grant and worked with a billboard company to put an anti-child-abuse PSA on a billboard.

🔊 They decided that kids needed to have a special child-abuse hotline—an easy-to-remember number they could call for help or just to talk about an abuse problem. After three years of trying, they got their hotline.

🔊 They wrote letters and spoke to housing authorities, reporting a drug house across the street from the school. About a year later, the house was torn down, and the kids were able to help build a new house in the area.

This is how Jogette sums up the experience: "I used to be shy, but because I had to communicate with so many people about fighting and dealing with crime, it opened me up. I've become more confident. It's important for everyone to speak what's on their minds. To risk nothing is to have nothing, do nothing, be nothing. Speaking out is taking that risk. If you don't do that, nothing will get done."

Jogette Garcia

# Conservation

## Preservation, thriftiness, moderation

"The earth we abuse and the living things we kill will, in the end, take their revenge; for in exploiting their presence we are diminishing our future."
*Marya Mannes*

A couple of years ago, I visited a hazardous waste facility just to see what it looked like. That's a place where dangerous chemicals, infectious waste (like hospital needles, things contaminated with blood), mine tailings, and other toxic materials are stored. The waste products were buried in mounds that looked like a cross between an Egyptian pyramid and a burial mound. Usually, pyramids and burial mounds are filled with treasures—the most valued possessions of the people who built them. I couldn't help but wonder "How might future civilizations judge us, when they dig up the pyramids from our time and find that they're filled with toxic garbage?"

You can learn a lot about people by looking at the things they throw away. Right now, that includes everything from disposable diapers to disposable dishes. You might ask yourself "What do I really need to throw away?"

## Conservation

*Conservation* means deliberately preserving or saving things. Often it refers to saving the environment—our water, land, plants, animals, and air—but you can conserve (or waste) many different things. *Examples:*

◆ material things including clothes, buildings, houses, and furniture
◆ food
◆ money
◆ friendships
◆ energy
◆ peace
◆ your own talents, physical health, and mental health
◆ time.

Can you think of other items or ideas you might add to this list?

"Dost thou love Life? Then do not squander Time; for that's the Stuff Life is made of."
*Benjamin Franklin*

Since conservation can involve everything in your life, you should decide what things are most important to you and work to preserve them or use them wisely.

## Thriftiness

Would you like to get rich? Here's how: *Spend less than you earn.* Do you think that someone who earns $500,000 a year is rich? Not necessarily, because he or she might be paying for an expensive home, a vacation cottage, five cars, designer clothes, and a yacht. In fact, this seemingly wealthy person might be close to bankruptcy.

When you're *thrifty*, you make your money go a long way. You plan ahead for your needs and budget your money carefully. If you simply can't live without designer clothes, you wait until they go on sale. You clip coupons, look for bargains, and shop at thrift stores, secondhand stores, garage sales, and tag sales.

Even small expenditures can add up quickly, and before you know it, your money is gone. Keep track of your spending habits. Make a plan to save part of your allowance or job earnings each week. Soon you'll be on your way to being rich!

# Moderation

"Moderation in all things."
*Terence (Publius Terentius Afer, c. 190–159 B.C.)*

*Moderation* means avoiding extremes, setting limits, and exercising restraint. When you use moderation, your life is in balance. You exercise . . . but you don't overexercise. You sleep . . . but not 12 hours a day. You eat . . . but you don't stuff yourself. You pursue your interests . . . but you don't get obsessed with them. You develop your talents . . . but you leave room for other things and people. You do your best . . . but you're not a perfectionist.

Consider something as basic as water. You can't drink too much, right? Wrong. Some people drink an excessive amount of water every day in an effort to lose weight. This drains nutrients from their body and can eventually damage their health. On the other hand, if you don't drink enough water, your body gets dehydrated. You feel dizzy and weak and can even pass out. So use moderation. Drink five to six glasses of water each day. And if you want to lose weight, try a combination of sensible eating and regular physical activity.

When you feel that your life is out of balance, stop, look, and listen. What is your body telling you? Do you have headaches, sore muscles, black shadows under your eyes? What is your mind telling you? Are you frantic, anxious, stressed out, bored? What are your friends and family telling you? Are they worried about you and advising you to slow down, take it easy, and make more time for them? What are your teachers telling you? If something seems out of whack, take a deep breath, plant both feet on the ground, and make a commitment to moderation.

On the other hand, maybe moderation isn't for you. Some great contributions—to the arts, sciences, medicine, politics, philosophy, religion, and other areas of human life and culture—have been made by people who went overboard with a talent, ability, interest, or passion. You'll need to decide for yourself when to step back and when to leap forward.

# Character Dilemmas

*For journaling or writing essays, discussion, debate, role-playing, reflection*

**Suppose that . . .**

**1** A developer wants to build new homes on the wetlands at the edge of your town. The wetlands would be lost, but your town would gain much-needed property tax revenues. Should people be allowed to build homes in wetlands and other undeveloped areas? Or should that land be preserved? Is a compromise possible? How could you determine how much land should be developed and how much should be saved?

**2** People in a South American country are buying up huge chunks of the rainforest, chopping down trees, and planting cash crops on the land. Sales of the crops are bringing in money the people need to raise their standard of living. Does your country have the right to insist that the South American people preserve the rainforest? Why or why not? Be sure to consider as many sides of this issue as possible.

**3** You live in a city where unemployment is high. A big company has just announced plans to build a factory downtown. The factory will provide hundreds of new jobs, but it might also pollute the air and contaminate the soil and water. What should your city do? What can you do?

**4** An old historical building in your city has been vacant for many years. The City Council has just announced plans to tear it down and build a parking ramp. What, if anything, should you do about this? What can you do?

**5** You have a friend who saves every penny she earns. She never has money for movies or snacks, and when she goes out with you and your friends, someone else always ends up paying her way. Can thriftiness ever be carried to an extreme? If so, how?

**6** In science class, you learn about a new lightbulb that uses less energy and lasts much longer than regular lightbulbs. The only problem is, they cost twice as much as regular lightbulbs, and your family is on a limited budget. Should you try to convince your parents to make the switch? What else can you suggest that would lower your family's monthly electric bill?

**7** Your brother has a special talent for music. Should he develop that talent exclusively? Should he spend hours every day studying and practicing? Should your parents make sure that he has the best teachers and opportunities available? What would that mean to you and your family? What kind of life might your brother have? On the other hand, what might happen if he decides not to develop his talent?

# Activities

**MAKE A VIDEO** of people at your school (students, teachers, staff) to show at a school assembly. Start by choosing a theme—conservation, thriftiness, or moderation. Come up with questions to ask the people you tape. *Examples:*

**?** What is our school doing to conserve energy? What should our school be doing? What ideas do you have?

**?** What is our school doing to be thrifty? What ideas do you have to help our school be more thrifty? Are you a thrifty person? How?

**?** Do you think that our school values moderation? Explain your answer.

**LEARN ABOUT THE NATURAL RESOURCES** of different countries around the world. You might consider the United States, a European country, an Asian country, an African country, and one or two other places (a polar region, a Caribbean island, New Zealand). What are each country's most important natural resources? What does each country do with its resources—conserve them, use them wisely, or waste them? Make and illustrate a chart showing your findings.

**LEARN ABOUT ENDANGERED SPECIES** around the world. Choose one to research in depth, then present your findings artistically. You might write a melody, song, or poem; produce a play or skit; choreograph a dance; prepare an art exhibit; make a quilt; make a diorama; create a slide show; or whatever else you'd like to do.

## CHECK IT OUT

*The Atlas of Endangered Animals* by Stephen Thomas Pollock (New York: Facts On File, 1993). Maps, pictures, symbols, and words focus on areas of the world in which human activity is threatening to destroy various animal species. Ages 12 & up.

**Endangered Species Homepage:**
**U.S. Fish & Wildlife Service**
*endangered.fws.gov*
Tons of information about U.S. animals and plants, including lists and counts by state, plus a foreign species index. You can also download a copy of the Endangered Species Act.

**National Geographic Wild World**
*www.nationalgeographic.com/wildworld*
Find lots of interactive maps of some of the Earth's richest, rarest, and most endangered areas. Also includes an extensive glossary and links to other organizations concerned about the environment.

**Yahoo's Endangered Species Links**
*www.yahooligans.com/Science_and_Nature/Living_*
*Things/Animals/Endangered_Species*
Part of Yahoo's "Yahooligans!" service for kids and teens.

___

**INTERVIEW AN ENVIRONMENTAL/CONSERVATION** expert in person or over the telephone. Write up your interview and submit it to your school newspaper. During the interview, ask questions like these:

**?**  What's the most pressing environmental/conservation issue we're facing today in our country? Our world?

**?**  What kinds of projects are you working on now? What are your plans for the future?

**?**  What can other people do to help with your project?

**PLAN AND CARRY OUT** an environmental/conservation project to benefit your school, neighborhood, or community. Invite a speaker to your class or club from a neighborhood beautification community, environmental group, or community council. Pick the speaker's brain to find out what projects are needed in your area. Then choose one to do and make a step-by-step plan for getting it done.[1]

> *Variation:* Find your own project by walking around your school or neighborhood or reading the local newspaper for ideas. To start you thinking, here's a list of 10 project ideas:
>
> **1.**  Adopt a zoo animal and fund-raise for a habitat.
> **2.**  Adopt a pothole in the street near your school and repair it.
> **3.**  Plant trees near your school or in a park.
> **4.**  Find homes for abandoned pets. Work with your local Humane Society or animal shelter.
> **5.**  Clean up litter.
> **6.**  Conduct an energy audit of your school.
> **7.**  Recycle used school paper.
> **8.**  Ask your school to purchase recycled paper.
> **9.**  Dispose of chemicals (from your school chemistry lab, cleaning service, etc.) safely.
> **10.**  Teach other kids about conservation.

**MAKE DECORATIONS** from recycled materials. *Examples:* Styrofoam, plastic rings from pop-can holders, lids, cans, paper, newspaper, magazines, paper or plastic grocery bags, old jewelry, old

clothes, dishes, paper towel tubes, egg cartons, etc. (including whatever you find under your bed). Decorate your classroom or your room at home.

**FIND OUT ABOUT HISTORIC BUILDINGS** and sites in your community. Is there anything listed on the National Register of Historic Places? Are there any National Trust for Historic Preservation sites? If not, do you know of any buildings or sites you feel should be identified for preservation? Are any currently scheduled for demolition? Contact your local Historical Society or History Center for information and advice. Ask how you can help.

___

## CHECK IT OUT

**National Register of Historic Places**
National Park Service
1849 C Street, NW
Washington, DC 20240
(202) 208-6843
*www.cr.nps.gov/nr*

**National Trust for Historic Preservation**
1785 Massachusetts Avenue, NW
Washington, DC 20036
1-800-944-6847
*www.nthp.org*

___

**LEARN HOW ATHLETES** conserve energy during competitions. You might interview members of your school football, basketball, gymnastics, or cross country teams. If your town or city has semiprofessional or professional sports teams, you might try to interview some of the players. Ask questions like:

**?**  Do you eat any special "energy foods" before competing?

**?**  How do you keep from burning out before a competition is over?

**?**  Are there any mental exercises you do that help you to conserve energy during competitions?

**?**  What's your attitude during competitions?

**PLAN YOUR LIFE** down to the minute. Someone who lives for 75 years lives for more than 39 *million* minutes. Figure out how many minutes remain between now and your 75th birthday. Make a pie chart showing how you plan to spend this time. How many min-

___

[1] See "Be an activist" in "Citizenship," page 39, and "Plan and do a service project" in "Caring," pages 23–24.

utes will you spend sleeping? Eating? Taking care of your body (bathing, washing, etc.)? Going to school? Studying and doing homework? Doing chores? Working? Playing, pursuing hobbies, vacationing? Praying, thinking, meditating? Volunteering? Goofing off? What else? For each segment of your pie chart, show the approximate number of minutes. Then analyze your chart. Is your life plan balanced?

**LEARN TO BUDGET YOUR TIME.** Make a list of all the activities you do during a typical day. (You can use the chart on page 66 or design your own chart.) For the next week, record how much time you actually spend on each activity. Next, on a clean copy of the chart, indicate how much time you'd *like* to spend on each activity. Try to follow this plan for at least a week. Afterward, review it and make any needed changes.

**LEARN TO BUDGET YOUR MONEY.** For the next month, keep track of your income (allowance, gifts, wages, payments for services, etc.) and expenditures (clothes, recreation, school lunch, gas, etc.) Record *everything* you earn and spend—*to the penny,* if possible. (You can use the chart on page 67 or design your own chart. If you need help designing a chart, ask your parents or teacher.) Then analyze your spending and saving habits. Are you spending too much? Could you be saving more? If you have money left over, add it to your savings account (or open a savings account). TIP: If you're spending too much, try this strategy: Whenever you see something you want, wait at least 24 hours before actually buying it. Better yet, wait a week. You may find that you no longer want it . . . and the money can go into your savings account.

> *Variation:* Carry a small pocket notebook everywhere you go. Use this to record your expenditures. Transfer this information to your chart.

## CHECK IT OUT

*The Kids' Guide to Money: Earning It, Saving It, Spending It, Growing It, Sharing It* by Steve Otfinoski (New York: Scholastic, 1996). How to earn money, save for a big purchase, understand the stock market, choose a worthy cause for charity, avoid getting ripped off, and more.

**GO SHOPPING.** Compare food prices, clothing prices, etc. Which products are most economical? Where are the best places to shop? Share what you learn with your family and friends.

**ENJOY FREE FUN AND GAMES.** Having a great time doesn't have to cost money. Share some no-pay play with your friends, club, and family. *Examples:*

- Ask a grandparent or elderly neighbor to tell you about the "good old days."
- Build sand castles or snow castles.
- Chase butterflies.
- Climb trees.
- Decorate each other's lockers.
- Feed squirrels.
- Go on a scavenger hunt.
- Go swimming.
- Have a laughing contest.
- Have a squirt-gun fight.
- Have a tickling contest.
- Have a tug-of-war.
- Have an arm-wrestling contest.
- Make "rock buddies" (decorate rocks with paint, stick-on eyes, paper feet).
- Make a fort from snow, blankets, etc.
- Make and fly paper airplanes.
- Make paper chains and hang them.
- Make paper boats and sail them.
- Make snow angels and snow sculptures.
- Make your own kite and fly it.
- Play hide-and-seek.
- Play tag.
- Rake leaves into a pile. Jump in.
- Read aloud to little kids.
- Roll down hills.
- Save seeds from fruits and vegetables. Plant them.
- Skip stones on a creek or river.
- Swing in the park.
- Take a hike.
- Walk in the rain.
- Watch birds.
- Watch for shooting stars.

# Time Chart

For the week of _____ _____, _____ through _____ _____, _____.
            month      date     year            month     date     year

| ACTIVITY | Mon | Tues | Wed | Thurs | Fri | Sat | Sun |
|---|---|---|---|---|---|---|---|
| Sleeping | | | | | | | |
| Eating | | | | | | | |
| Chores | | | | | | | |
| Homework | | | | | | | |
| Recreation | | | | | | | |
| Entertainment | | | | | | | |
| Practicing talents | | | | | | | |
| Exercise | | | | | | | |
| Personal hygiene | | | | | | | |
| Prayer, thought, meditation | | | | | | | |
| Service/ volunteering | | | | | | | |
| Other: | | | | | | | |
| Other: | | | | | | | |
| Other: | | | | | | | |
| Other: | | | | | | | |

# Income and Expenditures Chart

See "Learn to budget your money" on page 65.

| DATE | MONEY EARNED (from where?) | MONEY SPENT (on what?) | BALANCE |
|---|---|---|---|
| | | | |
| | | | |
| | | | |
| | | | |
| | | | |
| | | | |
| | | | |
| | | | |
| | | | |
| | | | |
| | | | |

**EXPLORE EXTREMES.** Make a poster showing how good things can become problems if taken to extremes (overuse/overdoing and underuse/underdoing). For example, you might put a drawing or photograph of exercise equipment in the center of your poster. To one side, show a kid watching TV, eating chips, drinking soda, and looking out of shape (underuse). To the other side, show a kid with hugely exaggerated muscles (overuse). You might title your poster "Too Little or Too Much: Either Can Be a Crutch." Here's a list of other things you might want to illustrate—or come up with your own list:

▲ communication

▲ computers

▲ conservation

▲ entertainment

▲ friends

▲ hobbies

▲ homework

▲ recreation

▲ sleep

▲ talents

▲ thriftiness

▲ volunteering/service

▲ work

**READ STORIES ABOUT CONSERVATION.** Look for these books:

📖 *The Ancient One* by T.A. Barron (New York: Tor Books, 1994). While helping her Great Aunt Melanie try to protect an Oregon redwood forest, 13-year-old Kate goes back five centuries through a time tunnel and faces an evil creature intent on destroying the same forest. Ages 12 & up.

📖 *Canyon Winter* by Walt Morey (New York: Puffin Books, 1994). Stranded for six months in the Rocky Mountains after a plane crash, a 15-year-old boy is taken in by an old hermit who teaches him the ways of the wilderness. Ages 11 & up.

📖 *The Weirdo* by Theodore Taylor (New York: Avon, 1993). Seventeen-year-old Chip Clewt fights to save the black bears in the Powhaten National Wildlife Refuge. Ages 13 & up.

# Character in *ACTION*

## Nick Pollack: Being Thrifty

When Nick Pollack needed a bike in fifth grade, he rummaged through the family "parts stockpile" out behind the old barn in LeSueur, Minnesota. He salvaged wheels from one old bike, chains from another, and brake equipment from a third. Then he created a new bike for himself while at the same time recycling a bunch of old parts.

Nick has learned to be thrifty and to save money, too. This was necessary because his parents lost their family farm when he was five years old. "I have to save for stuff I need," Nick explains. "If I don't, I don't get it. I've saved money for shoes, ink pens, pencils, a calculator, clothes, and that kind of stuff. I have my own bank account. If you don't learn to save now, you won't know how to save in the future."

Nick is large for his age, and farmers around his home hire him to unload beans out of granaries, unload hay when they're baling, and do yard work and other farmhand work. He's dependable and willing to do anything.

Nick's conservation efforts branched out into the environment when he was in seventh grade at the Minnesota New Country School, a year-round school. During the summer of 1995, teacher Cindy Reinitz led her students on a nature hike through Ney Woods, part of a Wildlife Game Refuge near Henderson, Minnesota. The day was so hot that Nick felt like a melting ice-cream cone. As he passed under some huge oaks and maples, he noticed frogs near the trees. Nick dove to the ground on his belly and grabbed one. But it was weird. Nick's frog had very thin, paralyzed legs. It was almost as if there were no muscles in them. Another girl found a frog that was missing its hind legs. The frogs were easy to catch because so many of them were deformed.

The class scrapped their nature hike and headed for the pond in Ney Woods. They visited the pond many times over the next few months. "I found at least 100 deformed frogs myself," Nick remembers. The big question was: What was causing the deformities? To find out, the students needed equipment for testing the soil, the water, and the creatures in the pond.

Once again, Nick hit the family "parts stockpile" and found some discarded C-clamps, glass jars, and a wooden pole. He used them to make a soil collector. "I attached the glass jar to the long pole so it was L-shaped. Then you could scoop out dirt from the bottom of the pond. But I sterilized the collectors first and then sealed them up. Then I made an invertebrate collector from two-liter pop jugs and dowel rods." According to Nick, you can tell a lot about a pond's water quality by finding out what invertebrates live there. If there aren't very many, the water probably isn't very good.

Ms. Reinitz's class sought the help of scientists to test their samples. They went to their state legislature and lobbied for funding. Nick testified before the Legislative Commission on Minnesota Resources. "We feel sort of attached to these frogs," Nick told the lawmakers. "We want to find out how to stop these deformities."

He and his classmates gave speeches at several hearings. As a result, the lawmakers allocated $123,000 for research on the frog problem alone. Then they set aside $28,500 to develop programs to involve students across the whole state. The Ney Learning Center received a $100,000 grant to build a classroom at the pond site. And the kids have a proposal out for nearly half a million dollars for education and further research.

In the spring of 1996, when the snow melted and the students returned to the pond, they discovered deformed toads, deformed turtles, and albino (colorless) birds. The problem seemed to be spreading. Then they had a breakthrough. Nick and his friends tested the pond water after a big rainstorm and found that it was very high in nitrates. Could nitrates from fertilizer runoff be causing the deformities?

Left to right: Nick Pollack, Minnesota New Country School teacher Tom Fish, and Kim Steiner checking the Ney Pond

"We don't know yet, because you have to take a whole lot of tests and put them together before you can guess," Nick says.

It might not even be the water. The frogs migrate up to a mile over the ground and could contact pollution along the way. So the problem isn't solved yet, and it may take years to correct. But Nick suspects that humans are the cause.

Today Nick is a confirmed conservationist. "Trees make money for you," he points out. "The food you eat comes from an animal that sacrificed its life for you. Don't waste paper or food. You can pick up trash and be resourceful instead of wasting things and buying stuff new.

"If we don't start saving now," he warns, "there won't be anything left for kids in the future."

## CHECK IT OUT

**Minnesota Pollution Control Agency**
*www.pca.state.mn.us/hot/frogs.html*
This site offers information about deformed frogs. It provides background information, frequently asked questions, publications you can download, research news, and links to other frog-related sites.

# Courage

**Bravery, boldness, daring, confidence, resolve**

> "You can't be brave if you've only had
> wonderful things happen to you."
> *Mary Tyler Moore*

When our daughter Annie was ten years old, she was bucked from a horse. She suffered a few bruises, but the worst bruise was to her courage. She cried and said that she never wanted to ride a horse again. This might have been okay, except that Annie had lived and breathed horses since she was old enough to pronounce the word. It had been her dream and her goal to ride in competition. Obviously, that couldn't happen if she remained afraid to get on a horse again.

My husband Larry encouraged her and told her how important it was to face those fears that defeat you and prevent you from becoming what you want to be. "Otherwise," he explained, "you're like a butterfly who's afraid to leave its cocoon."

Annie brushed away her tears, squared her tiny shoulders, and climbed back onto that spirited horse. She didn't know what would happen next, but she was willing to do it anyway. Although years later she'd win enough ribbons to wallpaper her room, she never demonstrated more courage—even in difficult competitions—than she did on that day when she was just ten.

## The Meaning of Courage

Some people confuse courage with foolhardiness. They assume that if you're brave, you'll try anything. But reckless behavior and courage aren't the same.

Courage means doing the right thing, even when it's scary or difficult. It means that you try your best to succeed, even when success isn't guaranteed. In fact, the greatest courage often follows failure. You pick yourself up and get back on the horse.

Courage means facing the monsters in your closet and under your bed—things you're afraid of, whether real or imagined.

71

*"You gain strength, courage and confidence by every experience in which you really stop to look fear in the face."*
*Eleanor Roosevelt*

There are many different kinds of courage. You'd need *physical courage* if your boat capsized and you had to swim to shore. But it might also take *mental courage* to swim one more mile when you were nearing exhaustion.

*Moral courage* is what enables you to stand up to your friends and say "No, I won't show you the answers to the test. That would be cheating." This is the kind of courage that helps you stay true to your beliefs and make good choices, even when your friends tease you or snub you. It gives you the strength to admit "I was wrong" or "I made a mistake" and to say "I'm sorry." It gives you the power to influence others when they're facing difficult decisions.

*"One man with courage makes a majority."*
*Andrew Jackson*

It takes courage to stand up to censure and tyranny and speak out against injustice. It takes courage to embark on a new experience or adventure—to start a new school, to make a new friend. It takes courage to break a bad habit or make a difference in the world. You need courage to solve problems, and courage to stand the pain of losing a friend or loved one.

Courage does *not* mean that you ski down the steepest slope without having the skill, dive off the highest rocks into a shallow lake, or drive your car too fast. Putting yourself in danger isn't brave, it's stupid. Although growing up involves taking some risks, those risks should be reasonable.[1]

Different people have different ways of being courageous. For example, you might be someone who can stand up in front of your history class and speak for ten minutes without notes. But for someone who's shy or lacks confidence, raising a hand and answering a question might require an extraordinary amount of courage.

---

[1] For more about risk taking, see "Imagination," pages 126–134.

Finally, you'll need courage to fulfill your dreams. You'll need courage to learn from others and from your own mistakes, to get up after you fall, to come back from a failure, to work hard when you're too tired, to keep going when you're alone. It takes courage to learn and grow, to let life be your teacher.

*"Life shrinks or expands in proportion to one's courage."*
*Anaïs Nin*

# Profiles in Courage

☀ Sir Isaac Newton did poorly in school. He was only allowed to stay in school because he was a failure at running the family farm. He grew up to become one of the most famous philosophers and mathematicians of all time.

☀ Admiral Richard E. Byrd was retired by the Navy as being "unfit for service." He became a legendary explorer who flew over the North Pole in 1926 and the South Pole in 1929.

☀ Thomas Edison was told by his teachers that he was too stupid to learn anything. He read all the books in his local library on his own and became the greatest inventor of all time, with more than 1,000 patents issued in his name.

☀ Rosa Parks, who was black, was ordered to give up her seat on the bus to a white man. She refused, forcing the police to remove, arrest, and imprison her—and sparking the Montgomery bus boycott. She became known as the mother of the American civil rights movement.

☀ Andrei Sakharov was a high-ranking Soviet physicist when he began opposing nuclear weapons tests and supporting human rights. He was exiled for many years as a result of his beliefs. He won the Nobel Peace Prize in 1975.

☀ Aung San Suu Kyi has spent her life working for democracy and human rights in her country of Myanmar (formerly Burma). From 1989–1995, she was under house arrest. She won the Sakharov Prize for Freedom of Thought in 1990 and the Nobel Peace Prize in 1991.

## CHECK IT OUT

Since 1901, the Nobel Peace Prize has been awarded to people of great courage. You'll probably recognize many of their names: Yitzhak Rabin, Nelson Mandela, Mikhail Gorbachev, the 14th Dalai Lama, Desmond Tutu, Lech Walesa, Mother Teresa, Anwar el-Sadat, Rigoberta Menchu, Henry Kissinger, Elie Wiesel, Martin Luther King Jr. Find out more about these courageous men and women by reading about their lives. Look for biographies and articles at your school or community library, search encyclopedias, or explore the resources of the Internet.

**The Nobel Foundation**
*www.nobel.se*

**The Nobel Prize Internet Archive**
*www.almaz.com*

# Character Dilemmas

*For journaling or writing essays, discussion, debate, role-playing, reflection*

**Suppose that . . .**

**1** Every afternoon when you walk home from school, a bully pushes you around, knocks your books to the ground, or calls you names. What might you do to stop the abuse and, at the same time, help the bully to change his behavior? What kind of courage would this take?

**2** A woman wants to run for election to the school board. She understands the problems facing the board and is very well qualified, but she doesn't have the money she needs for campaign expenses. A group of parents offers to pay for her advertising costs, but if she's elected, she must agree to vote the way they want her to vote on issues facing the board. What might the woman do? What type of courage will she need to do the right thing?

**3** You're at the mall with two friends who dare each other and you to shoplift. What might you do to keep your friendships and also stay out of trouble? What kind of courage will this take?

**4** You've signed up for summer camp with a friend, and you plan to room together. At the last minute, your friend changes her mind and decides to bunk with someone else. Will you still go to camp? What kind of courage will you need?

**5** You love to swim, and you're on the swim team, but your coach has just told you that you'll never be a good swimmer. What might you do about this? What type of courage will you need?

**6** Your twin brother needs a bone marrow transplant, and your marrow is a perfect match for his. You've been asked to be a donor, but you're afraid. Meanwhile, your volleyball team is heading for the league championships, and you're the star player. If you agree to be a donor, you won't be able to play in the championships. How might you gain the courage to make the right decision?

**7** Your school is having a talent contest. You have a special talent for writing poetry, and you read very well. There's just one problem. The thought of reading in front of a crowd makes your knees do a drum roll. What might you do to overcome your fear?

# Activities

**EXPLORE WHAT COURAGE MEANS TO YOU.** Consider several of the following situations (or come up with your own). Then talk about or write about actions or decisions that demonstrate courage or the lack of courage. *Example:* Following your parents' rules might mean that you refuse to watch a movie with your friends that your parents wouldn't want you to watch.

- following your parents' rules
- following school rules
- following community rules or laws
- applying for a job
- asking someone for a date
- learning to play a musical instrument
- sharing your talents
- admitting mistakes
- meeting new people

- being different (different abilities, background, race, etc.)
- being friends with someone that few people like
- standing up to peer pressure
- telling the truth
- trying to learn something new that you've always wanted to do
- wearing or not wearing certain clothes
- correcting a teacher, parent, or friend
- sticking up for someone else
- sticking up for your beliefs or convictions
- facing the unknown

ROLE-PLAY SITUATIONS that require courage. Choose a few of the situations described above to role-play with a friend or a small group. For each, demonstrate three possible approaches: 1) no courage, 2) lukewarm courage, and 3) courage. *Example:* A person who wants to ask someone for a date might show *no courage* by simply not asking, *lukewarm courage* by calling the person on the phone but not asking, or *courage* by asking. The person might also show courage by asking someone else if the first person says no.

WRITE IN YOUR JOURNAL[2] about the things you fear the most. How can you face your fears? How can you lessen your fears? Or write about something you know you should do but might be afraid to do. Then decide what you *will* do.

LEARN ABOUT A COURAGEOUS SCIENTIST. *Examples:*

- What kind of courage has Stephen Hawking demonstrated in his life? What has he learned about black holes? What has he contributed to our knowledge of the universe and its origins? Write an essay to share what you learn.

- How did Marie Curie show courage in her life and career? Find out about her life and struggles. Discover the connection between her work and her death from leukemia. Write a brief biography of this Nobel Prize winner.

- What happened when Vesto Melvin Slipher challenged Jacobus Kapteyn's theory of the universe? Were his ideas accepted or not? What kind of courage did it take to convince the scientific world that he was right? Compose a possible debate between Slipher and Kapteyn.

HAVE THE COURAGE TO BE HEALTHY.[3] Make a list of things you can do to achieve (or maintain) a healthy body, mind, and spirit. How might each of these require courage? *Example:* You decide to stop eating certain kinds of foods for health reasons. Your family doesn't want to change its eating habits. What might you do?

BE AN ENTREPRENEUR. It takes courage to start your own business. Here's how to begin:

1. Decide what you might want to do. Then try to find out if this is something that's needed in your neighborhood or community. *Examples:* cleaning, snow removal, baby-sitting, gardening, landscaping, dog walking, window washing, party organizing.

2. Estimate the costs of starting your business. How much money will you need to spend on materials? Advertising? A place to keep your equipment? Travel? What else?

3. Decide how much you'll charge for your services. TIP: Find out the "going rate." What do other people charge? What are people willing to pay?

4. Estimate how long it will take to recover your start-up costs and begin earning (and saving) money.

## CHECK IT OUT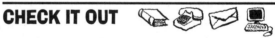

*Growing Money: A Complete Investing Guide for Kids* by Gail Karlitz (New York: Price Stern Sloan, 1999). A beginner's investment guide that covers savings accounts, stocks, bonds, and mutual funds. Ages 9–12.

*The Totally Awesome Business Book for Kids—And Their Parents* by Arthur Berg Bochner and Adriane G. Berg (New York: Newmarket Press, 1996). A financial expert and her 12-year-old son suggest 20 super businesses for kids ages 10–17, with special attention to jobs that help the environment.

---

[2] See "Endurance," pages 88, 89, and 92, for journaling resources. If you took the Fears Inventory on page 8, you might want to look back at it now. If you haven't yet taken the Fears Inventory, you might want to take it and write about it in your journal.

[3] See "Health," pages 103–114.

**The U.S. Small Business Administration**
Office of Marketing and Customer Service
409 Third Street, SW
Washington, DC 20416
1-800-827-5722
*www.sbaonline.sba.gov*
Created by Congress in 1953 to help America's entrepreneurs, the SBA is a wealth of information and advice. Call the national hotline to listen to recorded information on topics related to starting and running a business, or contact your local SBA office to request your own Small Business Starter Kit.

---

**LEARN ABOUT A HERO OR HEROINE** in history. Research a man or woman who fought tyranny, stood up for human rights, invented something important, was a leader, etc. Dress up like the person and tell his or her story to your class, club, or family.

**LEARN ABOUT A HERO OR HEROINE** of today. Choose someone you admire, then find out as much as you can about him or her. This might be someone famous or someone who has been an important role model in your own life—a grandparent or parent, teacher, friend, or neighbor. Find out about times when the person has acted courageously. If you choose someone famous, read a biography of the person or write to him or her.[4] If you choose someone you know personally, interview him or her. Afterward, think about what you have learned. How might this affect the decisions you make in your own life?

---

## CHECK IT OUT

*American Heroes: Their Lives, Their Values, Their Beliefs* by Robert Pamplin (New York: Master Media, 1996). Outstanding men and women of the 20th century including Billy Graham, Colin Powell, Elie Wiesel, Oprah Winfrey, Jackie Joyner-Kersee, Bill Cosby, and others share their stories of courage, integrity, and compassion. Ages 12 & up.

**The Giraffe Project**
PO Box 759
Langley, WA 98260
(360) 221-7989
*www.giraffe.org*

The Giraffe Project finds, commends, and publicizes people who "stick their necks out" for the common good. Write, call, or search their Web site for stories about real-life heroes of today.

**My Hero**
1278 Glenneyre #286
Laguna Beach, CA 92651
Fax (949) 376-9540
*myhero.com*
Check the Web site to read inspiring true stories about all kinds of heroes—teachers, artists, businesspeople, poets, explorers, athletes, freedom fighters, scientists, even pets. Submit your own story about someone you know who has shown courage, generosity, kindness, or ability. The stories are being developed into a TV series about role models for young people.

---

**GIVE AWARDS FOR COURAGE.** Place a "Courage Box" in your school, home, place of worship, or club. Put a stack of paper and a marker beside the box. Above the box, include a sheet of simple instructions. They might say "Write about an anonymous act of courage you've done or seen someone do." Design an award to be given each week to someone who has demonstrated courage.

---

[4] See "Choice," page 32, for information about *The Kid's Address Book.*

**GO UNDERGROUND.** Research the Underground Railroad, which helped slaves to escape from the United States South and reach freedom in the North and Canada before the Civil War. You might want to focus on the contributions of Harriet Tubman and Levi Coffin. Write a play about what you learn and perform it for an audience.

**CREATE A DIORAMA** depicting your favorite hero, heroine, or a moment in history when someone you admire acted with courage. Include a brief description. Place your diorama in your school library or clubhouse, or donate it to a local library. (This activity is more impressive if you do it as a group and create several dioramas.)

> *Variation:* Write a song describing your favorite hero, heroine, or a moment in history when someone you admire acted with courage. Perform it for an audience.

**LEARN A NEW SPORT OR ATHLETIC SKILL.** Choose one you feel uncertain about—maybe even one you fear. Practice it until you conquer your fear and feel comfortable and confident.

**PLAY A BALL-TOSS GAME ABOUT COURAGE.** You'll need a Nerf ball or other soft ball and a stopwatch. Divide into two teams. The leader or teacher starts the game by tossing the ball to a member of either team. That person has five seconds to think of an example of courage. If the person can think of one, he or she tells it to the group and earns a point for that team. If the person can't think of one, he or she tosses the ball back to the leader, who then tosses it to the other team. Keep alternating between teams. The first team to earn 5 points wins that round.

**READ STORIES ABOUT COURAGE.** Look for these books:

*Cracker Jackson* by Betsy Cromer Byars (New York: Viking, 1986). Jackson discovers that his former baby-sitter has been beaten by her husband. With the help of his friend Goat, Jackson attempts to drive her to a shelter for battered women. Ages 10–14.

*Journey to Jo'Burg: A South African Story* by Beverley Naidoo (New York: HarperCollins, 1986). Naledi and her brother Tino travel to Johannesburg to find their mother. While there, they witness firsthand the struggle for freedom in South Africa. Ages 10–13.

*Les Misérables* by Victor Hugo (New York: Fawcett, 1987). The classic story of the lives of several down-on-their-luck Parisians during the early 1800s. Ages 13 & up.

*Number the Stars* by Lois Lowry (New York: Dell, 1994). In Denmark during World War II, Annemarie and her family hide her best friend Ellen, who is Jewish, while Nazis track down Jewish families. Ages 10–13.

*So Far From the Bamboo Grove* by Yoko Kawashima Watkins (NY: Puffin, 1987). Eight-year-old Yoko escapes from Korea to Japan with her family at the end of World War II. Ages 10–14.

# Character in *ACTION*

## Merrick Johnston: The Courage to Follow a Dream

**M**errick Johnston sat at the feet of Vernon Tejas, a mountaineer and guide, listening to his stories of slippery slopes, of wind pelting snow in your face, of the tremendous rush when you reach the top of a mountain. She was nine years old, and right then she knew that she'd have to climb Mount McKinley someday.

Located in Alaska, Mt. McKinley is the tallest mountain in North America, 20,320 feet high at its peak. Much of it is covered by permanent snowfields and glaciers. The average temperature for June is 10–15 degrees, but the winds can blow up to 100 mph, and the wind chill can drop the temperature to 50–80 degrees below zero. During the 1995 climbing season, only 43 percent of the people who tried to climb it made it to the top. Six climbers died, and 22 needed to be rescued.

"At first, my mom didn't take me seriously—not until I was eleven," Merrick says. "I trained by doing gymnastics sixteen hours a week, snowboarding six hours a week, and hiking four hours a week in the mountains nearby."

Merrick needed a lot of courage to keep up her heavy schedule of physical activity. But she knew that if she wasn't physically strong, she would be a danger to the others on the climb.

"My mom and I hiked out back, and we gradually increased the loads in our packs and sleds. We climbed Mt. Goode, about 11,000 feet, using ropes, snowshoes, and crampons—boots with spikes," Merrick explains. She weighed just 90 pounds in a wet snowsuit, but she climbed with a 55–65 pound load. Although Merrick's favorite pastime is talking, she learned to entertain herself with her thoughts, and often when she was so exhausted she could hardly move, those thoughts were "I can do it. I can do it. I'm going to do it."

Merrick decided that when she climbed Mt. McKinley, she would also do something to help other children who weren't as fortunate as she was. She collected pledges from neighbors and other people in her community. The higher she climbed, the more money she would raise. The money would be donated to the Anchorage Center for Families, a family wellness center and child-abuse prevention agency.

On June 1, 1995, a beautiful, sunny day, Merrick began to fulfill her dream to climb Mt. McKinley. "My goal wasn't to reach the top. It was to *try* to reach the top." She paused at the base camp to build snowmen to mark the beginning of her journey.

"The worst part of the lower glacier was traveling in the heat and wearing a layer of clothes so we didn't sunburn," Merrick remembers. "We had two teams of four people. We had to load up sleds attached to

Merrick Johnston

our packs with all of our extra gear, food, and fuel, tow them ahead to our next camp, bury everything, and return to our other camp below and spend the night. The next day, if the weather was okay, we'd pack up our camp and set up our next camp where we had cached our supplies the day before. So we were really climbing the mountain twice. But it's safer that way, because if the weather gets bad you can stop and wait it out.

"We did that routine over and over until reaching our last camp at 17,000 feet. We planned to go from there to the top in one day, but we got snowed in for a week. Every night, we'd all go into one big tent and sing and giggle together. That's what kept me going."

Merrick needed a big dose of courage to pull her through the challenge of the climb. While climbing up to make camp at 11,000 feet, she fought strong gusts of wind and snow. The storm made it hard to see her own boots, and the load she carried felt like a ton of bricks on her back. She was the last person on a four-person rope team with her mother, another climber, and a guide in the lead.

Merrick had sunscreen for her lips and face tied onto a string around her neck. As she struggled forward, the string became twisted and caught up in the team's rope, tightening around her neck and choking her. Merrick panicked and started hyperventilating. The howling storm drowned out her pleas for help. Her mother, realizing there was a problem, yanked and shouted until she finally got the attention of the man ahead of her. But they couldn't make the guide aware of what was happening. He just thought that everyone was straining because of the steep slope and heavy loads. Merrick hung on like a pit bull for what seemed like hours. Finally, the guide stopped and Merrick was able to untangle herself.

On June 23, the climbers formed a single rope team for the final ascent to the summit. Merrick was second in line. She concentrated on each step, knowing that the summit ridge had a 7,000-foot drop off the right side. She thought again of the abused and disadvantaged kids back in the shelter. As she inched her way along a 100-foot ledge that was half the width of her foot, she felt grateful for her many hours of gymnastics practice.

At 1:35 P.M., Merrick heard the lead guy whoop. "We were on top of the clouds," she says. "I was the first one to touch the summit, and I saw a picture I'll never forget. The sun was setting, making the clouds look like pink cotton candy. I could see the blue shadow of the summit against the clouds. We were all struck dumb." She snuggled next to her mom, drank in the view, and felt a great rush of accomplishment.

Merrick Johnston was 12 years, 5 months, and 5 days old when she stood at the top of Mt. McKinley—the youngest person ever. Now she has her heart set on Mt. Vinson in Antarctica. And she has other goals as well. "I want to have the power to help people when I grow up," she says. "I want to be on top of things. I want to have an important job, like a heart surgeon. And I want to be a white-water rafting guide so I can play a lot, too."

Merrick in Alaska

# Empathy

**Understanding, compassion, charity, sensitivity, concern**

> "You can't understand another
> person until you walk a few miles
> in their moccasins."
> *Native American proverb*

Have you ever visited the Hoh rainforest in the Pacific Northwest? If you travel there, you'll discover the beautiful Sitka spruce, which grows abundantly in the shade of the forest's green canopy. There's something especially interesting about this tree. The young Sitka spruce seedlings have a hard time getting started alone in the dirt. There's too much competition from dense moss and other aggressive plants that spread a carpet along the forest floor. A seed must land on a fallen Sitka log in order to germinate, then live off the nourishment from the decaying trunk. The dying tree becomes a "nurse log" to new seedlings. The seedlings send roots into and around the log. Eventually the old log disappears, and all that remains are the new Sitkas standing in a colonnade on stilt-like roots.

If you have empathy, you can compare yourself to that nurse log. There's a deep connection between the decaying tree and the new seedlings that grow from it. Empathy is one step beyond service. You can care for people and serve them without knowing much about their thoughts and feelings.[1] For example, you might have a friend who reads to an elderly woman every week. That's a great service. But your friend might not know that the woman is weeping inwardly for a lost child, or that she's afraid of dying.

Empathy means that you can *sense, identify with,* and *understand* what another person is feeling. You can almost get inside the person's head and heart. You have a shared communion with him or her. You can connect and relate to what the person needs. For example, if your friend who reads to the elderly woman has empathy for the woman, your friend probably won't choose to read *The Giving Tree*. Shel Silverstein's story about a tree that sacrifices its life for a man might be too painful for the woman to bear, and your friend will realize this without being told.

When you shout from a hilltop, sometimes your words come back to you in an echo. You hear the same words you shouted, but they're not as loud. Empathy is like an echo. You don't add to what someone feels. You don't change the feelings. You accept and share them, but in a softer way, because it's almost impossible to feel with the same intensity of the other person's firsthand experience.

If you have empathy, you have *compassion* for others. In response, you might show them *charity*—kindness, benevolence, and goodwill. The

---

[1] See "Caring," pages 21–27.

word "charity" comes from the Latin for "Christian love," which is one way to understand it; if you're not a Christian, you might interpret it as "Mohammed-like love," "Buddha-like love," or whatever best describes your personal faith. Mother Teresa has often been cited as an example of charity because she not only served people in great need, she also lived with them. She "walked in their moccasins."

Empathizing with someone is *not* the same as pitying or feeling sorry for him or her. This is an important distinction. When you pity another person, you look down on him or her. You think "How awful" or "What a terrible situation that person is in" or even "Thank goodness I'm not in that situation." Pity sets you apart; empathy brings you together.

> "With compassion, we see benevolently our own human condition and the condition of our fellow beings. We drop prejudice. We withhold judgment."
> *Christina Baldwin*

# Character Dilemmas

*For journaling or writing essays, discussion, debate, role-playing, reflection*

**Suppose that...**

**1** There's a new student at your school who wears clothes that are different from what everyone else wears. How might you feel if you were 1) the new student, 2) a popular student, 3) an unpopular student, 4) a teacher, 5) the parent of the new student?

**2** Your state legislature has just passed a law requiring all public buildings—including schools, businesses, and houses of worship—to build wheelchair ramps within one year. How might you react if you were 1) a school administrator, 2) a person in a wheelchair, 3) a business owner, 4) a city planner, 5) a church administrator?

**3** Your city demolishes an entire block of low-income housing because it's in bad repair. How might you feel if you were 1) a person with a low income, 2) a developer who builds new houses, 3) someone who lives across the street from the newly razed block?

**4** Two girls have been best friends for years. One girl starts dating the other girl's boyfriend. How might you feel if you were 1) the girl who lost her boyfriend, 2) the girl who started dating her best friend's boyfriend, 3) the boyfriend?

**5** Your government has just announced major cuts in medical insurance for the elderly. How might you feel if you were 1) a government official, 2) a senior citizen, 3) a middle-aged person, 4) a child?

**6** A teenager signs an organ donor card. In the event of his death, his organs will go to other people who need them. How might you feel if you were 1) the person signing the donor card, 2) his parent, 3) a person awaiting an organ transplant, 4) a physician?

# Activities

**LEARN TO EMPATHIZE WITH ELDERLY PEOPLE.** Read stories, read books, or watch videos about elderly people. Then interview elderly people in your family, neighborhood, or senior citizens' centers in your community. Try to imagine what it might be like to be one of them. (Someday you will be!) Ask them how they feel about health care, food and housing, social security, family relationships, health and sickness, the future, and anything else you'd like to know about. Write about what you learn and share your findings with your family, class, or community.

## CHECK IT OUT*

*Driving Miss Daisy* (1989; PG). Jessica Tandy won an Oscar for her portrayal of an elderly Southern woman who can no longer drive. When her son hires a black man (Morgan Freeman) as her chauffeur, the two become faithful companions.

*Harold and Maude* (1971; PG). Bud Cort and Ruth Gordon star in this black comedy (and cult classic) about a friendship between Harold, a depressed 20-year-old, and Maude, a 79-year-old with a zest for life.

*On Golden Pond* (1981; PG). Henry Fonda and Katharine Hepburn won Academy Awards for their poignant portrayals of an 80-year-old man and his devoted wife spending a summer in Maine.

---

\* You must get permission from your parents to watch these movies. Better yet, watch them *with* your parents.

LEARN ABOUT THE NEEDS OF VARIOUS GROUPS in your community including 1) elderly people, 2) families, 3) children, 4) parents, 5) single parents, 6) people with disabilities, 7) people who are ill, 8) minorities, 9) immigrants, 10) homeless people, 11) women, and 12) men. Contact your city council or mayor's office for information; read your local newspaper; ask people who work or volunteer for service and charitable organizations. Compile your findings on a chart showing the differences and similarities among people's needs.

WRITE IN YOUR JOURNAL[2] about how it might feel to have LD (a learning difference or disability). If you have LD, write about how it might feel to have another kind of difference or disability.

## CHECK IT OUT

*Keeping a Head in School: A Student's Book About Learning Abilities and Learning Disorders* (Cambridge, MA: Educators Publishing Service, 1991). Stay on top of homework with this handy book. Ages 9–12.

### LDOnline
*www.ldonline.org*
An interactive site where parents, teachers, and kids can learn about LD. Includes information about LD and ADD (Attention Deficit Disorder), artwork and writing by young people with LD, recommended resources, and more. Be sure to visit the KidZone: *www.ldonline.org/kidzone*

### Yahoo's Disabilities Links
*www.yahoo.com/Society_and_Culture/Disabilities*
Links to sites, information, and databases about all kinds of disabilities.

TAKE FIELD TRIPS to increase your understanding of people whose lives and needs are different from yours. You might visit a children's hospital, juvenile detention home, halfway house for recovering alcoholics, home for unwed mothers, senior citizens' center or rest home, women's shelter, homeless shelter, food pantry, and any other place you're interested in. Each time you return from a field trip, write a story or a poem about your experience. IMPORTANT: Be sure to get permission from your parents,

your school, and the place or agency you want to visit. Go with a chaperon.

VOLUNTEER AT ONE OF THE PLACES you visit. Follow these steps:[3]

*1. Decide where you'd like to go and what you'd like to do.*[4] Consider these questions:

**?** What might benefit the most people?

**?** What might make the biggest difference?

**?** What can I afford (in terms of time, effort, etc.)?

**?** What's really possible for me to do?

*2. Talk to the administrator or volunteer coordinator.* Many organizations couldn't exist without strong support from volunteers, so they already have a system in place for accepting and training them. Ask what they need volunteers to do. This might be different from what you originally thought, and it might be different from what you'd like to do, so be prepared to be flexible—or to decide that you'd rather volunteer elsewhere. *Example:* If you want to be a volunteer at a children's hospital, you may have to be 16 to qualify.

*3. Once you find a good match, get any permissions you need to proceed.* Depending on where you want to volunteer, you may need permission from your parent(s), teacher(s), principal, youth leader, etc. You may need an adult chaperon.

*4. Decide how long you'll stay involved and what you want to achieve.* Set a schedule for yourself. When will you start? How much time will you spend volunteering each week or month?

*5. If you don't want to go it alone, invite others to join you.* Choose people who share your interest and can make a commitment.

*6. Firm up the details.* Will you need transportation back and forth? Any special materials, equipment, supplies, clothing, or skills? Are there any limitations or restrictions on what you can do or when and where you can do it?

---

[3] Adapted from *The Kid's Guide to Service Projects* by Barbara A. Lewis (Minneapolis: Free Spirit Publishing, 1995), pages 8–11. Used with permission of the publisher.

[4] See "Caring," page 24, for information about national programs that promote youth service.

---

[2] See "Endurance," pages 88, 89, and 92, for journaling resources.

**7. *When your term as a volunteer comes to an end, evaluate the experience.*** Discuss it with your team members, family, teachers, and friends. Talk it over with the people you served. Consider these questions:

**?** What did I learn?

**?** What did I accomplish?

**?** What were my feelings, fears, joys?

**?** Would I do it again?

**?** How could I improve on the experience?

**?** Will I repeat the experience? When? How soon?

**PRACTICE SEEING BOTH SIDES** of an environmental issue. Choose an issue that's currently being debated in your community. *Examples:* the use of a stream bed; air quality; dumping; the development of an area (for high-income housing, low-income housing, retail, industry, park, etc.). Invite speakers from both sides to address your class, school, or club and express their views on the issue. Afterward, ask your classmates and friends to vote on which person seemed most persuasive. Did you have an opinion or point of view before you heard the speakers, and did anything they said change your mind? Did you empathize more with one speaker than the other?

**FIND OUT THE AVERAGE ANNUAL INCOME** of a family in your town, city, or state. Then find out the average annual incomes of families in several countries around the world, including third world countries. (You might gather this information from almanacs, encyclopedias, or the Internet.) Calculate the differences and make a chart illustrating them. Could your family live on the amount of money earned by a family in Afghanistan? In Bangladesh? In Cuba? In India? In Zaire? How do you think families in these countries pay for food, clothing, housing, utilities (heat, light, water, telephone), medical expenses, transportation, education, and recreation? You might extend your research to include average life expectancy, infant mortality rates, and other topics. Afterward, think about how this information has affected your feelings about different peoples around the world. Can you begin to empathize with the struggles of families in poor nations?

**PRACTICE EMPATHIZING WITH YOUR PARENTS.** Each day, ask them how they feel about a different issue. *Examples:* family rules, money, working, the easiest/best part about raising children, the hardest/worst part about raising children, current events, their hopes/dreams for your future, etc. Do this for five days. Just listen to what they say—without arguing. Afterward, think about what you learned. Do you know your parents any better now? Can you see their point of view on certain issues? Can you understand where they're coming from and why? Tell them how you feel and practice having a discussion.

*Variation:* Practice empathizing with your siblings. Ask your older or younger brother(s) or sister(s) what frustrates them the most, what makes them happiest, etc. Ask if they have any advice for you.

**WALK IN SOMEONE ELSE'S SHOES.** Literally! Exchange shoes with a sibling, parent, classmate, teacher, or friend for an hour or a day. Talk about what you learned from the experience.

*Variation:* Imagine what it would be like to walk in the cold with *no* shoes. Or be courageous and do it. Ask your parents for permission first. Afterward, collect good used shoes (and money for new shoes) from your school or club and make a donation to a homeless shelter, second-hand store, or kids' shelter.

**LEARN ABOUT IMMIGRATION** in your town, city, or state. Check with organizations that sponsor immigrants to find out where people are coming from. If possible, arrange to meet with and interview recent immigrants. (You might need translators to accompany you.) Ask about the beliefs and customs they have brought with them to their new home. Try to empathize with their feelings and needs. Afterward, present your findings to your class or school. You might want to create a choral reading using different "voices" to tell about the immigrant experience and the beliefs and customs of the people.

**START AN INTERNATIONAL CLUB** at your school.[5] Post flyers announcing the club. Your goal should be to attract as many people as possible, preferably from a wide variety of ethnic groups and backgrounds. Talk about common concerns and problems, special needs, and times when you need support and

---

[5] See "Leadership," pages 160–161, for tips and a resource on how to start a club.

understanding. Get to know each other. Really listen to each other. Empathize. Decide on common goals and ways to achieve them.

*Variations:* Hold an International Fair with exhibits and presentations. Or have an International Talent Show, Music Show, Fashion Show, Food Festival, or Arts & Crafts Show. Invite students (and parents) to participate, perform, and share information about their lives and cultures.

## CHECK IT OUT

**Skipping Stones Magazine**
PO Box 3939
Eugene, OR 97403-0939
(541) 342-4956
*www.efn.org/~skipping*
This international multicultural children's magazine encourages an understanding of different cultures and languages. Ages 8–18.

**Kids Meeting Kids**
324 West 96th Street
New York, NY 10025
(212) 663-6368
*www.kidsmeetingkids.org*
This international organization promotes multicultural understanding, peace, fairness, and children's rights. Programs include pen-pal and peace exchanges, workshops, and a newsletter.

**Yahooligans! Cultures**
*www.yahooligans.com/School_Bell/ Social_Studies/ Cultures*
A site of links that celebrate cross-cultural communications. Learn about cuisines, currencies, gestures, holidays, languages, religions, and more.

CREATE A POSTER COLLAGE showing different types of ethnic clothing. If you can't find pictures in magazines, visit your library and look for books on costumes and fashions. Then draw pictures based on what you find. If you hold an International Fashion Show, take photographs of the show and use them to make your collage. Imagine how people's lives might be affected by the types of clothing they wear.

MAKE A JIGSAW PUZZLE (with cardboard or wood backing) showing different people. You might show men, women, and children; people from different ethnic or racial groups; people of different ages; people working at different types of jobs, or engaged in various kinds of recreational activities; etc. Donate your puzzle to a class of younger kids.

LEARN EMPATHY THROUGH MUSIC. Play different types of ethnic music over your school PA system each morning for 5–10 minutes to increase understanding and appreciation of various cultures. Ask students to bring in examples of music to play, and/or gather examples from your school or local library.

PRACTICE EMPATHY IN SPORTS. When someone on your team makes a mistake, pat him or her on the back or offer encouragement. When you compete with another team, try to imagine how they feel if they win or lose. Shake hands at the end no matter who wins. Help a teammate or competitor who falls. Develop concern for your teammates and competitors. Keep track of how this changes your attitude toward and feelings about sports. How does it affect your performance?

PLAY A "GUESS WHAT I'M FEELING" GAME. Divide into pairs. Face each other. Player A tells about an experience he or she had. Player B watches for facial expressions and concentrates on listening and understanding. Then Player A says "Guess what I'm feeling." Player B tries to identify the emotion the first player felt during the experience just described—happiness, sadness, anger, joy, fear, hurt, relief, frustration, etc. Then Player B tries to repeat what Player A said about the experience—as closely as possible, and empathizing with Player A's feeling. Afterward, the players switch roles and Player B tells about an experience.

READ STORIES ABOUT EMPATHY. Look for these books:

- *Belle Prater's Boy* by Ruth White (New York: Farrar, Straus & Giroux, Inc., 1996). Woodrow moves in with his grandparents after his mother mysteriously disappears. There he befriends his cousin, and together they learn to face the losses in their lives. Ages 12 & up.

- *Blubber* by Judy Blume (New York: Simon & Schuster Children's Books, 1982). Jill doesn't worry much about the grief that she and her classmates cause a fellow student—until Jill becomes a target herself. Ages 9–12.

- *Pink and Say* by Patricia Polacco (New York: The Putnam Publishing Group, 1994). Say Curtis describes his meeting with Pinkus Aylee, a black soldier, during the Civil War, and their capture by Confederate troops. Ages 9–13.

📖 *A Separate Peace* by John Knowles (New York: Bantam Books, 1994). Set at an elite boarding school for boys during the early years of World War II, this beloved classic (a best-seller for over 30 years) is a starkly moving parable of friendship, treachery, and tragedy. Ages 13 & up.

📖 *Visiting Miss Pierce* by Pat Derby (New York: Sunburst Books, 1989). In talking with an elderly woman about her past, Barry begins to examine his own situation as an adopted child. Ages 11–14.

# Character in *ACTION*

## Mia Mejorado: Compassionate Service

Mia Mejorado was 12 years old when she first started volunteering as a junior counselor at Delhaven Community Center a block from her home. The center ran a summer camp and was also the site of an after-school program in a low-income neighborhood, where Mia had grown used to hearing gunshots puncture the silence. Once she had to help rush the kids into an enclosed building because there was gunfire right next door.

"I was in charge of helping the kids play games, do artwork, or other activities," Mia remembers. "Every day, we took care of between 50 and 100 kids."

Mia had attended Delhaven Community Center as a child until she was too old at the end of sixth grade. Then she volunteered as a junior counselor. She was so responsible and mature that she was made a senior counselor during her first summer camp between seventh and eighth grades, more than a year earlier than anyone else.

During the seven years she volunteered at Delhaven, Mia helped many children. Once a tiny, sparrow-like girl attended a summer camp where Mia volunteered 24 hours a day, with only a few days off for breaks. "I felt so sorry for this little soft, delicate girl," Mia says. "All of the other girls in my group were happy to be away from home. But this one cried. So I kept her under my wing like a baby bird all day. I gave her piggyback rides and wiped her tears."

Mia pushed damp curls off the girl's forehead at night as she tucked her in. Then she remained beside the girl until she smiled and slept. Meanwhile, Mia remembered many dark nights she had spent alone while her parents worked. "I often longed for morning so I wouldn't feel the dead calm of the night or fear the noises or the sound of gunshots."

Mia also took care of mentally disabled adults who came from group and private homes on Saturdays for recreation activities. She spoon-fed them and wiped spaghetti sauce from their chins with gentle hands. She even changed their diapers. Sometimes she lost her own appetite, but she swallowed hard and carried on, sensing the adults' frustration and loneliness.

When Mia was 15, her best friend, who also worked at Delhaven, was killed in a car crash. The center started a scholarship fund in his memory. Mia walked about silently, fighting a sinking feeling in her chest. She moved robot-like among the children. But she understood their pain even better than before. Now she knew death.

Not long afterward, she was leading a group of mentally disabled adults at an amusement park. Several members of the group decided to go on the gondola ride. Mia watched, helpless and horrified, as one of the women fell 30 feet from the gondola to the concrete below. Mia rode in the ambulance with the woman to the hospital and waited there until 11:00 P.M., when she was taken back to the camp. She couldn't sleep, so she went to the shower area, sat on the tile floor, and cried through the night.

Although Mia had been a good student before the woman's accident, she grew uninterested in school. When she learned that the woman had been injured so severely that she would never walk or talk again, Mia's grades fell further to a rock-bottom low.

Her Delhaven supervisor, Tim Seal, understood Mia's problem and appreciated the thousands of hours she had volunteered for the center. He arranged for her to attend a new private school, Bishop Amat Memorial High School. Delhaven sponsored her with a scholarship.

In the warmth of her new school, Mia revived. She regained her enthusiasm for learning and continued to volunteer at Delhaven. Her grades soared to A's and B's. When she was 16, she was hired as the youngest person on the staff of Delhaven. They paid her a stipend of $75.00 a month, and she used some of the money for her school uniforms and books. She continued to donate countless hours in volunteer service.

Her life wasn't easy, however. Once she saw a man commit suicide, shooting himself in the mouth in the center's parking lot. She went back into the building, sat down in the corner of the bathroom, and cried.

Despite everything she's seen and experienced, Mia is generally cheerful, and she loves people. Sponsored by Delhaven, she's now attending Mount San Antonio College, where she plans to study education, recreation, law enforcement, or social work. When she turned 18, she was made the youngest member of Delhaven's Board of Directors. Her compassion and kindness have cushioned the hardships of many kids and adults.

"It's like a positive addiction," Mia explains. "Those little kids need someone to talk to. They need me. Even if I'm low, when I go there, they run up and hug me. They give me pictures they've drawn and pull on my hands. They need someone who'll always be there—someone they can depend on. I want to get married and have a family someday, but even if I do, I still want to adopt some kids."

Mia Mejorado

# Endurance

**Patience, stamina, strength in adversity and suffering**

In a test to check the effects of depression and stress, two groups of mice were given a series of electric shocks. One group was allowed to learn a way to turn off the shocks; the other group wasn't allowed any control over the shocks. The result of the test was that the second group was less able to fight off cancer cells.

When you have no control over the things that happen to you, you sometimes feel helpless, frustrated, depressed, guilty, or anxious. And your body doesn't like it. You often catch a cold because your immune system gets tired, overworked, and goes on vacation, leaving you with a headache and a box of tissues.

*Bad things happen to good people.* In fact, *bad things just happen.* Sometimes you have problems you cause to happen because of poor choices, such as not getting enough sleep or exercise, getting chilled, and not eating right. Then you really can't blame your immune system. But some things happen that you can't seem to control.

Endurance is *the ability to withstand hardship or adversity.* To endure means *to undergo hardship without giving in; to remain firm under suffering or misfortune without yielding.* When you have endurance, you stand strong, holding your balance physically, emotionally, and spiritually, without buckling under, losing hope, or surrendering. You're patient, holding your own and waiting until the turmoil subsides. You know and accept that bad things happen, and you don't blame anyone. Instead of thinking "My mom's in the hospital and it's the doctor's fault," you think "Okay, my mom's in the hospital. Now what do I need to do?"

"The thought that we are enduring
the unendurable is one of the things that
keep us going."
*Molly Haskell*

# Coping When Bad Things Happen

A zit blossoms on your forehead just before a first date. Or you miss the tying foul shot in the regional basketball playoffs. Or your friend spreads lies about you. Or your dad loses his job. Or you break a leg, catch pneumonia, or develop a serious illness. What do you do? If you have endurance, you cope in healthy, positive ways. You realize that making good choices can help you to avoid much suffering, but you also understand that doing things right doesn't always prevent misfortune from knocking at your door.

## Not-So-Cool Ways to Cope

*Escape or avoid your problems.* You crumple up your failed biology test and toss it in the trash. Or you vegetate in front of the TV, sleep more than you need to (although sometimes sleeping helps), eat constantly, or do something self-destructive (drive too fast, use alcohol or drugs, or take other unhealthy risks). Sometimes, when things get *really* bad, some people think that suicide is the answer. It isn't. Suicide is the final copout. You can't ever change your mind or come back from it.

> "Suicide is a permanent solution to a temporary problem."
> *Phil Donahue*

## CHECK IT OUT

*Straight Talk About Anxiety and Depression* by Michael Maloney and Rachel Kranz (New York: Dell, 1993). Case studies, self-corrective behavior, suggestions for coping, and how to get help. Ages 11–18.

*The Power to Prevent Suicide: A Guide for Teens Helping Teens* by Richard E. Nelson, Ph.D., and Judith C. Galas (Minneapolis: Free Spirit Publishing, 1994). Understanding the causes of suicide, recognizing the signs, and reaching out to save a life. Ages 11 & up.

**Covenant House Nineline**
1-800-999-9999
*www.covenanthouse.org*
Immediate crisis intervention, support, and referrals for runaways and abandoned youth, and those who are suicidal or in crisis. Help is available for children, teens, and adults.

**Suicide Awareness Voices of Education**
*www.save.org*
An extensive collection of links and articles about depression and suicide.

***

**Blame yourself.** This is *not* the same as accepting responsibility for your actions and choices. In fact, blaming yourself is a way of *avoiding* responsibility. If you tell yourself "I failed my biology test because I'm too stupid to learn that stuff," you've just given yourself an excuse for not studying anymore. And you can forget about doing better on future biology tests.

**Blame other people.** "I failed my biology test because Sarah made me go to a concert with her." You can probably see the false reasoning in this argument. Unless Sarah tied you up and dragged you to the concert, you *chose* to go with her.

**Blame chance.** "I failed my biology test because the bus came too early, and I missed it. I got to school ten minutes late and had to rush through the test." Chance happenings are totally out of our control, right? Yes . . . but what we do in response is up to us.

**Blame other things, forces, or powers.** "I failed my biology test because I had to go to work and didn't have time to study." That's not a good reason. That's poor planning. "I failed the test because God is punishing me." It may help to talk to a religious leader if you feel this way.

## Cool Ways to Cope

**Face and accept what happens in your life.** If you stop trying to escape and avoid disagreeable or painful events, if you stop looking for someone or something to blame, you can gather your strength and move forward. It's normal to feel depressed and discouraged at times. But if you're always angry, hurt, sad, or frightened, you get stuck and immobilized. And you may develop unpleasant side effects—headaches, back pain, overwhelming tiredness or lethargy. Even when what happens to you isn't your fault at all—if, for example, you contract a serious disease—you can't waste your energies wondering "Why me?" That won't make you better. It might even make you worse. Don't spin your wheels searching for fairness, because *sometimes life isn't fair.*

> "I accept the universe!"
> *Margaret Fuller*

**Express your feelings.** If someone hurts you, talk to him or her. If you're angry, that's okay. Express your feelings in a way that doesn't blame or hurt you or the other person. Focus on the behavior, not the person.[1] *Example:* "It really makes me mad when I hear that lies are being told about me." Talk about your feelings with someone you trust—a true friend who will listen and understand. Sing, dance, laugh, or cry. Crying can help you release your frustration.

**Write about your feelings.** Dr. James Pennebaker and Sandra Beall once did an experiment with 46 college students to find out how important it was to

***

[1] For more on this topic, see "Respect," pages 217–218.

express feelings related to problems. They divided the students into groups and asked them to write about their suffering. One group was told to stick to the facts; another group was told to also write about their feelings, frustrations, anger, and so on. The students who wrote about their feelings had higher blood pressure and heart rates after writing than the first group. Six months later, however, they had fewer illnesses, less tension, more peace of mind and insight, and were able to face painful things more easily. So get a journal to write in and let your feelings out. Learn from them; let sadness and suffering be your teachers.

## CHECK IT OUT

*Anne Frank: The Diary of a Young Girl* by Anne Frank (New York: Bantam Books, 1993). The diary Anne Frank kept during the two years she and her family hid from the Nazis in an Amsterdam attic is an eloquent testament to the human spirit. Ages 12 & up.

**Anne Frank Online**
*www.annefrank.com*
View a photo essay about Anne Frank's life, read excerpts from her diary, and learn about the Anne Frank Center USA.

*The Diary of Latoya Hunter: My First Year in Junior High* by Latoya Hunter (New York: Vintage Books, 1993). A young girl writes about the challenges of youth and the way it's shaped by the inner city. Ages 10–14.

*Zlata's Diary: A Child's Life in Sarajevo* by Zlata Filipovic (New York: Viking Press, 1994). Shortly before war broke out in Sarajevo, 11-year-old Zlata Filipovic began to keep a diary. Moving and inspiring, it puts a human face on an inhuman tragedy. Ages 11 & up.

***Get help if you need it.*** Sometimes it's not enough to write in a journal or talk to a friend. You might need to talk with an adult—a teacher, counselor, parent, religious leader, or someone else you trust. If people belittle or discount your feelings, you might end up feeling ashamed or worse. So find someone who will take you seriously and understand your fear and pain. If your body got sick, you'd go to a doctor. If your mind and soul are suffering, seek out a counselor, psychologist, or psychiatrist.

"I'm feeling burned out. Are you in?"

## CHECK IT OUT

**Kids Help Phone**
1-800-668-6868
*www.kidshelp.sympatico.ca*
Canada's only toll-free national telephone counseling service for children and youth ages 4–19.

**National Youth Crisis Hotlines**
1-800-HIT-HOME (1-800-448-4663)
Operated by Youth Development International
1-800-442-HOPE (1-800-442-4673)
Operated by Children's Rights of America

***Try to make it better.*** Take positive action. If you fail a test, study harder next time. If you tell a lie, admit it. If you break a window, repair it. If you have an illness, follow your doctor's advice. When you redirect your energy from suffering to making things better, you stop being a victim.

> "Although the world is full of suffering,
> it is full also of the overcoming of it."
> *Helen Keller*

***Take good care of yourself.*** Eat well. Get enough sleep. Leave time in your life for daydreaming, meditation, relaxation, recreation, and goofing off. Reward yourself for taking care of yourself.[2]

---

[2] See "Health," pages 103–114.

**Let go.** Have you ever seen a rotten tree branch wedged in a gutter? Before long, all kinds of junk are snagged by the branch. By itself, the tree branch isn't harmful, but the debris it collects can cause the gutter to clog and overflow. If you cling to your difficulties, you might obstruct your own progress. Try to let go of your problems and move on. Know what you can control and what you can't control, what you can change and what you're powerless to change. You'll be healthier, happier, and more successful in everything you do.

**Learn and grow from your experiences, including the ones that hurt.** You'll develop wonderful character traits as a result. You might become more patient, tolerant, understanding, and helpful. You might learn how to take better care of your body so you're healthier for the rest of your life. You might become more assertive and confident, and develop leadership skills. Your friends might respect you more for setting a good example. You might even become a hero! Best of all, you'll probably develop more empathy, understanding, and compassion for others.

# Character Dilemmas

*For journaling or writing essays, discussion, debate, role-playing, reflection*

Suppose that . . .

**1** Your best friend decides that she doesn't want to be friends with you anymore. How might you turn your suffering into a positive experience so you aren't hurt so badly? How might you stick up for yourself and, at the same time, treat your former friend kindly?

**2** You have a friend whose parents are getting divorced. Your friend is devastated. He starts missing school, and his grades begin to fall. He keeps to himself and ignores you and his other friends. How might you help your friend to cope? What could you say without being preachy?

**3** Lately your older sister has been crying a lot. You know that something has happened to hurt her. But every time you try to talk with her, she slams the door in your face. How might you help her, even if she won't tell you what's happened? Or should you just ignore her?

**4** Your father loses his job, and your family moves to another state. Once there, your mother starts working, too, and you end up taking on more of the housework. Your grades start to slip and your social life is nonexistent. What might you do to help your family and yourself endure these difficult changes and times?

**5** You feel like a loser, hate the way you look, and are convinced that you have no talents or abilities at all. You're sure that good things only happen to other people, never to you. What might you do to change your suffering into something positive? How might you change the way you feel about yourself? Be realistic.

**6** There's a young child in your family or neighborhood who has stopped speaking and hides from people. What might you do to help?

# Activities

WRITE IN YOUR JOURNAL about things that have hurt you physically or emotionally. Write about what you've done to feel better—or what you might do if you're still suffering. Then follow through.[3]

## CHECK IT OUT

*A Book of Your Own: Keeping a Diary or Journal* by Carla Stevens (New York: Clarion Books, 1993). Practical suggestions plus excerpts from diaries past and present. Ages 9–13.

*All About Me: A Keepsake Journal for Kids* by Linda Kranz (Flagstaff, AZ: Northland Publishing, 1996). A place to record problems, reflect on your life, and preserve memories of your best or hardest times. Ages 9–12.

WRITE A POEM that begins "I hurt most when. . . ." Or write a poem about suffering, what you can learn from it, how to face it, how not to hurt others—or anything else you want to write about.[4]

---

[3] See page 92 for a list of fiction books written in journal style.
[4] See "Communication," page 57, for a list of resources for young writers.

COLLECT STORIES, POEMS, DIARIES, or quotations by writers who have written about pain and suffering. *Examples:* William Shakespeare, Edna St. Vincent Millay, Edgar Allan Poe, William Wordsworth, Norman Vincent Peale. (You might also look through the Bible, the Koran, the Talmud, or other religious or reflective works.) What can you learn from them about endurance, patience, and strength? What are their attitudes toward adversity? Here are three quotations to get you started:

- "A *Wounded* deer—leaps highest." *Emily Dickinson*

- "Those who aim at great deeds must also suffer greatly." *Marcus Licinius Crassus*

- "I do not believe that sheer suffering teaches. If suffering alone taught, all the world would be wise, since everyone suffers. To suffering must be added mourning, understanding, patience, love, openness and the willingness to remain vulnerable." *Anne Morrow Lindbergh*

BRAINSTORM "CURES" FOR THE BLUES. Make a list of things you might do to help yourself feel better the next time you're down or depressed. (Be sure that your list includes "Talk to someone I trust" and "Get help if I need it.")

RESEARCH THE RELATIONSHIP between health and emotions.[5] Find out how eating and exercise can affect the way you feel. Invite a nutritionist to your class or club to give a presentation and answer questions.

> *Variation:* Interview a doctor or psychiatrist about depression and disease. Ask questions like:
>
> - Does depression weaken the body's ability to fight off disease?
> - Do some diseases cause people to feel depressed?
> - What kinds of help are available for people who are depressed?

LEARN WHAT GALILEO ENDURED. Research this famous astronomer (or another scientist you choose) to find out what kinds of opposition he faced during his lifetime and how he endured. Write a story or skit about his life.

CALCULATE HOW MUCH IT COSTS to get help. Suppose that you need counseling to help you endure a problem in your life. Find out how much money it would cost for six months of counseling by a 1) school psychologist, 2) social worker, 3) psychologist, 4) psychotherapist, and 5) psychiatrist. You'll need to find out how much per hour each type of counselor gets paid. Will you meet with your counselor once a month? Once a week? Twice a week? Figure the costs, then compare them on a graph or chart.

FIND OUT WHO NEEDS HELP ENDURING. Check your neighborhood or community. Visit a hospital, children's hospital, senior citizens' center, nursing home or rest home, juvenile detention center, or homeless shelter. (Be sure to get permission, and go with a chaperon.) Ask what you can do to help. TIP: Don't forget your own family.

MAKE ACTIVITY KITS FOR CHILDREN at a hospital or homeless shelter. Include pencils, crayons, markers, paper, coloring books, clay, glue, glitter, colored paper, pictures from magazines, yarn, safety scissors, etc. TIP: Be sure to contact the hospital or shelter first to find out what they want or need.

CREATE A SKIT that shows what to do when disaster strikes. Depending on where you live, choose one or more of the following topics: a tornado or hurricane, earthquake, fire, mudslide, drought, flood. Perform your skit for other students, younger children, your club or youth group, your community group, and anyone else who's interested.

LOCATE WORKS OF ART that depict suffering. Look through art books in your school or local library, or visit an art museum. You might start your search by looking for paintings by Cimabue, Donatello, Fra Angelico, Daumier, Picasso, Goya, Munch, Titian, Van der Weyden, Grunewald, and Dali. For each painting you find, decide what it means to you. What do you think the artist's attitude was toward suffering?

EXPLORE THE HEALING POWERS OF MUSIC. Many people around the world believe that music has special healing powers. What do you think? Form your own opinion by listening to many different types of music. You might want to start with music categorized as "relaxation," "healing," or "New Age." Ask at your local library or music store, or find a local radio station that plays relaxing music.

---

[5] See "Health," pages 103–114.

*Variations:* Create your own music when you're feeling down. Play a musical instrument or sing. How does this make you feel? Better? Worse? No different? You might try writing a song or a tune. Do you agree or disagree with William Congreve's famous quotation, "Music has charms to soothe a savage breast/To soften rocks, or bend a knotted oak"?

**EXPLORE THE HEALING POWERS OF EXERCISE.** When you're feeling blue or have a problem, try jogging, going for a brisk walk, taking a bike ride, playing racquetball—anything that raises your heart rate and makes you sweat. When you exercise, your brain releases endorphins into your bloodstream. Endorphins are chemicals that give you a natural "high." When you're through exercising, see how you feel.

**EXPLORE THE HEALING POWERS OF PETS.** Researchers have found that pets and companion animals improve our everyday health and well-being. Medical studies suggest that blood pressure is lowered and hospital stays are shortened when patients have access to pets. The next time you've got the blues, spend time with your pet (or a friend's pet). See how you feel during and afterward.

**PLAY A "HANG IN THERE" GAME.** Divide into teams, brainstorm some problems that cause sadness or suffering, then try to come up with as many ideas as you can for coping with those feelings. Think of 1) things you might do to lessen or eliminate the problem, 2) things you might to do make yourself laugh, 3) things you might do to help yourself endure the problem, and 4) things you might to do reward yourself. Award 1 point per idea. The team with the most points (or the most creative ideas) wins. *Example:* Someone steals $25 that you needed for a new pair of $50 running shoes. Ideas:

1. Report the theft to someone who might help you; find a way to earn $25.

2. Make a "Most Wanted" poster showing a $20 bill and a $5 bill; offer candy kisses for information leading to the recovery of your money; make a list of embarrassing or funny things a thief might accidentally steal and get caught with.

3. See if you can borrow $25 from a friend, parent, or sibling; see if you can borrow a pair of running shoes; try to find running shoes on sale for $25 instead of $50.

4. Do something you enjoy. Climb rocks, take a bike ride, draw, paint, listen to music, or treat yourself to an ice-cream sundae.

**PLAY A "PASS THE CANE" GAME.** Canes are supports you can lean on when you need help walking. Friends are supports you can lean on when you need help enduring. Sit in a circle (around a campfire, if possible) and pass a cane. The person with the cane shares a story about a time when he or she was hurt or suffering. If you don't feel like talking when the cane reaches you, simply hand it to the next person. If you do feel like talking, hold the cane while you talk.

**READ STORIES ABOUT ENDURANCE.** Look for these books:

*After the Dancing Days* by Margaret I. Rostkowski (New York: Harper & Row, 1986). Just after World War I, 13-year-old Annie is forbidden to maintain her friendship with a badly disfigured soldier. The experience changes her views on heroism and patriotism. Ages 12–14.

*The Brave* by Robert Lipsyte (New York: HarperCollins, 1991). Seventeen-year-old Sonny, a boxer, has left the Indian reservation for the streets of New York. He tries to harness his emotions by training with Alfred Brooks, who left the sport to become a police officer. Ages 13–17.

*Hatchet* by Gary Paulsen (New York: Simon & Schuster, 1996). Brian is still dealing with his parents' divorce when he chooses to visit his father on the oil fields of Canada. His trip takes a life-threatening turn when the small plane he's flying in crashes, stranding him in the Canadian widerness. Ages 11–14.

*Julie of the Wolves* by Jean Craighead George (New York: Harper & Row, 1972). While running away from her family and an unwanted marriage, a 13-year-old Eskimo girl becomes lost on the North Slope of Alaska, where she's befriended by a wolf pack. Ages 11–14.

*Weasel* by Cynthia C. DeFelice (New York: Macmillan, 1990). Nathan is alone in the frontier of 1839 as his father recovers from an injury. During that time, he meets the renegade killer Weasel and makes a surprising discovery about revenge. Ages 9–12.

Books written in journal or diary style:

📖 *Amelia Writes Again!* by Marissa Moss (Berkeley, CA: Tricycle Press, 1996). A 10-year-old writes about her life—and her struggles with friendship, privacy, and loyalty—in the journal she receives for her birthday. Ages 8–12.

📖 *Catherine, Called Birdy* by Karen Cushman (NY: Clarion Books, 1994). A 13-year-old daughter of an English country knight keeps a journal in which she records the events of her life, including her longing for adventures beyond the usual role of women and her efforts to avoid being married off. A Newbery Honor Book and ALA Notable Children's Book. Ages 11–14.

📖 *Don't You Dare Read This, Mrs. Dunphrey* by Margaret Peterson Haddix (New York: Simon & Schuster, 1996). Sixteen-year-old Tish Bonner first resents having to keep a journal for English class, then finds solace in writing about problems she can't discuss—such as being abandoned by her mother. Ages 12–16.

📖 *Ellen Anders On Her Own* by Karen Hirsch (New York: Macmillan, 1994). Eleven-year-old Ellen gains insight into her changing friendships after reading her deceased mother's girlhood diary. Ages 9–12.

📖 *Heads or Tails: Stories from the Sixth Grade* by Jack Gantos (New York: Farrar, Straus & Giroux, 1994). Jack's diary helps him to deal with problems including dog-eating alligators, a terror for an older sister, and next-door neighbors who are really weird. Ages 9–12.

# Character in *ACTION*

## Ryan Schroer: Carrying the Torch

Ryan Schroer was 16 years old when he was asked to carry the Olympic Torch across town in Columbus, Indiana. "That is, my wheelchair and I carried the torch," Ryan chuckles.

Ryan was born with cerebral palsy, a condition that severely impairs muscle control. But he didn't let that stop him. At three years old, he taught himself to read by pulling out the Yellow Pages of the phone book and learning letters and words. His parents realized that he was very bright and needed to be in a regular school, where he's stayed all the way through high school. With the help of an aide, and a computer for writing assignments and tests, he's able to function very well. Although he's been identified as moderately mentally handicapped because of poor eyesight and lack of motor skills, he's an honor roll student.

"I'm lucky," Ryan insists. "I don't have a terminal disease. I try not to look at myself as disabled, because if I do I might want to take the easy way out."

When he was nine years old, he took his first step with the help of leg splints and a walker. When he was 15, he was trudging down his street, listening to the radio attached to his walker, when he felt pain in his left hip. It had slipped out of its socket and required surgery. After six weeks of lying in bed and still keeping up on his school work, Ryan developed kidney stones. Just as he started getting stronger, he felt pain in his back and learned that he had two cracked vertebrae.

"At that point, I was ready to die," Ryan explains. "I asked God to take me if He wanted me. But then I told myself 'You know, you shouldn't listen to that negative side of your mind.' So I didn't give up." He struggled through painful physical therapy and returned to school.

He became a reporter for the school newspaper, *The Triangle*, using a tape recorder and his computer to do interviews and articles. Then one day Ryan heard an announcement over the school PA system. The basketball team needed managers. "Something popped into my head and told me that I'd be perfect for that job. Something else in my head said 'No, you have too many limitations.' But I've learned not to listen to that negative voice. So I wheeled into Coach Preda's office and told him there were some things I couldn't do, but ask me to fold a towel, and hey! I can do that! A couple of weeks later, Coach Preda came up to me in the gym and told me that I could keep the statistics for all the home games."

One of his teachers designed a system of circles and boxes so Ryan could track the statistics for each game with two colored pencils. "When Coach Preda uses my charts in the locker room at halftime, it gives me a good feeling because I know I'm making a contribution to the team. I've always wanted to be part of a team."

Then Ryan received a surprise: the United Way nominated him as one of the people who would carry the Olympic Torch through Columbus before the Atlanta games. "I didn't want to do it at first, because I thought they had selected me because I'm disabled. I wanted to give the honor to my English teacher and good friend, Rick Weinheimer. He taught me to respect myself, and I thought he deserved it more than me. But then he got nominated, too. So I wanted to carry it with him.

"The torch was placed in a holder in my wheel-chair, and I carried it from Northside Middle School to North High School. Then I handed it off to Mr. Weinheimer. It was the most poignant moment of my life. I felt a sense of history, joy, sadness—like I wanted to bust out crying. I heard music in my head. The whole town turned out and my whole school.

"I want to go on making a contribution to life. I'm going to college and maybe study communication. I hope I can continue to influence people. I like to be noticed for *who* I am, not *what* I am. But I don't wish I was able-bodied anymore. I used to. I can experience some regular things, but then I can do things other people can't." Ryan smiles. "I can speed down the school hallway really fast. Being this way gives me a unique view of the world."

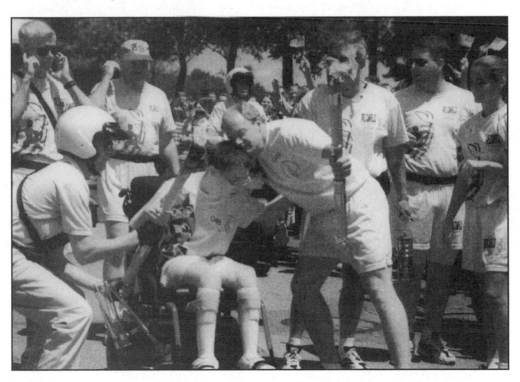

Ryan Schroer (center) passing the Olympic Torch to his teacher, Rick Weinheimer

# Forgiveness

**Pardon, absolution, leniency, mercy, grace**

> "And throughout all eternity
> I forgive you, you forgive me."
> *William Blake*

There's an old Zen story that tells of two monks who were walking along the banks of an overflowing river. They saw a young woman who was afraid to cross. Although the monks had taken vows never to touch a woman, the older monk picked her up and carried her to the other side of the river. The younger monk seethed in anger all day. The two didn't speak until sunset, when they were allowed to break their vow of silence. Then the younger monk, enraged, accused the older monk of defiling himself and the whole order. The older monk simply answered "I put the woman down on the other side of the river early this morning. It is only you who have been carting her around throughout the day."

You're not going to get through life without people stepping on your toes and sometimes even stealing your shoes. You've probably already experienced people lying about you, cheating you, betraying you, taking your friends, homework, or possessions, telling you you're stupid, and worse. You may have suffered physical pain, injury, or abuse from people you love. These things should never happen . . . but they happen.

What should you do? What's best for you. Drop your anger and desire for revenge like a hot potato, because if you don't, the person who wronged you will hurt you twice. *Example:* Your brother takes your bike without asking, ruins the gear shifter, then dumps the evidence in the trash behind a store.

Okay, he's hurt you once. If you seethe in anger like the younger monk, you'll put a stop to your own personal growth and probably hurt your health, too. Wham! Your brother has hurt you twice—and you still don't have your bike.

> "Hate is like acid. It can damage the vessel
> in which it is stored as well as destroy the
> object on which it is poured."
> *Ann Landers*

Here's the secret of forgiveness: When you forgive others or yourself, *you stop being a victim*. You stop suffering. You can turn your pain into strength. You can improve your health, your sense of peace, and your happiness.

"Great," you might say, "but forgiveness is easier said than done." And you'd be right. Developing positive character traits isn't for wimps, and forgiveness is one of the hardest of all traits to form. You can do it, though. Here's how.

# How to Forgive Others

**1. Acknowledge and accept what was done to you.** Don't ignore it or bury it. Buried things rot. Life isn't fair, bad things happen to good people, and wrongdoers aren't always punished. This doesn't mean you should give up or give in.

**2. Report the offense.** If the other person broke the law, report him or her to the police. If the person broke a school rule, report it to your teacher or principal. If the person broke a family rule, tell your parents. You're not being a tattletale. Offenders should be held accountable for what they do.

**3. *Let your feelings out.*** Go ahead; get mad. Yell and cry if you want to. Let your anger out in a nonviolent way. Anger held inside can make you sick. Jog, run, throw a football, pound the floor, pound your pillow, or wad up your dirty socks and throw them at the wall.

**4. *Talk with a caring, understanding adult or friend.*** Explain what happened and how you feel. Get professional help if you need it.[1]

**5. *Write about your feelings in your journal.*[2]** Let them out. Or pound out your feelings on a piano or other musical instrument. Or draw your feelings. Do whatever works for you.

**6. *Tell the offender how you feel.*** Sometimes other people aren't aware that they've hurt you. Focus on the problem, not the person. Explain, don't blame. *Example:* You might say "I needed that bike to get to my job. Now I either have to walk or lose my job. This is a real hardship for me, and I don't know what to do." Don't say "You idiot! You stole my bike and ruined it. You're a thief and a liar. I hate you!" The first approach might turn your brother into an ally—someone who sympathizes with your problem. The second approach will put him on the defensive.

**7. *Ask the offender to make things right.*** Ask the person to return what was taken or fix what was broken. *Example:* "Will you help me repair my bike? Will you help me pay for the parts I need?" Sometimes this is possible, sometimes it isn't.

**8. *If this is appropriate for you, talk with God or another Higher Being/Higher Power you have faith in.*** Ask to be relieved of your anger and desire for revenge. Ask to be healed of your hurt. Ask for the ability to understand what's happened and put it behind you. Ask for the strength to forgive.

**9. *Forgive the offender.*** Take charge of your own attitudes, reactions, and feelings. Anger is a choice, revenge is a choice, hatred is a choice—

"I really NEED a bike. What am I going to do?"

and forgiveness is a choice.[3] When you're ready, say "I forgive you." If you're sincere, you should feel a sense of calm and relief. Your body and spirit will be healthier. Don't worry about justice; leave that to the law, to the offender's own conscience, or to a Higher Power.

> "It is by forgiving that one is forgiven."
> *Mother Teresa*

**10. *Find a way to serve the offender.*** "WHAT?" you might ask. Yes, you read it right! This step is not for the faint of heart. Only the truly courageous can take it. But this is where you grow the most and gain the most—and that's why it's worth a try.

For this step, focus on the *person,* not the problem. See the human being complete with faults, weaknesses, worries, doubts, deficiencies, and insecurities. Then ask yourself "How can I serve this person? How can I help him or her? What can I do to make his or her life better—without expecting anything in return?" An answer will come to you. You might even do a "secret service" or a random act of kindness.[4]

---

[1] See "Endurance," pages 87 and 88, for crisis hotlines.
[2] See "Endurance," pages 88, 89, and 92, for journaling resources.
[3] See "Choice and Accountability," pages 28–34.
[4] See "Caring," page 24.

Serving someone who hurt you can be very healing. When you do this, you defeat the wrong that was done to you. You're free. You win!

**11. Repeat any of these steps as often as you need to until they stick.** Be patient with yourself. Forgiveness takes time.

# How to Forgive Yourself

"If you haven't forgiven yourself
something, how can you forgive others?"
*Dolores Huerta*

What if you're the person who committed the offense? Who hurt someone else? Who behaved badly? You can hope that the other person will forgive you, but that's not something you can control. What you *can* control is how you treat yourself.

You can't change the past. You can't go back in time and undo the wrong you did. But you can do good in the present. And you can start by forgiving yourself. Here's how.

**1. Admit what you did.** Take responsibility for your actions. You can't forgive yourself until you acknowledge that you did something wrong. Maybe you made a mistake; everybody does from time to time. Or maybe you deliberately hurt someone. Either way, *you* did it, and *you* need to admit it.

Think of your wrong or mistake as the first link in a chain that imprisons you. Each time you lie about or deny what you did, you're adding another link. Admitting it breaks the chain.

**2. Let yourself feel guilty.** But be aware of what kind of guilt you feel. If your guilt leads you to look in the mirror, admit what you did, and feel sorry for it, you'll grow from your experience. If your guilt makes you turn away from the mirror in shame and self-loathing, get help.

**3. Talk with a caring, understanding adult or friend.** Explain what happened and how you feel. Get professional help if you need it. Talking about wrongs and mistakes can be healing. You might ask for advice, if that seems appropriate. Then do what you think is best.

**4. Say you're sorry and ask the person you wronged to forgive you.** Be sincere. And be prepared; the person might throw a tomato in your face. It's not your problem if the person doesn't accept your apology. You can't control what he or she says, does, or feels. You can only control what *you* say, do, or feel. Try not to get angry if the person doesn't immediately respond the way you'd like. Forgiveness takes time. However, most people will soften if you ask for forgiveness and really mean it.

**5. Accept the consequences of what you did—unless they seem unjust.** Then you have the right to be assertive and work for a better solution. *Example:* You steal $10 from the cash register in the school cafeteria. Someone sees you and reports you to the

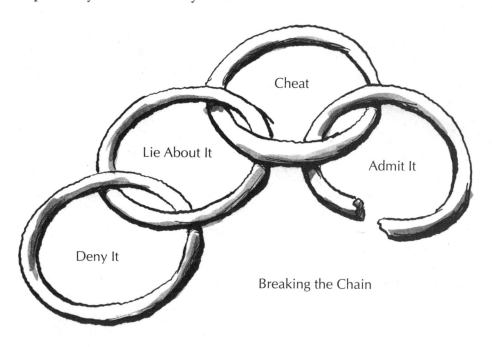

Breaking the Chain

principal, who calls you into his office and confronts you. You say "What I did was wrong. I'm really sorry, and I'll pay it back. Please forgive me. I won't ever do it again." The principal gives you a date by which he expects you to pay back the money. He also gives you a month's worth of detentions. And you know that you've lost his trust and respect and will have to earn them back—if you can. Those consequences are fair.

But what if the principal makes you pay the money back *and* expels you from school for the rest of the year? Those consequences aren't fair. Ask a parent, teacher, or counselor for help. If you're convicted of breaking the law, get a lawyer. If you can't afford to pay for a lawyer, ask the court to appoint one for you. You have the right to expect fair and just consequences for what you did.

**6. *Do what you can to make things right.*** Give back the money. Paint over the graffiti. Tell the truth about a friend. Admit that you cheated, then take the test over—or accept a failing grade.

**7. *Try to find a way to serve the person you hurt.*** If this isn't possible, do kindnesses for other people.

**8. *If you have a faith tradition that encourages you to look to a higher power, ask that higher power for forgiveness.*** Ask for the strength not to repeat the wrong or mistake. Ask for patience if the person you hurt hasn't forgiven you.

**9. *Forgive yourself.*** Don't bad-mouth yourself or carry around a load of guilt. This can make you sick in your mind and your body. Sometimes it's easier to forgive others than it is to forgive yourself. When you forgive yourself, you can learn from your actions and mistakes. You're free to use your energy to keep growing and becoming the kind of person you want to be.

# Character Dilemmas

*For journaling or writing essays, discussion, debate, role-playing, reflection*

**Suppose that . . .**

**1** Your sister steals money from your room. You go through all the steps of forgiving others, but she won't cooperate. She just keeps stealing from your room. What might you do?

**2** You're jealous of a big guy on the football team, and you want to replace him on first string. So you lie and tell the coach and everyone else that he's muscular because he uses steroids. He gets dropped from the team, and you feel terrible about it. You finally go to him, tell him what you did, and ask his forgiveness. He punches your lights out. What might you do? Fight back? Tell the coach? Let it go? Try to make things right? Predict and evaluate the results of each action.

**3** A man is mistakenly identified as a murderer and sent to prison for life. He knows he's innocent, and the real killer is still on the loose. What might the man do with his life? Is it possible for him to get justice? How can he free himself from his own anger and the injustice committed against him?

**4** Your best friend is driving home from school one day when she's broadsided by a drunk driver. As a result of the accident, she loses the use of her legs and must spend the rest of her life in a wheelchair. What are some specific things you might to do help your friend overcome the anger and hatred she feels for the drunk driver?

**5** You're taking a math test when you happen to gaze to your right. You're lost in thought, and you're not even aware that your head is turning; in fact, you don't even see anything. But your teacher notices, walks over to your desk, looks at your paper, looks at the paper of the person sitting on your right, and accuses you of cheating because your answers happen to match. You tell the truth—you weren't cheating—but she doesn't believe you. She tears up your paper in front of the class and announces that you'll be getting an F. What might you do to release yourself from the anger you feel toward your teacher?

**6** An elderly widow in your neighborhood has just lost her home. The Internal Revenue Service (IRS) has taken it because, they claim, her husband didn't pay income taxes for 20 years. How might she handle her anger toward the IRS—and her dead husband? What might she do? In your opinion, were the IRS's actions fair and just?

**7** One of your friends is shot in the arm by a gang member for warning the police about a gang fight. The police can't prove that the gang member did the shooting, and after a few months in the detention home, he walks free. Now he's threatening to kill your friend. What might your friend do? Consider the possible consequences of each course of action your friend might take.

# Activities

**BRAINSTORM WAYS TO "LET OFF STEAM"** when you're angry. Make a list. Keep your focus on positive, helpful things rather than negative, harmful, or vengeful things.

## CHECK IT OUT

*Don't Rant and Rave on Wednesdays! The Children's Anger-Control Book* by Adolph Moser, Ed.D. (Kansas City, MO: Landmark Editions, 1994). Like *Don't Pop Your Cork on Mondays!* (see page 4), this book is written for younger kids ages 6–9, but the information it contains makes it worth reading at any age.

*Everything You Need to Know About Anger* by Renora Licata (NY: Rosen Publishing Group, 1994). Discusses the causes of anger, how it affects people, and ways to control it. Ages 12–18.

**WRITE IN YOUR JOURNAL**[5] about someone you're angry with. Write about how you feel; write about what you'd like to do. Or write about an experience someone else has had.

**COLLECT NEWSPAPER OR MAGAZINE STORIES** about crimes, wrongdoings, and mistakes. Bring them to your class or club and rewrite them so they have positive endings. Imagine how each victim might overcome his or her anger and desire for revenge and arrive at positive new solutions.

## CHECK IT OUT

**True Stories About Forgiveness**
*www.triadonline.com*
On Easter Sunday, 1996 (April 7), the *Greensboro News & Record* published a series of stories on the subject of forgiveness. Reporter Lex Alexander interviewed five people including a man who was wrongly convicted and imprisoned for rape, a woman who put her mother in a psychiatric hospital, and a man whose sons were murdered. The series also includes

an article on how various religions—Christianity, Judaism, Islam, Buddhism, and Hinduism—view forgiveness. If you can't access the Web site and you'd like to read the stories, see if your local library subscribes to the *News & Record* and has back issues on file or on microfiche. Or contact:

**The Greensboro News & Record**
PO Box 20848
Greensboro, NC 27420
1-800-553-6880

**WRITE A MYTH** about how forgiveness came into the world. You might want to start by reading myths or folktales from various cultures to get a feel for how they're written. (Your local library will have many books about myths for you to explore.) Afterward, consider presenting your myth as a play, reading it aloud to your classmates and younger students, illustrating it, or sharing it in other ways.

**INVITE A PSYCHOLOGIST OR PSYCHIATRIST** to your class to discuss the harmful effects of holding on to guilt, harboring grudges, wanting revenge, etc. Ask the expert's advice on ways to handle anger, being a victim, and so on.

**WRITE A REPORT ABOUT MENTAL** or physical illnesses that result from harboring anger, guilt, grudges, and other responses to being wronged. You might interview your school counselor or psychologist, if one is available.

**RESEARCH THE LIVES** of one or more famous people who have overcome hatred, injustice, guilt, or being victimized and have made a significant contribution to the world. Make a chart showing 1) their names, 2) the injustices they suffered or obstacles they faced, 3) how they responded to and/or triumphed over the injustices or obstacles. *Example:* 1) Anne Frank 2) lost her home, her family, and ultimately her life to the Holocaust. 3) During the time she spent in hiding, she kept a diary that has inspired millions of people.[6]

**ESTIMATE WHAT IT COSTS YOUR COMMUNITY** to counsel people who have been victimized by crime, abuse, or other wrongs done to them. Contact victims' rights organizations, battered women's shelters,

---

[5] See "Endurance," pages 88, 89, and 92, for journaling resources.

[6] See "Endurance," page 88, for information on Anne Frank's diary and a related Web site.

Child Protective Services (the government agency responsible for investigating reports of child abuse, neglect, and abandonment), and other organizations and agencies that work with victims. See if you can find out approximate hourly counseling fees, numbers of counselors, and average caseloads. Using those figures, try to come up with an estimate.

**SURVEY YOUR SCHOOL, NEIGHBORHOOD,** or community to determine how many people are holding grudges—against individuals, groups, agencies, organizations, etc. Come up with three or more questions to ask each person you survey. *Examples:*

**?** Is there anyone you're angry with right now?

**?** How long have you been angry? An hour? A few days? A month? Longer?

**?** What are you doing about your anger?

Organize your survey results on a chart or graph.

**CREATE A BOOK OR BOOKLET** about forgiveness. You might want to write a story and illustrate it, create a comic book, or write a how-to book explaining how to forgive. Bind your finished work and donate it to your school library. If it's a picture book, share it with younger children.

**CREATE A SERIES OF SYMBOLS** illustrating different feelings and emotions related to forgiveness. *Examples:* hurt, anger, frustration, sadness, acceptance, guilt, being apologetic, forgiveness.[7]

**VOLUNTEER AT A HOSPITAL,** home, or treatment center for children with behavioral disorders. Ask for training to help those who have pent-up anger, aggression, or hostilities.

**FOLLOW THE STEPS** on pages 94–96 or 96–97 if there's someone you need to forgive (someone else or yourself). Keep a diary of what you experience, how you feel, and what happens as a result of your efforts. If you think you need professional help to resolve some of the issues you're facing, get a referral from your school psychologist, community counseling center, youth leader, or religious leader.

**PLAY A YARN GAME.** Sit in a circle with a ball of yarn. One person starts the game by holding the yarn ball and telling about a time when he or she forgave someone else. Then the first person hangs on to the loose end of the yarn and tosses the ball to another person, who relates a personal experience about forgiveness. That person then loops the yarn around his or her finger and tosses it to a third person, and so on. At the end of the game, you'll have a network of crossed yarn strings that might resemble a spider's web. Talk about how your common experiences connect you, as the yarn connects you. TIP: If someone doesn't want to tell a personal story, he or she can tell a story that happened to someone else (without naming names).

**READ STORIES ABOUT FORGIVENESS.** Look for these books:

*The Fear Place* by Phyllis Reynolds Naylor (New York: Atheneum, 1994). When 12-year-old Doug and his older brother Gordon are left camping alone in the Rocky Mountains, Doug faces his fear of heights and his feelings about his brother. Ages 9–12.

*Glennis, Before and After* by Patricia Calvert (New York: Atheneum, 1996). When her father is sent to jail for a white-collar crime and her mother is hospitalized with a breakdown, 12-year-old Glennis goes to live with her aunt and learns that not all prisons are made of stone. Ages 12 & up.

*Honor Bright* by Randall Beth Platt (New York: Bantam Doubleday Dell, 1997). While visiting her grandmother during the summer of 1944, a 14-year-old girl helps to heal the wounds that have been inflicted upon three generations of women. Ages 14 & up.

*Nick* by Alma Yates (Salt Lake City, UT: Deseret Book Co., 1995). Aaron Solinski's summer job in northern Utah leads to more than he expected, including meeting his old friend's kid sister Nadine (Nick) and running into his estranged father. Ages 12 & up.

*Walk Two Moons* by Sharon Creech (New York: HarperCollins, 1994). As Sal and her grandparents follow the route her mother took when she suddenly left home, Sal tells about her friend Phoebe, whose mother also left. Ages 11–14.

---

[7] See "Positive Attitudes," page 18, for a resource about symbols.

# Character in *ACTION*

## Andrew Papachristos: Forgiving Others

Andrew Papachristos grew up in the Rogers Park neighborhood on Chicago's North Side. He remembers the way it used to be. "It was ethnically diverse," he explains, "with practically every religion, ethnic group, and race within one mile. We were black, white, Hispanic, Russian, Italian, Greek, everything. My parents were part owners of Kamar's Restaurant and had been for many years. We served free dinners on Thanksgiving and Christmas, and a lot of the neighborhood ate there every day. I worked there. It was a place for people to come and hang out."

By the time Andy became a teenager, things were changing. "Our strong neighborhood started to deteriorate. People joined gangs and began running drugs. There was violence, theft, and beatings. People became afraid. So the community got together and started a Crimestoppers Group for parents. My parents worked with the community, and I joined the Guardian Angels. Rather than watch my neighborhood be taken over by crime, I decided to do something about it."

Andy was 16 when he joined the Guardian Angels, an organization of trained volunteers who patrol neighborhoods, make citizens' arrests, and offer protection to anyone in need. "I became a patrol leader," Andy explains. "So I got really involved. The gang members—many were my old friends—didn't like that. "

Andy's parents scrimped, saved, and sent him to Loyola Academy, a private Catholic high school. "I'm really grateful for that," he says, "because Loyola gave me a different way of being accepted. It gave me a choice."

As Andy walked home from the train after school each day, he'd usually find at least two gang members waiting for him. Dressed in baggy pants, baseball caps cocked to one side, gold chains swinging from their necks, they'd stop him at street corners and taunt him. "Hey, Charlie's Angel! What you trying to do, bro? We're going to get you. You can't stop us." Then they'd block his path, push him, and insult him and his family.

Andy tried to talk with them, then ignored them, and sometimes shoved back and ran. Having been trained by the Guardian Angels to defend himself, he learned to block the gang members' punches and blows. Sometimes he had to fight back to get past them.

The gang members didn't like Guardian Angels patrolling the streets and protecting the store owners because it interfered with their extortion business. Gang members collected "protection" money from store owners. If the owners refused to give it to them, the gang members would break the store windows, steal, and set businesses on fire.

Andrew Papachristos

Soon Andy's family started receiving threats. Gang members followed his sister home from work during the summer, shouting trashy names at her. They wrote letters to his parents threatening to burn down their restaurant and harassed them on the phone. They tromped into the restaurant during business hours and shouted "You can't stop us. We're going to get you." They broke windows in the restaurant, and each time the alarm went off, Andy's family would get a call from the police. Andy and his dad would drag themselves out of bed at 3:00 A.M. and go to the restaurant to shut off the alarm. Then they'd reset the alarm so the gang members couldn't get inside and loot the restaurant. They'd have the windows repaired and start over.

Gang members hit their family car. They broke the windows and covered it with graffiti three times. They stole a car belonging to one of Andy's aunts and burned down another aunt's garage. After each incident, they bragged about it on the street or left threatening notes so Andy and his family would know who had attacked them.

Despite the torment, Andy stayed with the Guardian Angels. He became a youth counselor and tried to help other kids choose alternatives to gangs, drugs, and violence. He and his family were role models in their neighborhood.

Then one night the telephone rang. It was a neighbor. "You'd better get down here. They set the restaurant on fire!" Andy, his parents, and his sister tore out of their apartment and raced to the restaurant.

"I sat there under the tracks where the elevated train goes over, just watching the blaze," Andy remembers. "They had poured gasoline down the ventilation shaft in the ceiling, then thrown a Molotov cocktail down it. The explosion set the ceiling on fire. I saw the roof collapse." The blaze shot 20 feet into the air. There was nothing anyone could do.

"I can't describe how I felt," Andy says. "They had gotten us where it hurt. The restaurant was all we had. We had no house, no fancy car. We were just

Andy (left) with another Guardian Angel

a regular family trying to make a difference. Now everything we had was gone.

"At first, I wanted revenge. I was steaming mad. But my family and I talked about it, and I cooled down. Then I was just happy that no one was hurt. The blaze was so big that it also destroyed the three businesses around our restaurant: a shoemakers' shop, a tavern, and a convenience market.

"There was no proof, so the gang members got off free. The insurance company went bankrupt, and we got nothing. My parents didn't blame me or themselves. I went to work at a grocery store, my father got a job as a draftsman, and my sister worked at the university. My mom got jobs at retail stores."

When Andy saw the gang members on the street, bragging to let him know who had done this to his family, Andy curled his fists into balls but controlled his anger. "Either you hold a grudge forever, or you say 'That's over with. Now what are you going to do?' If you hold a grudge, you're driven by rage and revenge. You end up hurting other people and yourself. You have to let it go."

Not long after the fire, Andy's parents brought in three foster children, kids involved in gangs and drugs. Then his family helped to start Communities Dare to Care, a one-of-a-kind organization that works directly with youth at risk. Andy counseled the kids, showing them another way. "There's a saying that goes something like this: 'If you ever get a chance to get out of your situation, you've got to reach down and bring someone else up with you.' Other organizations like to work with kids who offer more hope for change. We work with the throwaways, the dropouts, the kids who live on the streets or in gang houses."

Andy still sees the gang members who burned down his family's restaurant. "They're on the street all the time. One of them is in jail for something else . . . It's hard to forgive," he admits. "But if I had sought revenge, I would have become what I hate the most. I would have been stuck there. Instead, I wanted to do something with my life. So I'm going to college to study criminal justice. I'm now the director of Communities Dare to Care, and we're incorporated. I'm writing grants for funding."

He pauses, thinking back on the events of the past few years. "It's funny," he says, "but if you give something good back to the community, it's easier to forgive."

## CHECK IT OUT

**The International Alliance of Guardian Angels**
*www.cyberangels.org*
This is the site for CyberAngels, an all-volunteer Internet safety organization founded in June, 1995, by senior members of the Guardian Angels. Visit the site to learn more about the Angels and pick up some CyberStreetSmarts tips on how to take care of yourself online.

# Health

**Being physically, mentally, and emotionally healthy**

"We are indeed much more than what we eat, but what we eat can nevertheless help us to be much more than what we are."
*Adelle Davis*

Imagine that someone gives you a fancy new car. As you read your owner's manual, you discover that it likes to guzzle high-octane, expensive supreme gas. You decide that your car should have less expensive tastes, so you feed it regular gas. After a year or so, the engine coughs, sputters, and dies. Because a new engine costs thousands of dollars, you decide to get a different car instead.

Your body is like a fancy car. It requires high-quality fruits, vegetables, grains, and proteins to keep its engine running—but if something goes wrong with your body, you can't replace it. "Wait!" you might say. "My Great Aunt Harriet is 105 years old, and she chain-smokes cigars and eats french fries every day." Maybe so, but what does that have to do with you? It's true that some people have heredity on their side. No matter how they abuse their bodies, they seem to be okay. Most people aren't like that, however. And you can't be sure which side of the family your genes come from. Maybe your Great Uncle Harry died at age 30.

You are what you eat, and you'll definitely be healthier if you give your mind and body the fuel it needs. When you were younger, you may have learned about the Four Basic Food Groups: 1) meat, fish, poultry, and eggs, 2) dairy products, 3) vegetables and fruits, and 4) grains. More recently, the U.S. Department of Agriculture has recast the Four Basic Groups into a Food Guide Pyramid that places more emphasis on bread, cereal, rice, and pasta, less emphasis on meat, poultry, and fish. The Pyramid (see page 104) also includes recommended numbers of daily servings from each group. It's a great place to start learning how to eat right.

---

## CHECK IT OUT

**U.S. Department of Agriculture**
Washington, DC 20250
(202) 720-2791
*www.usda.gov*
The USDA is an excellent source of up-to-date information about nutrition. Write or call to find out about current publications, or visit the Web site and explore the Food and Nutrition Information Center (FNIC) section. Links on the FNIC homepage *(www.nal.usda.gov/fnic)* will take you to a list of publications and databases including the Food Guide Pyramid, Dietary Guidelines for Americans, and an index of Food and Nutrition Internet Resources.

---

Maybe you've defined some food groups of your own—burgers, shakes, sugar, caffeine, and chips. The good news is, you can retrain your taste buds to be just as happy with sweet grapes as they are with sugary shakes.

You might have special nutritional needs. Maybe something that's good for your sister isn't good for you. For example, you may have an allergy

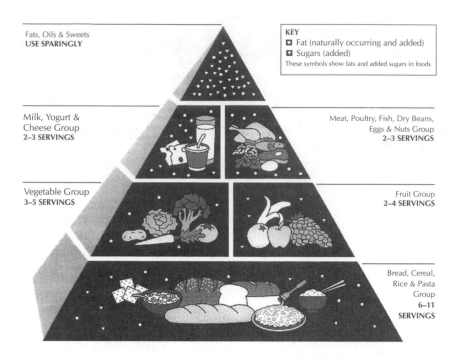

**KEY**
◨ Fat (naturally occurring and added)
◨ Sugars (added)
These symbols show fats and added sugars in foods

Fats, Oils & Sweets
**USE SPARINGLY**

Milk, Yogurt &
Cheese Group
**2–3 SERVINGS**

Meat, Poultry, Fish, Dry Beans,
Eggs & Nuts Group
**2–3 SERVINGS**

Vegetable Group
**3–5 SERVINGS**

Fruit Group
**2–4 SERVINGS**

Bread, Cereal,
Rice & Pasta
Group
**6–11
SERVINGS**

to milk. Start with the Pyramid, pay attention to your body, use your common sense, and talk to your doctor if you have any questions. Everybody—every *body*—is different.

# How to Be Physically Healthy

> "When it comes to your health, I recommend frequent doses of that rare commodity among Americans— common sense."
> *Vincent Askey*

***Listen to your body.*** Do you get lightheaded if you go more than four hours without eating? Maybe you need to eat more often and increase the amount of protein you consume. Or maybe it's a sign that you're eating too much sugar. Change your eating habits and see what happens.

***Eat a variety of wholesome foods.*** Use the USDA's Food Guide Pyramid as a guideline. Many people are vegetarians who get their protein from dairy and non-meat products; evidence shows that this, too, is a

healthful way to live. Some vegetarians are vegans ("vee-guns") who don't consume any animal products (meaning no dairy products or eggs). This diet can be very healthful as long as it includes protein from other sources like beans, grains, and nuts.

## CHECK IT OUT

*A Teen's Guide to Going Vegetarian* by Judy Krizmanic (New York: Puffin, 1994). This book covers all the bases, from nutritional requirements to dealing with anxious parents and friends. Ages 12 & up.

**The Vegetarian Youth Network**
PO Box 1141
New Paltz, NY 12561
*www.geocities.com/RainForest/Vines/4482*
An informal grassroots organization run by and for teenagers who support compassionate, healthy, globally aware vegetarian/vegan living. If you contact the VYN in writing, enclose a self-addressed stamped business-size envelope.

***Keep the lid on fats, oils, and sweets.*** An occasional splurge won't hurt you, but don't make fried foods the focus of every meal. And go easy on the sugar. A single bottle of soda contains anywhere from 30–50 grams of sugar—about 7–9 teaspoons. (Think about eating nine teaspoons of sugar. Doesn't that make you sick?) Sugar by any other name—glucose, sucrose, fructose, corn syrup—is still sugar, as are the so-called "natural" sugars.

Sugar sends you on a rollercoaster ride. You rise and then you drop. You drink a soda or eat a candy bar, and you experience a buzz and burst of energy. Then your pancreas starts secreting insulin, which carries the sugar to your liver. Then your liver kicks into overdrive to get rid of the extra blood sugar. Before you know it, you're crashing, cranky, and looking for another sugar fix.

Before Sugar

Right After Sugar

Sugar Crash

***Avoid caffeine.*** If you drink four cans of soda or four cups of coffee a day, you're probably hooked on caffeine—unless you're a decaf drinker. How can you tell if you're a caffeine fiend? Try going without it for a day or two. If you get a headache that goes away when you drink caffeine, that's a sure sign.

Caffeine can make your heart race, keep you awake at night, give you stomachaches and scary dreams, and make you so jittery that you start drumming your fingers on your desk (and driving everyone around you crazy). And it's not only in soda and coffee. Caffeine is also found in chocolate, cold capsules, cough syrups, and headache medication. When in doubt, read the product label.

***Limit your salt and sodium intake.*** Too much salt can raise your blood pressure. A little goes a long way, and you can train your tongue to like less. TIP: Try some fresh-ground black pepper or an herbal flavoring instead.

***Exercise regularly.*** When you exercise, you strengthen your cardiopulmonary system, stimulate your vital organs, and keep your body flexible. For most people, it's sufficient to exercise for at least 30 minutes three to four times a week. If you need advice on what to do and how often to do it, ask your gym teacher or a coach at your school or community center. If you've been a slow-moving sloth until now, talk with your doctor before starting an exercise program.

***Get enough sleep.*** Most people need to sleep an average of eight hours a night. Some need less sleep; others need more. Too much sleep can be an escape—a way to avoid problems or responsibilities. If you find yourself sleeping 10–12 hours every night and taking naps during the day, ask yourself what's happening in your life. Is there something you need to face, fix, decide, or do?

***Stay away from alcohol, drugs, and smoking.*** Studies indicate that as much as 85 percent of all crime is related to alcohol and drugs. According to the National Safety Council, more than 4 million American teenagers have serious problems with alcohol. Most teens don't use drugs, but millions do. The American Cancer Society estimates that cigarette smoking causes 87 percent of all deaths from lung cancer; more than 3,000 teenagers start smoking each day. Alcohol, drugs, and cigarettes are the main causes of early and preventable illness, disease, disability, and death in the United States today.

Be smart and don't start. If you've already started, quit. Help is available from many sources, including toll-free information and counseling hotlines.[1]

## CHECK IT OUT

### Drug Information Database
*www.drugfreeamerica.org*
Comprehensive, accurate, up-to-date information from the Partnership for a Drug-Free America, the organization behind many of the antidrug TV and print ads you see.

---

[1] See also "Cleanliness," page 49, for how to contact SADD (Students Against Driving Drunk).

**National Clearinghouse for Alcohol and Drug Information (NCADI)**
1-800-SAY-NO-TO (1-800-729-6686)
PO Box 2345
Rockville, MD 20847-2345
*www.health.org*
Part of the U.S. Department of Health and Human Services, NCADI is the world's largest resource for current information and materials about substance abuse prevention. Ask about free fact sheets, brochures, pamphlets, posters, and videos. On the Web site, be sure to visit:
**For Kids Only**
*www.health.org/features/kidsarea*
**Girl Power!**
*www.girlpower.gov*
**Tips for Teens**
*www.health.org/govpubs/ph323*
**A Guide for Teens**
*www.health.org/govpubs/phd688*

---

***Don't obsess about your weight.*** Instead, find your *set point*—your own healthy weight. You'll feel better, look better, and stay healthier if you find the weight your body wants to be. Don't worry if your set point isn't the same as your friends'; your bodies are different. When you're eating sensibly, aren't always hungry, have plenty of energy, and generally feel "balanced" and comfortable, you're there. Avoid excesses (eating too much or too little), which can lead to eating disorders.

There are three types of eating disorders, and they affect *both* females and males, although more girls than boys tend to have problems with them.

- *Bulimia nervosa* involves eating too much (binge eating) and then getting rid of it (purging).

- *Anorexia nervosa* involves self-imposed starvation.

- *Compulsive eating* involves bingeing without purging, which leads to obesity and constant dieting.

All three types can become so serious that they require treatment. In some cases, eating disorders lead to death. As in this true story....

Claire[2] was a popular 14-year-old at her junior high school. She was a hard worker and a cheer-

---
[2] Not her real name.

leader with high grades. But she was afraid of getting "fat," so she began secretly purging after she ate. Soon she discovered that if she put a small amount of baking soda in water and drank it, the mixture would taste so disgusting that she automatically threw up.

One morning, Claire's mother heard a scream from the upstairs bathroom. She rushed upstairs to find Claire doubled over in pain, and as Claire choked out what was wrong, her mother learned that Claire had dumped *several teaspoons* of baking soda into a glass of water and swallowed it down.

You might remember from science experiments what happens when you mix baking soda with vinegar. The "volcano" erupts, or the cork shoots sky-high off the top of the soda bottle. That's what happened to Claire. The baking soda mixed with the acid in her stomach, producing large amounts of carbon dioxide. The pain grew excruciating as Claire's abdomen swelled like a basketball.

Although Claire's mother rushed her to the hospital, it was already too late. The swelling had cut off the blood supply to Claire's organs. During the night, this bright young woman with everything to live for died of organ failure.

---

## CHECK IT OUT

*Food Fight: A Guide to Eating Disorders for Pre-Teens and Their Parents* by Janet Bode (New York: Simon & Schuster, 1997). This comprehensive guide to eating disorders discusses their causes, symptoms, and solutions. Ages 11 & up.

*Taking Charge of My Mind & Body: A Girls' Guide to Outsmarting Alcohol, Drug, Smoking, and Eating Problems* by Gladys Folkers, M.A., and Jeanne Engelmann (Minneapolis: Free Spirit Publishing, 1997). Facts about alcohol, drugs, smoking, and eating problems, myths and reality checks, warning signs, stories from girls who have "been there," and strategies for building resistance skills. Ages 11–18.

**National Eating Disorders Association**
603 Stewart Street, Suite 803
Seattle, WA 98101
(206) 382-3587
*www.nationaleatingdisorders.org*
Information and referrals to clinics, counselors, and support groups in your area.

**Something Fishy**

*www.something-fishy.com*

Lots of information about eating disorders and related issues, personal stories from girls and women, a chat room, links to other sites, and more, all presented in a friendly, caring style with fun graphics.

---

***Protect yourself against contagious diseases.*** Make sure that your immunizations are up-to-date. (Public health clinics often give them free of charge.) Even if you had all of your shots when you were younger, pay a visit to your doctor and ask if you're due for any new immunizations or boosters. Medical experts now say that adolescents 11–12 years of age may need the hepatitis B and varicella virus vaccines; a second dose of the measles, mumps, and rubella (MMR) vaccine; a tetanus and diphtheria toxoid (Td) booster; and others.

## CHECK IT OUT

**The National Immunization Information Hotline**

1-800-232-2522
Spanish: 1-800-232-0233

Information about vaccine-preventable diseases, who should be immunized, when vaccines should be given, where vaccinations are available, and how to obtain free publications. Operated by the American Social Health Association under contract with the Centers for Disease Control (CDC).

---

***Protect yourself against sexually transmitted diseases (STDs) and unwanted pregnancies.*** The best way to protect yourself is by abstaining from sexual activity until you're married. Get the facts about STDs (including HIV/AIDS) and pregnancy. If someone is pressuring you to be sexually active, talk to an adult you trust. Ask for help and support in saying no.

## CHECK IT OUT

*AIDS: Answers to Questions Kids Ask* by Barbara Dever (Santa Barbara, CA: Learning Works, 1996). Questions and answers about the risks and dangers of infection, activities to increase AIDS awareness and develop skills in saying no, and biographical sketches of Ryan White, Magic Johnson, and others. Ages 9–13.

**National HIV/AIDS Hotline**

1-800-342-AIDS (1-800-342-2437)
Spanish: 1-800-344-SIDA (1-800-344-7432)
TTY: 1-800-AIDS-TTY (1-800-234-7889)

Confidential 24-hour information and referral hotline backed by the Centers for Disease Control (CDC).

**National STD Hotline**

1-800-227-8922
Spanish: 1-800-227-8922

Information and referral hotline backed by the CDC.

**Planned Parenthood Federation of America**

*www.plannedparenthood.org*

Information about pregnancy, STDs (HIV), etc., with many links to other sites. To reach the Planned Parenthood office nearest you, call 1-800-230-7526. Ask your parent or guardian to get information for you, if you are interested.

---

***Protect yourself against the sun.*** Wear sunblock or sunscreen whenever you plan to spend time in the sun, especially between 10:00 A.M. and 2:00 P.M., when the ultraviolet (UV) rays are strongest. UVA rays can contribute to aging, wrinkling, and skin cancer; UVB rays can cause sunburn, skin cancer, and cataracts. UVC rays—the strongest ones—are normally filtered out by the ozone (except where there are holes).

***Protect yourself against accidents and injuries.*** See "Safety," pages 234–244.

## CHECK IT OUT

*Teenage Health Care: The First Comprehensive Family Guide for the Preteen to Young Adult Years* by Martha M. Jablow and Gail B. Slap, M.D. (New York: Pocket Books, 1994). Dr. Gail Slap, a "Dr. Spock for teenagers," teams up with Martha Jablow to present a complete guide to teenage health, covering the confusing changes that take place during puberty, common medical conditions during adolescence, risky behaviors, and more. Ages 11–18.

# How to Be Mentally and Emotionally Healthy

*"The brain is a world consisting of a number of unexplored continents and great stretches of unknown territory."*
*Santiago Ramon y Cajal*

*Follow these simple tips for maintaining good mental and emotional health:*

Run it out.

Talk it out.

Wash it out.

Then move on!

*Give your brain a break.* Like your body, your brain needs regular rest and relaxation. When you sleep and dream, your brain produces chemicals and proteins to replace those you used while you were awake.

*Exercise your brain.* Like your body, your brain thrives on regular exercise. It stays flexible and gets stronger. So keep your brain active! Read, think, ask questions, solve problems, learn and try new things. (Homework is good brain exercise.) TIP: Staying *physically* active is one of the best things you can do for your brain. Studies have shown that aerobic exercise improves memory, thinking, and mental response time.

*"No brain is stronger than its weakest think."*
*Thomas L. Masson*

*Eat well and healthfully.* Like your body, your brain needs nourishment. Although researchers can't agree on any specific foods that improve brain functioning, they do agree that a varied, balanced diet is what your brain needs most.

## CHECK IT OUT

*The Brain* by Jim Barmeier (San Diego, CA: Lucent Books, 1996). Explores how the human brain works and examines new technologies that are helping us to learn more about it. Ages 11–15.

**Neuroscience for Kids**
*faculty.washington.edu/chudler/neurok.html*
Experiments, activities, brain games, facts about the brain and nervous system, resources, links, and *much* more, all for elementary and secondary students and their teachers. This fun and fascinating site is maintained by Eric H. Chudler, Ph.D., a Research Assistant Professor at the University of Washington in Seattle.

---

*Feel your feelings.* Don't worry about "feeling bad" from time to time. It's okay to sometimes feel sad, frustrated, angry, worried, guilty, and/or afraid. Be brave and face your emotions. Peek inside yourself and try to figure out why you're feeling a certain way. Recognizing, acknowledging, and experiencing your feelings is good for you. It's only when you try to shove painful or uncomfortable feelings out of sight that they grow into monsters. So give yourself permission to cry, to go outside and throw rocks at the dirt or into a lake, to scream or stomp your feet. Release your "bad" feelings in ways that don't hurt you (or anyone else). If you have feelings you just can't handle—if you're overwhelmed or knocked flat by powerful emotions—find an adult you trust and can talk to.[3]

*Avoid escape routes.* It's tempting to want to dodge painful or uncomfortable feelings. It's easy to sleep too much, watch too much TV, put things off until tomorrow, skip school, ignore homework, evade responsibilities, retreat into a shell, or numb yourself with alcohol, drugs, or food. You can't run away from your emotions. Wherever you go, they go, too.

*Accept the sad or bad things that happen in your life.* This doesn't mean that you throw your hands in the air and just give up. Instead, it means that you take sad or bad things in stride.[4] Why kick yourself over and over again for missing the final free throw in the last game of the season? Why beat yourself up for losing a friend? Don't waste your energies on things you can't change. Learn from these experiences and move on.

*Help yourself to feel better.* You can do it. Here's how:

1.  Focus on things you *can* change. Brainstorm things you *can* do that won't hurt you or other people.

---

[3] If there's no adult available, see "Endurance," pages 87 and 88, for crisis hotlines.
[4] See "Endurance," pages 86–93, and "Forgiveness," pages 94–102.

**2.** Write down your feelings in your journal.[5] Write about what happened and how you feel. This can release some of your tension, sadness, and anger.

**3.** Draw your feelings. Don't worry about what your drawing looks like. Don't worry about making mistakes. Just draw.

**4.** Listen to soothing music.

**5.** Do something you enjoy. Read a book, ride your bike, take a walk, watch a video, pet your cat, spend time with a friend.

**6.** Meditate or pray.

**7.** Practice relaxing. Stretch out spread-eagle style, or sit in a comfortable chair. Relax every muscle as you breathe in and out. Think or say to yourself: "I can face this. I can fix this. I can do this."[6]

**8.** Do a service for someone. You'll be amazed at how good you feel if you focus on helping someone else. This won't make your problems go away, but it will increase your ability to handle them. Try it and see.

**9.** Set a time limit on your sad feelings. Decide that you *will* feel better in an hour, four hours, a day, or a week.

**10.** If steps 1–9 don't work, get a second opinion. Talk with someone you trust who cares about you. Brainstorm solutions together. Or seek professional help. Ask your parent, school counselor, youth group leader, or religious leader to recommend someone you can call. If you had a toothache, you'd go to the dentist. Don't let your emotions fester.

---

## CHECK IT OUT

### Facts for Families
*www.aacap.org/publications/factsfam*
An award-winning series of fact sheets on problems and issues that affect children and teens, developed by the American Academy of Child & Adolescent Psychiatry (AACAP). Available in English, Spanish, and French.

### Mental Help Net
*www.mentalhelp.net*
A guide to over 6,000 mental health resources including information about anxiety, depression, and substance abuse; professional resources in psychology, psychiatry, and social work; journals and self-help magazines.

---

# Character Dilemmas
*For journaling or writing essays, discussion, debate, role-playing, reflection*

**Suppose that . . .**

**1** Someone you know is infected with a highly contagious disease. How might you help the person and still protect yourself?

**2** Nearly 14 percent of the children in the United States don't have health insurance.[7] Should the U.S. be responsible for ensuring that *all* citizens have access to health care? Or only *some* citizens? (Which ones?) What about illegal aliens? Who should fund the health care system?

**3** Only 75 percent of all two-year-olds in the United States have been immunized against preventable diseases.[8] Some parents object to immunization for religious or personal reasons; others just don't get around to having their children immunized. Do parents have the right to keep their children from being immunized? Why or why not? Which is most important—the parents' freedoms of religion and expression, or the children's health?

**4** Almost 21 percent of all children in the United States are living in poverty.[9] Who should feed the thousands of kids who go to bed hungry each night? Are the parents responsible? The government? The schools? State health agencies? How do you think this problem should be addressed?

**5** A new policy says that people with HIV (the AIDS virus) may keep their identities private.

---

[5] See "Endurance," pages 88, 89, and 92, for journaling resources.
[6] See "Peacefulness," pages 175–176, for a relaxation exercise.

[7] This is true, by the way. *Source:* The U.S. Bureau of the Census Current Population Survey, March, 1995.
[8] This is also true. *Source:* The Centers for Disease Control and Prevention, *MMWR Weekly Report,* 1995 statistics.
[9] True again. *Source:* The U.S. Bureau of the Census Current Population Survey, March, 1996.

Some people are *against* the policy, believing that the public should be told when someone has HIV so they can protect themselves from infection. Other people are *for* the policy, believing that the patients' privacy should be protected because of the negative ways in which people with HIV are treated (and the specific ways in which the virus is spread). What do you think? Would it make a difference if you knew what kind of work someone with HIV was doing? *Examples:* A bank teller; a food service worker in your school cafeteria; a doctor; a teacher; a landscaper; an airline pilot; the manager of a restaurant; a bus driver; a musician in an orchestra; a day-care provider.

# Activities

**BRAINSTORM THE EFFECTS** of poor health and nutrition on people in the U.S. or other countries. Think of as many ways as you can in which people's lives are affected.

**BRAINSTORM THE VARIOUS "ESCAPE ROUTES"** people take to avoid facing their feelings. *Examples:* sleeping too much, eating too much, watching too much TV. Combine your list with other people's lists. How many different "escape routes" can you come up with?

**WRITE A LETTER TO THE EDITOR** of your local newspaper, a newsletter, or school newspaper. Express how you feel about hunger, malnutrition, health care, being an organ donor, or any other health-related issue you feel strongly about.

**FAST FOR A DAY.** Try going without food for one day to see how it feels to be hungry. Then write in your journal about the experience. IMPORTANT: Get your parents' permission first. Make sure you're in good health. Don't take part in any strenuous physical activity while you're fasting.

**RESEARCH AND REPORT ON SOMEONE** who has made important contributions to health and medicine. *Examples:* Albert Schweitzer, Jonas Salk, Florence Nightingale, Pearl Kendrick, Alexander Fleming, May Chinn, Sigmund Freud, C. Everett Koop, Gertrude Elion.

**RESEARCH AND REPORT ON A HEALTH CARE** topic or issue. *Examples:* nutrition, food preparation, smoking,

exercise, teen pregnancy, heart disease, stress management, allergies, asthma, environmental health, HIV/AIDS, etc. Come up with a creative or unusual way to present what you've learned. *Examples:* Create a board game; write and illustrate a comic book; make a slide show or video. You might want to research both conventional and alternative approaches to your topic or issue.

---

## CHECK IT OUT

**National Center for Complementary and Alternative Medicine**
*www.nccam.nih.gov*
This site is run by the National Institutes of Health and offers sound advice on alternative health options.

**Healthfinder**
*www.healthfinder.gov*
An excellent source of medical information online, sponsored by the U.S. Government, Healthfinder offers hundreds of health-related sites pre-screened for accuracy.

---

**CALCULATE YOUR TARGET HEART RATE** (THR). Here's the formula:

$$\frac{(220 - \text{your age}) \times 70\%}{6} = \text{Your THR}$$

Your THR is the specific heart rate that offers you the most benefits during periods of physical activity. It's the rate your heart should be at (or near) while you spend 20–30 minutes walking, biking, swimming, running, playing tennis, or whatever activity you choose. Check your pulse rate at your wrist or at the carotid artery alongside your Adam's apple while you're still active. (After 10 seconds of rest, a healthy heart is already starting to return to its normal rate.) If your pulse is above your THR, you're working too hard. If it's below your THR, you need to work a little harder.

> *Variation:* Check your pulse after you've been sitting or resting. Check it after 20–30 minutes of activity. Compare your resting rate with your active rate.

**CALCULATE THE COST OF HEALTH CARE** in the United States. As of the second quarter of 1996, the U.S. spent 13–14 percent of its GDP (Gross Domestic

Product) on health care. The total GDP was $7538 billion ($7.5 trillion). Check your calculations by reading the answers printed upside down at the bottom of the page.

> *Variations:* Find out how health insurance costs have increased over the past 10 years. Plot your findings on a line graph. Call or visit a local hospital to ask how much it costs, on average, for 1) outpatient treatment, 2) an overnight stay, 3) a visit to the emergency room, 4) a week-long stay. How much does insurance cover, on average?

**RESEARCH WORLD HUNGER AND DISEASE.** In which countries is hunger most common? Most severe? Where are the world's "hot spots" for disease? Make a map showing the results of your research. Include facts, figures, names of diseases, and other information you find. TIP: Contact the American Red Cross or CARE to request information.

## CHECK IT OUT

*The State of the World Atlas: A Unique Visual Survey of Global, Political, Economic, and Social Trends* by Michael Kidron, Ronald Segal, and Angela Wilson (New York: Penguin USA, 1995). This acclaimed atlas provides a unique view of current affairs by translating key political, economic, and social indicators into 50 full-color maps and graphics.

**American Red Cross**
PO Box 37243
Washington, DC 20013
1-800-435-7669
*www.redcross.org*

**CARE**
151 Ellis Street, NE
Atlanta, GA 30303-2440
1-800-521-CARE (1-800-521-2273)
*www.care.org*

**ENCOURAGE PEOPLE TO BECOME ORGAN DONORS.** Unless you're opposed to organ donation for religious or personal reasons, contact your local hospital to see how you can help encourage people to become organ donors. You might make cards to hand out that include a phone number to call. Or

you might distribute flyers or brochures that the hospital has available.

**ROLE-PLAY WITH YOUR FRIENDS,** class, youth group, or club various ways young people can say no to sexual pressure and avoid STDs or unwanted pregnancy. FACTS: Over 1,400 babies are born to teenagers mothers every day in the U.S., and 27 percent of girls drop out of school because of pregnancy. In 1991, young women ages 15–19 had 314,000 abortions.

**VOLUNTEER AT A FOOD BANK,** soup kitchen, or other place where meals are served to homeless and hungry people.[10] Be sure to get permission from your parents, and go with a chaperon.

**TAKE NEEDY CHILDREN ON A PICNIC.** Contact a shelter or other service organization. Prepare sack lunches for children there and take them on a picnic. Be sure to check the food handling license requirements for your area, get proper permissions, and go with a chaperon.

**REACH OUT TO A FRIEND.** Do you know someone who's abusing alcohol or other harmful drugs? Try talking frankly with him or her. See if your friend will agree to get help. You might suggest that he or she talk to a parent, teacher, school counselor, school social worker, youth leader, or clergy member, or call a hotline. (Look in your Yellow Pages under "Drugs" and "Alcohol" for local hotlines.) If you have Internet access, check out NCADI's "A Guide for Teens" (see page 106).

> *Variation:* Start a substance-abuse awareness and prevention campaign in your school, club, or community. You can obtain many of the materials you might need from the resources listed on pages 105–106.

**START AN EXERCISE CLUB WITH YOUR FRIENDS.**[11] Decide on a time and place to meet, and get an adult sponsor if you want to make your club official. Choose a variety of activities to do together (aerobics, running, jogging, biking, hiking, swimming, etc.). You might designate an "activity of the week" or just get together and burn off calories dancing to music.

**MAKE A MURAL, BULLETIN BOARD,** or poster illustrating the USDA's Food Guide Pyramid (see page 104) for your classroom or school.

---

13% × $7538 billion = $979,940,000,000. 14% × $7538 billion = $1,055,320,000,000.

---

[10] See "Empathy," pages 81–82, for tips on volunteering.
[11] See "Leadership," pages 160–161, for tips on how to start a club.

*Variations:* Evaluate the meals served in your school cafeteria according to the Food Guide Pyramid. Does the cafeteria offer plenty of choices in the various groups the Pyramid recommends? Survey students to learn if they're making healthful choices. Report your findings to your school principal, along with any recommendations for improvements. Should the cafeteria make any changes in the meals served? Should your school start an "Eat Right" campaign to encourage students to make better choices? Be sure to talk with the cafeteria folks to get their side.

**LEARN ABOUT THE NUTRITIONAL VALUE** of fast foods. Which is better for you, a McDonald's Quarter Pounder with Cheese or a Taco Bell Taco Salad? An Arby's Roast Beef Sandwich or Kentucky Fried Chicken? Many fast-food restaurants now have nutrition information available to hand out. Report on your findings.

## CHECK IT OUT

### Fast Food Facts
*www.olen.com/food*
Request a copy of this free brochure from the Attorney General's Consumer Division that includes the calorie, fat, sodium, and cholesterol counts of menu items from popular fast-food restaurants. Or visit the interactive "Food Finder" Web site and search for information about specific restaurants and menu items.

---

**DESIGN AND CREATE BUTTONS** to make people more aware of hunger, malnutrition, the need to have children immunized, and other health issues in your community. Hand them out at a school assembly, a local mall (get permission first), a community council meeting, or to anyone who might be interested or concerned.

**RESEARCH SONGS FROM THE GREAT DEPRESSION.** Visit your city or country library to find old records, tapes, or sheet music from songs popular during the Great Depression, which began in 1929 and lasted through most of the 1930s. TIPS: Look for recordings by Woody Guthrie and those on the Folkways or Rounder records; check Library of Congress and Smithsonian recordings; research old blues recordings. What impact do you think this music might have had on the mental health of people living during the Depression era?

**PLAY A FOOD GROUPS MEMORY GAME.** To prepare:

**1.** Make one card for each of the food groups defined by the USDA's Food Guide Pyramid (see page 104). You should have 6 group cards.

**2.** Make cards illustrating different food items within those groups. Make two identical cards illustrating each type of food. *Examples:* Two milk cards; two carrot cards; two cereal cards; two apple cards; two candy-bar cards; two pork-chop cards. You can make as many food cards as you want, but 25 pairs is a good number to start with.

To play:

**1.** Lay out the 6 group cards, face up, in a line on the floor or a large table.

**2.** Place the food cards upside down below the group cards. Shuffle them well.

**3.** The first player turns over two of the food cards. If they match, the player places them under the card of the group they belong to, earns two points, and takes another turn. If the cards don't match, the player returns them to the floor or table, face down, and mixes them in. Then it's the next player's turn.

**4.** The game continues until all of the food cards have been matched and are under the group cards.

**READ STORIES ABOUT HEALTH.** Look for these books:

*Amazing Gracie* by A.E. Cannon (New York: Delacorte, 1991). Gracie has a lot to deal with during her sophomore year when her mother, a victim of depression, remarries, a new brother moves in, and the family moves to Salt Lake City. Ages 13–16.

*Blubber* by Judy Blume (New York: Simon & Schuster Children's Books, 1982). Jill doesn't worry much about the grief that she and her classmates cause a fellow student—until Jill becomes a target herself. Ages 9–12.

*The Hunger Scream* by Ivy Ruckman (New York: Walker, 1983). Lily, a Colorado high school senior, progressively withdraws from her family and friends as she loses weight in an effort to protect her independence. Ages 12 & up.

# Character in *ACTION*

## Ashley Johnson: Kids' Café

Ten-year-old Ashley Johnson pulled the giant plastic trash bag over her head and popped her head and arms through the holes. She had stapled labels from junk foods on the bag: cookies, bubble-gum, greasy chips, and other fattening stuff. The skit she was about to perform (and had helped to write) would teach other kids about the importance of eating healthful foods. Ashley and friends from her fifth-grade class were taking a bite out of poor nutrition by being part of Kids' Café, a nationwide program that provides meals, activities, and friendship to children at risk of hunger.

It all started when Ashley and her classmates at Dilworth School met with their teacher, Gloria Jones, to brainstorm about the problems in the world. They got excited about the idea of reducing hunger among kids, and they decided to begin in their own community of Charlotte, North Carolina. Usually Kids' Cafés are run by adult volunteers. This one would be the first in the nation that allowed kids to help kids.

Ashley and her friends spent months planning and finding partners. They got help from Second Harvest, the national network of all food banks in the United States. They partnered with North Carolina Harvest, which recovers restaurant surplus food, and the Metroline Food Bank. The American Culinary Federation of Chefs offered to do the food preparation. Tonight's program was called "Blast Off to Good Nutrition," and Ashley had helped to decide what would be on the menu. The hungry kids would enjoy such creative dishes as "Meteor-Shower Rice," "Big Dipper Juice," and "Alien Green Beans."

"We did it all after school," Ashley explains. "First we had disadvantaged kids come in from the projects. They were different ages—first to sixth grade—and we talked to them and got to know them. We asked them what they wanted us to do. They asked for a puppet show and skits. So we made up a paper-plate puppet show and wrote four skits."

In the skits, Ashley played the role of a character she invented, Chef-Boy-R-U-Junky, wearing her decorated trash bags. She'd say lines like "I've improved my diet this week. I had sugar-sweetened cereal, chocolate milk, and orange pop for breakfast." Then another Dilworth student, Jonathan Kite, playing the part of Astronaut Food Dude, would enter in a football helmet and baseball pants to help the kids in the audience analyze Chef-Boy-R-U-Junky's breakfast. The kids from the project learned that if they ate that way, they wouldn't get the nutrition they needed.

Ashley says "One little boy came up to me and said 'Is that *really* what you ate for breakfast? That's really bad!' Another boy promised to eat more vegetables."

Ashley Johnson

The Dilworth students were part of Kids' Café from February until May, 1996. Twice a week, they ate dinner with kids from the project at a local YWCA. They also planned art activities, wrote and taught nutrition lessons, and mapped out the meals. Each time the two groups met at Kids' Café, they hugged each other. In between times, they wrote love letters and thank-you notes.

"The children my students served weren't the only ones who benefited," Mrs. Jones remembers. "My students would come in before school and stay after school to work on Kids' Café. They were constantly planning. Parents told me how much this carried over into their homes. My students changed their own eating habits, and so did some of their family members. Parents said this was the most exciting curriculum they had ever seen—and the most meaningful."

Ashley agrees. "Kids' Café helped me to understand some of the problems in the world, and the different ways we can help. It meant a lot to me to see the children's faces when we worked with them each week. They were happy. Plus it was a good leadership experience. I had never worked on a project where the adults stepped aside and let the kids do the work."

Ashley (left) wearing her Chef Boy-R-U-Junky costume

# Honesty

**Truthfulness, sincerity, honor,
fairness, trustworthiness, being genuine**

**M**artin was sprawled in front of the TV, sort of doing his math, when the phone rang. "Answer it!" his sister hollered from upstairs. "And if it's Robert, tell him I'm not home."

"Why should I?" Martin asked, looking up as his sister rushed into the family room.

"You idiot! Just answer the phone! I don't want to hurt his feelings. He's going to ask me to go to the junior dance with him, and I want to go with Alex. So tell him I'm not here . . . if it's Robert."

Martin still hesitated as the phone rang for the fifth time.

"Look, if you're feeling guilty, I'll go stand on the front porch," his sister said. "Then I'm really *not* home." Martin's sister ran out the front door just as he answered the phone.

Would Martin be lying if it were Robert calling and Martin said his sister wasn't home? Have you ever manipulated the truth in this way? What might Martin have done to handle the problem with his sister better?

Suppose you have a brother who has had a really rotten day. A bad-hair, drop-your-lunch-tray, step-in-dog-doo-day. He comes home, throws his books on the kitchen table, and stomps off toward his bed-room as your mother follows him, asking "What's wrong, dear?" He barks "Nothing!" and slams his door in her face. Is he being honest with your mom? With himself?

Dishonest thoughts can lead to dishonest actions. The truth is, your brother doesn't want to tell your mother what's wrong, because to do that he'd have to face what's wrong. Did he make a poor choice? A foolish mistake? Did he fight with a friend? Talk back to a teacher? Whatever it is, he'd rather not think about it. And he certainly doesn't want to tell your mom about it . . . too embarrassing. So he covers up the truth, lies to your mom, then tops it off by being rude. Now he has *three* problems instead of just one. And until he admits *to himself* what's wrong, he can't make any of them better.

It's okay to look stupid, make mistakes, and have bad days. Everyone does. If your brother had stopped to think about that, he might have told your mom "I had a rotten day, and now I want to be alone for a while." That would have left him with the *one* problem he had to begin with, plus quiet time to consider what to do about it.

In most cases, honesty isn't just the best policy. It's also a lot simpler than the alternative.

# Eight Great Reasons to Tell the Truth

*"Half the truth is often a great lie."*
*Benjamin Franklin*

1.   Telling the truth lets everyone know what really happened. There's less chance of misunderstanding, confusion, or conflict.

2.   Telling the truth protects innocent people from being blamed or punished.

3.   Telling the truth allows everyone to learn from what happened.

4.   You usually get into less trouble for telling the truth than for lying (and getting caught).

5.   Other people trust you more when you tell the truth.

6.   You don't have to tell (and remember) more lies to keep your story straight.

7.   You gain a reputation for being truthful—a trait most people value.

8.   Telling the truth helps you to feel secure and peaceful inside.

I told Jared I couldn't meet him at the park because I had to do an errand for my mom... but I told Mom I couldn't do the errand because I had to help Mr. Kennedy in the biology lab... but I told Mr. Kennedy I couldn't help him because I was meeting Jared at the Park... Where am I supposed to be? Help!

You could probably come up your own list of great reasons for telling the truth. And you might want to do just that, if it helps you to stay on the truth track. Meanwhile, here are ten tips to keep in mind for times when you're tempted to go the other way.

# Ten Tips for Being More Truthful

1.   **Make a commitment to tell the truth.** Say to yourself "Starting today, I'm someone who tells the truth." Then honor your commitment.

2.   **Tell someone about your commitment**—a close friend, a parent, a teacher, someone else you trust. Keep that person informed of your progress.

3.   **Think before you give a dishonest answer, explanation, or reason.** Consider the consequences. You'll probably decide that it's easier to tell the truth.

4.   **Be careful of when and how you use exaggeration, sarcasm, or irony.** Maybe you're trying to be funny, or maybe you want to discourage further questions or conversation. Either way, you don't want to give people the wrong information. *Example:* You missed three problems on your math test, and you're upset because that dropped you down a grade. You dad asks "How was your math test?" and you answer back "I blew it!" He ends up thinking you did a lot worse than you really did—and worrying as a result.

5.   **Be careful not to twist the truth or leave out part of it.** *Example:* Gloria says to Marcus "Tell Hosea I don't know if my folks will let me go to the party with him." What Gloria means is that her parents might not let her go to the party, period. But Marcus says to Hosea "Gloria's dad probably won't let her go to the party with *you*." Now Hosea thinks that Gloria's dad doesn't like him, doesn't think he's good enough for his daughter, doesn't trust him—or maybe Gloria doesn't want to go with him. Marcus's little twist could greatly change how Gloria and Hosea relate to each other in the future.

**6. *Don't indulge in little white lies;* don't get caught up in cover-ups.** *Example:* "My sister's not home" means she's not home. Standing outside on the porch doesn't count.

**7. *Watch out for silent lies.*** When you know about a lie and choose to keep quiet about it, you're allowing the lie to live on. Silence equals complicity.

**8. *When you catch yourself lying, throw your mouth into reverse.*** Do it then and there. *Example:* "What I meant to say is I missed three problems on my math test, which means I'm getting a B instead of an A."

**9. *Talk to yourself.*** (Not out loud, or people might think you're a little strange.) Ask yourself "How do I really feel about this? What's the best thing to do? How can I keep my commitment to myself?"

**10. *Treat yourself when you tell the truth even when it's hard to do.*** Pat yourself on the back. Indulge yourself. Take an evening off. Do whatever works for you.

> "Truth, like surgery, may hurt, but it cures."
> *Han Suyin*

Being honest means more than telling the truth. When you're honest, you're *sincere.* You have a *sense of honor and fairness.* You're *trustworthy* and *genuine.* And you're not just honest on the outside; you're honest on the inside, too. You don't lie to anyone, including yourself.

This sounds hard, and sometimes it is. But you probably know someone who has these qualities. And if you're fortunate, that person is your friend.

### CHECK IT OUT

*The First Honest Book About Lies* by Jonni Kincher (Minneapolis: Free Spirit Publishing, 1992). This book explores the truth about lies and encourages you to develop honesty as a personal value. Experiments, examples, and games explore the nature of lies and promote active questioning and truth-seeking. Ages 13 & up.

# Sincerity

***When you're sincere,*** you don't flatter people to try to make them like you or think well of you. *Example:* A friend comes to school wearing a new blue shirt. The first thing he asks you is "How do I look?" Actually, he doesn't look that good. You don't say "You look great" to his face, then laugh about him later behind his back. That's not being sincere. On the other hand, you don't say "You look awful" because there's no need to hurt his feelings.

Admittedly, this is a tricky situation. You might say "You look nice in blue." Or you might say "You look nice in blue, but I like your old blue shirt better." It depends on what kind of relationship you have. You'll have to be the judge of what's best.

When you're sincere, you're free from hypocrisy and pretense. You express your feelings openly and honestly. Your speech is natural, without double messages or hidden agendas. People know they can count on you to say what you mean and mean what you say.

> "The most exhausting thing in life, I have discovered, is being insincere."
> *Anne Morrow Lindbergh*

# Honor and Fairness

You overhear a teacher blame a student for taking the lunch money from her desk. In fact, you saw another student take it. Would you be lying if you said nothing? Technically, no. Would this be the honorable thing to do? No again.

***When you have a sense of honor,*** you do the right thing.[1] You might have to spend some time figuring out *how* to do the right thing, and you might have to play out a few scenarios in your mind before taking action, but you know that staying silent isn't an option. In this case, you might tell the teacher what you saw and let her handle it. Or you might go to the student who took the money and suggest that he give it back. Explain that if he doesn't, you'll have to tell the teacher. You're not going to sit by

---

[1] See also "Integrity," pages 135–141.

and let the other student be blamed for something he didn't do.

> "Lying is done with words and
> also with silence."
> *Adrienne Rich*

Having a sense of honor isn't easy. It means that you're true in all you say and do. Your life exemplifies truth, and people can trust you to do and be what you say. You stand up for the truth even when silence is more comfortable. If you hear one person telling a lie about another, you stick up for the person being lied about.

Having a sense of honor can also mean that you're patient and understanding with someone who might have lied. You don't tolerate the lie, but you can forgive the liar,[2] because you know that it's only human to make poor choices and mistakes.

**When you have a sense of fairness,** you don't take things you don't deserve.[3] These "things" might include awards, praise, money, or credit for good ideas or a job well done. If you win first prize in an essay contest because a teacher spent hours listening to you and making suggestions, you don't just take the prize and smile. You take the prize, smile, *and* thank your teacher.

Having a sense of fairness means that you don't tell your employer that you worked a half-hour more than you did. You don't tell your trombone teacher that you practiced every day when you didn't. You don't let your dad pay you to mow the lawn and then do a shabby job. If the cashier at the grocery store gives you change for a $20 bill when you paid with a $10 bill, you don't keep the extra change. You give it back. And if you don't discover it until after you get home, you *take* it back.

# Being Trustworthy and Genuine

**When you're trustworthy,** your parents know that you'll be home by curfew. They don't have to worry

(although they *will* worry, of course, until you walk through the door). They don't have to remind you or hound you. Similarly, if your parents go out for the evening or away for the weekend and leave you in charge of the house, they know that you'll take good care of it. You won't let your friends in for a wild party, even if your friends show up uninvited and make fun of you for not letting them in.

Being trustworthy means that if you promise to meet your math teacher at 7:00 A.M. for a makeup test, you arrive on time. And if you forget to do your homework, that's what you tell your teacher—not some phony story.

"But wait!" you might say. "If I tell my teacher I forgot to do my homework, he'll yell at me." So what? If your teacher yells, that's *his* problem. What you do is *your* problem. When you're trustworthy, you accept the consequences of your actions.[4]

Being trustworthy doesn't mean that you're perfect. It means that when you make a mistake, other people can count on you to tell the truth and take responsibility. *Example:* Your club leader asks you to call 10 people on a phone list she gives you. If you're trustworthy, you call them. And if you forget to call them, you're *still* trustworthy if you admit it and promise to call them right away. Basically, being trustworthy means that you're a No-Excuses Kid.

**When you're genuine,** the "real you" is the one people see. You're the legal tender dollar bill, not the counterfeit. You're authentic.

Some people have a hard time being genuine. Maybe they're insecure, or they're afraid that other people wouldn't like their "real" selves. So a boy whose father was a so-so boxer brags that his dad was a middleweight champion. Or a girl pretends that her family is rich because that makes her feel more important around her friends. Or politicians develop public selves that are very different from their private selves, hoping to win more votes that way.

Being genuine means that you don't bother with games, ruses, and masquerades. You are what you are, and other people know that. They can relax around you and be genuine, too.

---

[2] See "Forgiveness," pages 94–102.
[3] For more on fairness, see "Justice," pages 142–153.

[4] See "Choice and Accountability," pages 28–34.

*"I yam what I yam."*
*Popeye*

# Character Dilemmas

*For journaling or writing essays, discussion, debate, role-playing, reflection*

**Suppose that ...**

**1** Your four-year-old nephew asks you if Santa Claus is real. You can tell by the way he asks that he still wants to believe in Santa Claus. Are you lying if you say yes? Give a reason for your opinion, and look at both sides.

**2** You're living in Belgium during World War II, and you're secretly hiding a Jewish family in your attic. The police show up at your door and ask if you're harboring Jews. Do you lie or tell the truth? Are there times when you might make a greater mistake by telling the truth than by lying? Give other examples to support your opinion.

**3** A salesperson at a clothing store works on commission. (This means that she earns a small salary plus a percentage of anything she sells.) A customer tries on a suit that's much too tight for her. When the customer asks "How do I look?" is it the salesperson's responsibility to tell the truth? Why or why not?

**4** You're a doctor, and one of your patients has severe heart disease. You discover that he also has incurable cancer. Should you tell him about the cancer, knowing that the stress of hearing the news might bring on a heart attack? Or should you say nothing and do your best to treat him?

**5** The President of the United States (or the leader of your country) has learned about a new communications device that will allow the U.S. government to discover where other countries store their weapons. The same device can also be used to snoop on people in the U.S. Is the President obligated to tell the people about the new device? Why or why not?

**6** One night, while your parents are away, your brother drives your mother's car without her permission. He doesn't hurt it, and he even puts gas in the tank on his way home. The one thing he *doesn't* do is put the keys back exactly where he found them. Later, your mom asks you both if anyone moved the keys. Your brother says "Not me." He avoids looking at you. What might you say and why? Should you cover for him, stay silent, or tell?

# Activities

**WRITE AND PERFORM A SKIT** in which you and a friend debate the saying "Honesty is the best policy." This saying has been credited to two famous people: Miguel de Cervantes (1547–1616), author of *Don Quixote,* and George Washington (1732–1799), the first President of the United States. To add interest to your debate, one of you might play the role of either Cervantes or Washington (in costume, of course).

**DISCUSS WITH YOUR CLASS, CLUB,** or family what it means to "live a lie." Brainstorm examples of lies that people might "live" and reasons why they might do this.

**LIST EXAMPLES** of what honesty means to you. *Example:* "Honesty means stopping for a red light even when no one is around." Ask your friends to make similar lists. Combine your lists in a booklet to share with your class, school, club, family, or faith community.

**ROLE-PLAY HOW YOU MIGHT RESPOND IF:**

- a friend invites you to his house to watch an R-rated movie, and your parents have made you promise not to watch R-rated movies

- a friend asks you to keep a secret, then tells you she's planning to run away from home

- a friend you're shopping with slips a CD into his jacket and walks out of the store without paying for it

**RESEARCH WHISTLE-BLOWERS.** A whistle-blower is someone who goes public about an unfair, unsafe, or unethical practice in his or her workplace or somewhere else. *(Example:* An employee learns that his company is illegally dumping toxic waste into a stream, then takes the story to the local media.)

Whistle-blowers may get fired or face other types of abuse. Ask your librarian to help you search newspaper archives for stories about whistle-blowers. For each story, decide if you think the whistle-blower did the right thing.

> *Variation:* Talk about what journalist Bill Moyers has said about whistle-blowers: "They're not always right, they don't always win, and they're not always likable. They break the china and rattle the cages of conformity. What would America be without them? They keep the high and mighty on their toes and the majority on notice." Based on what you learned from your research, do you agree or disagree?

**STUDY HONESTY (AND DISHONESTY)** in advertising. Read ads in newspapers and magazines and watch them on TV. When do advertisements exaggerate, make promises that seem unrealistic, and make comparisons with other products that seem unfair? Do they use words like *always, never, perfect,* and *best?* Collect examples of your research. Compile an "Honesty in Advertising?" booklet. Include your evaluation of each advertisement and a list of guidelines that you think would help to ensure honesty and fairness in advertising.

> "Advertising may be described as the science of arresting the human intelligence long enough to get money from it."
> *Stephen Leacock*

## CHECK IT OUT

*Caution: This May Be an Advertisement: A Teen Guide to Advertising* by Kathlyn Gay (Danbury, CT: Franklin Watts, 1992). Examines the persuasive techniques used by advertisers and their effects on consumers. Ages 14–18.

**Adbusters**
The Media Foundation
1243 West 7th Avenue
Vancouver, BC V6H 1B7
Canada
1-800-663-1243
*www.adbusters.org*
A quarterly magazine published in Vancouver, *Adbusters* is for people who are tired of TV and magazine ads full of stereotypes, sexism, and propaganda. You might ask your library to subscribe. The Web site includes articles from past issues, previews of upcoming issues, and more.

**LEARN ABOUT THE RELATIONSHIP** between honesty and health. Invite a mental health expert to your class to talk on this topic. Are honest people more or less healthy than dishonest people? Are there any diseases or illnesses that seem to be linked to dishonesty and guilt?

**LEARN ABOUT HONESTY** in scientific or medical research. Interview researchers at a local university. Do this in person or, if there's no university nearby, by telephone, mail, or email. (To identify researchers you might want to interview, check the faculty biographies on the university's Web site.) Ask each person a series of questions about honesty in research. You might ask questions like these:

**?** Can you give any examples of researchers who have exaggerated or minimized test results to try to prove something?

**?** What happens to people who manipulate research results and get caught?

**?** How common is manipulation of research results in your area of study?

**?** Are there any safeguards in place to increase the chances of honest research and reporting? If so, what are they?

**?** Do you know of any cases where results were manipulated and something terrible happened?

**COMPARE NATIONAL HONESTY** with local honesty. Contact the National Crime Prevention Council and request the latest statistics for juvenile robbery, burglary, or shoplifting. Next, contact your local police department and request similar numbers from them. Are your local statistics higher or lower than the national numbers? Make a graph to show what you've learned and share it with your class, school, or community.

> *Variation:* Meet with your local police, city or community council, juvenile justice department, or intervention program to make a plan for lowering crime local statistics. Ask how you can help.[5]

---

[5] See "Safety," pages 234–244.

# CHECK IT OUT

**National Crime Prevention Council (NCPC)**
1000 Connecticut Avenue, NW, 13th Floor
Washington, DC 20036
(202) 466-6272
*www.ncpc.org*

**RESEARCH CULTURES PAST OR PRESENT** to learn their views of honesty. *Examples:* Did ancient Greece have the same ideas about honesty as medieval England? How did Native Americans during the 1800s view honesty as compared to the Caucasians who were expanding westward across North America? Choose 2 or 3 cultures and investigate how the concept of honesty has varied. Write a report about what you learn, or write a skit that demonstrates the differences in how honesty has been perceived (and practiced).

> *Variations:* Make a scroll showing how the concept of honesty has changed through time. Learn how other cultures have punished people for dishonesty (lying, stealing, cheating), and display your findings on a chart or graph. Or draw cartoons showing how dishonesty is treated in different cultures.

**FIND OUT HOW YOUR SCHOOL** handles dishonesty. Does your school have a student handbook? If so, what does it say about cheating, stealing, lying, plagiarism, and other honesty-related issues? What are the consequences for students who are dishonest? Do the consequences seem fair or unfair? Survey students to collect their opinions about the consequences, and report your findings to the administration.

> *Variation:* If your school doesn't have a student handbook, form a committee to create one. Your committee should include members of the administration, the faculty, and the student body. You might start by collecting examples of student handbooks from other schools. Contact the schools directly or search schools' Web sites (TIP: Educational institutions—schools, colleges, and universities—have Internet addresses ending with *.edu*). Some universities have student "honor codes." Under the terms of these "honor codes," students are allowed to take exams unsupervised. Do you think that an honor code would work in your school? If so, suggest that it be included in your handbook.

**SURVEY YOUR CLASS OR SCHOOL** to find out how honest students are. You can copy and use the survey on page 123 or write your own questions. Distribute the surveys and set up a collection box where people can return their completed surveys anonymously. Afterward, score the surveys and compile the results. Graph them and display the graph in your classroom or school. On your graph, you might want to compare males to females (which gender seems to be more honest?) and/or different age groups or grades. Your graph should include information about how the surveys were scored. *How to score the surveys:* Give 3 points for each "Yes," 2 points for each "Maybe," and 0 points for each "No." *How to evaluate the scores:* 27–30 points = Very Honest; 22–26 points = Mostly Honest; 18–22 points = Bends the Rules; 17 points or fewer = Needs to Reevaluate What Honesty Means. (NOTE: You may disagree with this scoring scale. That's okay. The point of this survey is not to judge, but to get people thinking and talking about honesty. You might want to discuss the scale with your teacher and come up with a different version to use with your class or school.)

**COLLECT PICTURES OF PEOPLE** throughout history who have been known for their honesty. *Examples:* Abraham Lincoln ("Honest Abe"), George Washington ("I cannot tell a lie"). Use your pictures to create an Honesty Mural.

> *Variation:* Ask your friends and classmates to tell about times when they were honest. Take their pictures and display them along with brief stories about their honesty.

**HOLD A JINGLE-WRITING CONTEST.** Invite people to write and record jingles about honesty or dishonesty. Award prizes for the best three. Play the winning jingles over your school intercom, or take them to a local radio station and ask if the station will play them on the air.

**PLAY A "WINK THE TRUTH" GAME.** The purpose of this game is to create a group story that's half true and half lies—and to discover how hard it is to keep a story straight if you need to remember many facts and lies. You'll need a group of at least 4 people (more is better). To play:

1. Begin by agreeing on what the story will be about. Try to keep the topic simple. *Examples:* A day at school; something specific that happened at

school or near the school; how the basketball team played at the last game.

2.   The first player starts the game by saying two sentences about the topic. One sentence is true, and one is a lie. It doesn't matter what order the player says them in, but he or she must wink when telling the lie. *Example:* "Mrs. Brody was standing at the door of the school this morning when we arrived." (True.) "She was wearing red shoes." (A lie; wink.)

3.   The second player repeats the first player's sentences and adds two more sentences to the story, winking for each lie.

4.   The third player repeats all four sentences said by the first two players, adds two more sentences, and winks three times.

Continue until the story gets very complicated and people start forgetting which parts are true and which parts are lies. Afterward, talk about the game. Is it hard to keep a story straight if you have to remember many facts and lies?

**READ STORIES ABOUT HONESTY.** Look for these books:

*Jennifer-The-Jerk Is Missing* by Carol Gorman (New York: Simon & Schuster, 1994). Thirteen-year-old Amy is baby-sitting Malcolm, an eight-year-old with a reputation for making up stories. When he tells her he's witnessed the kidnapping of a schoolmate, Amy doesn't know if she should believe him. Ages 10–14.

*One-Eyed Cat* by Paula Fox (New York: Bradbury Press, 1984). Eleven-year-old Ned has tried to be the perfect person that his minister father wants his to be, but is filled with guilt after shooting a stray cat with his new air rifle. Ages 10–13.

*Spying on Miss Muller* by Eve Bunting (New York: Fawcett Book Group, 1996). At a Belfast boarding school at the start of World War II, 13-year-old Jessie must deal with her suspicions about a teacher whose father was German and with her own father's drinking problem. Ages 11–14.

*Water Sky* by Jean Craighead George (New York: HarperCollins Children's Books, 1987). While living in Barrow, Alaska, with friends of his father, a boy learns the importance of whaling to the native Eskimo culture. Ages 11–14.

*Your Move, J.P.* by Lois Lowry (New York: Dell, 1991). Lovestruck J.P. goes out of his way to impress his new interest, but things get complicated after a simple lie gets out of control. Ages 9–13.

# Survey

*This is an anonymous survey. Don't write your name anywhere on it! Please drop your completed survey in the collection box in* _____.

location

| | Yes | No | Maybe |
|---|---|---|---|
| 1. If you were driving five miles per hour over the speed limit, and a police officer stopped you and asked how fast you'd been driving, would you tell the truth? | ❑ | ❑ | ❑ |
| 2. If you cheated on a test and didn't get caught, would you tell the truth if your teacher later asked if you cheated? | ❑ | ❑ | ❑ |
| 3. If you arrived home one night 30 minutes after curfew and your parents weren't there, would you tell them that you had been late? | ❑ | ❑ | ❑ |
| 4. If you found a wallet in the street with $200 in it, would you try to return it to the owner? | ❑ | ❑ | ❑ |
| 5. If a cashier at a checkout stand mistakenly undercharged you for something you bought, would you tell the cashier about it and pay the correct amount? | ❑ | ❑ | ❑ |
| 6. If you knew you could sneak into a concert without paying, would you buy a ticket anyway? | ❑ | ❑ | ❑ |
| 7. If someone you wanted to impress thought you were rich (and you really weren't), would you tell that person the truth about yourself? | ❑ | ❑ | ❑ |
| 8. If your parents promised to pay you a lot of money if you earned all A's and B's on your next report card, and if you could keep them from finding out your real grades, would you tell them the truth if you *didn't* earn all A's and B's? | ❑ | ❑ | ❑ |
| 9. If you promised your teacher that you'd complete a task by a certain date, would you keep your promise? | ❑ | ❑ | ❑ |
| 10. If you knew that a friend stole $10 from someone else's locker, would you report him or her? | ❑ | ❑ | ❑ |

*Please be sure to complete this information:*

You are a        ❑ male      ❑ female

What grade are you in? _____

How old are you? _____

## THANK YOU for taking this survey!

# Character in *ACTION*

## Jana Benally: Telling the Truth

Jana Benally grew to be five feet eleven inches—a tall Navajo—and a star on her high school volleyball team in Blanding, Utah. She spiked, blocked, and scooped up impossible smashes from the other team before they hit the floor. Her team members trusted her skills and depended upon her honesty.

But Jana hadn't always been completely honest. When she was in fourth grade, she lied to her teacher when he asked her if she were chewing gum. "I quickly swallowed the gum and said 'No,'" Jana remembers. "The dumb thing about it was that I didn't need to lie. He probably would have just asked me to spit it out. I felt so guilty, I couldn't think about anything else, and I vowed I would never lie again."

But she did lie again, and she cheated, too. "In fifth grade, my friends and I had a huge social studies assignment. We were all good students and liked to finish our assignments ahead of time. So we divided up the parts and copied from each other." Then her teacher, who conducted secret raids on her students' desks, found three of their notebooks in one desk, all with the same answers. The teacher called in the girls and their parents for a talk.

When Jana and her parents went to see her teacher, Jana's stomach dropped, and all she could see were her teacher's big, round, horrified eyes, with eyelashes that poked straight up as if they were drawn on her eyelids. Jana burst into tears and confessed. This time, she promised herself that she would never cheat again—or lie. For real.

And she didn't, even under pressure. Tremendous pressure. When she was a sophomore at San Juan High School, her team played Morgan High School in the state volleyball championship. The game was tight. Morgan would score, then San Juan would score. Jana leaped, dove, smashed the ball, and wiped the sweat from her forehead between plays.

Near the end of the game, the score was 12 to 14, with Morgan ahead. Morgan only needed one more point to win the state championship. Morgan served to San Juan, and Jana's team passed the ball to the center. Jana set it up and spiked it down hard on Morgan's side of the net. A Morgan player dove for the ball and miraculously dug it up from the back row. The Morgan setter went underneath it and set the ball up to the offhand hitter, who spiked it to San Juan. Jana blocked the ball and it smashed down, in-bounds, on Morgan's side.

The referee blew his whistle and yelled "Side out!" San Juan got the ball, and Jana knew that her team could tie the game and maybe even win. But there was just one problem. As Jana had blocked the spike from Morgan, she had felt the underside of her

Jana Benally

arm brush the net. The referee hadn't seen it. Nobody knew but Jana.

She hesitated for a moment. Then she grabbed the net, motioned to the referee, and said "I touched the net."

Jana's coach glowered and shouted at her. "Let the ref call the game!"

The referee called "Time out!" As he studied Jana's face, his eyes widened into circles. He paused. Then he blew the whistle, called the net ball, and gave the point to Morgan.

Jana took a long, scorching shower before she left the locker room. It was quiet. Her shoes squeaked as she crossed the empty gym floor. No one on her team had blamed her—but they hadn't congratulated her for being honest, either. No one had said much of anything to Jana after the game. But she knew that it took a whole team to win or lose, and she didn't blame herself, either. Although the state championship was blown away, Jana smiled, because inside she knew she had really won.

# Imagination

## Creativity, risk taking, inventiveness

*"All acts performed in the world begin
in the imagination."*
*Barbara Grizzuti Harrison*

Have you ever plopped down on the grass and gazed up at the clouds? You might have imagined dragons, animal shapes, or even saucers in the billowy wisps. You probably did that as a child, too, and you should do it again and again, even when you're 80.

Do you remember lying in bed scared when you were little? You probably shivered and pulled the quilt up under your chin, afraid to move because a large, dark monster was swaying beneath the window. You might have screamed, and when someone switched on the lights, you saw that the monster was only your own shirt hanging over a chair and blowing in the breeze. Your mom or dad might have said "See? There's no monster. You're just imagining things. Now stop being silly and go to sleep!" These words were meant to help you feel brave, but they might have had a different effect that wasn't as positive. They might have made you feel so embarrassed that you buried some of that rich "make-believe" imagination.

Imagination is a ripe, tempting fruit when you're young. You might have hidden some of that fresh sweetness as you grew older, partly because you might have been teased or scolded for it. Or you might have buried your imagination altogether. But don't panic. It's still there, although you might need to dig a little to find it.

*"Creative minds have always been known
to survive any kind of bad training."*
*Anna Freud*

If you've ever been hurt, your pain can become your molding clay for creating something that other people can feel, too. If you've ever been happy, you can call on those emotions and invent ways to communicate them to others. If you've ever been scared, who knows? Maybe you're the next Stephen King or R.L. Stine.

You imagi-"nation" is your private country where you're the only person with a passport. Imagination is born in the deepest parts of your

mind, and it can only be limited by your own thoughts. Imagination is the power to see things you can't see, hear things you can't hear, smell or taste things you can't smell or taste, and design or change the puzzle pieces of your own life.

Everything that humans have ever created or accomplished was first envisioned in someone's thoughts. Young people are especially good at imagining because they don't always know the way things are "supposed to be." You're free to wander uncharted streets in your mind. You haven't set up roadblocks that say "Stop! You can't do that!" or "Dead end!" or "Detour! That won't work!"

Sometimes harnessing your imagination is elusive, like trying to catch a shadow. The harder you try, the more unreachable it seems. At other times, imagination creeps up on you, most often when you aren't concentrating on it. You build and strengthen your imagination's muscles by relaxing, letting go, and removing all the obstacles.

Your imagination can go wild in your sleep. There's a period called REM (Rapid Eye Movement) sleep when you do most of your dreaming. Did you know that you have more than 1,000 dreams in a single year? Those dreams stimulate your imagination and even help you to solve problems in your sleep. Watch people who are sleeping, and if you see their eyes wiggle behind their lids, you'll know they're in REM sleep.

Albert Einstein once said "Imagination is more important than knowledge." Why do you think he said that? Do you think he meant that it wasn't important to study and learn? Hardly! Try interpreting his words this way: You can have all the tools of knowledge in the world at your fingertips, but unless you also have a dream of something you might build, those tools will lie there uselessly.

Bertrand Russell, another great thinker, once said "It is only through imagination that men become aware of what the world might be." Do you agree or disagree?

# Creativity

*"Make visible what, without you, might
perhaps never have been seen."*
*Robert Bresson*

When you use your imagination to design, build, change, or rearrange things, you're using *creativity*. Creativity is what you do with your imagination. Creativity is the car your imagination rides to its destination.

You might not be creative at drawing, but you might be creative in your ability to see solutions to problems, or in movement (such as running, dancing, or kicking). You might be creative in analyzing angles, arranging furniture, or calming someone who's angry. You might be creative in the way you cook, sing, fly a kite, race your bike, wear your clothes, or come up with alibis for not doing your homework.

Creative people aren't only artists, writers, musicians, and dancers. They're teachers, industrial workers, telephone operators, doctors, athletes, plumbers, singers, newspaper reporters, mothers, fathers, kids, electricians, even bank robbers. In other words, *everyone* is creative in some (or many) ways.

"Not me," you might say. "I'm not creative!" If that's what you think, you haven't dug deeply enough to uncover your own unique gifts. Your mind is a gold mine of creativity. Here's how to bring up your treasures for the world to see:

**B**rainstorm many ideas. Let yourself be silly, nonsensical, absurd. Explore new things, unusual things, unexpected twists.

**R**elax. Rest. Leave spaces in your searching.

**A**lone. Don't be afraid to be alone. Committees can come up with great ideas, but you need solitude to explore your own creative mind.

**I**nvestigate new ways of looking at things. Learn from experts. Turn ideas upside down; make them larger or smaller. Redesign the form, change the colors, change the order, put things together that don't fit together.

**N**otice what you're *not* searching for. Stop and look behind your thoughts. Go in the opposite direction for a while.

**S**truggle. Work hard. Practice. Get help. Don't give up at what you like to do or want to learn.

**T**rust your hunches. Even when experts insist that your idea is dumb, lame, impractical, or impossible, don't give up until *you* prove it wrong. As movie director Frank Capra once said, "A hunch is creativity trying to tell you something."

**O**pportunities. Keep your eyes and ears open for opportunities. Look for chances to learn new things, develop new talents, listen to people whose ideas are different from yours, and go places you haven't been.

**R**ecord your mistakes. Track your progress so you'll learn from your errors, wrong turns, and side trips. (Who knows, you might discover something interesting along the way.)

**M**ake things up wherever you are. Train your eyes, ears, and mind to redesign whatever you're looking at, thinking about, or listening to: the doorway, a melody, a street sign, an advertising jingle, a dance, a picture, bacteria under a microscope, the shoes on your feet, the bus, a garden, a phrase, your teacher's hairpiece. . . .

## CHECK IT OUT

*A Whack on the Side of the Head: How to Unlock Your Mind for Innovation* by Roger von Oech (New York: Warner Books, 1993). Learn how to open your mental locks, break rules, use impractical ideas as stepping-stones to practical ideas, and more. Ages 13 & up.

### Creativity Web
*members.ozemail.com.au/~caveman/Creative*
This Australian site includes information on Mind Mapping and Lateral Thinking, a Children's Corner, quotations, humor, creativity basics, and more.

### GoCreate.com
*www.gocreate.com*
Tools, techniques, resources, links, references, and more to promote and enhance creativity. Be sure to visit the QuotAmaze part of this site, where hundreds of quotes about creativity are linked in a random, free-association way. Use it to kickstart your thinking.

# Risk Taking

> "You can't steal second base and still keep your foot on first."
> *Frederick Wilcox*

When you allow yourself to be creative, you take risks. Not daredevil risks; not foolish, jumping-off-of-cliff stunts. Creative risk taking means daring to explore your talents, taking off your mask, and letting people see the real you. The biggest risk of all is having the courage to be yourself.[1] That sometimes means making mistakes and doing things over again. Or falling down and getting back up. Or failing at something so many times that you don't think you can stand to try again . . . then trying again. (You succeed when you try *one more time* than your total number of failures.)

## Successful Failures

- Giacomo Puccini's music teacher told him that he had no talent for music. Puccini went on to become one of the world's greatest composers, famous for operas including *La Bohème* and *Madame Butterfly*.

- Charles Goodyear was determined to find a way to make rubber flexible. He had some success by treating rubber with sulfur, but it wasn't good enough. One day he accidentally dropped a rubber-sulfur mixture onto a hot stove—and discovered vulcanization.

- When Marian Anderson wanted to sing in Constitution Hall in Washington, D.C., on

---

[1] See "Courage," pages 71–78.

Easter Sunday, 1939, she was barred because she was black. So she gave her concert on the steps of the Lincoln Memorial and drew a crowd of 75,000. Her open-air concert was a triumph over bigotry and helped to solidify her position as an international star.

 Charles Darrow was an unemployed engineer when he invented the game Monopoly. He first presented his game to a toy company in 1935, and they gave him 52 reasons for rejecting it. Today the game is so successful that Parker Bros., the publisher, prints more than $40 *billion* in Monopoly money each year—more than twice the amount of real money printed by the U.S. Mint.

> "People fail forward to success."
> *Mary Kay Ash*

## CHECK IT OUT

*Inventor's Workshop: You Can Invent* by Belinda Recio (Philadelphia: Running Press, 1994). This handbook gets readers thinking from the perspective of an inventor. Included materials also allow for trying one's own hand at inventing. Ages 9–12.

*The Kid's Invention Book* by Arlene Erlbach (Minneapolis: Lerner, 1996). Tells about young inventors, their creations, and how the inventions came to be. Ages 9–12.

## 16 Ways to Take Risks

1. Color outside the lines.

2. Change the rules in a game so everyone has more fun.

3. Wear clothing you design instead of wearing what your friends like.

4. Write the truth in your journal about how you feel, what you dream, what you worry about, what you plan to do with your life, what gives you nightmares, and what you hope for yourself and the world.[2]

5. Solve a math problem in a new or unusual way—different from the established or "proper" way.

6. Take dance lessons if you're a boy. Take shop class if you're a girl. Explore any talent that interests you, especially one you "shouldn't" explore because you're the "wrong" gender, age, race, or whatever.

7. Speak up for what you believe.

8. Make new friends.

9. Go new places. (Whenever you have the chance to travel, take it.)

10. Challenge the old way of doing things if you see a better way. Shake up the status quo.

11. Go with your hunches.

12. Dare to make mistakes and look ridiculous.

13. Keep trying even when others are laughing at you.

14. Spend time alone.

15. Reach farther than you think you can reach.

16. Don't stop at 16.

> "Go for the moon. If you don't get it, you'll still be heading for a star."
> *Willis Reed*

# Character Dilemmas

*For journaling or writing essays, discussion, debate, role-playing, reflection*

**Suppose that . . .**

**1** You get an assignment from your geography teacher to draw a map of the United States, showing the products each state specializes in, like corn, mining, and so on. You'd like to add three-dimensional objects to your map—a real corn kernel, a small piece of ore. Your teacher is very strict and doesn't allow students to change the rules. What should you do? Is it worth the risk to do the assignment your way? What might happen if you *always* follow assignments exactly?

---

[2] See "Endurance," pages 88, 89, and 92, for journaling resources.

**2** Manuel's grandparents have left him a trust fund to pay for his college education. But Manuel's father died recently, and his mother needs financial help raising the three younger children. What should Manuel do? Should he risk his trust fund? Can you come up with other creative solutions to Manuel's dilemma?

**3** Your friend Erica is thinking about entering an after-school speech contest. She writes very well, and she has wise things to say, but she's very shy. You talk her into entering. Meanwhile, Erica's mother tells her that she has to come home every night after school to baby-sit her brothers. Her mother also tells her not to bother with the speech contest; Erica is "too shy" and "shouldn't waste her time." When Erica tells you about these latest developments, she bursts into tears and says that her mom is right; entering the contest was stupid. What might you do to help your friend regain her confidence, stay in the contest, and not get in trouble with her mother?

**4** A young man lives in a primitive culture whose traditions dictate that reading is evil. The young man yearns for knowledge and feels that there's much to be learned from other cultures. Some missionaries secretly give him books and start teaching him how to read. The young man knows that if he's caught, he'll be shamed and banned from becoming a tribal leader, and no young women from his tribe will ever want to marry him. What do you think the young man should do? Can you think of other examples in which a culture might prevent a person from becoming what he or she wants to be? Does this ever happen in the United States? In other countries? If so, where and how?

**5** You've been asked to serve on an international committee of scientists, researchers, and ethicists. The purpose of the committee is to consider the implications of cloning and determine standards. Most of the world's countries have agreed to abide by the standards set by your committee. What are some of the issues you might raise? What position might you take? Will you recommend strict standards or more lenient standards? Will you decide that cloning should be allowed or forbidden?

**6** You're someone who's afraid to take risks. You like it when things are safe, predictable, and planned out. One day you come across this quotation by author Erica Jong: "The trouble is, if you don't risk anything, you risk even more." What does this say to you?

# Activities

**IMAGINE EACH OF THE FOLLOWING SITUATIONS.** What would you do? Talk them over with your friends or family. TIP: Be aware that there might not be one "right" or "best" response.

▲ You're a girl and you want to play football on your high school team.

▲ You're a boy who has a beautiful, high voice and loves to sing, but everyone makes fun of your high voice.

▲ You're a talented artist and you want a $250 set of watercolors, but your parents won't buy them for you.

▲ You love to write poems, but your English teacher tells you that your poetry is "trite and unimaginative."

▲ Your P.E. teacher tells you that you're too short to play basketball.

▲ You're in a wheelchair and you want to learn how to swim.

▲ You're totally bored in school and would rather spend your time reading and studying on your own.

**LEARN ABOUT RISK TAKERS IN NATURE.** Are there any animals that seem to be creative risk takers? *Example:* When a goose flying with its flock becomes ill or is shot or wounded, two other geese drop out of formation and follow the stricken goose down. They stay with the goose to protect it until it recovers or dies. Then the two protectors must launch out *on their own* to find another flock or catch up with their original flock. Can you find other examples?

**RESEARCH CREATIVITY AND RISK TAKING** in science. You might learn about Copernicus, Galileo, Thomas Edison, and/or Marie Curie. In what ways were they creative? What risks did they take? What were the consequences of those risks? Were their discoveries or inventions accepted at first?

**RESEARCH THE RISKS THAT ASTRONAUTS** take. You might want to start by learning about the early days of the space program. What were the risks taken by Alan Shepard, the first U.S. astronaut to fly into space? Or John Glenn, the first U.S. astronaut to orbit the earth? Or Neil Armstrong, the first man to set foot on the moon? Or the crew of the *Apollo 13?* Compare the risks taken by astronauts in the 1960s to those taken by astronauts today.

## CHECK IT OUT

**NASA Human Space Flight**
*spaceflight.nasa.gov*
Up-to-the-minute information about the International Space Station and its astronauts.

**The NASA Homepage**
*www.nasa.gov*

**INVENT A NEW WAY TO TEACH THE MULTIPLICATION** tables to younger children. Or concepts of carrying, place value, or anything else that requires practice and memorization to learn.

> *Variation:* Design a game for teaching a math concept to younger children. Play it with your younger brother or sister, or volunteer at an elementary school, hospital, or shelter.[3] TIPS: You might create a board game (like Monopoly, Candyland, Chutes & Ladders, or Life); a card game (like Go Fish or Concentration); or a mime game patterned after Charades.

**MAKE A COMIC BOOK** showing imaginative, creative, risk-taking, and inventive events in the history of your state or province, your country, or the world. Narrow your focus a bit by choosing a theme. *Examples:* inventions, science, art, literature, music, military/warfare, medicine/health, technology, communication, language development, transportation, finance, sports, recreation, agriculture, industry, business, philosophy, archaeology, or anything else you choose.[4]

---

[3] See "Empathy," pages 81–82, for guidelines on how to volunteer.
[4] See "Choice and Accountability," page 32, for a resource about comics.

## CHECK IT OUT

For inspiration when preparing your comic book, visit your library or bookstore and look through one (or more) of the cartoon histories by Larry Gonick including *The Cartoon History of the Universe* (New York: Doubleday, 1990, 1994) and *The Cartoon History of the United States.*

When deciding what events to portray, you might want to start by paging through *The Timetables of History* by Bernard Grun (New York: Touchstone Books, 1991). There are other *Timetables* books on *African-American History, American History, Jewish History, Science, Technology,* and *Women's History.*

---

**RESEARCH RISK TAKERS IN HISTORY.** Pick your favorite hero or heroine from history and write a report on him or her. Answer these questions: 1) What risk-taking activities did the person do? 2) How were the person's ideas/activities accepted at first? 3) What obstacles did the person overcome? 4) When did the person's ideas become widely accepted?

**BOLDLY GO WHERE YOU'VE NEVER GONE BEFORE**—in your imagination. Make a list of all the places you'd like to go someday. Pick one, then invent a new vehicle to take you there. Make a three-dimensional model to show your class or club as you explain how your vehicle works.

**CREATE A COMMERCIAL** to "sell" people on a talent you have. *Example:* If you play the piano, you might start by playing a recording by another pianist. Tell how long you've been studying and/or playing. Explain how you might use your talent to make a contribution to others. End by performing—perhaps the same piece you played at the beginning of the commercial. Record your commercial on videotape.

> *Variation:* If everyone in your class creates a 1-minute commercial, you might show them all at your school's Open House or Parents' Night.

**ESTABLISH A MENTOR FILE.** Gather names, telephone numbers, and descriptions of experts and other talented people in your community who are willing to help young people develop their talents. You might look for leaders in music, art, architecture, writing, drama, medicine, science, space, technology, math, engineering, law, etc. Ask if they'd be willing to be listed in a Mentor File. Explain that students might be calling on them for advice, assistance, or guidance. IMPORTANT: If you meet with your mentor in person, go with a chaperon.

**ORGANIZE AND PRESENT A TALENT SHOW** for your class, club, or school. Remember that there are many types of talents: visual (drawing, painting, sculpture, graphics), performing arts (singing, dancing, playing an instrument, doing a karate demonstration), public speaking (speeches, debates, recitations, readings), etc. Your talent show might include a dramatic skit, a speech contest or debate, a math/science/history competition, and/or a science fair.

**INVITE SPEAKERS WITH SPECIAL TALENTS** to speak to your class, club, or school. Ask them to talk about how they first became aware of their talents, how they developed their talents, who encouraged them to develop their talents, what advice they might have for someone else who's interested in developing those talents, etc.

**PLAY A "HUMAN SCULPTURES" GAME.** This game promotes free expression and creativity, courage and risk taking, flexibility and trust. Start by dividing into groups of 3. One person is the artist; one is the model; and one is the "clay." To play:

**1.** The artist and the "clay" must close their eyes and keep them closed until step 5. If it helps, the artist may want to wear a blindfold.

**2.** The model sits comfortably and poses with whatever facial expression he or she chooses (smiling, frowning, happy, angry, peaceful, thoughtful, etc.).

**3.** The artist feels the model's face and head (gently) for 15 seconds.

**4.** The artist sculpts the "clay" (the third person) in the same expression the model was wearing (again, gently). The artist can't go back and reexamine the model's face. He or she must sculpt from memory.

**5.** The artist and the "clay" open their eyes to see if the "clay" matches the model.

**READ IMAGINATIVE STORIES.** Look for these books:

*The Dark is Rising* by Susan Cooper (New York: Atheneum, 1973). On his 11th birthday, Will learns that he's one of the "Old Ones," a group of people with special powers. Will must quickly harness his powers to defeat the forces of evil and save his sister. Ages 10–13.

*The Hobbit* by J.R.R. Tolkien (New York: Galahad Books, 1989). Bilbo Baggins, a home-loving hobbit, is enticed to join a party of adventurers in search of treasures. Ages 11 & up.

*The Phantom Tollbooth* by Norton Juster (New York, Random House, 1961). Neither words nor numbers can excite young Milo. One day, a tollbooth appears, allowing Milo to enter into a land where numbers and words are constantly at war with one another. Ages 9–13.

*Rondo in C* by Paul Fleischman (New York: Harper & Row, 1988). As a young piano student plays Beethoven's Rondo at her recital, each audience member is stirred by memories. Ages 6–10.

*Topsy Turvies: Pictures to Stretch the Imagination* by Mitsumasa Anno (New York: Walker/Weatherhill, 1970). Optical illusions form structures in which strange little men can go up stairs to get to a lower place, hang pictures on the ceiling, and walk on the walls. All ages.

# Character in *ACTION*

## Wren Gleason: Worth the Risk

"If you can prove that you're as good a player as the boys, then you can stay on that team. If you can't, you'll have to play on the girls' team." Fourteen-year-old Lauren Gleason (Wren) listened carefully to the coach's words. Was it worth the risk? What if she blew it? Could she take the pressure?

Wren had been playing lacrosse with boys ever since she was 12. When she first tried out for the Amherst team, it was coed, and five girls made it. The other four eventually dropped out, but not Wren. She remained the only "co" on the team. An aggressive, spirited player, she proved herself by pounding many goals for the team during the next two years. Suspicious at first, the boys grew to accept and even depend on her. In seventh grade, Wren was the second most valuable player in the league, having scored the second highest number of goals during the season.

With her imaginative and creative spirit, Wren had more interests than lacrosse alone. She invented a "Cats Only Restaurant" out of cardboard that was small enough for cats to get into, but not dogs. She and her Odyssey of the Mind team put on a skit using all recycled goods. They made ears from sponges, vests from plastic, bow ties from bubblewrap, and shoes from boxes. Their skit took them to the state competition.

An artist and award-winning speaker, Wren also composed her own music for guitar and piano (and played it for her school). But she loved sports best, especially lacrosse.

Then, when she was in seventh grade, the ground rules changed. The Lacrosse Club started a new team for girls. "You can't play on the boys' team now because we have a girls' team. You'll have to play there," the director told her.

"But why?" Wren asked. "I don't want to be on the all-girls' team. The guys and I play well together. We're a good team." It wasn't fair, she thought. She began to doubt if she should stay on the boys' team. Then some of her teammates threatened to quit if she couldn't play on their team. And she decided she'd try to "prove herself," as the coach had told her she'd have to do.

After the first game, when she had scored two winning goals, both teams lined up to slap hands and congratulate each other. They pulled off helmets and toweled sweat from their faces. Wren watched as the captain of the opposing team walked past his teammates and snarled "Not only did you get beaten by an Amherst team, but you got beaten by a team with a *girl* on it."

Wren ignored the insult, wiping her eyes. But her teammates hollered and shook their fists. Wren's friend Brent shoved the other captain and knocked him to the ground. Then the other captain

Wren Gleason

shouted at Wren "Get back in the kitchen where you belong!"

Wren bit her lips and said nothing. Brent punched the guy. Players shoved, yelled, and threatened each other until Wren's coach broke it up. Although she had been insulted, Wren glowed through red cheeks. Once again, her team had stood up for her.

Then her coach brought her back down to earth. "Wren," he said, "I'm not sure how other coaches in the future will like having you on their team. When they lose, they'll always blame it on you. Think about it."

She thought about it, but not for long. She was too busy playing lacrosse. As an attack person on both right and left, she blasted the goal again and again. She averaged one score per game in eighth grade. (That's a lot when the average score for an entire game is 2 to 3.)

What's next for Wren? She's been told that she can't play lacrosse with the boys in high school. That doesn't surprise her—and it won't stop her. She's already planning her strategy. "I guess I'll have to make a big scene and pass a petition or something," she says. "I know it will be hard, but I'm willing to fight for it, because lacrosse is my favorite sport.

"Besides, I'm not just doing it for me. I'm doing it for all girls, for anyone who follows me."

# Integrity

**Consistency, constancy, honesty, honor**

> "One must not conceal any part of what
> one has recognized to be true."
> *Albert Einstein*

The chameleon is a curious lizard-like reptile. It can change colors from green, yellow, cream, or brown to blend with its surroundings. People can be like chameleons, changing their behavior and attitudes to please and accommodate others. For the chameleon, changing is a survival skill that protects it from predators. For people, changing can mean that they're not being true to themselves. In their eagerness to blend in, they sacrifice their integrity.

"Integrity" is one of those words that can be hard to define. If you look it up in a dictionary, you're likely to find definitions like these: "Steadfast adherence to a strict code of moral, ethical, or artistic values; incorruptibility; the quality or state of being whole, entire, undiminished, or unimpaired; soundness; the quality or state of being undivided; completeness." When you read between the lines, you can probably come up with a simpler definition: *Being yourself.* All day, every day, regardless of who's around. This doesn't mean that you'll never change. As long as you keep growing and learning, you'll continue to change in some ways. But *who you are*—your essential self—will stay rock solid.

When you have integrity, you're honest with yourself and others.[1] But integrity involves more than telling the truth. You talk the talk *and* walk the walk. You match what you do to what you believe. You have confidence in yourself because you know yourself. Other people have confidence in you because they can depend on you to be consistent and constant. Your friends look to you as a leader because they trust you; parents, teachers, and employers give you more freedom and responsibility.

Your integrity encompasses every part of your life, including your relationships with people (family, friends, neighbors, classmates, teachers), institutions (schools, faith communities, places of employment, organizations), society (community groups, clubs), your country (town, city, state), and yourself. You don't brag, exaggerate, name-drop, try to impress other people, or put them down with insults or cutting sarcasm. And you do the right thing, even if it isn't the easiest or most popular thing.

---

[1] See "Honesty," pages 115–125.

You don't deceive people into thinking you have more money than you do. You don't tell some of your friends that you hate cigarettes, then light up with others so they'll think you're cool. You don't pretend to like someone and later stab him in the back. If you do, the time will come when you're not fooling anyone but yourself. When chameleons in nature change colors, they fade into the background, but people who act like chameleons stick out like sore thumbs.

> "One must live the way one thinks or end up thinking the way one has lived."
> *Paul Bourget*

When you have integrity, you're true to your values. Look for role models who can guide you in developing good values. Seek out honorable, trustworthy, genuine people in the present; study good examples from the past. Your values should not bring harm to other people, things, your country, or the world. They should support, respect, strengthen, and build.

What's great about having integrity is that you can approach each new situation calmly because you don't have to struggle inside to decide how to act. Your integrity protects you from making poor choices. Integrity is the cornerstone of building good character.

Values ⟷ Behaviors

**INTEGRITY**

Thoughts and Beliefs ⟷ Actions and Words

# Character Dilemmas

*For journaling or writing essays, discussion, debate, role-playing, reflection*

**Suppose that . . .**

**1** Your friend Evan is popular, well liked, and a great soccer player besides. Your school's soccer team is competing for first place in the district, and Evan is key to winning. During math class this morning, you saw him cheat on an important test. No one else noticed. If the teacher found out, Evan would be kicked off the soccer team. Is it your responsibility to report what you saw? Is it anyone's responsibility? What are the consequences of reporting? What might be the consequences of *not* reporting?

**2** You're paying for school supplies at your local discount store. The store is part of a huge chain with hundreds of stores across the country. When the cashier rings up your purchases, she undercharges you $10 by mistake. You could call it to her attention . . . or you could donate the $10 to a local homeless shelter you've been helping. You wouldn't be keeping the money for yourself, and the shelter needs it more than the big corporation that owns the store . . . right? Do you put the $10 in your wallet and leave? Why or why not?

**3** A friend asks you to trade shirts for a day. The style and color of your friend's shirt makes it look like a gang shirt. You don't like gangs, and you don't want anyone to think you're in a gang, but your friend is being very persuasive. If you say no, he'll accuse you of being a coward and broadcast it to the whole school. And it probably wouldn't hurt to wear the shirt for just one day. If anyone thinks you're in a gang, that's *their* problem for being judgmental. Do you agree to the trade? How might you handle this situation with integrity?

**4** Someone you know is always true to her beliefs. She believes in cheating, lying, backstabbing, and putting herself first, and that's what people can count on her to do. Does this person have integrity? Or does having integrity mean being true to the *right* values? Who decides which values are right and which are wrong?

**5** You're baby-sitting for a neighbor who's told you not to have your friends over when you sit. Around 10:00, two of your friends show up uninvited. The kids are in bed asleep, so you let them in. When one friend spills his root beer on the carpet, you make them both leave. You scrub the carpet and manage to remove the stain. Do you need to tell your neighbor that you let your friends inside the house? After all, you sent them home. The stain is gone. Your neighbor will never know they were there. If she did, she might never trust you to sit again. What should you do?

**6** Your neighbor puts his house up for sale, knowing that it needs a new roof that would cost thousands of dollars. His realtor advises him to say nothing about the roof to prospective buyers. "You won't be lying," the realtor says. "You don't have to say anything unless they ask." Do you agree? If you were your neighbor, what would you do?

# Activities

**WRITE IN YOUR JOURNAL**[2] about what integrity means to you. Do you have integrity? How do you know? Who are the integrity role models in your life? Write about a time when someone you know showed integrity. Tell how this affected you personally.

**EVALUATE THE INTEGRITY OF POLITICAL** candidates. If you're near an election time, read the papers, watch TV, and listen to campaign speeches and promises. Which promises do you think are made just to win votes? Are candidates exaggerating problems or making promises that probably can't be kept? How can you tell? Which candidates seem to have the most integrity? Consider volunteering to help them. Call their campaign offices and ask what you can do. You might answer phones, do surveys, pass out flyers, or encourage people to go to the polls on election day.

> *Variation:* Research the campaign promises of one or two elected officials who've been in office for two years or longer. Have the officials done what they promised to do? Present your findings in a speech to your class or community.

**RESEARCH PERSONALITY DISORDERS.** Interview a psychiatrist or search the Internet for up-to-date information on mental illnesses that can lead to personality changes, disorders, or multiple personalities. Write a paper based on your findings. Is it possible that mental illness turns some people into "chameleons"?

---

[2] See "Endurance," pages 88, 89, and 92, for journaling resources.

## CHECK IT OUT

**Internet Mental Health**
*www.mentalhealth.com*
A free encyclopedia of mental health information, designed by Canadian psychiatrist Phillip W. Long, M.D. Includes information on the 52 most common mental disorders, the 67 most common psychiatric drugs, links to other mental health sites, and more.

**National Institute of Mental Health**
*www.nimh.nih.gov*
The official site of this U.S. Government agency includes a large "public information" section with information on specific mental disorders, diagnosis, and treatment.

---

**INTERVIEW A RESEARCHER** who is working with humans or animals. TIP: Call a university, an engineering laboratory, or a medical facility. Ask questions about integrity in research, like the following:

**?**    What kind of research are you doing?

**?**    What is the purpose of your research?

**?**    What will your research add to our knowledge? Who or what will it help?

**?**    Who are your research subjects (people or animals)?

**?**    What procedures are you using?

**?**    If you're working with human subjects, what do you tell them about your research? Do they know exactly what's happening and why? Have you told them the purpose of your research?

**?**    Will you do any follow-up testing?

**EVALUATE THE INTEGRITY** of the U.S. government during World War II, when American soldiers were exposed to atomic radiation in the Pacific and in the American desert (Nevada and New Mexico). Find out 1) what the U.S. government told the soldiers, 2) whether the soldiers were informed about the health hazards of radiation exposure, 3) if the soldiers have experienced any health problems since then, 4) what the government has done to support or not support the soldiers. Form an opinion based on what you learn. Do you agree or disagree with the government's actions? Justify your opinion in a speech or report.

RESEARCH ATTEMPTS TO REGULATE INTEGRITY in government. *Examples:* The Ethics in Government Act (1978, 1983, 1985, amended 1990); the Public Officials Integrity Act (1978). Do you think it's possible to enforce the integrity of public officials? Why or why not? Debate this issue.

> *Variations:* Research one or more of the following: Watergate (1972–1974); Iran-Contra (1985–1990); Whitewater (1985–still under investigation as of this writing). What happened in each case? What issues of integrity did the investigations uncover?

## CHECK IT OUT

*What Was Watergate?* by Pamela Kilian (New York: St. Martins Press, 1990). Written especially for young adults and students, this book recounts the events of the Watergate scandal, which resulted in the resignation of President Richard M. Nixon. Ages 12–16.

**The Center for Public Integrity**
910 17th Street, NW, 7th Floor
Washington, DC 20006
(202) 466-1300
*www.publicintegrity.org*
Created in 1989, the Center for Public Integrity is a nonpartisan research organization that focuses on ethics and public services issues. It uncovers stories about political deception, scandal, fraud, and abuse and reports them to the public, helping people to understand the issues and hold public officials accountable. Founder and executive director Charles Lewis is a former investigative reporter and producer for "60 Minutes."

SURVEY YOUR CLASS OR SCHOOL to find out how important integrity is to the students. You can copy and use the survey on page 140 or write your own statements. Distribute the surveys and set up a collection box where people can return their completed surveys anonymously. Afterward, score the surveys and compile the results. Graph them and display the graph in your classroom or school. On your graph, you might want to compare males to females (does one gender seem to be more concerned about integrity than the other?) and/or different age groups or grades. Your graph should include information about how the surveys were scored. *How to score the surveys:* For statements 1, 3–6, and 9, give 1 point for each "No." For statements 2, 7, 8, and 10, give 1 point for each "Yes." *How to evaluate the scores:* 9–10 points: This is a person who values integrity. 8 points or fewer: This is a person who might want to reexamine what integrity means to him or her. (NOTE: You may disagree with this scoring scale. That's okay. The point of this survey is not to judge, but to get people thinking and talking about integrity. You might want to discuss the scale with your teacher and come up with a different version to use with your class or school.)

TALK TO YOUR FAMILY ABOUT INTEGRITY. Ask your parents, brothers, sisters, grandparents, aunts, uncles, etc. what they think integrity means. You might begin your discussion with one of the "Character Dilemmas" on pages 136–137. You might ask each person "In your opinion, who in our family has the *most* integrity? Why do you think this is true?"

> *Variation:* Ask each family member to choose an aspect of integrity that he or she wants to work on. Chart your progress individually or as a family.

CREATE AN INTEGRITY MOBILE. List some examples of what integrity means to you. Illustrate them and hang them from a mobile in your classroom, club, or room at home. *Example:* If you write "Integrity means standing up for your beliefs," you might illustrate a person standing and saying "I believe. . . ." Can you think of ways to illustrate integrity in dress, speech, action, patriotism, communication, teaching, medicine, politics, etc.?

WRITE A CHANT ABOUT INTEGRITY with your class or club. You might write it into your class goals or club charter. *Example:*

> What you say is what you do.
> Integrity is being true.
> In speech, in action, and in dress
> You do what's right and don't impress.

PLAY A "TOSS THE ARTICHOKE" GAME. This is a game of confusion, laughs—and discovery. You'll need a group of 5–10 people and 5–10 used tennis balls. Paint each tennis ball a different color. (You don't have to paint the whole thing. A big spot of color is sufficient.) Each color represents a different thing. *Examples:* Red = artichoke; green = hyena; orange = can of soda; blue = teddy bear. Make a list of what each color represents. When you're ready, have the players stand in a circle. To play:

1. The leader takes one ball and passes it to the person on his or her right, saying "This is an artichoke" (or whatever the ball stands for).

2. That person passes the same ball to the right, saying "This is an artichoke." The ball continues around the circle.

3. Meanwhile, the leader starts a second ball around the circle, saying "This is a hyena."

4. The leader continues introducing new balls into the circle until all 5–10 are circulating.

5. Without warning, the leader says "Reverse!" and the balls have to travel to the left.

Continue until the game completely falls apart. Afterward, talk about what happened. Ask questions like this:

**?** Is it hard to keep track of who you are if you look like everyone else?

**?** If you try to be something you really aren't, is it easy to lose your identity?

**?** If you call a ball an artichoke, does it become an artichoke?

**?** If you tell someone else that a ball is an artichoke, does that make it an artichoke?

**READ STORIES ABOUT INTEGRITY.** Look for these books:

*The Hero and the Crown* by Robin McKinley (New York: Greenwillow, 1984). The daughter of a witch sets out to win people's trust and to gain the Hero's Crown. On the way, she fights dragons, meets a wizard, and battles an evil mage. Ages 11–14.

*Nothing but the Truth: A Documentary Novel* by Avi (New York: Orchard, 1991). A ninth grader's suspension for singing "The Star Spangled Banner" during homeroom becomes a national news story. Ages 13–17.

*The Story of Ruby Bridges* by Robert Coles (New York: Scholastic, 1995). Six-year-old Ruby must confront the hostility of white parents when she becomes the first African-American girl in Frantz Elementary School in New Orleans in 1960. Ages 8–11.

*The Unbreakable Code* by Sara Hoagland Hunter (Flagstaff, AZ: Northland, 1996). John is afraid to leave the Navajo reservation until his grandfather explains how Navajo language, faith, and ingenuity helped to win World War II. Ages 9–12.

*The Well: David's Story* by Mildred T. Taylor (New York: Dial Books for Young Readers, 1995). In early 1900s Mississippi, David Logan's family shares their well water with white and black neighbors in an atmosphere of potential racial violence.

# Survey

*This is an anonymous survey. Don't write your name anywhere on it! Please drop your completed survey in the collection box in* _____.
location

|  | | Yes | No | Sometimes |
|---|---|:---:|:---:|:---:|
| **1.** | I wear certain types and styles of clothing to impress other people. | ❏ | ❏ | ❏ |
| **2.** | I tell the truth even if it means I'll get into trouble. | ❏ | ❏ | ❏ |
| **3.** | The language I use (polite or crude, respectful or obscene) changes depending on who I'm with. | ❏ | ❏ | ❏ |
| **4.** | I exaggerate to impress other people. | ❏ | ❏ | ❏ |
| **5.** | I use sarcastic humor to put other people in their place. | ❏ | ❏ | ❏ |
| **6.** | I give in to peer pressure. | ❏ | ❏ | ❏ |
| **7.** | I maintain the same standards with everyone I know—friends, family, teachers, neighbors, etc. | ❏ | ❏ | ❏ |
| **8.** | I come home when I say I'm going to. If I can't be there on time, I call ahead to report the reason. | ❏ | ❏ | ❏ |
| **9.** | I sneak into games or concerts to avoid paying. | ❏ | ❏ | ❏ |
| **10.** | I'm the kind of person my parents and friends think I am. | ❏ | ❏ | ❏ |

*Please be sure to complete this information:*

You are a          ❏ male          ❏ female

What grade are you in?          _____

How old are you?          _____

## THANK YOU for taking this survey!

# Character in *ACTION*

## Winfred Rembert Jr.: Integrity in the Face of Danger

When eleven-year-old Winfred Rembert Jr. first moved with his family to New Haven, Connecticut, neighborhood gang members tried to get him to sell drugs. "It wasn't like they asked anyone. It was like a telling," Winfred remembers. He ignored them and walked away. Gang members continued to harass him, one time stealing his new basketball. Winfred refused to fight.

When he was 15, gang members tried to lure him into drug dealing in the school cafeteria. They promised him fast money. "They were throwing money down on the cafeteria table, you know, trying to bribe me," he explains. But Winfred ignored them again and went about his business of growing up. He grew *way* up—to 6 feet 3 inches by the time he was 16 and a basketball player for Hillhouse High School. And he still refused to sell drugs or to join the gang.

One evening, Winfred was in his backyard when a parking lot attendant tore across the street to tell him his family was in a gang fight. His 14-year-old brother Edgar didn't like drugs either, and the gang had roughed him up and damaged his bicycle.

Winfred dropped his basketball and charged up the block. In the distance he could see his mom, dad, and brother trying to fight off the gang. As Edgar fought back, a kid Winfred had known at school for three years pulled a gun and aimed it at Edgar. His mother was standing right by Edgar's side.

Winfred pumped his legs like pistons, leaped through the air, and shoved Edgar, knocking him out of the line of fire. Then he threw his body across his mother just as the gun discharged. Winfred clutched his stomach and fell backward, taking the bullet meant for his brother.

While Winfred was lying in the hospital, a news reporter asked him if he regretted having sacrificed himself for his brother and mother. Although Winfred swallowed hard, he shook his head. When another reporter asked him why he thought the gang member had shot him, Winfred replied "I think he shot me to make a point to the neighborhood that you can't say no to them. They never before had anyone stand up to them and actually say no."

The gang member was arrested on a first-degree assault charge. Winfred had two operations. The bullet was extracted and he recovered. He still sometimes wakes up in the night with a fleeting pain in his abdomen.

Winfred's integrity didn't go unnoticed. Albertus Magnus College, a private liberal arts college in New Haven, offered him a full scholarship for standing up for his beliefs. He accepted and chose to study sociology with an emphasis on criminal justice.

Winfred knows exactly why he refused to join a gang or sell drugs. "I want a better life," he insists. "I was doing something I believe in, and that's why I wasn't afraid. You've just got to do what you think is right."

Winfred Rembert Jr.

# Justice

**Fairness, equality, tolerance**

## Justice

**Y**ou're driving down a city street where the posted speed limit is 35 miles per hour, but you're doing 50. You're stopped by the police and given a speeding ticket. Is this justice?

What if you were doing 50 because you're late for work? You explain this to the officer, but she gives you a ticket anyway—and advises you to get up earlier tomorrow so you won't have to speed. Is this justice? Would it be justice if the officer decided *not* to give you a ticket because you had a "good reason" to speed?

"I'm positive I wasn't driving too fast. Are you sure your radar is accurate?"

And what if were doing 35 and you got stopped anyway? When you ask the officer why she stopped you, she explains that a robbery just happened nearby. The robbery was committed by a young black man. You're a young black man, and the street you're driving down is in a predominantly white neighborhood. Is this justice? What do you think?

Here's how *Merriam Webster's Collegiate Dictionary*[1] defines justice:

1  **a:** the maintenance or administration of what is just esp. by the impartial adjustment of conflicting claims or the assignment of merited rewards or punishments
   **b:** JUDGE
   **c:** the administration of law; *esp:* the establishment or determination of rights according to the rules of law or equity
2  **a:** the quality of being just, impartial, or fair
   **b:** (1): the principle or ideal of just dealing or right action
   (2): conformity to this principle or ideal: RIGHTEOUSNESS
   **c:** the quality of conforming to law
3:  conformity to truth, fact, or reason: CORRECTNESS

"What is just" means what is reasonable, proper, righteous, deserved, and lawful. "Impartial" means treating and affecting everyone equally, without bias. Getting a speeding ticket for going 15 miles over the limit is justice, even if you had a good reason. Getting stopped because you're a black man in a white neighborhood is not justice.

---

[1] *Merriam Webster's Collegiate Dictionary,* Tenth Edition (Springfield, MA: 1993).

Think about all the ways the word "justice" is used. The United States Pledge of Allegiance ends with the words ". . . with liberty and justice for all." Superman fights for "Truth, Justice, and the American Way." So do the members of the Justice League of America, to name other comic book characters. We have a criminal justice system to deal with people who commit crimes, and a juvenile justice system for those who aren't yet adults. A person who "flees justice" runs from the law; if he's caught, he's "brought to justice." In the days of the Wild West, "frontier justice" often meant taking the law into your own hands. If you're given a task, assignment, or job and you "do it justice," you're giving it a good effort. "Social justice" calls for the fair distribution of goods. If we lived and practiced social justice, all children would have a safe place to live, clothing to wear, food to eat, and adequate medical care.

The legendary U.S. defense attorney Clarence Darrow once said "There is no such thing as justice—in or out of court." What do you think he meant by that? Do you agree?

> "Justice cannot be for one side alone,
> but must be for both."
> *Eleanor Roosevelt*

---

## CHECK IT OUT

*What Are My Rights? 95 Questions and Answers About Teens and the Law* by Thomas A. Jacobs, J.D. (Minneapolis: Free Spirit Publishing, 1997). Covers laws related to the family, school, workplace, growing up, and more that pertain specifically to teens. Ages 12 & up.

---

# Fairness

> "Fairness is what justice really is."
> *Potter Stewart*

You probably learned about fairness long before you heard the word justice. As a child, you were taught to "play fair," "be fair," and "act fair." This usually meant taking turns, sharing, and waiting your turn in line. When someone wouldn't take turns, refused to share, or cut into the line, you hollered to your parent or teacher "So-and-so isn't being FAAAAAAIIIIIIIRRRRRRR!"

When you're fair, you're impartial and honest. You make decisions free from bias, prejudice, favoritism, or self-interest ("what's in it for ME?"). You follow the established rules, and you don't cheat. Your family, friends, and teachers know that they can trust you and count on you. When you announce that you're throwing a pizza party for everyone in your class, you really do invite *everyone*—even the kid who steals your lunch and calls you names. People who have a sense of fairness make good leaders and mediators.

# Equality

> "As long as you keep a person down, some
> part of you has to be down there, to hold
> him down, so it means you cannot soar
> as you otherwise might."
> *Marian Anderson*

If your parents give you and your brother the same opportunities to go to school, take guitar lessons, and do the dishes, you might say that they're treating you as equals. Does this mean that you *are* equals? What if your brother is older than you are? What if you're older than he is? What if he does better in school than you do? What if you do better in school than he does? What if you're both boys? What if you're a girl? And what does equality really mean?

Most people struggle with this concept at one time or another. It's complicated, and there are no easy answers. To some people, equality means treating everyone the same. But everyone *isn't* the same, so this doesn't always work and can create big problems. Take school, for example. In a class of 30 students, some will be gifted, some will be "average" (another tricky word!), and some will have learning differences and need special help with things that average students learn more easily and gifted students might already know. What if the teacher treats everyone exactly the same? The average students might be okay with this, but the gifted kids and those who struggle to learn probably *won't* be okay.

The Declaration of Independence says that "all men are created equal." Does this mean that women aren't created equal? Is that what the signers meant to say, or was the word "men" supposed to include women, too? If it was, why did women have to fight for the right to vote, and why did it take until 1920 (and a constitutional amendment) before they were given that right? Does "all men" include men (people?) of all races and cultural backgrounds? If so, why do we need affirmative action . . . or do we?

> "Men their rights and nothing more;
> women their rights and nothing less."
> *Susan B. Anthony and Elizabeth Cady Stanton*

You might have asked yourself questions like these. Or you might have talked about equality with your family, friends, classmates, and teachers. Keep asking, talking, and thinking about equality, because it's important to do so. What you feel and believe about equality will determine how you treat other people throughout your life—and how you expect them to treat you. Continue gathering information and opinions, then form your own conclusions about equality. You might start with these basic ideas:

▲ Equality isn't about sameness. It's about access, rights, and opportunity.

▲ Every person is unique, and all people should be able to reach their full potential without encountering artificial barriers of gender, race, religion, class, or cultural background.

▲ Hatred, harassment, discrimination, and prejudice have no place in a society that promotes equality.

## CHECK IT OUT

Three organizations that fight for equality and fairness are:

**Anti-Defamation League (ADL)**
823 United Nations Plaza
New York, NY 10017
(212) 490-2525
*www.adl.org*

**National Association for the Advancement of Colored People (NAACP)**
4805 Mt. Hope Drive
Baltimore, MD 21215
1-877-622-2798
*www.naacp.org*

**National Organization for Women (NOW)**
PO Box 96824
Washington, DC 20036
(202) 628-8669
*www.now.org*

# Tolerance

> "Every bigot was once a child
> free of prejudice."
> *Sister Mary de Lourdes*

You've probably heard the word "tolerance" often over the past few years—at school, in your faith community, and at home. We all need to learn to be more tolerant of others, regardless of whether their "differences" are due to race, cultural background, gender, age, intelligence, physical capabilities, or any other reason.

When you're tolerant, you have sympathy for beliefs or practices that are different from your own. You may not share or even agree with them, but you recognize their right to exist. You don't let prejudice and bigotry determine who your friends will be. You treat people with respect no matter who they are.

Why should you be more tolerant? Here are four great reasons:

**1. The more tolerant you are, the more open you are to learning about other people.** Have you ever had a preconceived notion about a person or group, then found out you were wrong once you got to know them? What if you hadn't gotten to know them? You'd still be stuck in your old ways of thinking. When you're not learning, your brain becomes stale.

**2. *The more you learn, the less you fear.*** Remember when you were sure there were monsters under your bed? Or how afraid you were the first time you went swimming and put your face in the water? Then you looked under the bed or dunked your face in the water a few more times and suddenly you weren't afraid anymore. Unlearning prejudices works the same way. Once you learn that you have nothing to fear, you become willing to try more new things, ideas, and relationships. As you practice tolerance and become more comfortable with other people's differences, curiosity replaces fear. Your mind opens. You start respecting other people's opinions, practices, behaviors, and beliefs. You gain a deeper understanding of yourself and others. It's easy to hate a stereotype, hard to hate a friend.

**3. *The less you fear, the more comfortable you feel around all kinds of people.*** Wouldn't you like to feel safer and more secure anytime, anywhere? Studies have shown that people who get along with different kinds of people are emotionally and physically healthier—and more successful in their careers—than those who don't.

**4. *The more people you know (especially different kinds of people), the more interesting your life becomes.*** What if you were allowed to read books by only one author? If you had to wear blue jeans, a white T-shirt, and black sneakers every day? What if you were never permitted to try anything new, not even a new soft drink or computer game? What if all of your friends looked, thought, and behaved exactly alike? What if they all had to be the same age, religion, gender, and race?

How can you learn to be more tolerant of others? Here's how:

**1. *Be willing to meet new people.*** Don't ever judge a whole group of people by one person's actions.

That's poor deductive reasoning, and it leads to prejudice and discrimination.

**2. *Be willing to listen and learn.*** Ask people to tell you about their backgrounds, beliefs, and traditions. Sometimes this can challenge your own ways of thinking and make you reexamine your own ideas. It can also open the door to new friendships and experiences.

**3. *As you're learning about differences, look for similarities.*** You probably have more in common than you know.

> "If four-fifths of the world's population consists of people of color, why are they still called 'minorities'?"
> *Lynn Duvall*

## CHECK IT OUT

*Respecting Our Differences: A Guide to Getting Along in a Changing World* by Lynn Duvall (Minneapolis: Free Spirit Publishing, 1994). Real-life examples, activities, and resources encourage readers to become more tolerant of others and savor the rich diversity of America's changing culture. Ages 13 & up.

**Teaching Tolerance**
400 Washington Avenue
Montgomery, AL 36104
(334) 264-0286
*www.splcenter.org/teachingtolerance/tt-index.html*
A national education project dedicated to helping teachers foster equity, respect, and understanding in the classroom and beyond. *Teaching Tolerance* magazine is available free to teachers.

# Character Dilemmas

*For journaling or writing essays, discussion, debate, role-playing, reflection*

**Suppose that . . .**

**1** In Florida in 1993, a young boy named Gregory Kingsley tried to sue his mother for divorce. He wanted to be adopted by a family that had been caring for him. The Circuit Court ruled that Gregory had the right to do this. His mother took the case to the District Court of Appeals (a higher court), which overruled the lower court and said that Gregory did *not* have this right. What do you think? Should children have the legal right to divorce their parents? Should they have the right to choose which parent to live with when parents divorce? What should the parents' rights be?

**2** There are two different ethnic groups in your school. They don't like each other and are constantly arguing, pushing each other around, and even fighting. One day, a new student arrives, and soon you start to think that you'd like to have him for a friend. The problem is, you're in one group and he's in the other. What should you do? What might be the consequences of your actions? Could you accept the consequences?

**3** A college has a limited number of scholarships to award. How should it decide which students should receive the scholarships? Should the decisions be based on 1) financial need (which would help students from low-income families), 2) affirmative action (which would help women students and those from minority groups), or 3) merit (which would help students who have earned good grades and high test scores in high school)?

**4** You know that one of your neighbors doesn't pay her income taxes. Instead, she reports her earnings in a way that takes illegal advantage of tax shelters. Do you think that people should have the right to decide whether or not to pay taxes? Who should decide how much they must pay? What, if anything, might you do about your neighbor?

**5** A student in your class at school has been very ill this year. You learn that he needs a heart transplant; in fact, if he doesn't have one soon, he'll probably die. His parents belong to a religion that doesn't allow heart transplants, and they refuse to let your friend have the surgery. Do parents have the right to decide whether their children get medical help? Do they have the right to decide what kinds of medical help their children can have? Explain your answer—but first, try to see both sides of this dilemma.

**6** You're an employer, and you're looking for someone to fill a job. Your favorite applicant is a man. But because of affirmative action, you have to hire a woman. What are the pros and cons of affirmative action? What do you think is the best thing to do in your situation?

# Activities

GUESS THE PUNISHMENT OR CONSEQUENCE for each of the following crimes or infractions. Try to be just and fair. If you do this activity with your class or club, you might brainstorm punishments and consequences as a group. Afterward, invite a law student or an attorney to visit your class or club. Share your guesses, then ask for a legal point of view.

- During a locker search of your school, two cans of beer are discovered in a student's locker.

- The governor of your state accepts a bribe from a lobbying group.

- Your best friend borrows his parents' car without their permission, and the two of you go to a movie.

- Your older sister "borrows" money from your dresser without permission.

- The school secretary dips into the school lunch money to buy food for her family.

- A high-ranking officer in the military sells government secrets to another country.

- A drunk driver hits a child, causing minor injuries, and drives away.

- The owner of a small, struggling business doesn't report all of his earnings on his income tax return.

- One of your neighbors grows marijuana in her basement.

- Gang members graffiti your school.

- A student at your school has a handgun in the glove compartment in her car. She says it's so she'll feel safe.

- One of the clubs at your school refuses to let a new student join. You overhear the president say that it's because the new student is of a different race.

**LEARN ABOUT FAIRNESS AND EQUITY LAWS.** Research one or more of the following, then report your findings to your class or club. You might do this orally, in writing, or creatively (make a bulletin board or poster, have a debate, create a comic book, perform a skit, etc.).

⚖ The Civil Rights Act of 1964 (Public Law 88-352) prohibits race-based discrimination in public places including hotels, restaurants, and buses.

⚖ The Civil Rights Act of 1965 (Public Law 89-110) makes it illegal to use literacy tests and other unfair practices to prevent citizens from voting.

⚖ Title VII of the Civil Rights Act of 1964 protects people against sexual harassment, including unwelcome sexual advances, contact, or conditions of employment.

⚖ Title IX of the Educational Amendments of 1972 bans discrimination on the basis of sex. It applies to any educational program that receives federal funds, including school athletic programs.

⚖ The Civil Rights Act of 1964, the Rehabilitation Act of 1973, and the Americans with Disabilities Act of 1990 provide equal opportunities for persons with disabilities. Under these laws, schools that receive federal funds must provide accessible facilities for *all* of their students.

⚖ The Equal Rights Amendment (ERA) states that "Equality of Rights under the law shall not be denied or abridged by the United States or any state on account of sex." Written in 1921 by suffragist Alice Paul, the ERA has been introduced in Congress every session since 1923 but has never been ratified by the 38 states needed to make it a law. Find out why. Do *you* think it should be ratified? Why or why not?

## CHECK IT OUT

*Guide to American Law: Everyone's Legal Encyclopedia* (St. Paul, MN: West Publishing Company, 1983, supplemented annually). If you enjoy reading about landmark laws, look for this 12-volume set and its supplements at your library reference desk or local law library. It's written in language that even non-lawyers can understand.

**HOLD A MOCK TRIAL** of a fairy tale character. *Example:* Put Goldilocks on trial for breaking and entering, or the Wolf for destroying the Three Little Pigs' property. Make sure that your trial is just and fair. Write the history of the case. Assign people to play various roles: judge, defendant, prosecuting attorney, defending attorney, witnesses, experts, bailiffs, clerks, jurors. Allow time afterward for discussion and analysis.

**FIND OUT IF THERE'S A TEEN COURT,** Youth Court, or Student Court in your state, county, or community. If there isn't, contact your principal, mayor, state representative, or governor and ask that one (or more) be established. Teen courts are becoming increasingly popular alternatives to juvenile court for first-time offenders ages 16 and under including kids caught drinking, using drugs, or exhibiting other problem behaviors. The jurors, attorneys, bailiffs, and clerks are all teens; the judge is usually, but not always, an adult. The teen jurors decide on the punishment, which usually involves service, educational classes, and future jury service on the court rather than the traditional fines and sentences. When the defendant completes the sentence, the misdemeanor charge is usually dropped from his or her record. Since most teens must wait until age 19 to have their teen crimes erased, many young offenders are choosing to be tried in teen courts instead of regular courts.

## CHECK IT OUT

**American Bar Association**
Division for Public Education
541 North Fairbanks Court
Chicago, IL 60611-3314
1-800-285-2221
*www.abanet.org*
The ABA has materials available to help teachers hold lively mock trials in the classroom. It also offers a free packet of information about teen/youth/student courts, including a national directory of existing courts.

**Center for Civic Education**
5146 Douglas Fir Road
Calabasas, CA 91302-1467
(818) 591-9321
*www.civiced.org*
The Center for Civic Education wrote the national standards for civics and government education (available on their Web site), as well as CIVITAS and other educational materials concerning concepts, principles, and values of democracy for K–12.

**Constitutional Rights Foundation**
601 South Kingsley Drive
Los Angeles, CA 90005
(213) 487-5590
*www.crf-usa.org*
The Constitutional Rights Foundation provides educational materials and sends out an excellent newsletter that includes discussions about law-related topics.

---

**MAKE A TIMELINE ABOUT PRAYER IN SCHOOLS.** In 1962, the U.S. Supreme Court ruled in *Engel v. Vitale* that a school district can't compel students to pray in schools. Since then, there have been many lawsuits involving prayer in schools. Research several and show them on a timeline. TIP: See the *Guide to American Law* (page 147).

> *Variation:* Debate both sides of this issue. Consider these questions: 1) Should students be *allowed* to pray in school? 2) Should they be *encouraged* to pray in school? 3) Should they be *prevented* from praying in school? 4) Who has the right to decide?

> "As long as there are tests, there will always be prayer in schools."
> *Anonymous*

**LEARN ABOUT THE INTERNET** and free speech. Research one or more current "hot topics." *Examples:* Should certain types of information be censored? What if Person A posts instructions for how to build a bomb and Person B finds them, uses them to make a bomb, and kills a dozen people? Should Person A be held accountable for the bombing? Should scientific information be screened before it's made public? Should people be allowed to slander each other? Should people be fined or punished for using bad language? For posting or accessing pornography? Learn as much as you can about your issue and write an essay that considers both sides.

*Variation:* Research the history of the Telecommunications Act of 1996 and/or the Communications Decency Act (CDA) of 1966.

---

## CHECK IT OUT

**The Electronic Frontier Foundation**
*www.eff.org*
A nonprofit civil liberties organization working to protect privacy, free expression, and access to public resources and information online, as well as to promote responsibility in new media.

**National Coalition Against Censorship**
*www.ncac.org*
An alliance of 50 national nonprofit organizations, they work to educate the public about the dangers of censorship. Also provides many links.

---

**WRITE IN YOUR JOURNAL**[2] about how it feels to be treated unfairly. Think about a time when it happened to you. Maybe you were accused of something you didn't do. Maybe a parent or teacher didn't believe you when you told the truth. As you write, consider these questions:

1. How did you feel then?

2. How do you feel now?

3. What might you do to prevent that from happening again?

4. Is there anything you can do to clear the air between you and the person who treated you unfairly? Can you talk with him or her? Or is it too late?

5. Do you need to apologize for anything?

6. Do you need to replace or fix anything?

7. Have you tried forgiving the person who treated you unfairly?[3]

8. What have you learned from the experience?

**IMAGINE THAT YOU'RE A PARENT** with four children. You have $25 a week to hand out in allowances. Your children are 1) a 15-year-old boy, 2) a 12-year-old girl, 3) an 8-year-old boy, and 4) a 5-year-old boy.

---

[2] See "Endurance," pages 88, 89, and 92, for journaling resources.
[3] See "Forgiveness," pages 94–102.

What percentage of the $25 will each child get? How will you determine this in a way that's fair to everyone? Will the amount stay the same each week? Why or why not?

**CREATE A FAMILY FAIRNESS CHART.** Who does what around your house? Do some people do all or most of the chores? Is there a way to divide up the work that's fair to everyone? Make a chart listing all of the different jobs that need to be done, from feeding the cat to washing the dishes, taking out the trash to mopping the floors. Hold a family meeting to discuss your chart. See if your family members will agree to sign up for jobs.

**CONSIDER THE PROS AND CONS** of coed team sports. Should team sports include boys/men and girls/women on the same teams, or should players be separated by gender into different teams or leagues?[4] Does it make a difference which type of league or competition is involved? Think about college vs. high school, middle school, or elementary school; community vs. national leagues; football vs. basketball, soccer, tennis, swimming, or other sports you can think of. Break up into small groups and discuss this issue. Be sure to consider all sides. Then choose a spokesperson and share your conclusions with your class, club, or friends.

> *Variation:* Is this an issue in your school or community? If it is, write a letter to the people who organize athletic competitions and teams and express your views. Or pass a petition, collecting names of those who agree (or disagree) that teams should be coeducational. Present your petition to those who have the power to make the decision.

**RESEARCH CURRENT ANNUAL SALARIES** for people in various professions. You might include professional athletes, corporate executives, teachers, electricians, librarians, plumbers, physicians, dentists, engineers, computer programmers, construction workers, etc. For athletes and executives, be sure to include money earned from other sources (endorsements, bonuses, stock options, etc.). Once you've gathered your information, make a graph that compares the salaries. Do they seem fair to you? Why or why not? Draw your conclusions and

report them to your class. TIP: In 1996, boxer Mike Tyson fought three times and earned $75 *million* in purses. NBA star Michael Jordan earned $52.6 million—$12.6 million from basketball and $40 million from other sources.

**PRETEND THAT YOU'RE IN CHARGE** of deciding the order in which patients receive heart transplants. There are five patients who need immediate transplants: 1) a heart specialist who has already saved hundreds of lives, 2) a four-year-old child, 3) a convict at a local prison, 4) a talented pianist, and 5) a mother of four children. Who will receive the first transplant? The second? The third? How will you decide? Create a list of requirements (in order of importance) for persons receiving heart transplants. Make your list as fair and just as possible. Share and discuss your list with classmates, friends, and family members.

**PLAY A RELAY GAME.** This game is an object lesson in fairness, but no one should know that but you (and anyone who helps you to organize it). The players should think that they're simply going to play a game, with no advance warning of what's *really* about to happen.

**1.** Divide the group into two teams—boys and girls. (Or you might divide them into groups by hair color, eye color, who's wearing brown or green, or any other criterion you choose.) It doesn't matter if the teams have equal numbers of players.

**2.** Have the teams stand in two lines behind a starting line. Mark off another line several yards away.

**3.** To play, team members take off their shoes, run to the marked-off line, and return. Before the next person on the team can start running, the first person must put his or her shoes back on—ties, clips, and all. Then the first person goes to the back of the line and the relay continues.

**4.** After 2–3 people from each team have finished their runs, stop the game and announce a change in the rules. *Example:* "Since there are more girls than boys, and since girls' shoes are usually harder to take off and put back on, we're going to give the girls an extra advantage. They can run to the line and back, but the boys have to walk." Or

---

[4] See "Imagination," pages 133–134, for a true story on this topic.

you might shorten the relay distance for one team, make it okay for one team to start running before their team member finishes putting on his or her shoes, or whatever you choose. The point is to deliberately create an unfair situation. If some people start complaining, ignore them or tell them to stop.

Continue the relay, changing the rules once or twice more. Stop when almost *everyone* is complaining that the rules "aren't fair." Afterward, talk about what happened. Ask questions like these:

**?**   How did it feel to play this game?

**?**   What was it like to be on the team that received special privileges? What was it like to be on the other team?

**?**   Does it make a difference if the rules of a game are fair for everyone? Why or why not?

**?**   Does it make a difference if the rules aren't fair for some people? Why or why not?

**BRAINSTORM LISTS OF WAYS** in which people are and aren't equal. Brainstorm ways in which you, your class, your family, and/or your community can help people to be more tolerant of differences.

**LEARN ABOUT HUMAN RIGHTS.** According to the preamble of the United Nations' Universal Declaration of Human Rights, "recognition of the inherent dignity and of the equal and inalienable rights of all members of the human family is the foundation of freedom, justice and peace in the world." You might choose to research a particular human rights document or declaration, or you might look into the status of human rights in a particular country or part of the world. You might gather information from one or more human rights organizations—and you might decide to join one and do your part to promote human rights. Come up with a creative way to report your findings to your class, school, family, community, or club.

## CHECK IT OUT

*Contemporary Human Rights Activists* by Eileen Lucas (New York: Facts On File, 1997). Meet men and women around the world who are working on human rights and civil rights issues. Ages 12–16.

**Human Rights Watch**
485 Fifth Avenue
New York, NY 10017-6104
(212) 972-8400
*www.hrw.org*
This coalition of human rights groups attracts some of the best researchers in the field.

**Human Rights Web**
*www.hrweb.org*
Extensive up-to-date information about human rights, an online primer for new human rights activists, and links to human rights organizations.

**University of Minnesota Human Rights Library**
*www.umn.edu/humanrts*
The Universal Declaration of Human Rights, Declaration of the Rights of the Child, and many more, plus links to other human rights sites.

---

**SURVEY YOUR SCHOOL** to find out how tolerant students feel it is. You can copy and use the Tolerance Survey on page 152 or write your own questions. Distribute the surveys and set up a collection box where people can return their completed surveys anonymously. Afterward, compile the results and write an article for your school newspaper, or announce the results over your school PA system. Work with your school's administration to make a plan for carrying out the suggestions for improving tolerance. IMPORTANT: Use your survey to bring people together, not to further divide them into groups.

**START A MULTICULTURAL CLUB** at your school.[5] Post flyers announcing the club, and/or advertise it over your school PA system, in your school newspaper, on community bulletin boards, or on the radio. Your goal should be to bring together people from different cultures to share fun and activities. Find a supportive adult to act as your sponsor, decide on a time and place to meet, then let the club members

---

[5] See "Leadership," pages 160–161, for tips on how to start a club.

choose their own activities (biking, skiing, jogging, swimming, service, etc.).

**HOLD A CULTURAL APPRECIATION WEEK** at your school or in your community. Schedule various activities throughout the week that spotlight and celebrate cultural differences.[6] (Or schedule the activities at any time throughout the year.) *Examples:*

✳ Have a multicultural fashion show, talent show, music festival, and/or food festival.

✳ Display multicultural books and crafts.

✳ Make a bulletin board or a series of posters that reveal the richness of different ethnic groups. Include clothing, art, music, inventions, etc.

✳ Invite ethnic leaders from the community to speak.

✳ Organize ethnic dances.

✳ Invite people from different cultural groups to sing for an assembly. Have them teach songs to the group so everyone can sing along.

✳ Show films from various countries and cultures around the world.

✳ Hold a forum or panel discussion for members of various cultural groups to discuss problems, similarities, and opportunities.

✳ Research and provide scholarship information for members of various ethnic groups.

**MAKE NEW FRIENDS.** Seek out and talk with people from various ethnic and cultural backgrounds. Sit with someone new at lunch. Invite someone to go with you to a movie or other activity.

**READ STORIES ABOUT JUSTICE,** fairness, equality, and tolerance. Look for these books:

📖 *Gemini Game* by Michael Scott (New York: Holiday House, 1994). Liz and BJ O'Connor, teenage owners of a computer game company, find themselves in serious trouble after players of their virtual reality computer game fall into a coma. Their only hope is to flee from the police, locate a copy of their game, and correct the programming. Ages 12–16.

📖 *The Hate Crime* by Phyllis Karas (New York: Avon Flare Books, 1995). For high-school sophomore Zack, being Jewish has never been a big deal—until someone paints anti-Semitic graffiti on the Temple Israel. Ages 13 & up.

📖 *The House of Dies Drear* by Virginia Hamilton (New York: Macmillan, 1968). A story about the secrets walled within an old house reaches back to the days of slavery and the underground railroad. Ages 10–14.

📖 *The War with Grandpa* by Robert Kimmel Smith (New York: Dell, 1984). Upset that he's forced to give up his room when his grandfather moves in, Pete decides to declare war to get it back. Ages 9–13.

📖 *The Well: David's Story* by Mildred Taylor (New York: Dial, 1995). In the early 1900s, David's rural Mississippi family shares their well water with black and white neighbors. Ages 8–12.

---

[6] See "Empathy," page 83, for multicultural resources.

# Tolerance Survey

*This is an anonymous survey. Don't write your name anywhere on it! Please drop your completed survey in the collection box in* _____.
                                                                              location

                                                              **Yes**   **No**

1. Do you think the students in our school are tolerant?    ❑    ❑

2. Do you think the teachers are tolerant?    ❑    ❑

3. Do you think the administration and staff (principal,    ❑    ❑
   secretaries, custodians, cafeteria workers, etc.)
   are tolerant?

4. Have you personally experienced intolerance? If so, describe your experience.
   (Please DON'T name names.)

   _____

   _____

   _____

5. In your opinion, what are the worst tolerance problems at our school?

   _____

   _____

   _____

6. What would you do to improve tolerance at our school?

   _____

   _____

   _____

*Please be sure to complete this information:*

You are a                   ❑ male        ❑ female

What grade are you in?       _____

How old are you?       _____

What is your race or
ethnic/cultural background?    _____

## THANK YOU for taking this survey!

# Character in *ACTION*

## Shagufta Bhatti: Teaching Tolerance

When Shagufta Bhatti was in elementary school, the other students stared at her colorful *shalwar kameez*—the ethnic clothing she wore. They asked her about her long, loose pants and shirt that billowed down to her knees. "They look like pajamas," kids said. "Why do you wear them? Aren't you hot, especially in summer?"

Shagufta told her parents "I can't concentrate on school. There are too many questions about my clothes." So her parents, devout Muslims, agreed that she could wear "regular clothes" to school if she wore her ethnic clothing at home and at other times when she was out in public. Shagufta was relieved.

In junior high school, she felt the stab of prejudice when students associated her with terrorism and torture because of her ethnic background. Except for her best friends, who always stood by her, many kids looked at her with mistrustful faces, eyes wide with suspicion.

Then Shagufta's social studies teacher stopped her one day in the hall and asked her if she wanted to join the Council for Unity (CFU), a multicultural club that promotes diversity education and violence prevention. Founded in 1975 by New York City high school teacher Robert DePena following a racially motivated killing, CFU has spread to many high schools and middle schools.

It sounded good to Shagufta. It was just what she needed, even though the thought of opening up to others scared her. She was shy, partly because she respected the Muslim tradition that encouraged women to be obedient, modest, and quiet.

Shagufta and other members of the group organized and hosted an ethnic fair where African, Asian, Jewish, Latino, Caribbean, Muslim, and Russian cultures shared tasty ethnic foods. "I helped make banners, posters, and we had activities which taught the 1,200 high school students about different cultures," Shagufta explains. "Then we had an ethnic fashion

Shagufta Bhatti (seated, front left) wearing her *shalwar kameez*

show. I was afraid at first, afraid of looking silly. I didn't want to model my ethnic clothing, but we all did it. We used it to educate the junior high students. People liked it. I was surprised."

In high school, Shagufta became a member of the CFU executive board. She and her friends planned a Jewish Passover Seder around the holiday season. They collected, wrapped, and delivered toys to over 1,700 disadvantaged kids at Christmas. They collected money for charities, shopped for seniors, and got involved in cultural awareness programs.

One of the activities Shagufta liked best was Group Dynamics. A multicultural group of kids sat in a classroom in a circle, facing one another. They talked about problems and discussed ways to change their behaviors. They gained each other's trust and understanding and learned how to support each other. Shagufta developed skills as a mediator and helped other students to settle disputes before they blew up.

Gradually Shagufta overcame some of her shyness and learned how to approach people, communicate better, and express her feelings. She shared her traditions of fasting during Ramadan, the ninth month of the Muslim calendar; of praying privately while facing Mecca; of not eating pork or drinking alcohol; of arranged marriages. Her culturally different friends nodded their heads in understanding because they, too, had unique customs that other people understood and respected.

"We are a melting pot," Shagufta now believes. "We came together from diverse lands to form a new, colorful nation. We should judge people by character, not by color."

## Setting a good example, leading others, being a good follower

# Leadership

Two fourteen-year-olds saved a busload of school kids on one hot, sticky afternoon in Fayetteville, North Carolina. When the driver suffered a heart attack and the bus careened down a busy highway, sheared a utility pole with sparks flying, and headed toward the trees, Carl Boney and Michael Etowski stumbled to the front of the bus and took charge. Carl forced his body between the driver and the steering wheel and steered the bus away from the trees and back into the rushing traffic. He could barely reach the brake with his toe. But the driver's foot was pressed heavily against the gas pedal, and every time Carl let up the pressure on the brake, the bus lunged forward again. Meanwhile, Mike grabbed the keys and turned them. The engine sputtered and died.

Neither Carl nor Mike had a driver's license. They didn't have the knowledge or skill to drive a bus. And they didn't have time to think of all the reasons why they *couldn't* do it. They just did it, and because they took charge, 36 kids on the bus were saved from injuries or death.

Leaders are people who see a problem and fix it, even if they don't always know how. They step forward, sometimes in an emergency, and do what needs to be done. They get others to help them. Being a leader takes courage and confidence.

There are many different kinds of leadership. They include:

- *Leadership of the moment.* You take charge in a crisis, like Carl and Mike did.

- *Leadership by example.* You set a good example in your family, with your friends, or anywhere else. This is a wonderful type of leadership, because you become the ruler or yardstick by which other people measure themselves. You're an inspiration.

- *Community leadership.* You become president of the chess club, captain of the hockey team, a scout leader, a deacon in your church, chair of the community council, a senator, a lieutenant in the military, vice president of your school, and so on.

- *Job leadership.* You direct others, organizing their work and activities.

- *Trail-blazing leadership.* You walk into unexplored territory and create a path for others to follow. You invent a new mousetrap, set a new record for the high jump, discover a vaccine against cancer, or start a new business.

If you're a leader, then someone or something is following you, because to lead means to go out in the front of others. History is full of leaders—from dictators like Adolf Hitler, who forced people to follow him and slaughtered those who didn't, to Albert Schweitzer, who led by example and service. Mohandas Gandhi, Eleanor Roosevelt, Attila the Hun, Shakespeare, Buddha, Jesus, Marie Curie, and probably your next-door neighbor have all been leaders.

> "Leadership is action, not position."
> *Donald H. McGannon*

The best leaders are those who care about other people, have integrity, and love to serve.[1]

## 12 Character Traits of Good Leaders

**1.  They serve others.** Among the greatest leaders are those who serve the people. They care about others and work to help them. Or they care about animals, the environment, or other important issues.

**2.  They develop leadership in others.** They trust and believe in the people who follow them. They share. They delegate. They give credit to others for their ideas and contributions, rather than hogging all the glory for themselves.

**3.  They listen to others and communicate well.** They accept advice and criticism without exploding or wilting.

**4.  They are good planners and decision makers.** They work with their followers to set and achieve goals.

**5.  They inspire others** to walk farther than they think they can, to be better than they ever imagined they could be.

**6.  They learn and grow.** They are constantly learning better ways to do their jobs.

**7.  They have positive attitudes.** They are usually or often cheerful, enthusiastic, hopeful, alert, energetic, and resilient.

**8.  They have integrity.** They are true to what they say. They set a good example of honesty and trustworthiness.

**9.  They take responsibility** for their own actions and decisions. As leaders, they also take responsibility for the actions and decisions made by their followers.

**10.  They take risks.** This doesn't mean that they balance on one foot at the edge of a cliff. It means that they're willing to try new ideas and to experiment.

**11.  They take good care of themselves.** They balance work with play. They jog, play racquetball, golf, or walk. They eat healthful foods so their bodies have the right fuel. They take time to think and relax.

**12.  They are good followers.** They look for people who are good examples. They realize that they don't know everything, and they still have a lot to learn. They seek out mentors.

Do you notice anything special about this list? You're right; it includes many of the character traits discussed in this book. You might want to create your own list of traits you believe are important to being a good leader. If you'd like to be a leader yourself (or if you're already a leader but would like to improve), carry your list with you and refer to it from time to time.

---

[1] See "Caring," pages 21–27, and "Integrity," pages 135–141.

*Principle-Centered Leadership* by Stephen R. Covey (New York: Simon & Schuster, 1992). The author of *The Seven Habits of Highly Effective People* explains how individuals can improve their leadership skills by focusing on universal principles rather than personal priorities. Ages 13 & up.

*Stand Out: How You Can Become a Strong Leader* by Bill Sanders (Ada, MI: Fleming H. Revell Company, 1994). A comprehensive guide for teens who want to improve their leadership skills, written in a fun, motivational way. Ages 14–18.

# Followership

> "We don't need any more leadership training; we need some followership training."
> *Maureen Caroll*

Even leaders don't lead all of the time. Many learn to lead by following others. You'll probably spend some of your time being a leader, and some of your time being a follower. Knowing how to follow is just as important as knowing how to lead. A skyscraper wouldn't be able to stand without its supports.

Followership doesn't mean that when you see a bully punch someone, you join in. It doesn't mean that you jump into a lake because your friends do— not without checking it out first.

Sometimes followership means following your own instincts. For example, you might have a bad feeling about going to a party. Even though your friends are all going, you decide to skip it, and later you learn that kids there were drinking. Or you might have a good feeling about joining a school club. Even though you're feeling shy or scared, you give it a try, and it turns out to be one of the best things you've ever done.

Do you remember the story about "The Pied Piper of Hamelin" and how the children followed him out of town? That's not the kind of follower you want to be. Have you heard about lemmings, the rodent-like creatures that follow their leader off the edge of a cliff and into the sea? Have you ever followed someone and gotten into trouble? *Before you decide to follow a leader, you should know where the leader is going.*

Here's how to be an intelligent follower:

**T**hink before you follow.

**H**elp to make the plan, if you can.

**I**magine the ending before you begin. Where will this lead you? Into a positive experience—or down a dark, dead-end alley?

**N**ever do anything that will hurt yourself, other people, or other things.

**K**eep thinking and rethinking as you go. Do you have new information? Do you need to back up, stop, or change directions?

Intelligent following saves time, gives you new opportunities, and offers the chance to learn and grow from others. Wouldn't it be awful if you had to be an Olympic swimmer, invent air-conditioning, design the microchip, lead a safari, serve as your state's governor, write the Constitution, and discover cures for diseases, all at the same time? If we couldn't be good followers, there would be no progress in history, because we couldn't learn from each other.

# Character Dilemmas

*For journaling or writing essays, discussion, debate, role-playing, reflection*

**Suppose that ...**

**1** You're present at a speech given by the great English statesman, Benjamin Disraeli (1804–1881), when he says "I must follow the people. Am I not their leader?" What do you think he means by that? Can you give examples of how you could be a leader by following?

**2** In the heat of battle, a soldier doesn't have time to ask his commander what to do. Should the soldier follow his own instincts or wait for orders? Imagine different scenarios before making your decision.

**3** A country has a very charismatic leader. Most of the people follow him without really knowing or asking where he's going. What might be the pros and cons of this? Can you think of examples from history where people followed charismatic leaders and things turned out well? Can you think of examples from history where following a leader was destructive or disastrous?

**4** You have a friend who does *everything* adults ask and expect of her. She follows their lead to the letter. Is this good, or is this a problem? Or is it both good *and* a problem? Justify your answers. Look at both sides.

**5** You want to be a biomedical engineer someday—someone who does genetic research, or designs replacement parts for human bodies, or works in the area of cloning. What leadership qualities will you need to reach your goal? Could those qualities ever get you in trouble? How?

**6** A friend goes to hear a speaker one evening, and the next day he's very excited about it. He tells you that the speaker answered questions that had been bothering him for a long time, and made him feel as if his life had meaning. You've heard about this speaker, and you know that he leads a cult. His followers include many teenagers who have run away from home and renounced their families. What might you say to your friend? What might you do to keep him from making a mistake?

# Activities

**WRITE LEADERSHIP AND FOLLOWERSHIP** metaphors. A metaphor is a figure of speech that compares two things that aren't necessarily alike. *Examples:*

▲ Leadership is the first peach blossom that blooms on the tree.

▲ Followership is the soil the tree grows in.

Afterward, choose your best metaphors and illustrate them.

**WRITE IN YOUR JOURNAL**[2] about how it feels to be a leader. Write about how it feels to be a follower. Which do you prefer? Which feels more comfortable to you? Why?

**ROLE-PLAY EXAMPLES OF HOW A LEADER** might act in each of the following situations if 1) he or she sim-

ply *told* his or her followers what to do (a dictator leader), and 2) he or she *worked with* his or her followers to accomplish a goal (a cooperative leader). *Examples:* 1) A big sister tells her little brother "Get your ugly face out of my room!" 2) A big sister asks her little brother "Do you like to be alone sometimes? Me, too. I'd like to be alone for a while right now. Can you help me?"

- A teacher wants her students to stop acting out and start paying attention.

- A military leader wants male soldiers to treat female soldiers respectfully.

- A baby-sitter wants the three kids she's sitting to go to bed on time.

- The captain of a basketball team wants her players to improve.

- The President wants to convince Congress to pass a new law.

- Parents want their children to be more polite and responsible.

- A religious leader wants his congregation to become more involved in community service.

**READ AND DISCUSS** this excerpt from Joseph Campbell's book, *The Hero's Journey:*[3]

> They thought it would be a disgrace to go forward as a group. Each entered the forest at a point that he himself had chosen, where it was darkest and there was no path. If there is a path, it is someone else's path, and you are not on an adventure.

**?** What do you think this means?

**?** Why did "they" think that "it would be a disgrace to go forward as a group"? Did they want to go it alone? Why?

**?** Why did each person choose the darkest part of the forest, where there was no path?

**?** What does the last line mean? What do you think Campbell meant by the word "adventure"?

**?** Why did "they" not want to follow someone else's path?

**?** What does this selection have to do with leadership and followership?

---

[2] See "Endurance," pages 88, 89, and 92 for journaling resources.

[3] *The Hero's Journey: The World of Joseph Campbell* by Joseph Campbell (New York: Harper & Row, 1990).

**RESEARCH MAJOR ADVANCES IN SCIENCE.** Try to find out 1) how each one changed the world, and 2) how each one affected those who followed and made use of the advances. Include both positive and negative results. Choose from among the following examples or come up with your own.

- stone tools (the Paleolithic era, about 2.6 million years B.C.)
- the wheel (about 3500 B.C.)
- the compass (A.D. 83, invented in China)
- printing (Pi Cheng, 1041; Johannes Gutenberg, the mid-1400s)
- the microscope (Zacharias Janssen, around 1590)
- the revolver (Samuel Colt, the early 1830s)
- the mechanical harvester or reaper (Cyrus McCormick, around 1831)
- the electric lightbulb (Thomas Edison, 1879)
- the fire escape (Harriet Tracy, 1883)
- the medical syringe (Letitia Geer, 1899)
- wireless electronic communication (Guglielmo Marconi, 1895)
- the airplane (Orville and Wilbur Wright, 1903)
- plastic (Leo Hendrik Baekeland, 1909)
- the Theory of Relativity (Albert Einstein, 1909)
- penicillin (Alexander Fleming, 1928)
- nuclear fission (Otto Hahn, Lise Meitner, and Fritz Strassman, 1938)
- electronic computer with memory storage capability (Frank Hamilton of IBM, 1948)
- mercaptopurine and other disease-fighting drugs (Gertrude Elion, 1954)
- fiber optics (John Tyndall, 1870; Narinder S. Kapany, 1955)
- space flight (the Soviet *Sputnik,* 1957)
- the microchip (Jack St. Clair Kilby, 1958)
- the heart transplant (Christiaan Barnard, 1967)
- virtual reality (Jaron Lanier, VPL Research, 1985)
- all-optical processor (AT&T, Bell Laboratories, 1990)

**LEARN MORE ABOUT LEADERSHIP.** Check your library for books by and about leaders. Search the World Wide Web for sites about leaders and leadership. See if you can identify certain character traits that leaders seem to have in common. Try to come up with a Top 5 or Top 10 list of character traits. Share your list with your family, class, or club.

## CHECK IT OUT

*Cool Women, Hot Jobs . . . and how you can go for it, too!* by Tina Schwager and Michele Schuerger (Minneapolis: Free Spirit Publishing, 2002). Twenty-two women describe what they do, how they got there, and why they love it. Ages 11 & up.

**Congressional Youth Leadership Council**
1110 Vermont Avenue, NW, Suite 320
Washington, DC 20005
(202) 638-0008
*www.cylc.org*
CYLC provides outstanding high school juniors and seniors nationwide an opportunity to study leadership, citizenship, and government in the nation's capital. Visit CYLC's Web site to find out more; click on "Taking Issue" to read what national leaders (and students) have to say about today's "hot topics."

**FIND OR MAKE AN ABACUS.** The first hand-held calculator, the abacus was used by the Chinese as early as 3000 B.C. Use your abacus to tutor or help younger children to learn about place values.

**MAKE A HISTOGRAM ABOUT LEADERSHIP.** Choose five of the following leaders from history, or create your own list:

- Susan B. Anthony
- Yasser Arafat
- Benazir Bhutto
- Hillary Rodham Clinton
- Queen Elizabeth II
- Louis Farrakhan
- Indira Gandhi
- Mohandas Gandhi
- Mikhail Gorbachev
- Thomas Jefferson
- Barbara Jordan
- Martin Luther King Jr.

✳ Chandrika Kumaratunge

✳ Nelson Mandela

✳ Golda Meir

✳ Ruth Perry

Rate each leader on a scale of 1–10, depending on whether you agree or disagree that his or her contributions were/are positive and valuable. Show your results on a histogram. (A histogram is a bar graph with the bars touching each other, leaving no gaps.)

## CHECK IT OUT

**Roberto Ortiz de Zárate's Political Collections**
*www.terra.es/personal2/monolith*
Based in Spain, written in English, this fascinating site includes a chronological listing of contemporary political leaders, a country-by-country review of world leaders, a list of women world leaders, a list of the first African rulers, and links to many related sites.

CHOOSE A LEADER from world history or the history of your country—someone you especially admire. Write a story or skit showing how that person's leadership changed history for the better. Present your story or skit to your class, club, or family. You might dress up as the person to make your presentation more interesting.

RESEARCH LEADERSHIP IN THE FALL of the Berlin Wall. Learn about the events leading up to and following the fall of the Wall in 1990 and the people who shaped and influenced those events. You might want to look into Lech Walesa's formation of the Solidarity trade federation in Poland (1980); Mikhail Gorbachev's policy of *glasnost* (openness) toward the West (1988–91); the ouster of East German leader Erich Honecker in October, 1989; the unification of Germany in October, 1990; the independence of Latvia, Lithuania, and Estonia (1991); and other related events. How have they affected Eastern and Western Europe? The relationships between European countries and the United States? Present the results of your research in a timeline and a report.

JOIN A NATIONAL YOUTH ORGANIZATION that promotes leadership training and development. *Examples:* Boy Scouts, Girl Scouts, 4H, Camp Fire.

*Variation:* Many national clubs and organizations for adults have youth programs and/or divisions. *Examples:* American Legion (Boys State/Boys Nation, Girls State/Girls Nation), American Red Cross (American Red Cross Youth Program), Kiwanis International (Key Clubs), Lions Clubs International (Leo Clubs, Lions-Quest), NAACP (Youth and College Division), Optimist Club (Junior Optimist Octagon), Rotary Clubs (Rotary Youth Leadership Awards), YMCA (Youth in Government, Black/Minority Leaders, more). Contact local chapters for more information.

## CHECK IT OUT

*The Directory of American Youth Organizations* by Judith B. Erickson is a guide to hundreds of adult-sponsored, nonprofit national organizations for young people, including clubs, groups, troops, teams, societies, lodges, and more. It's available online at: *www.nydic.org/nydic/dayo.html*

START A NEW CLUB in your school or community. *Examples:* a service club, sports club, exercise club, reading club, hiking club, environmental club, collector's club, or . . . ? Use these steps as guidelines:

1. Find a sponsor—an adult who will support your club and provide leadership and guidance when needed.

2. Write a proposal for your club. Include:

   ✔ the name of your club

   ✔ the people (kids? community members?) it will serve

   ✔ what you will do (the purpose of your club)

   ✔ when and where you will meet

   ✔ how long your club will last

   ✔ a budget (for supplies, etc., if needed)

   ✔ where the money you need will come from (dues? donations? a fund-raiser?)

3. Present your proposal to the principal, faculty, club coordinator, or community leader.

4. Advertise your club so your friends can join. Make and display posters, pass out flyers, make an announcement over your school's PA system.

# CHECK IT OUT

*Join the Club! The Fun Guide to Starting Your Own Club* by Jennifer Hulme (Hatboro, MA: Legacy Books, 1994). A roundup of all the key phases of forming a successful club.

---

**START AN AWARDS PROGRAM** at your school to honor the Leader-of-the-Month and the Follower-of-the-Month. Form a committee to oversee the awards program. Publicize the program and create a way for students, teachers, and administrators to nominate candidates. Design trophies, certificates, or ribbons to give to each month's winners. Display their photographs on a school bulletin board.

**BE A LEADER IN YOUR FAMILY.** Plan a family activity for one night each week—something that will bring everyone together. You might read stories aloud, make cookies, tell jokes, walk, hike, sing, or anything else your family might enjoy. If some family members aren't interested at first, don't give up. Keep trying, and you might find that everyone joins in eventually.

**MAKE LEADERSHIP MOBILES.** Show the contributions of various leaders from the past or present. You might pick famous leaders and not-so-famous leaders, such as the teenager in your neighborhood who organizes after-school activities for younger kids.

**RESEARCH THE LEADERSHIP ROLES** played by professional athletes. Why do people admire athletes so much? What roles do professional sports play in society today? Should athletes have certain responsibilities, based on the fact that young people look up to them? If so, what should those responsibilities be? You might choose 2–3 famous athletes and research their influence on young people. In your opinion, are they good leaders or not? Give reasons for your decision.

**PLAY A "LEAD OR FOLLOW" GAME.** Go outside with a group (your class, family, or club) and identify two trees or other landmarks that are close together. Label one "Leadership" and the other "Followership." As you read the following questions, each member of the group should stand beside the landmark that describes the role they would choose to play in each situation.

- **Student government:** Would you rather be the president of the student council *or* a member of the student council?

- **Fashion:** Would you rather be the first to wear a new style of clothing *or* wait until many people are wearing it?

- **Adventure:** Would you rather lead a safari *or* follow the guide?

- **Sports:** Would you rather be the captain of a team *or* a player on a team?

- **Medicine:** Would you rather discover the cure of a disease *or* be a doctor who uses the cure to help patients?

- **State or national government:** Would you rather be a senator *or* a citizen who follows the rules and laws established by senators?

- **Cooking:** Would you rather make up a new recipe *or* use one from a cookbook?

- **Literature:** Would you rather write a book *or* read one?

- **Public speaking:** Would you rather give a speech *or* hear one?

- **Business:** Would you rather start your own business *or* work for someone else?

- **Performing arts:** Would you rather sing, dance, *or* play an instrument or be an audience member?

- **Technology:** Would you rather create your own Web site *or* explore other people's sites?

- **Science:** Would you rather make important discoveries *or* teach about discoveries that others have made?

Afterward, discuss with the group what this game has taught you about yourselves and each other. Are there some people who almost always prefer to be leaders? Who almost always prefer to be followers? Are there certain types of leadership that seem more popular than other types? How might it be possible to be *both* a leader and a follower?

READ STORIES ABOUT LEADERSHIP and followership. Look for these books:

- *Being Danny's Dog* by Phyllis Naylor (New York: Atheneum Books for Young Readers, 1995). Twelve-year-old Danny and his ten-year-old brother T.R. move to Rosemary Acres with their mother, find new friends , and discover that their new community has strict rules. Ages 10–13.

- *The Daffodils* by Christi Killien (New York: Scholastic, 1992). When the Daffodils softball team elects a "sophisticated" girl to lead them, former captain Nichole struggles with the growing pains of her team and her teammates to prove herself a winner on and off the field. Ages 11–14.

- *Ender's Game* by Orson Scott Card (New York: Tor Books, 1994). After Earth is nearly destroyed by alien forces, the world government begins preparing a new generation of military geniuses to fend off the next attack. Games are crucial to the young soldiers' training, but they're no challenge for Ender Wiggin. Ages 14 & up.

- *What's an Average Kid Like Me Doing Way Up Here?* by Ivy Ruckman (New York: Delacorte Press, 1983). Seventh grader Norman Gates considers himself an extremely average kid. When his dad leaves to climb mountains and his mom returns to teaching, Norman decides to take on the unordinary task of saving his school from being closed for good. Ages 10–14.

- *A Wrinkle in Time* by Madeleine L'Engle (New York: Dell, 1997). Meg Murray and her friends beome involved with unearthly strangers and a search for Meg's father, who disappeared while engaged in secret work for the government. First published in 1962, this book is a beloved classic. Ages 10–15.

# Character in *ACTION*

## Northridge Elementary: No Ifs, Ands, or Butts

"What can you kids do to leave your mark on your generation?" Ms. Vivian Meiers asked her sixth-grade class at Northridge Elementary in Bismarck, North Dakota. "You're going to graduate from high school in the year 2000. What can you do to change or improve society?"

The students had been studying the harmful effects of alcohol and other drugs—especially smoking—in a health unit. They had learned that for each cigarette you smoke, you lose about 5½ minutes of life expectancy. They had also learned that approximately 400,000 deaths per year—from lung cancer, heart attacks, and high blood pressure—are related to smoking. "Some of those deaths are from second-hand smoke," Ms. Meiers told them.

One of the students drew a picture of Joe Camel in a wheelchair, his face blue, on a respirator. He wrote "How cool is this?" across his picture and mailed to the R.J. Reynolds Tobacco Company. "We're not stupid," he told the tobacco company, "but we can be swayed by colorful pictures and cool advertisements."

He let the company know that they were *not* doing a service to society by advertising to young people.

Student Ashley Burke wanted to know "Why is it legal for adults to produce things that are bad for kids?"

"We live in a democratic society," Ms. Meiers explained. "There are many choices to make, and you have to learn very early to make the right choices, or bad choices can destroy your life. So, what can you do to leave your mark?"

"Wouldn't it be cool if we all promised not to smoke?" one student asked.

"We could be a smokeless society," another added. "We could all pledge to stay away from tobacco, because chewing tobacco is bad, too."

"Yeah. It can cause cancer of the mouth."

"Why not get other kids to make a promise with us? We could all sign a pledge or something to be tobacco-free in the year 2000."

Ms. Meiers offered to contact the other sixth-grade teachers in the Bismarck Public School District.

Almost 60 teachers told their students about the Northridge kids' idea. Of the 950 sixth graders in the Bismarck area, 867 followed the leadership of Ms. Meiers' class and signed the pledge.

The Heart and Lung Clinic in Bismarck put up the money for a full-page advertisement in the *Bismarck Tribune* that listed the names of more than 500 kids who signed the pledge. The caption read "Class of 2000. No ifs, ands, or butts. Choose to be tobacco-free."

That all happened in 1994. Since then, many of the students in Ms. Meiers's sixth-grade class have returned to Northridge Elementary to visit their former teacher. They've told her that they're still keeping the pledge and want to do it forever. Ms. Meiers plans to conduct a survey of the kids just before they graduate to learn how many kept their promise.

The students weren't just thinking of their own future. In Ashley Burke's words, "We tried to set an example for the younger kids to follow."

Teacher Vivian Meiers's students at Northridge Elementary School

## Loyalty

**Faithfulness, steadfastness, obedience**

> "Unless you can find some sort
> of loyalty, you cannot find unity and
> peace in your active living."
> *Josiah Royce*

# Loyalty

**W**hen you're loyal to someone or something, you're faithful, constant,[1] and dependable.[2] You stay true-blue no matter what anyone else says or does. It doesn't matter to you whether your position is popular or not. You stand firm anyway.

But loyalty, like justice and equality,[3] can mean different things to different people. For example, imagine that you have a friend who's sneaking out at night without her parents' knowledge. You're worried about your friend, and you're afraid that she might get into serious trouble. Your sense of loyalty compels you to tell her parents what you know. But your friend might see this as being totally *dis*loyal—and it could damage your friendship.

When deciding where to place your loyalty, ask yourself "Does this person (group, organization, idea) deserve my loyalty?" Find out as much as you can ahead of time. If it's a person, is this someone you admire? For what reasons? Does he or she set a good example? If it's a group or organization, what does it stand for? Is it working to make a difference in your neighborhood or community? If it's an idea, is this something you can

believe in and support 100 percent? When you give your loyalty, you give an important part of yourself. Don't do it lightly!

You should be loyal to your parents and family, even if you don't always agree with them, and even if they make serious mistakes. Being loyal to them doesn't mean you have to copy everything they do or be exactly like them. But you can still be constant in your love for them, and you can try to help them. You might be loyal to your friends, employer, school, club, scout troop, and your faith community. You might be loyal to your country and the planet. You might also be loyal to values such as truth and wisdom. What about your own talents, interests, and passions? You can be loyal to them, too.

---

[1] For more on constancy, see "Integrity," pages 135–141.
[2] For more on dependability, see "Responsibility," pages 225–233.
[3] See "Justice," pages 142–154.

Have you ever told a friend "You're worthless and stupid! You have a terrible, awful personality! Nobody likes you!" Probably not, because if you did, that person wouldn't be your friend anymore. Have you ever said anything like that to *yourself*? If so, you're not being loyal to you. You're beating yourself up, and you're hurting your own chances for success. Your negative feelings about yourself will show when you try to make new friends, apply for a job, or want to join a committee or a team. Be loyal to yourself and your principles. Be your own best friend. Stick up for yourself and never let yourself down.

*Sometimes loyalties change, and that's okay.* For example, you might belong to one religion now, then decide at some point later in your life that you feel more comfortable with another. Or suppose you're loyal to a gang. That's an obvious reason to switch your loyalty. Be loyal to friends who support each other (and you) in making positive, safe choices.

If you ever wonder whether someone or something deserves your loyalty, remember the three R's:

1. *Reason* it out. Use your brain.

2. *Remove* your loyalty if you discover that you've placed it where it doesn't belong.

3. *Replace* it somewhere that's worthy of it.

When you're loyal to people, things, and ideas that deserve your faithfulness and constancy, you'll be happier and more fulfilled. You'll be supported and encouraged to develop your talents and become the person you want to be. You'll have closer relationships with people you can trust.

# Obedience

Have you ever watched a horse being broken? At first the horse rears high in the air, straining and yanking against the harness, and all he receives for his efforts is a stiff neck, sore muscles, and exhaustion. Most smart horses eventually learn that as long as they struggle, the battle continues and they get nowhere. Not until a horse learns to work *within* the harness does he become the trusted friend and animal who's able to serve, lead, and experience new adventures.

You have many harnesses you have to learn to work within. And sometimes your harnesses feel like ropes around your neck. You're not allowed to run wild and free, doing whatever you want with no consequences. For example, suppose that your big sister decides she doesn't need to obey the speed limit while she's driving down the interstate. Yank! The harness pulls tight and she finds herself with a speeding ticket.

Or suppose that your friend decides to walk into a bike shop and ride out on a mountain bike without paying for it. Ouch! The harness pulls tight and he's charged with shoplifting.

Or suppose you think it's unfair for you to have a curfew, to be forced to go to school or religious services, to be expected to do chores. Home and family rules, school rules, the rules or laws of your religion, and the laws of your community and country might all feel like harnesses to you. But as long as you fight and strain against them, you'll get jerked around, and you might end up with less freedom than you already have.

When you're obedient, you submit to authority. You mind people who are in charge of you—your parents, teachers, and other authority figures. Laws and rules might feel like harnesses, but they make it possible for us to live together. Without them, life would be chaos. Imagine what would happen if there were no traffic laws, no laws against stealing each other's property, no laws against killing each other. Imagine a hospital or airport with no controls. Even the most primitive people made laws that everyone was expected to obey.

If you spend a lot of time and energy resisting your "harnesses," here's something you might want to know: *When you learn to work* within *the rules, you gain the trust and confidence of the people who make the rules*—like your parents, for example. And when that happens, the rule-makers are more likely to change some of the restrictions you feel are unfair—and change them in your favor.

For example, suppose that your parents have given you an 8:00 P.M. curfew on weekends. All of your friends are allowed to stay out later, and you'd like your curfew extended to 9:00 or even 10:00. You can either 1) stay out as long as you want on weekends, no matter what your parents say, or 2) obey your curfew for a few weeks or months, then talk to your parents about extending it. Which behavior do you think will lead to the later curfew you want?

*It's important to know that there are times when you should not be obedient.* You shouldn't obey a team captain who tells you to cheat. Or an adult who tells you to try marijuana or another drug. You should never obey *anyone* who tries to make you do something you know is wrong—even if it's a parent. Find another adult you can trust and ask for help. And you should speak out against social injustice whenever you can.

If you're ever in doubt about whether to obey something, ask yourself "If I obey this, will I bring harm to myself, to anyone or anything else, or to my country?" If the answer is yes, don't do it. If you don't know the answer, or you're not sure of the answer, seek the advice of an adult you trust. In time, you'll learn to judge for yourself what to obey and what not to obey.

> "Loyalty to petrified opinion never yet broke a chain or freed a human soul."
> *Mark Twain*

# Character Dilemmas

*For journaling or writing essays, discussion, debate, role-playing, reflection*

**Suppose that . . .**

**1** Your best friend confides in you that he's been smoking marijuana almost daily. He insists that it's not a problem and tells you not to worry about him. Do you keep his confidence, or do you talk to his parents or a teacher? What might be the results of each choice?

**2** A cult leader asks you to do something that's against the law, such as not attending school. Will you obey him or not? What might be the consequences of following the cult leader? What might you do to remain loyal to your government and avoid disobeying laws?

**3** You're a member of a committee that's studying animal rights. Should dogs be trained and taught to perform dangerous tricks and stunts in movies, or is this taking advantage of their loyalty? Would it be okay to use pigs instead of dogs? Why or why not?

**4** You and a friend both work for a large grocery store. She's in the produce department, and you're a cashier. One day, you catch your friend stealing produce. She tells you to be a loyal friend and keep quiet, because she only takes the produce that's getting old and will be thrown out anyway. Then she gives it to a local food bank twice a week. If you tell on her, she'll lose her job, the food bank will lose the produce she brings, and some people will go hungry. How might you be loyal to your friend and your employer? Consider and discuss the consequences of your choices.

**5** A war breaks out between your country and another country. You don't believe in violence of any kind, but you get drafted to serve in your country's army. Do you obey your country's orders to fight in the war, or do you stay loyal to your own beliefs and refuse to fight? (During the Vietnam War, when South Vietnamese government forces backed by the United States fought against North Vietnam's Vietcong forces, many young people in the U.S. called themselves "conscientious objectors" and refused to fight. Some fled to Canada and other places to avoid the draft; others were sent to prison.) Should you obey your country's laws even if you don't agree with them? What might happen if people choose to obey only those laws they agree with? Look at both sides of this issue. Can you come up with any solutions?

**6** Your older sister runs a day-care center in her home, which isn't far from where you and your parents live. Whenever you stop by, the children are either in playpens or cribs, and often they're crying. You suspect that they spend most of their time there and aren't getting the attention they need. When you ask your sister about it, she tells you to mind your own business. You're worried about the children, but you don't want to get your sister in trouble, and she and her husband really need the income from the day-care center. What should you do? Where should your loyalties lie—with your sister or the children in her care?

**7** Your state law says that anyone who offers first aid at the scene of an accident (except for trained rescue teams) will be held responsible for any injuries that might result from the first aid. One day, you witness an accident between a motorcycle and a car. You're the only other person around. The driver of the car is unconscious, and the cyclist is bleeding profusely from a head wound. Do you leave the scene, hunt for a phone, and call for a trained rescue team? Or do you try to help and risk injuring the accident victims? Consider both sides of this issue. What would you do? What do you think is the *right* thing to do?

# Activities

**WRITE A SATIRE** about someone who obeys without considering the consequence. TIP: Satire uses *irony*, a figure of speech in which you say the opposite of what you mean. *Example:* After watching a movie with your friends, you say "That was definitely the *best* movie I've ever seen," when in fact it was the *worst* movie you've ever seen, and you and your friends all know that.

> *Variation:* Write an *allegory* instead of a satire—or an allegory that's also a satire. An allegory uses symbolic fictional figures to represent truths or make generalizations about human existence. Some famous allegories are John Bunyan's *The Pilgrim's Progress* and George Orwell's *Animal Farm.* You might write about a group of obedient sheep, for example.

**MAKE A LIST** of all the people, places, ideas, things, etc. you could be loyal or obedient to. Decide which ones require loyalty, which ones require obedience, and which ones require both. *Examples:* You're *loyal* to your friends, but you don't *obey* them. You *obey* traffic laws, but you don't feel *loyal* to them. You're *loyal* to your parents and you also *obey* them.

> *Variation:* Make a list of people, places, ideas, things, etc. you feel loyal to. Rank them from most important to least important. Compare your list with the lists of other people in your class, club, or family. Are there similarities? Differences? Add up the responses and compile a list of loyalties, ranked from the one most often listed to the one least often listed. Put your results on a computer spreadsheet and discuss them.

**WRITE NURSERY RHYMES OR JINGLES** about loyalty and/or obedience. It's okay if they're corny. *Example:*

> Your mother said "Come home at four."
> Your best friend said "Let's play some more."
> Your doctor said "Rest and stay quiet."
> Your brother said "Let's have a riot."
> Your pastor taught you "Be polite."
> Your coach insisted "Fight, fight, fight."
> How can you tell what you should do
> Or whom to be obedient to?

**DEBATE THIS ISSUE:** "Be it resolved that from this time forward, it shall be more important to be obedient than to be loyal in every part of your life." Or turn this statement around and debate it from the other side.

**RESEARCH THE STEPS** in the scientific method. Decide how important you think it is to follow the steps exactly. Are there times when it might be better *not* to follow the steps? Give reasons for your opinions. Can you give examples from the history of science of people who made both types of decisions?

**ESTIMATE THE PERCENTAGE OF DRIVERS** who disobey the speed limit posted in your school zone. Start by calling your local police department to find out how many drivers have received speeding tickets in your school zone area during this school year. Then call your state transportation department to learn approximately how many drivers travel through your school zone on each school day. Combine these figures to arrive at your estimate. What can you do to get drivers to slow down?

**RESEARCH CIVIL DISOBEDIENCE.** Learn about times in history when people have willfully disobeyed laws for causes they believed in. *Examples:*

- the Boston Tea Party

- the Revolutionary War (George Washington, Thomas Paine)

- the attack on the Bastille fortress in Paris

- the French Revolution

- the Women's Suffrage movement (Susan B. Anthony, Elizabeth Cady Stanton)

- the Civil Rights movement (Rosa Parks, Martin Luther King Jr., Medgar Evers)

■   the movement for the independence of India (Mohandas Gandhi, Jawaharlal Nehru)

■   the Vietnam War protests

■   the Tiananmen Square protests

Were these actions right or wrong? Justify your conclusion. How can you know whether to follow a cause that calls for civil disobedience? Write an opinion paper on this issue.

> *Variation:* Read and study some important civil disobedience documents. Look in your library or on the World Wide Web for "Civil Disobedience" by Henry David Thoreau (originally titled "Resistance to Civil Government") and "Letter from a Birmingham Jail" by Martin Luther King Jr. Decide if you agree or disagree with what the writers have to say.

## CHECK IT OUT

*People Power: A Look at Nonviolent Action and Defense* by Susan Neiburg Terkel (New York: Dutton, 1996). Covers the definition, principles, and methods of nonviolence, including civil disobedience, with vivid photographs and factual accounts of nonviolent acts and demonstrations. Ages 13 & up.

**Nonviolence.Org**
*www.nonviolence.org*
This site is home to many nonviolence groups in the United States including the Fellowship of Reconciliation, Jewish Peace Fellowship, Muslim Peace Fellowship, and War Resisters League. It also includes links to magazines, newsletters, peace organizations, international organizations, regional peace centers, other WWW sites, Web pages on specific issues, and discussion groups.

**LEARN ABOUT SYMBOLS THAT INSPIRE** loyalty and obedience.[4] Make an illustrated chart or poster showing different symbols.

▲   Analyze the symbolism of state flags. *Example:* Utah's flag shows a honey bee, symbolizing industry and hard work.

▲   Find out about other state symbols. *Examples:* state flowers, birds, slogans, etc.

▲   Research other important symbols from history. *Examples:* the cross; the swastika; signs of the Zodiac; etc.

*Variation:* If you live in a state that doesn't have a state flower, bird, slogan, etc., and you believe it should (or if you think the symbols it does have could use improvement), ask a legislator to be your sponsor and teach you how to promote your idea.

**CREATE SYMBOLS FOR YOUR CLASSROOM,** school, club, or group. What about a flag? A flower? A bird? A slogan? A rock? What else can you think of that might be interesting and fun? Have a contest, invite people to submit their ideas, and choose the best one(s) by popular vote.

> *Variation:* Create school loyalty banners. Individual classes, clubs, teams, etc. can brainstorm their own slogans and symbols, then use them on big, colorful banners. (The more, the better!) Hang all of the banners around the school. You might want to have a contest and choose the best one by popular vote.

**WATCH A DOG OBEDIENCE** training demonstration. Invite a trainer to your class or club, or arrange to attend a demonstration or class. Afterward, discuss what you observed. Is there any connection between dog obedience training and "people obedience training"? Are people ever trained like animals? Can you give examples? How would you teach obedience to your children?

**TAKE A FIELD TRIP** to your state legislature or city government. Learn why and how laws and ordinances are created. (You're expected to obey them, so you should know as much as you can about them.)

**WORK TO CHANGE A SCHOOL** or district rule. Sometimes old rules no longer apply because times and circumstances have changed, or they could use some dusting off and updating. *Example:* Does your school or district prevent you from leaving the classroom for field trips or service projects unless you travel on buses? There are probably good reasons for the older rule, but there might be a way to change or adapt it so you can travel in cars with parent drivers/chaperons. See what you can find out; see what you can do. Be sure to consider the issue from both sides.

**PRACTICE BEING OBEDIENT** for a whole day. Do what your parents and teachers ask you to do without arguing or making excuses. At the end of the day, write about it in your journal.[5] Was this a positive or negative experience, or both? Did you feel trapped or more free?

---

[4] See "Positive Attitudes," page 18, for a resource on symbols and symbolism.

[5] See "Endurance," pages 88, 89, and 92, for journaling resources.

*Variation:* Practice being obedient for a whole week. Afterward, assess the pros and cons. Was your life easier or harder? More pleasant or less pleasant? Do you think that your behavior improved your relationship with your parents and teachers? Why or why not?

**LEARN ABOUT ARTISTS** who "disobeyed the rules." The history of art is full of artists, schools, and movements that broke with tradition. *Examples:*

- Impressionists (Cézanne, Degas, Monet, Cassat, Renoir)
- Fauvists (Matisse, Vlaminck, Rouault)
- Cubists (Picasso, Braque, Léger)
- Dadaists and Surrealists (Duchamp, Dali, Miró, Chagall, Magritte)
- Abstract Expressionists (Pollock, de Kooning, Rothko)
- Pop Artists (Warhol, Lichtenstein, Jasper Johns)

Choose one or more artists or groups, then try to find out what rules they disobeyed. Did they create new rules for others to follow? Find copies of their paintings to display on a bulletin board or poster, or make transparencies to show on an overhead projector. Discuss the pros and cons of 1) staying loyal to traditional styles and 2) breaking away from traditional styles.

**RESEARCH THE POWER OF MUSIC** to shape public opinion and inspire loyalty or disloyalty. Listen to and analyze some of the protest songs and singers of the Great Depression (Woody Guthrie), the Civil Rights movement ("We Shall Overcome"), the Vietnam War era (Bob Dylan, Joan Baez), and other periods in history. How does this music make you feel? How do you think these songs and singers affected people at the time? Then listen to and analyze patriotic songs and anthems ("The Star-Spangled Banner," "America the Beautiful," and patriotic songs from other countries). How does this music make you feel? How do you think patriotic songs influence loyalty?

**STUDY SPORTS LOYALTY.** Why do some sports and teams inspire more loyalty than others? Is such loyalty healthy or unhealthy, or does it depend on the circumstances? Give examples to support your ideas and conclusions.

**PLAY "SIMON SAYS"** with your class, club, or family. You probably learned this game when you were younger, but in case you didn't, here are the rules:

**1.** The leader gives a command such as "Simon Says 'Jump'" or "Simon Says 'Touch your head with your right index finger.'" Each command must begin with "Simon Says." Everyone in the group must do what the leader says.

**2.** If the leader gives a command without first saying "Simon Says," everyone in the group must *not* do what the leader says.

**3.** Anyone who doesn't follow a "Simon Says" command is out of the game. Anyone who *does* follow a command that doesn't start with "Simon Says" is out of the game. The last person remaining becomes the leader for the next round of the game.

*Variations:* Instead of "Simon Says," you might play "Teacher Says," "Mother Says," "Father Says," "Friend Says," and so on.

When you're through playing the game, talk about what happened. Discuss questions like these:

**?** Should we always do what someone says?

**?** Does it depend on who says it?

**?** Why is it important to listen very closely when someone tells us to do something?

**READ STORIES ABOUT LOYALTY** and obedience. Look for these books:

- *Drummers of Jericho* by Carolyn Meyer (San Diego: Harcourt Brace, 1995). A 14-year-old Jewish girl goes to live with her father and stepmother in a small town and soon finds herself the center of a civil rights battle when she objects to the high school band marching in the formation of a cross. Ages 12–15.

- *The Light in the Forest* by Conrad Richter (New York: Knopf, 1953). Young John was taken from a small Pennsylvania frontier town by the Lenni Lenape Indians and raised by one of the tribe's greatest warriors. When he's 15, word reaches the village of a new treaty which states that all white prisoners must be returned, but John, or "True Son," cannot believe it applies to him. Ages 10–14.

📖 *The Lion, the Witch, and the Wardrobe* by C.S. Lewis (New York: HarperCollins Children's Books, 1994). Four English children, spending a holiday in an old estate, find their way to the land of Narnia. They have many strange adventures, become kings and queens, meet the royal lion, Aslan, and become involved in the battle between good and evil. A classic, originally published in 1950. Ages 8–12.

📖 *On My Honor* by Marion Dane Bauer (New York: Dell, 1997). When his best friend drowns while they are swimming in a treacherous river they had promised never to go near, Joel is devastated and terrified at having to tell both sets of parents the terrible consequences of their disobedience. A Newbery Honor Book. Ages 9–13.

📖 *The Slave Dancer* by Paula Fox (New York: Bantam Doubleday Dell Books for Young Readers, 1982). Jessie is kidnapped and taken aboard a slave ship to play his fife while the slaves are forced to exercise. When the ship is destroyed in a storm, Jessie and a young black boy named Ras must try to survive together. Ages 11–14.

# Character in *ACTION*

## Ana Zavala: A Life of Loyalty and Obedience

When Ana Zavala was three years old, she and her parents lived in a tiny one-room cement house in Mexico. They had no running water and only one light in the middle of the ceiling. Everyone slept in the same bed.

Ana's parents wanted a better education for Ana, so they moved the family to Texas and became migrant farm workers. During the spring, they harvested onions, melons, and oranges in Texas. Then they drove to Michigan for the summer, where they picked cucumbers and tomatoes until the middle or end of October. Ana didn't learn English until she was in kindergarten, when a kind student teacher took her under his wing and tutored her.

Each fall when her family returns to Mission, Texas, Ana has to catch up on two months of missed schoolwork. "It is difficult for me, but I have faith in myself that I can do it," she says. "I also have to develop new friends each year." She manages to get all A's and B's on her report cards, and she is very friendly.

You might think that 14-year-old Ana would feel like rebelling against her migrant life, but she doesn't. "My parents didn't finish school, but they want their kids to," she explains. "They have always worked hard and show patience to us. I am proud of them." And Ana's parents are proud of her for being smart, obedient, and loyal to her family.

Ana's life isn't easy. Each day before she goes to school, she must clean her room, dress, and make her own breakfast. At 3:00 P.M. she hurries home to set the table and make supper for her family, which now includes ten-year-old Silbia and four-year-old Pedro. Ana prepares meals like soup, ground beef and beans, a salad, tortillas, and rice, with lemonade or Kool-Aid to drink.

By 4:30, she hurries to Silbia's school to pick her up. Her grandmother brings Pedro home at the same time. Then Ana helps Silbia with her homework (especially math) and also helps Pedro learn the alphabet, numbers, and colors. Sometimes she coaches Silbia on making friends. "Don't worry," Ana encourages her sister. "Have patience. Don't be shy. Don't be afraid of the other kids. Tell them about yourself. Do the same games they like to do. You're sweet. Just be friendly and they'll like you."

Her parents arrive home after 5:00 and the family has dinner together. At 7:30, Ana goes to her bedroom and does her homework until around 9:00. Then she goes to sleep.

On Saturdays, the whole family spends the day shopping for groceries and washing their clothes at the laundromat. They all attend church together on Sundays in freshly washed and ironed clothes.

When a boy called Silbia "dumb," Ana stuck up for her little sister. She sticks up for her parents when kids ask "Why don't they get a real job?" In response to rude questions, Ana says "My parents don't have an education. But they are hard workers, and I respect them a lot." She also speaks highly of the United States. "I love my country. I feel good inside when we all stand up and say the Pledge of Allegiance or sing 'The Star-Spangled Banner.' I feel proud of all the people in the past in the United States, and I'm happy to be a part of it." Ana sees herself as a first-generation American, a pioneer who plants for those will who harvest after her.

Sometimes she gets frustrated. "Once I wanted to join a volleyball team. But I couldn't because I have to come home right after school. It made me feel sad, but I had to accept it." She knows that her family depends on her help. Meanwhile, she's making plans for her future. "I'd like to help kids learn their English and do well in school," Ana says. "I want to be a teacher or a nurse, because I want to help people who are injured or teach them how to read and write."

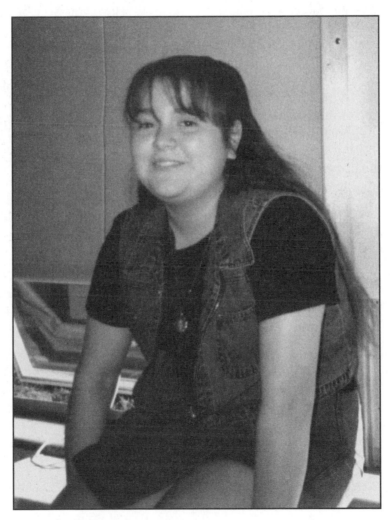

Ana Zavala

# Peacefulness

## Conflict resolution, calmness, cooperation, compromise, patience

"If you want to make peace with your enemy, you have to work with your enemy. Then he becomes your partner."
*Nelson Mandela*

Several years ago, a riot broke out at Cleveland High School in Reseda, California, involving over 200 kids. "You couldn't walk down certain hallways without being jumped," one of the senior boys said. As a result of the uproar, teachers and students met together and designed a program to reduce racial tension and to stop violence before it happened. Former gang leaders took leadership in organizing and developing it. They learned peaceful ways to resolve conflicts.

Your disagreements may or may not be as violent as this. Either way, you'll be happier and get along with your friends and family better if you learn how to resolve differences. Peace is more than the absence of conflict. It doesn't mean that no one ever disagrees. It means that *people know how to resolve their disagreements.* And they're willing to work together to do it.

It seems that conflict and violence are everywhere around us. We hear about wars, revolutions, ethnic conflicts, and violent crimes daily on the news. Some of us live in violent cities, neighborhoods—even homes. If you watch a lot of TV, you witness hundreds of acts of violence each week, because for some strange reason people think violence is entertaining.

Have you ever been in a store or at a shopping mall and seen a frustrated parent trying to discipline a child? Maybe the child has just smacked his little brother or sister. The parent grabs the older child, spanks him on the bottom, and shouts "That will teach you to stop hitting!" Do you think it will? Why or why not? What has the child really learned from that lesson?

You can't control what other people do, but you can control how *you* react to different situations. For example, let's say you're walking into class when another student bangs right into you, causing you to stumble and drop your books. You could shove her back, which might cause a fight. You could yell "Watch where you're going!" and she might bang into you again, just to prove that you can't tell her what to do. You could say nothing and silently seethe, which might give you an upset stomach. Or you could smile and say "Whoops! I guess you didn't see me!" Maybe it was an accident after all. And even if it wasn't, at least your conflict will probably end there. And she might even offer to help you pick up your books.

Peacefulness is more than avoiding violence. It doesn't mean that people never lose their tempers or act impulsively. It means that *people know how to talk to each other and work out their differences.* They're willing to *cooperate and compromise.* Peacefulness is a great way to avoid an upset stomach. When you're a peaceful person, you feel calm and serene inside most of the time.

Of course, there will be occasions when you feel frustrated, upset, or helpless. Maybe you don't get the A or B you want on your science test. Or you try out for a team, give it your best, and don't make it. Or you lose your job. Or your best friend decides to be best friends with someone else. Or you think your parents treat you unfairly. When things happen to you that you can't control, life feels scary and uncertain, and you might be tempted to blow up or strike out at others. You want to do something—anything—to show that you're still in charge of your life. But if you've made the decision to be a peaceful person—and if you've learned how to be peaceful—you won't just react. You'll act in a way that's best for you and doesn't harm anyone or anything else. You'll calm down, hold your tongue, find a quiet place inside yourself, and think through what to do next. Maybe you can't get what you want right away. Maybe you'll have to be patient and wait. Or maybe you'll have to give it up and move on. Your peacefulness will guide you.

> "The more peace there is in us, the more peace there will be in our troubled world."
> *Etty Hillesum*

# 12 Ways to Resolve Conflicts Peacefully

*1. Practice.* Just like learning to swim or play the piano, learning to settle problems peacefully takes practice. Role-play with your family and friends different ways to resolve conflicts.

*2. Talk about problems before they become conflicts.* Try to resolve minor disagreements before they grow into major disputes.

*3. Use "I-messages."* When you say "YOU make me angry" or "YOU shouldn't do that" or "YOU need to change your behavior," you're blaming the other person and putting him or her on the defensive. And the other person might respond "Yeah, but YOU make ME angry, too!" or "Are YOU going to stop me?" or "What about YOUR behavior?" Before you know it, you're having an argument.

"I-messages" are different. You start them off with "I," not "You." You talk about your feelings, not the other person's failures or mistakes. You give a reason for your feelings, which helps the other person understand your point of view. And you ask for what you want and need, which gives the other person the chance to do the right thing. "I-messages" encourage cooperation. *Examples:*

- Instead of "YOU make me so mad when you borrow my bike without asking," try "I feel angry when you borrow my bike without asking, because then it's not there when I need it to get to soccer practice. I want you to ask first."

- Instead of "YOU're always interrupting," try "I feel frustrated when someone interrupts me, because I lose my train of thought and can't remember what I was trying to say. I need you to wait until I'm finished speaking."

*4. Talk about the possible reasons behind the conflict.* Try to find out where it started (as opposed to "who started it"). *Examples:* "I guess I stayed up too late last night. I'm kind of grumpy today." "Maybe I didn't explain things clearly enough, and that's why you misunderstood me." "Maybe I didn't listen carefully enough, and that's why I misunderstood you." Try to identify any "accidental messages" that might have led to the conflict. *Examples:* If you're a shy person who doesn't talk much, others might misinterpret this as meaning that you're conceited or not interested in them. Or something you meant as a joke might be heard as sarcastic or rude.

*5. Talk about the problem without placing blame.* *Examples:* "I don't like to be treated that way." "I hate being late to movies." Try to give the other person the benefit of the doubt. Maybe she didn't mean to insult you. Maybe he couldn't help being late to the movie.

*6. Be a good listener.* Remember that you have *one* mouth but *two* ears. This means that you can listen twice as hard as you talk! Let other people know that you care about what they're saying. Look at them while they're speaking. Acknowledge what they say (nod your head, say "yes" or "umm" or "uh-huh"). Ask questions if you need more information. Don't interrupt while they're talking. And give them your full attention. Turn off the TV and log off the Internet during serious conversations (and even not-so-serious conversations).

**7.   *Be willing to cooperate.*** When you and another person are involved in a conflict, you *both* have a problem. If you can work together to solve it, you'll *both* benefit. That's why it pays to cooperate.

**8.   *Be willing to compromise.*** Decide what's really important to you and what you're willing to sacrifice to resolve the conflict. Give a little and you might get a lot.

**9.   *Choose people to act as mediators or peacemakers*** in your school, family, or club. When a conflict arises, a mediator/peacemaker steps in and helps the people involved in the conflict to talk, listen, cooperate, compromise, and look for solutions. Some schools train students to be peer mediators. See if your school does this. If it doesn't, talk to your principal about starting a peer mediation program.[1]

**10. *Identify adults you trust and respect,*** and call on them if you need them. If you can't resolve your conflict among yourselves or with a mediator/peacemaker, get help from an adult.

**11. *Agree to disagree.*** Some conflicts simply can't be resolved to everyone's satisfaction. When that happens, the best you can do is agree to disagree. Set some ground rules if you can. *Examples:* "Even though we disagree, we can still respect each other." "Live and let live." "We won't let our disagreement escalate into verbal or physical fights."

**12. *Learn from experience.*** After each conflict, review in your mind what happened, why it happened, and how the conflict was resolved (if it was resolved). You may want to write about it in your journal.[2] Was there anything you could have done differently? Should have done differently? Did you learn anything that you might be able to use to resolve future conflicts? Did you learn anything that you might be able to use to *prevent*

future conflicts? *Example:* Make rules in your classroom and family so everyone knows what's expected of them.

> "Peace is the skillful management
> of conflict."
> *Kenneth Boulding*

## CHECK IT OUT

*Tug of War: Peace Through Understanding Conflict* by Terrence Webster-Doyle (Middlebury, VT: Atrium Society Education for Peace Publications, 1990). Describes the roots of war, how we create "The Enemy," and a new way to handle violence. Ages 10 & up.

**Educators for Social Responsibility**
Resolving Conflict Creatively Program
23 Garden Street
Cambridge, MA 02138
1-800-370-2515
*www.esrnational.org*
Through its Resolving Conflict Creatively Program, Educators for Social Responsibility (ESR) teaches teachers how to respond nonviolently in conflict situations. Tell your teacher about this organization. The "Steps for Mediation" on page 180 are from ESR. If you visit the Web site (hosted by Ben & Jerry's Ice Cream company), click on "RCCP," then click on "Kids' Conscious Acts of Peace Project" for activities you can print out and distribute in your school, and on "Kids Keeping the Peace" for tips, games, activities, and success stories.

# 10 Positive Ways to Handle Anger and Frustration

Are you someone who gets into a lot of arguments and fights? Do you sometimes feel mad at the world? Do other people either pick fights with you or avoid you? Do some people act as if they're afraid of you? If you answered yes to any of these questions, you might need to learn ways to handle your anger and frustration. Here are some you can try.

**1.   *Acknowledge the problem.*** *Examples:* "I get into fights easily." "I lose my temper quickly." "I feel

---

[1] See "Be a mediator" on page 178 for information on how you can be a mediator.
[2] See "Endurance," pages 88, 89, and 92, for journaling resources.

frustrated a lot of the time." "I boss other people around." "I act like a bully."

**2. Talk about it with an adult you trust.** You can talk about it with your friends, too, but a skilled adult who's been trained in conflict resolution techniques can give you solid advice and strategies to try. You might talk with a school counselor, psychologist, youth group leader, or spiritual leader.

"I get so ANGRY when that happens!"

**3. Practice talking about difficult things in a calm, soft voice.** Breathe deeply and talk slowly. This might feel strange to you at first, but it works.

**4. Stop and think before you act or react.** Try to predict the consequences of your words or actions. Do you really want to get into a fight? To keep an argument going? To hurt someone else or risk getting hurt?

> "When angry, count ten, before you speak;
> if very angry, a hundred."
> *Thomas Jefferson*

**5. Try to imagine how the other person feels.**[3] How would *you* feel if you were that person? If you were the focus of someone's anger or frustration?

---

[3] See "Empathy," pages 79–85.

**6. Try to figure out why you behave the way you do.** *Example:* Maybe someone in your life reacts to stress by getting angry and attacking others with words (or hands, or fists). Maybe you're following this person's example. When you understand some possible reasons for your behavior, it's easier to make a change.

**7. Work to change negative habits into positive ones.** According to brain experts, habits actually create "grooves" or "channels" in your brain. The good news is, you can create new "grooves" or "channels." Think about how you want to act and react in the future. Visualize a new you—calmer, more peaceful. Role-play positive responses to negative situations. Make a plan for what you'll say and do the next time you feel angry or frustrated. And practice, practice, practice.

**8. Find ways to calm and soothe yourself when you're feeling angry or frustrated.** Try these:

- **Listen to peaceful music.** Look in your library's music collection under "relaxation." Or find a radio station that plays "smooth jazz" or New Age music. Many people enjoy recordings that blend music with nature sounds (birds singing, waves on a beach).

- **Get physical.** Walk, jog, hike, bike, climb, swim, shoot baskets, kick a ball—whatever you enjoy doing. This is a great way to release anger and frustration.

- **Do a calmness/relaxation exercise.** Here's an example:

  1. Lie on your back with your arms and legs extended. (Or sit in a comfortable chair.)

  2. Relax every muscle in your body, one by one. Think of your shoulders and relax them. Think of your back and relax it. Think of your facial muscles and relax them. Work your way down your body. Tell all of your tense muscles to loosen and go limp.

  3. Breathe in slowly. Picture the fresh air flowing into your lungs, and your blood carrying oxygen to every part of your body—from the top of your head to the tips of your toes. Feel peace and calmness flowing into and through your body. (You might want to count "One" as you breathe in.)

4. Breathe out slowly. Picture your breath carrying the anger, frustration, stress, and tension out of your body and releasing it into the air. (You might want to count "Two" as you breathe out.)

5. Picture your brain as a clear, calm place (a lake in the woods? a desert at sunset?).

6. Listen to the silence. Release all of your thoughts. Think of nothing at all. Experience the peacefulness.

**9. *Take good care of your body.*** [4] Eat well and get enough rest. If you're hungry and/or tired, full of sugar or caffeine, problems can seem bigger than they really are.

**10. *Have faith and hope.*** For some people, this means believing in a Higher Being/Higher Power. For others, it means adopting a positive, optimistic attitude toward life. [5]

> "Peace is a journey of a thousand miles and it must be taken one step at a time."
> *Lyndon B. Johnson*

# Character Dilemmas

*For journaling or writing essays, discussion, debate, role-playing, reflection*

**Suppose that . . .**

**1** You're walking home from school one day when you see someone punching your little brother. What do you do to help your brother, the other kid, and yourself to bring about a peaceful resolution?

**2** Your sister loves to argue with you. You don't enjoy it, but you go along, mainly in self-defense. The two of you have been arguing for years. What might you do to change the habit you and your sister have developed? Come up with a strategy and specific steps.

**3** You have a friend whose parents can't agree on how to discipline their children. Sometimes your friend is given a lot of freedom; at other times, his parents impose unfair restrictions on him. This has made your friend totally confused. How important is it for parents to be consistent? Give examples of rules parents might set—and exceptions to those rules. How might parents win their children's peaceful cooperation? What can happen when parents don't agree on how to discipline their children?

**4** Two countries in another part of the world have gone to war, and some of your country's leaders want to send military forces to help one side. Other leaders feel that your country should stay out of the war. Without outside aid, it's likely that the two countries will keep fighting for many years. But if your country sends soldiers to the war, many will die. Should peace be pursued at any price? Or are there times when peace isn't possible? Explain your views.

**5** You're in a school where there's a lot of rivalry between different groups of students. Usually it's verbal, but sometimes fights break out. What might you do to help the groups cooperate and get along?

# Activities

**BRAINSTORM A LIST OF ACTIVITIES** that might encourage peaceful behavior, calmness, cooperation, compromise and patience. *Examples:* Don't watch violent movies or TV programs; listen to soothing music; do relaxation exercises.

**WRITE IN YOUR JOURNAL** [6] about a time when you had a misunderstanding, disagreement, or fight with someone else. How did you feel about it at the time? How do you feel about it today? Is there anything you can do to make things better now, or is it too late? What could you have done at the time to avoid the misunderstanding, disagreement, or fight? What might you do in the future to avoid similar conflicts?

**ROLE-PLAY WAYS TO AVOID** misunderstandings or fights in the following situations:

▼ Someone insults your sister.

▼ Someone steals your homework.

▼ Your employer wrongly blames you for taking money from the cash register.

---

[4] See "Health," pages 103–114.
[5] See "Positive Attitudes," pages 14–20.

[6] See "Endurance," pages 88, 89, and 92, for journaling resources.

🔻 Your mother grounds you for breaking a lamp when your brother was the one who did it.

🔻 A gang member says that he'll rough you up if you don't smoke a joint with him.

🔻 A bully threatens to beat you up after school.

🔻 A girl in your class won't share the basketball with you at recess.

🔻 You loan your skis to a friend, and he wrecks them.

🔻 Your teacher wrongly accuses you of cheating on a test.

🔻 You're playing soccer when you get fouled (another player kicks your shins), but the referee calls the foul on you.

🔻 Your parents won't let you stay out as late as you want to.

**BRAINSTORM SOME "WIN/LOSE"** and "win/win" scenarios. In a win/lose scenario, one person/side wins and the other loses. In a win/win scenario, both people/sides benefit. *Example:* Your little brother's favorite TV program is on at the same time as a movie you want to see. In a win/lose scenario, you'd tell your brother to get lost and then watch your movie—or your parents would order you to let him watch his program. In a win/win scenario, you'd program the VCR to record your movie while your brother watched his program. Then you could watch your movie later, after he went to bed. Come up with win/lose and win/win scenarios for the situations in the role-playing activity above.

*Variation:* Draw cartoons or create a comic book[7] illustrating win/lose and win/win scenarios.

**RESEARCH ONE OR MORE HISTORICAL** conflicts—wars, battles, and/or revolutions. Find out 1) what issues were central to the conflicts (possession of land? resources? ideology? ethnic differences? something else?), 2) how the conflicts were resolved (if they were resolved), and 3) whether these were win/lose or win/win scenarios. Make a chart comparing the results.

---

[7] See "Choice and Accountability," page 32, and "Imagination," page 131, for resources related to comic books.

**SET UP A "PEACEFUL PLACE"** in your classroom. Talk with your teacher about turning a corner of your classroom into a place where people can go to be quiet, calm, and thoughtful. Work with your class to decorate it with posters and other artwork. Fill a bookshelf with books about peace. Have cassette players with headphones available and tapes of soothing music. Make and decorate a "Peaceful Place" sign to hang on the wall.

*Variation:* Work with your family to set up a "Peaceful Place" in your home.

**WORK TO MAKE YOUR SCHOOL** a safe and peaceful place to learn and grow. Here are some ideas to try:

▲ Pass a proclamation calling for a peaceful school. *Example:* "Whereas our school needs to be a safer and more peaceful place for students to learn, and whereas the school needs to be a safer and more peaceful place for teachers to teach, now, therefore, be it resolved that from this time forth all people in our school will work to create a safer and more peaceful school." Make copies available for people (students, faculty, and staff) to sign. Collect as many signatures as you can, then present the signed proclamation to your principal.

▲ Encourage your principal to make conflict resolution training available to students, faculty, and staff.

▲ Gather information from organizations that are helping schools become safer. Assess and analyze the information you collect. Work with a committee to draw up a list of suggestions, actions, and goals to try. Share what you learn with your principal. Your school might decide to work with one of the organizations you contact.

---

## CHECK IT OUT

Three organizations that help schools become safer are:

**National School Safety Center**
141 Dusenberg Drive, Suite 11
Westlake Village, CA 91362
(805) 373-9977
*www.nssc1.org*

**Peace Education Foundation**
1900 Biscayne Boulevard
Miami, FL 33132-1025
1-800-749-8838
*www.peace-ed.org*

**Safe and Drug-Free Schools Program**
1250 Maryland Avenue, SW, Portals 604
Washington, DC 20202
1-800-624-0100
*www.ed.gov/offices/OSDFS/index.html*

See also the Educators for Social Responsibility resource on page 174.

---

BE A MEDIATOR. Intervene in conflicts and help the people involved to find a solution. You can follow this procedure from The Resolving Conflict Creatively Program.[8] Start by asking yourself:

🕊 Am I the right person?

🕊 Can I assist without taking sides?

🕊 Will both parties let me assist?

🕊 Is this the right time to intervene?

🕊 Are the parties relatively calm?

🕊 Do we have enough time?

🕊 Is this the right place?

If you can answer yes to these questions, continue with the Steps for Mediation on page 180.

LEARN WHAT PEOPLE AROUND THE WORLD are doing to promote peace. Check your library for books about peace and biographies of peacemakers.[9] Search the World Wide Web for information about organizations, foundations, and associations working for peace. You'll be amazed by how much you find . . . and you might be inspired to get involved.

> *Variation:* Choose one of the national or international organizations working for peace, research it deeply, and present your findings in a detailed report. If you do this as a class, as individual students or teams, you'll compile a wealth of information you can share with each other, your school, and your community. Some organizations have special programs for children and youth.

## CHECK IT OUT

Three of the many organizations working for peace are:

**Association of World Citizens**
55 New Montgomery Street, Suite 224
San Francisco, CA 94105
(415) 541-9610
*www.worldcitizens.org*

**Fellowship of Reconciliation**
PO Box 271
Nyack, NY 10960
(845) 358-4601
*www.forusa.org*

**The King Center**
449 Auburn Avenue NE
Atlanta, GA 39312
(404) 526-8900
*www.thekingcenter.org*

To learn about more organizations working for peace, go to:

**Yahoo's Nonviolence Organizations Links**
*dir.yahoo.com/Society_and_Culture/Issues_and_Causes/Peace_and_Nonviolence/Organizations*

---

RESEARCH THE EFFECTS OF VARIOUS INVENTIONS on peace and conflict in the world. Find out who invented them (or when they were first used) and how they have been used since. Choose examples from this list or create your own list:

- gunpowder
- rocket
- gun
- submarine
- locomotive
- telegraph
- machine gun
- dynamite
- telephone
- television
- jet-propelled aircraft
- radar

---

[8] Reprinted with the permission of Educators for Social Responsibility © 1997 Educators for Social Responsibility, Cambridge, MA.

[9] See "Courage," page 73, for Nobel Peace Prize resources.

- nuclear fission
- communication satellite
- genetic engineering
- Internet

*Variation:* The inventor of dynamite also invented other explosives including liquid nitroglycerin. He was a life-long pacifist who wished his inventions to be used only for peaceful purposes, and he was very unhappy when they were adopted by the military. Find out his name, research his life, and discover the surprising use to which he put his fortune.

**FIND OUT WHAT HAPPENS WHEN NATURE** isn't peaceful. Research the effects of cyclones, hurricanes, tornadoes, floods, fires, earthquakes, volcanoes, etc. (Or choose *one* instance of *one* type of natural disaster and research it in detail.) Do some natural disasters seem to happen for a reason? Do natural disasters ever have positive results? Do you think that humankind will ever be able to channel, contain, or control nature? Would this be a good thing or a bad thing? Explain your answer.

**STUDY HOW DIFFERENT SHAPES AND PATTERNS** affect our sense of calmness and peace. *Example:* Buckminster Fuller built three-dimensional spherical structures from triangles. One of his geodesic domes is in Quebec, Canada; another is in Epcot Center in Disney World. If you've seen one in person, maybe you can remember how it made you feel. If you haven't seen one in person, look at pictures and decide how it makes you feel.

*Variation:* Research different types of architecture. Are there buildings that create a sense of calmness, serenity, and peace? Are there buildings that create a sense of excitement or exhilaration? Tour your own town or city and prepare a report on several buildings. (Be sure to bring a camera so you can illustrate your report with photographs.) Or study famous architects, schools of architecture, or buildings around the world. *Examples:* Frank Lloyd Wright, Le Corbusier, the Taj Mahal, the Parthenon, Gothic architecture, Modernist architecture, etc.

**LEARN HOW COLORS CAN AFFECT FEELINGS** of peacefulness. Would you rather be in a red room or a blue room? A white room or a black room? Why? For centuries, artists, designers, psychologists, and scientists have been studying the effects of color on human emotions. Some colors are perceived as "warm" (red, yellow, orange), while others are perceived as "cool" (blue, green, gray). The warm colors are believed to create feelings of excitement, cheerfulness, and aggression; the cool colors are believed to create feelings of calmness, security, and peace. Find out more about this. Start noticing the colors around you—in classrooms, fast-food restaurants, libraries, and other public buildings. Make a colorful chart showing the results of your research. (Based on what you learn, you might decide to paint your room a different color.)

**START A PEACEMAKERS CLUB** at your school.[10] Decide what your goals will be. Will you work to make your school more peaceful? How will you do this? Will you work to make your community, country, or world more peaceful? How? Plan specific projects to do together. IMPORTANT: Make sure that your club's rules include ways to handle conflicts or disagreements among the members. And don't forget to have fun!

## CHECK IT OUT

Maybe the members of your Peacemakers Club will want to make pen pals with other kids around the world. Or maybe this is something you'll want to do on your own. Here are two pen-pal organizations you can contact:

**Peace Pals**
26 Benton Road
Wassaic, NY 12592
(845) 877-6093
*www.worldpeace.org/peacepals.html*

**World Pen Pals**
PO Box 337
Saugerties, NY 12477
(845) 246-7828
*www.world-pen-pals.com*

**START A PEACEMAKER-OF-THE-MONTH** awards program to honor individuals who promote peace at your school. Anyone who works for peace is eligible to receive the award—students, custodians, faculty, staff, parent volunteers, etc. Publicize the program and create a way for members of your school community to nominate candidates. Design trophies, certificates, or ribbons to give to each month's winners. Display their photographs on a school bulletin board.

---

[10] See "Leadership," pages 160–161, for tips on how to start a club. See also the "Kids Meeting Kids" resource on page 83.

See "Be a mediator" on page 178.

# Steps for Mediation

## I. Introduction

1. Introduce yourself as a mediator.

2. Ask those in the conflict if they would like your help in solving the problem.

3. Find a quiet area to hold the mediation.

4. Ask for agreement to the following:
   —try to solve the problem
   —no name calling
   —let the other person finish talking
   —confidentiality

## II. Listening

5. Ask the first person "What happened?" Paraphrase.

6. Ask the first person how she or he feels. Reflect the feelings.

7. Ask the second person "What happened?" Paraphrase.

8. Ask the second person how he or she feels. Reflect the feelings.

## III. Looking for Solutions

9. Ask the first person what she or he could have done differently. Paraphrase.

10. Ask the second person what she or he could have done differently. Paraphrase.

11. Ask the first person what she or he can do here and now to help solve the problem. Paraphrase.

12. Ask the second person what she or he can do here and now to help solve the problem. Paraphrase.

13. Use creative questioning to bring disputants closer to a solution.

## IV. Finding Solutions

14. Help both disputants find a solution they feel good about.

15. Repeat the solution and all of its parts to both disputants and ask if each agrees.

16. Congratulate both people on a successful mediation.

**PLAN A PEACE DAY, WEEK, OR MONTH** at your school. Invite influential people from your community (the mayor, police, members of the town council, etc.) to speak about peace. Invite student volunteers to choreograph a peace dance, decorate bulletin boards with peace messages, make peace posters, write and perform songs about peace, etc. End with a Peace Party. You might ask local businesses to sponsor your party by donating money for refreshments and decorations.

> *Variation:* Search the World Wide Web for "Peace Day" or contact some of the organizations listed on page 178. You may be able to coordinate your Peace Day, Week, or Month with a national or international effort.

**SUPPORT OR OPPOSE A LAW OR ORDINANCE** involving peace or violence. Contact your state house and ask for a list of bills currently being considered that deal with these issues. Once you've looked over the list, choose a bill to support or oppose. *Examples:* a bill about gangs, family violence, gun control, etc. Then contact the sponsor of the bill and ask how you can help.

**MAKE A PEACE THERMOMETER** for your classroom or home. Draw a large thermometer on a piece of posterboard. Label the different levels of peace. *Examples:* Sunny sky, no clouds (peace, cooperation); cloudy and windy (people are using angry words and insults); stormy (hitting, shoving); hurricane (major conflicts). String a bead through a long piece of yarn and tape the ends of the yarn to the top and bottom of the thermometer. Slide your bead up and down depending on the "climate" of your classroom or home.

**PLAY AN "OFF-KEY CHOIR" GAME.** Invite everyone in your family, class, or club to sing a familiar song together. Ask some people to sing it one note higher or lower. Or ask everyone to sing their own favorite song, all at the same time. What happens? A lot of noise—and a reminder that when we sing the same song, on the same key (and when we cooperate to reach the same goals) the results are a lot more pleasant and harmonious.

*Variation:* Try playing any game—volleyball, Monopoly, Chutes and Ladders, etc.—without following the usual rules. Instead, everyone can make up their own rules. Is this possible? Why or why not? What happens?

**READ STORIES ABOUT PEACEFULNESS** and conflict resolution. Look for these books:

*The Big Book for Peace* by Lloyd Alexander, Natalie Babbitt, and Ann Durrell (New York: Dutton Children's Books, 1990). More than 30 prominent children's authors and illustrators teach about the importance of a peaceful world. Ages 12 & up.

*Journey Home* by Yoshiko Uchida (New York: Atheneum, 1978). Twelve-year-old Yuki and her family have just been released from Topaz, one of the camps in which many Japanese-Americans were sent to live during World War II. Their return to Berkeley is filled with disappointment and resentment by others, but Yuki soon discovers that coming home is a matter of heart and spirit. Ages 11–14.

*Never Cry Wolf* by Farley Mowat (New York: Bantam, 1985). Biologist Mowat describes the summer he spent in the Canadian Arctic watching and tracking the activities of a family of wolves, learning that these graceful and intelligent creatures barely resemble the ferocious wolves of legend. Ages 13 & up.

*Peace Tales: World Folktales to Talk About* by Margaret Read MacDonald (North Haven, CT: Shoe String, 1992). Folktales from around the world invite young readers to think about peace and how they can make it a reality. Ages 10 & up.

*The Story of Ferdinand* by Munro Leaf (New York: Puffin, 1988). Ferdinand grows up to be the biggest and strongest bull in his neighborhood. His friends are anxious to be chosen for the bullfights, but Ferdinand is happiest when he can sit in the shade and smell the flowers. Originally published in 1936. Ages 5–9.

# Character in *ACTION*

## Michael Hwu: Building Peace

Fifteen-year-old Michael Hwu considered himself lucky. His family was close, and they lived in a quiet neighborhood in Pasadena. He worked hard at school, earned high grades, and didn't bother anyone. Violence was something that happened to other people, not the Hwus.

So Michael wasn't at all prepared for what he saw one day when he arrived home from school. Two police cars were parked in front of his house. But what made his heart pound was the ambulance also parked there, its lights flashing.

Michael raced up the front steps and through the double doors of his home. Inside, papers were strewn everywhere. Chairs were overturned, and books were scattered across the floor.

His sister, Michele, ran towards him, crying. "They broke in and robbed us, and they shot Dad in the leg!"

Michael sat on the front porch in shock. Later, when he went to the hospital to visit his dad, he found him lying between white sheets, his leg in a cast and suspended in the air, his face swollen and bruised. Michael learned from his dad what had happened that day. There had been a knock at the door, and when his dad went to answer it, three teenagers had forced their way into the house and started beating him. One had a gun. He grabbed a pillow to muffle the sound, shot Michael's dad in the leg, and threatened to kill him if he didn't open the safe.

That's when Michele arrived home. The teenagers forced her to open the safe. Meanwhile, Michael's dad bluffed and told the boys that the safe had a secret alarm attached to it. They quickly grabbed the family's passports, other papers, jewelry, and a stereo, then dashed out the door.

Not long afterward, Michael's family moved to Seattle to live with Michael's grandmother. They hoped that Seattle would be less violent than Pasadena, and

they could regain some peace and composure there. Michael began attending Shorecrest High School for his junior year. During an English class, the teacher discussed the increase in violence across the country. "No one in the class could relate to what the teacher was saying," Michael remembers. "At least, no one but me. Everyone else was saying that violence didn't affect them. That bothered me, because you shouldn't have to experience violence firsthand before you do something about it. I didn't want my friends to go through the same thing my family and I had experienced."

Michael felt frustrated, and his frustration built up inside him. But Michael's father had taught him

Michael Hwu

how to restore peace within himself before going to sleep at night. Michael lay in bed and thought about the things he had done during that day, what he needed to do tomorrow, and what he wanted to do in the future. He thought about the past and pondered ways to resolve problems and conflicts. In this relaxed state of reflection, it came to him: He would keep feeling frustrated until he did something to promote peace in a world that seemed to be growing more violent.

"I knew I couldn't just sit on the sidelines anymore," Michael explains. "I had to do something about violence. I went to the Center for Human Services at my school and talked to the people there. I started volunteering in a number of ways—doing substance abuse counseling, helping people complete high school, doing job readiness training."

Along the way, Michael learned about a group called Mothers Against Violence in America (MAVIA). He contacted them and asked what else he might do to promote peace. They told him about Students Against Violence Everywhere (SAVE), a student-initiated, proactive organization with chapters in elementary, middle, and high schools in Washington State and California, and explained how he could start a chapter at his school. Michael wrote a proposal for a SAVE chapter at Shorecrest High School and gave it to his principal. He also proposed organizing a series of youth forums at the local middle school and elementary school. The principal accepted Michael's proposal.

Michael organized six youth forums. He invited former gang members to speak, and they told the students what it's like to be in a gang and how to get out. He invited Guardian Angels to speak at another forum.[11] Michael also got involved as a peacemaker or mediator whenever he saw a situation on the verge of erupting. One night at a school dance, he noticed a friend and another guy bang into each other, then start arguing and shoving. Michael stepped in immediately and asked them to chill. "That was all it took," he says. "They just needed someone to step in so no one looked bad in front of their friends."

Michael believes that being *peaceful* is not the same as being *passive*. "You can't just be nonviolent," he claims. "You have to be active in the community to keep peace. You have to know your neighbors and not lose touch with your values."

---

## CHECK IT OUT

**Mothers Against Violence in America (MAVIA)/ Students Against Violence Everywhere (SAVE)**
105 14th Avenue, Suite 2A
Seattle, WA 98122
1-800-897-7697
*www.mavia.org*
Contact MAVIA to learn more about SAVE. Visit the Web site to read the current issue of the SAVE Newsletter, read a list of projects that SAVE students have participated in and organized, and find out how to start a SAVE chapter.

---

[11] See "Forgiveness," page 102, for more about the Guardian Angels.

# Problem Solving

## Resourcefulness, ingenuity

> "Problem solving means weeding out all the things that don't work until you find something that does. Mistakes need not be failures. They can be steps toward finding solutions."
> *Barbara A. Lewis*

When my fourth, fifth, and sixth grade students at Jackson Elementary in Salt Lake City discovered a hazardous waste site three blocks from their school, they flew into action, like an army of termites trying to eat the Sears Tower. It was a huge problem. Some 50 thousand barrels had been stockpiled over 40 years. Most of the things the kids tried in the beginning didn't work. For example, they conducted a survey of the neighborhood looking for ground wells so they could ask health officials to take water samples to test for toxic chemicals—but all the wells had been cemented over. They called the health department—and health officials told them there was nothing the kids could do. They passed a petition around the neighborhood asking for the removal of the barrels—and the petition was threatened with a lawsuit three times.

Was my students' project doomed to failure? No! Along the way, they learned many things that didn't work, and some that did. Through a process of problem solving, they eventually got all the barrels removed, and the site was cleaned up. It took 10 years, a lot of mistakes, some failures, and hard work, but they succeeded.

My students were in good company. People who make great contributions or discoveries always have problems to solve along the way.

Alexander Fleming took advantage of an apparent failure in an experiment, and by shrewd observation discovered penicillin. Here are more success stories that started out as failures:

- Beethoven's music teacher once proclaimed "As a composer, he is hopeless."

- Walt Disney was fired by a newspaper editor because he had "no good ideas."

- The legendary tenor Enrico Caruso once had a music teacher who told him "You can't sing. You have no voice at all."

- Madame Schumann-Heink, who later became a famous opera star, was told by the director of the Imperial Opera in Vienna that she would never be a singer and should buy a sewing machine.

- Leo Tolstoy flunked college.

- Werner von Braun failed ninth-grade algebra.

- Louis Pasteur was rated as "mediocre" in chemistry when he was at college.

- Dr. Seuss's first book, *And to Think That I Saw It on Mulberry Street,* was rejected by 23 publishers.

- Abraham Lincoln began the Black Hawk War with a captain's rank and came out as a lowly private.

- Louisa May Alcott was told by an editor that she wouldn't ever be able to write something that would have popular appeal.

184

- During World War II, a scientist named James Wright kept trying to invent artificial rubber, but all he got was a lump of flexible, bouncy stuff. He thought he had failed completely. In fact, he had invented Silly Putty.

- At the first TV station that hired her, Oprah Winfrey tried to be a reporter—and failed. But she couldn't be fired because of the terms of her contract, so her producers assigned her to a local morning talk show. That was the beginning of Oprah's incredibly successful career.

> "Go ahead and make mistakes. Make all you can. Because remember, that's where you'll find success."
> *Thomas J. Watson*

Successful problem solving requires several good character traits. If you glance at the list of character traits in the Contents, you'll see that any number of these are needed to solve problems. You have to *know yourself* and your own capabilities. It helps to be *optimistic* and have *hope* in your efforts. You need to *care* enough to try your best. Problem solving means making *choices*—and accepting the consequences when your choices don't turn out the way you want them to. And so on down the list. You might even think of problem solving as a "chemical reaction" that combines your best character traits to create a new "solution."

## CHECK IT OUT

*Mistakes That Worked* by Charlotte Foltz Jones (New York: Doubleday, 1991). Explores many inventions—Coca-Cola, Post-it Notes, Frisbees, cheese, chocolate chip cookies, aspirin, and more—that all happened by accident. Ages 9–13.

# 10 Ways to Fail at Problem Solving

Do you want to know how *not* to solve problems? Here are ten strategies that are almost guaranteed to lead to failure.

1. ***Fight against the problem.*** Many people think they can solve a problem by swimming upstream against it. That works for salmon, but not for problem solving. Instead, study the problem and try to understand it. Learn about it. Examine it from as many angles as you can. Then you'll know how to approach it.

2. ***Deny or ignore the problem.*** Do you remember the fable about the ant and the grasshopper? The ant worked hard to prepare for winter, but the grasshopper played. When winter came, the ant was ready, but the grasshopper was cold and hungry. If you deny or ignore a problem, it won't go away. It will just be harder to solve when you're finally forced to face it.

3. ***Have a bad attitude about the problem and your own ability to solve it.*** Shouting "Having a curfew STINKS!" won't win any points with your parents. Thinking "I can't talk to them, so why bother?" won't help, either.

4. ***Don't finish what you start.*** Some people are afraid to carry out their solutions for fear that other people will criticize them. Or they procrastinate and don't get around to finishing. Either way, the problem isn't solved.

5. ***Be afraid of making mistakes.*** Problem solving can be scary. What if you do something wrong? Make a mistake? Goof up? (In fact, doing nothing is usually a *bigger* mistake.)

6. ***Give up.*** Stop before you reach a solution. Stop before you start working toward a solution.

7. ***Be afraid of the competition.*** Some people don't solve problems for fear that others might do it better.

8. ***Get a false or inaccurate picture of the problem.*** If you think it's smaller or less serious than it is, you won't devote enough time and effort to solving it, and you're likely to fail. If you think it's bigger or more serious than it is, you'll devote too much time and effort to solving it—which could cause even more problems.

9. ***Rely on luck to solve the problem or make it go away.*** What some people call "luck" is really the result of thought, energy, commitment, and the willingness to take advantage of good opportunities.

> "I find that the harder I work, the more
> luck I seem to have."
> *Thomas Jefferson*

**10. Rely on other people to solve problems for you.** If you depend on others to solve problems and make decisions for you, this prevents you from learning and growing. Plus you have to be satisfied with what they come up with, even if it's not what you want.

# 10 Steps to Successful Problem Solving

As you read through these steps, you might notice some similarities to the scientific method—a procedure scientists have used for centuries to solve problems.

**1. See if there's a problem to solve.** You can't solve it if you can't see it. Identify it. Describe it. *Example:* "Uh-oh, I'm failing algebra."

**2. Research your problem.** Find out the history of your problem. What's involved? Who's involved? What's the extent of your problem? Ask questions about it. Talk to experts about it. *Example:* Your test and quiz grades have been slipping for the past few months. You've neglected to turn in several homework assignments, which also affects your grade. You go to your algebra teacher and say "Uh-oh, I'm failing algebra."

**3. Get help.** See if there's anyone who can work with you to solve your problem. *Example:* Your teacher tells you there's an after-school tutoring club for people who need help with algebra.

**4. Make a hypothesis or guess about what you think might solve your problem.** *Example:* "Maybe if I start going to the tutoring club, I can bring up my grade and pass the class."

**5. Experiment and observe.** Try your solution and watch what happens. *Example:* You start attending the tutoring club. You observe yourself to see if your grades improve.

**6. Form a theory based on your observations.** Think about what you've learned so far. Is it enough

to solve your problem? If not, think *beyond* what you've learned. *Example:* "Attending the tutoring club might not be enough. Maybe I need to start doing my homework."

**7. Make a decision based on your theory.** *Example:* "I should spend more time studying and complete all of my homework assignments."

**8. Make a plan based on your decision.** *Example:* "I'll pay more attention in class, write down the homework assignments, go to the tutoring club three times a week, and do my homework every night." Follow your plan.

**9. Learn from your mistakes.** Mistakes can be good teachers. *Example:* "Now I know that I can't bluff my way through algebra."

**10. Revise your theory.** *Example:* "Tutoring plus homework equals success in algebra."

BONUS: Successful problem solving can help you to *prevent* future problems. *Example:* "I guess I should start working harder in chemistry *before* that becomes a problem, too."

> "Each problem that I solved became
> a rule which served afterwards to
> solve other problems."
> *René Descartes*

# Character Dilemmas

*For journaling or writing essays, discussion, debate, role-playing, reflection*

**Suppose that . . .**

**1** You want to go to the algebra tutoring club, but you can't stay after school. Both of your parents work outside the home, and you have to take care of your little sister. What might you do to solve your problem?

**2** Your parents are divorced. You live with your mother, but you want to live with your father. What might you do?

**3** You're the mayor of a town in which two different groups are competing for the same budget money. One group wants a hospital expansion with better facilities for people who are mentally disabled. The other group wants a hospital expansion for children with birth defects. Both groups have urgent needs that can't wait for future funds. If you half-fund both groups, neither will be able to reach its goal. How might you decide which project should have priority? Or is there another way to approach this problem?

**4** You're a teacher with 39 students in his class, and because of budget cuts you don't have enough desks and books to go around. Ten of your students have serious behavior problems, and you believe that they would learn better in another school that specializes in teaching kids with behavior problems. But that school is overcrowded, too. You have several problems. What are they? What might you do about each one? Where will you start?

**5** You overhear two gang members talking about plans to graffiti the school and neighborhood. You think they know that you overheard them, but you can't be sure. If you tell on them, they might retaliate. If you don't tell, your school and the neighborhood will be defaced. What will you do?

**6** You live in a small town that doesn't have a public library. You work to build a team of people to work on this project, and the town donates a building and books. Just as you're about to begin renovations, you learn that the building is going to be demolished for a new sports park. Your group has no money to buy another building. How might you solve this problem?

# Activities

**CONNECT WITH STUDENTS FROM OTHER SCHOOLS** around your state, country, or world to find out how they solve problems. You might do this over the Internet or join a pen-pal organization.[1] Ask them how they deal with issues like these (or think of your own ideas):

- communicating with parents
- doing homework
- having a job and going to school at the same time
- curfew
- getting along with peers
- handling peer pressure
- reducing crime
- getting school supplies
- getting medical care.

**START A PROBLEM-SOLVING NOTEBOOK** or journal.[2] Write about the problems you face in your daily life and how you solve them. Write about what works and what doesn't work.

**LEARN ABOUT THE ORIGINS** of famous discoveries, inventions, and talents. Each one started out as a problem to be solved. You might want to start by asking yourself something you've always wanted to know. *Examples:* How do they get the lead into a pencil? How did they discover the age of the earth? How do they get music onto a CD? Then visit the library or log on to the Internet and look it up! See if you can figure out the problem-solving steps each discovery required.

---

[1] See "Peacefulness," page 179, for a list of pen-pal organizations.
[2] See "Endurance," pages 88, 89, and 92, for journaling resources.

## CHECK IT OUT

*How Do They Do That? Wonders of the Modern World Explained* by Caroline Sutton (New York: Quill Books, 1982). Answers questions including: How do they create spectacular fireworks? How do they splice genes? How do they dig tunnels underwater? Ages 13 & up.

*Tricks of the Trade for Kids,* edited by Jerry Dunn (Boston: Houghton Mifflin Company, 1994). Learn how to draw cartoons from a Disney animator, how to build mighty biceps from Arnold Schwarzenegger, how to start a successful business from Mrs. Fields of cookie fame, and more. Ages 9–14.

**WRITE A NEW ENDING TO A STORY, POEM,** or play that ends in a sad or disappointing way. You might have to work backward in the text to discover where the problem started, then rewrite that part, too.

**HOLD A SPEECH CONTEST** in which the contestants describe problems and propose solutions.[3] You might have a theme for the contest, such as a particular school or community problem (tolerance, theft, gangs, drugs and alcohol, sports ethics, etc.). Or you might broaden your theme to include city, state, or national issues (health care, child care, urban development, foreign relations, etc.). Give prizes for Best Speech and Best Solution.

**HAVE A CLASS, CLUB, SCHOOL, OR FAMILY** debate on this topic: "Be it resolved that from this time forward, all children in our town (city) under 16 years old will be in their homes by 9:00 P.M." Divide into two teams: *affirmative* (in favor of the statement) and *negative* (against the statement). TIP: Remember that when you debate a topic, you don't necessarily agree with the side you present. After the debate, switch sides so everyone has the chance to debate both the pros and cons of the topic.

**BRAINSTORM A LIST OF SOLUTIONS** for these problems (or other problems you'd rather brainstorm about):

- low self-esteem
- acne
- losing your homework

---

[3] See "Communication," pages 52–53, for tips on public speaking.

- a sibling who teases you
- making new friends
- finding a boyfriend or girlfriend.

**RESEARCH SOLUTIONS TO PROBLEMS** caused by natural disasters. What might people do to reduce the impact of tornadoes, hurricanes, floods, earthquakes, fires, and other events? Report your findings to your class or club. *Examples:*

1.   Research the Mt. St. Helens volcanic eruption on May 18, 1980. What happened when the volcano erupted? What have people learned from this disaster? Make a chart or poster illustrating what you learn.

2.   Research the impact of forest fires. What happens to the local populations of animals, plants, and trees? What happens to the people who live nearby? How do firefighters problem solve during a forest fire? What are the positive aspects of a forest fire? What happens to the forest as it recovers from a fire? Present your findings in an oral report.

3.   Investigate earthquake detection. How do scientists know when an earthquake is going to happen? How accurate are their predictions? What kinds of instruments do they use to problem solve? Write a report on your findings.

## CHECK IT OUT

**Cascades Volcano Observatory**
1300 SE Cardinal Court
Building 10, Suite 100
Vancouver, WA 98661
(360) 993-8900
*vulcan.wr.usgs.gov*
Part of the U.S. Geological Survey, the Cascades Volcano Observatory keeps a close watch on Mt. St. Helens.

**Forest Service**
U.S. Department of Agriculture
PO Box 96090
Washington, DC 20090
(202) 205-8333
*www.fs.fed.us*
Contact the Forest Service or visit the Web site to learn about fire management and current or recent fires.

**U.S. Geological Survey**
12201 Sunrise Valley Drive
Reston, VA 20192
(703) 648-7411
*www.usgs.gov*
Contact the USGS or visit the Web site for information on California quakes, hazards and preparedness, studying earthquakes, and more.

---

**INVITE A FINANCIAL PLANNING EXPERT** to speak to your class, school, or club. Learn about ways to solve the problem of making your money grow—now and in the future. How and where should you invest your money? How can you make sure to have enough money to meet your needs? [4]

**PREPARE A COLLEGE EDUCATION BUDGET.** Many students (and their families) are facing the problem of how to finance their college education. It's never to soon to start thinking about this, since college can be *very* expensive. Imagine that you'll be going to college at some point in the future—seven years from now? four years from now? next year? Choose a college or university you think you'd like to attend. Find out the current costs for tuition and room and board. (Ask your guidance counselor or librarian how to do this, or search the Internet.) Try to estimate costs for books and supplies, transportation, recreation, clothing, and medical expenses. You might want to start by researching current expenses. Then try to predict what expenses might be when you actually start college. What might you start doing *now* (individually and with your family) so you'll be ready when the time comes?

---

## CHECK IT OUT

*College Financial Aid Made Easy* by Patrick L. Bellantoni (Atlanta, GA: Tara Publishing, updated often). Describes in depth the variety of financial resources available to college undergraduates, including application information and financial planning suggestions. Written in a clear, easy-to-use style appropriate for high school students, parents and guardians, and school counselors. Ages 15 & up.

---

[4] See "Conservation," pages 61–70, for a discussion of thriftiness, an activity on budgeting your money, and a reproducible "Income and Expenditures" chart.

**FinAid: The Financial Aid Information Page**
*www.finaid.org*
A free, comprehensive, independent, objective guide to student financial aid, maintained by the author of *The Prentice Hall Guide to Scholarships and Fellowships for Math and Science Students,* sponsored by the National Association of Student Financial Aid Administrators (NASFAA).

---

**FIND OUT WHAT SUPPLIES** your school needs. Books? Lab equipment? Computers? Sports equipment? Musical instruments? Interview teachers and your principal to learn about the most urgent needs. Then work with your class, school, or club to plan and carry out a fund-raising effort. TIPS: You might 1) sell services (car washes, talent shows, tours, etc.), 2) ask for donations, 3) sell goods (cookies, buttons, books, candy, yo-yos), or 4) apply for grants.

**LEARN HOW PEOPLE WITH SPECIAL NEEDS** have been treated historically. How have people who are disabled, mentally incapacitated, or terminally ill been treated in the United States? What problem-solving techniques have been used to help them? How have people with special needs been treated in other countries and cultures? Show your findings on a histogram. (A histogram is a bar graph with the bars touching each other, leaving no gaps.)

> *Variation:* Use your problem-solving skills to decide what people might do today to improve the acceptance and care of people with special needs.

---

## CHECK IT OUT

**disABILITY Information and Resources**
*www.makoa.org*
A gateway site to vast amounts of information about people with disabilities, laws, products, services, and more.

---

**VISIT A HOLOCAUST MUSEUM** or war memorial. You might do this as a field trip with your class or school. Afterward, write a letter to the editor of your school or town newspaper describing what you saw and experienced. Can you think of other ways to solve disagreements besides killing people and fighting wars? You might end your letter with a suggestion or two. TIP: If there are no museums or memorials within visiting distance, search the Web for sites you can visit online. *Example:* The United States Holocaust Memorial Museum in Washington, D.C. has a Web site at: *www.ushmm.org*

**LOBBY YOUR LEGISLATURE.** Sharpen your problem-solving skills by supporting a bill (potential law). Follow these steps:

**1.** Call a legislator who represents your home or school district. (To learn the names of legislators in your area and the districts they represent, call your state house and ask, or check at your library.) Ask your legislator's intern to send you a list of bills currently under consideration in an area that interests or concerns you. (*Examples:* bills dealing with aging, poverty, hunger, substance abuse, homelessness, kids, disease, teen pregnancy, graffiti, possession of weapons, nutrition, or crime.) Ask the intern to include the bill numbers, descriptions of each bill, and the names and telephone numbers of their sponsors.

**2.** Choose one bill you'd like to support.

**3.** Research both sides of the issue.

**4.** Contact the bill's sponsor(s) and ask what you can do to help support the bill. You might offer to write letters, lobby in person, pass out flyers, testify before legislative committees, build local support, or advertise the bill.

> *Variation:* Lobby on a local level. Contact your city or town offices and find out how you can support an ordinance.

**IDENTIFY AND SOLVE A SCHOOL PROBLEM.** Look around your school for things that need fixing, improving, or changing. Survey students, teachers, and administrators to get their input and perspective. Then follow the 10 steps on page 39. (You might need to adapt them to fit your project.) Afterward, reward yourself and your team for all the hard work you've done. Have a party!

**PAINT THE TOWN.** Contact the human services department in your town or city and get the name of a family or senior whose house needs painting. Use your problem-solving skills to find an adult sponsor, get the permissions you need, gather a team of workers (friends, family members, classmates, kids in your club or faith community), and get the job done.

**LEARN HOW EDITORIAL CARTOONS** and comics have portrayed real-life problems. Editorial cartoons in particular focus on current events and news (elections, social problems, scandals, etc.); some comic strips have editorial content (for example, *Doonesbury*). You might choose a particular period from history (the Great Depression, the Vietnam War, the most recent national election), then visit your library and look at cartoons and comics from newspapers published during that time. Think about these questions as you're doing your research:

**?** How do cartoonists treat problems? Mostly seriously, or mostly as jokes?

**?** Do cartoonists have the power to influence public opinion?

**?** Do cartoonists ever suggest solutions to problems? Are they realistic or exaggerated?

Share what you've learned with your class, club, or family. You might want to create a comic book or a series of cartoons to present your findings.[5]

**LEARN HOW MUSIC AND ART** can help people cope with problems, such as physical and mental illnesses or accidents. Interview a psychologist.

> *Variations:* Are there places in your community where people are lonely? *Examples:* a senior citizens' home, children's shelter, homeless shelter. Cheer them up with a musical talent show. Get your whole class or club involved. Find people who sing and play musical instruments. Prepare a program and present it. Invite the people you're performing for to sing along with you. TIP: Choose songs that are easy to learn and sing (such as rounds), or popular songs that many people are likely to know. Or plan a summer music program for latchkey kids. Use your problem-solving skills to get the permissions, adult sponsors, and equipment you need.

**FIND OUT ABOUT THE SPORTS PROGRAMS** available to children and teens in your community. Are there enough programs, locations, and choices (softball, soccer,

---

[5] See "Choice and Accountability," page 32, and "Imagination," page 131, for resources related to comics.

tennis, volleyball, swimming, etc.) that anyone who wants to participate has the opportunity? Are they adequately funded? Are they affordable? Do the teams have the supplies and equipment they need? Survey local schools, neighborhood groups, park employees, etc. Maybe you won't find a problem. But if you do, brainstorm solutions and, if you can, carry them out.

**PLAY A "CHOOSE A SHOE" GAME.** Have everyone in your class or club take off one shoe. Put all of the shoes in a pile in the middle of the room. Blindfold each player in turn and ask him or her to find a shoe that fits (other than his or her own shoe). Keep playing until everyone has a shoe. Then talk about what happened. Discuss questions like these:

**?** Was it hard to find a shoe that fit?

**?** Did being blindfolded make it even harder?

**?** Do you need to see the whole problem to find a solution that "fits"?

**?** Is it easier to find a "fit" when you have a number of choices available to you? (In other words, does it help to have many possible solutions to choose from?)

*Variation:* Have other players give the blindfolded players verbal instructions to direct them toward specific shoes ("go right," "go left," "reach down"). Then talk about how it helps to have knowledgeable people in the team who can "see" all of the available solutions.

**READ STORIES ABOUT PROBLEM SOLVING,** resourcefulness, and ingenuity. Look for these books:

*The Book of Changes* by Tim Wynne-Jones (New York: Orchard, 1995). Six witty short stories full of magic, real-life ghosts, and unlikely heroes. Meet Clarke, who doesn't have the nerve to peddle *TV Guides* door-to-door; Tobias, who once again has left his long-term school project for the last minute; and Dwight, who uses his Donald Duck impersonation—and some timely advice from the school nerd—to thwart the neighborhood bully. Ages 8–13.

*The Car* by Gary Paulsen (San Diego, CA: Bantam Doubleday Dell Books for Young Readers, 1995). A teenager left on his own travels west in a kit car he built himself. Along the way, he meets two Vietnam veterans who take him on an eye-opening journey. Ages 12 & up.

*The Happiest Ending* by Yoshiko Uchida (New York: Atheneum, 1985). When 12-year-old Rinko learns that a neighbor's daughter is coming from Japan to marry a stranger twice her age, she sets out to change the arrangement and gains new insight into love and adult problems. Ages 8–13.

*Island of the Blue Dolphins* by Scott O'Dell (New York: Bantam Doubleday Dell Books for Young Readers, 1997). Records the courage and self-reliance of a Native American girl who lived alone for 18 years on an isolated island off the coast of California. Originally published in 1960. Ages 10 & up.

*The Tar Pit* by Tor Seidler (New York: Farrar, Straus & Giroux, 1991). Trying once again to skip math class, Edward Small wanders to an old tar pit and discovers a dinosaur jawbone, but no one will believe him. After a terrible nightmare in which his dinosaur destroys everything in sight, Edward realizes he's his own worst enemy and decides to change his attitude toward school and the people around him. Ages 10–14.

---

## CHECK IT OUT

If you'd like to find a book that might help you deal with a specific problem or challenge you're facing in your life, visit your local public library and ask the reference librarian for *Bookfinder* or *The Best of Bookfinder.* Published by American Guidance Service, this valuable resource groups and describes books by topic. (Sample topics include peer pressure, communication with parents, jealousy, resourcefulness, decision-making, loneliness, depression, and talents.) Your library might even have *The Bookfinder* on CD-ROM.

---

# Character in *ACTION*

### Christine Sargent: Solving Problems

"You have to be aware of your surroundings, watch, and keep one hand free, like when you're coming out of a grocery store," 15-year-old Christine Sargent explains. She's addressing a group of women in the self-defense class she teaches with her friend, Rita Trujillo. "Self-defense means that you're in control of your body and aware of your surroundings."

Christine and Rita grew interested in self-defense for women when they learned that girls as young as eight months and women as old as 80 years had been raped or physically abused in Taos, New Mexico. Together they founded the Taos Women's Self-Defense Project. They were the youngest of the first 12 people to be trained as instructors; the other women involved were all between 30 and 60 years old. Christine's mother, a psychotherapist, spearheaded the project.

First, Christine and Rita had to raise the money to fly trainers to Taos from the Los Angeles Commission on Assault Against Women. The trainers spent four hours with the Taos group, then left them with books and videos to study. Christine and Rita devoted two nights a week for a year to their training.

"Each of us would learn a skill and then teach the others," Christine says. "After being certified as instructors, we taught many classes for teens and women of all ages. We taught them *awareness* techniques, like watching your space and paying attention to how close you are to other people, and *assertiveness* skills so they could stand up for themselves. We also taught them *physical* techniques, like kicking, punching, and how to identify targets.

"We worked with seventh, eighth, and ninth grade P.E. classes. We warned them that when you're at a party, you have to be aware and assertive if someone hits on you. You have to use your voice effectively, make eye contact, and pay attention to your body language. Stand firm and don't slouch. Look strong and sound like you mean what you say. You need to be respectful in the way you speak to other people, but you should always be alert to what's going on. You have the right to protect yourself."

"Often, women don't know how to assert themselves," Rita adds. "In our society, girls are trained to be polite, nice, and submissive. We have to learn how to be strong individuals and follow our instincts."

Christine has used her problem-solving skills in her private life, too. For a while, she devoted so much time to the defense project that she had to figure out how to weave in her other activities. She

Christine Sargent

practiced the piano every night after school, and as soon as she got her driver's license at age 15, she drove an hour and a half to her piano lessons. She maintained an A average at Taos Junior High, participated in the science fair, and tutored kids at an elementary school.

She even helped a shy first grader who had a problem asserting himself with other kids. While tutoring him, Christine taught him how to play games such as "Duck, Duck, Goose" so he'd feel more confident about joining groups. She also participated in the student senate, was a member of the honor society, and got involved in other activities as well. But she kept her weekends for fun—something she still tries hard to do. As Christine says, "You can be a problem solver without being boring."

Rita Trujillo (left) and Christine Sargent

# Purpose

## Direction, goals, focus, vision

Suppose you have a friend who lives in the Springhill Housing Development somewhere in your city, and one day you tell him that you'd like to visit him. You know that you've seen a sign for the development in the eastern part of your city, so you set off in that direction. Without any specific instructions, you search for two days along main roads until finally you find a sign for the Springhill Housing Development.

You drive into the development and discover that it contains over 600 homes. After another two days of knocking on doors, you finally get lucky and locate someone who knows your friend. Of course, by then your friend has grown weary of waiting for you.

You probably would never do anything like this. It doesn't make good use of your time, and it doesn't win any points with your friend. Instead, you'd ask him for directions before you left home. Your friend would describe signposts to watch for along the way. You'd know to take I-15 to the Valley Hill Shopping Center exit, go left four blocks, turn right at Lexington (the corner with the Mom & Pop Gas Station), travel through two stoplights, and so on until you reached his home.

Although the idea of setting out on a journey with no directions seems hard to believe (and silly besides), some people live their lives this way. For example, suppose that you want to be a chemical engineer someday. You have a vague idea that being a chemical engineer is somewhere out there in your future. You might know the general direction to go in, but if you don't know any of the signposts along the way, you might wander indefinitely and never achieve your goal.

What are some of the signposts on the way to becoming a chemical engineer? First, you'll want to know what kinds of classes to take in school. If you don't take some chemistry and math, you'll have a longer and harder road to travel. You should probably do your best to earn good grades, since that will help you get into college. To finance your college education, you may need to work summer jobs, save money, and apply for scholarships. You'll need to do some research to discover the best colleges and universities to apply to and what kinds of scholarships might be available to you.

Thinking about and planning your future will help bring your dreams into focus. When you concentrate on something important to you, it usually becomes clearer and stronger in your mind. When you ignore something, it often becomes weaker and more indistinct.

What if you don't know what you want to be? That's okay. You can still find general signposts to help you go in positive directions. You can still do all kinds of wonderful things in your lifetime. It's also okay to change your mind and your direction as you journey through life. But you can achieve things faster and easier if you plan far ahead, and some things take a long time to reach—and require many signposts and steps along the way.

# Finding a Purpose

"We are told that talent creates its own opportunities. But it sometimes seems that intense desire creates not only its own opportunities, but its own talents."
*Eric Hoffer*

You might think of "what you want to be" (or "who you want to be") as your *purpose*. Purpose is very personal. It's that special something inside of you that you want to develop and pursue. Purpose gives your life meaning and enables you to make a contribution in your own unique way.

How can you find your purpose? You might start by asking yourself "What do I like to do most?" You have special talents that make you what you are. You can do things that nobody else can do, or do them in ways that nobody else can duplicate. When you match your talents with a need, you can find a purpose. Here are more questions to ask yourself as you think about your purpose and what it might be:[1]

? What are my talents?

? What's easy for me to do?

? What's hard for me to do?

? What are my interests?

? What do I do in my spare time?

? Who needs me or my skills?

? What do I dream about?

? Who are my heroes?

? What kinds of people do I like to be around?

? Do I like to be around people?

? Do I like to be around animals?

? Would I rather be outdoors or indoors?

? What things do I *dislike* doing?

? What things worry me?

? What things would I like to see improved?

? How would I design the ideal future for my town, city, country, or world?

You might want to jot down some responses to these questions in a notebook or journal.[2] Look back at your responses from time to time. Are there more questions you might ask yourself? Can you develop your responses further and go into more detail? If you're *purposeful* about your purpose, you should find it becoming more clear as the months and years go by.

# Setting Goals

"Goals determine what you're going to be."
*Julius Erving*

The signposts and steps you follow on the way to your purpose are your *goals*. Setting goals is a skill you can learn. Here's how to do it:

*1.  Get ready to do some serious goal-setting.* Here are four things you'll need:

● some uninterrupted quiet time

● someplace where you can think and work comfortably

● something to write with

● something to write in or on.

---

[1] If you completed the Self-Portrait on pages 12–13, you might want to look back at it now. Some of your responses contain clues to your purpose.

[2] See "Empathy," pages 88, 89, and 92, for journaling resources.

Take a walk, find a quiet corner at the library or your school media center, or go to your room and hang a "Do Not Disturb" sign on your door.

**2. *Set your long-range goals for the next 10 years.*** Write down all of the things you'd like to accomplish during this time. Keep your purpose in mind. Your long-range goals should support your purpose.

> *Example:* You like being around animals. One of your long-range goals might be to work as a veterinarian. So you write down "To work as a veterinarian," "To have my own veterinary practice," "To find cures for diseases that affect animals," and "To attend a college or university that has a program in veterinary medicine."

**3. *Prioritize your long-range goals.*** Number them in order of their importance to you. Then look at numbers 1, 2, and 3. These are your Top Three long-range goals. Congratulations!

> *Example:* Your Number 1 long-range goal might be "To have my own veterinary practice."

**4. *Set your medium-range goals for the next 3–5 years.*** Write down all of the things you'd like to accomplish during this time. Include details. Keep your purpose AND your long-range goals in mind. Your medium-range goals should help you achieve your long-range goals. They're related!

> *Example:* You write down "To find out which colleges and universities offer the best veterinary medicine programs," "To get a part-time job working for a veterinarian," "To read as many books as I can about being a veterinarian," and "To learn more about running a business."

**5. *Prioritize your medium-range goals.*** Number them in order of their importance to you. Now you have a Top 3 list of medium-range goals. You're making real progress!

> *Example:* Your Number 1 medium-range goal might be "To find out which colleges and universities offer the best veterinary medicine programs."

**6. *Set your short-range goals for the next year or two.*** Write down all of the things you'd like to accomplish during this time. Keep your purpose AND your medium-range goals in mind. Your short-range goals should help you achieve your medium-range goals.

> *Examples:* You write down "To ask my guidance counselor about veterinary schools," "To interview veterinarians about their education and what their work is like," "To search the Internet for veterinary schools and ask for copies of their catalogs," and "To check out a book from the library about being a veterinarian."

**7. *Prioritize your short-range goals.*** Number them in order of their importance to you. Now you have a Top 3 list of short-range goals. Good work!

> *Example:* Your Number 1 short-range goal might be "To check out a book from the library about being a veterinarian." (Guess what: This is something you could do today. *Taking action on your goals is what makes them happen.*)

**8. *Record all of your Top 3 goals in a notebook or journal and date them.*** Check your lists often to remind yourself of your goals—once a day or once a week. Whenever you reach one of your goals, check it off and write down that date in your notebook.

**9. *Revise your lists as you reach your goals.*** Whenever you reach one of your top goals, choose another one to replace it.

**10. *Revise your goals as needed.*** Things change. People change. You're changing right now. Don't be afraid to look back at your goals and start over if you need to. What's important is to *always have goals.*

You might be thinking that goal-setting seems too hard or complicated. Remember that it's a skill, and learning any new skill takes practice. If you want to play the piano, you have to practice. If you want to make the swimming team, that takes practice, too. Improving your score on your favorite video game is something that comes after hours of practice. Isn't it worth it to practice a skill that can shape your whole life? One that you'll use again and again throughout your life? After all, you'll always have things you want to achieve and accomplish.

Here are just a few of the good things that come from being a goal-setter:

✳ You feel more independent. You're not waiting for someone else to decide your life for you. You're doing it yourself.

✳ You feel more capable. You're not waiting and hoping for things to happen. You're *making* them happen.

★ You feel more in control of your time. You can look back at each week and know that you've accomplished something. This frees you to have more fun!

★ You feel more confident that you'll eventually fulfill your purpose. Remember, goals are the steps that get you there.

You might be thinking that goal-setting seems too simple or easy. How can making lists have such a powerful effect on your life? After all, you're just writing down a bunch of words! But before you decide that goal-setting isn't for you . . . *try it.* Look around for other goal-setters and talk with them. (TIP: Successful people and high achievers are usually goal-setters.) Then promise yourself to follow this process for at least three weeks. By then, you'll have a good idea of whether it works for you. If you don't like this process after three weeks, you might try it again, and then again, because it can help you to focus your energy in finding and fulfilling your purpose.

Many young people (and adults, too) have a general idea of where they might like to be in 5, 10, or 20 years from now. But they don't have the discipline to do the *daily planning* that enables them to accomplish the "little things" on the way to achieving their long-range goals. If you can train yourself to do this—and you must *do it for yourself*—then you'll be on your way to fulfilling your purpose.

You create your own future in your mind. Vision comes before doing. Goal-setting helps to make your vision come true.

> "The victory of success is half won when one gains the habit of setting goals and achieving them. Even the most tedious chore will become endurable as you parade through each day convinced that every task, no matter how menial or boring, brings you closer to fulfilling your dreams."
> *Og Mandino*

# Character Dilemmas

*For journaling or writing essays, discussion, debate, role-playing, reflection*

**Suppose that . . .**

**1** You're a talented musician, a top scorer on the soccer field, plus you're very interested in medicine. How might you decide which is the best career or direction for you to choose? Give reasons.

**2** One of your friends is suddenly given the opportunity to attend a day-long leadership workshop out of state. Unfortunately, she already has a music recital scheduled for the same day, and she sent out invitations several weeks ago. So she (reluctantly) decides to skip the leadership workshop. Do you think she might ever have another opportunity like that, or does "opportunity knock" only once? Do you think your friend made the right decision? Why or why not?

**3** The mayor of a city has made a plan for the city's future direction. Her plan includes developing a large park as a business area, which would lead to economic growth the city needs. When the mayor's plan is made public, many people protest. They think that the park should be left alone. Should the mayor follow her plan for the city, or should she listen to the people? Explain your answer.

**4** You go to a sleepover at a girlfriend's house, expecting that it will be an all-girls party. When you arrive, you discover that your friend has invited boys to spend the night, too. You don't want to be a party-pooper, but you're not comfortable with boys sleeping over. Should you ask your friend to tell the boys to leave? Should you stay at the party and keep quiet? Should you go home? What might you do in the future to avoid similar problems and misunderstandings?

**5** You're confused about your future, and you have no particular vision of what you want to be someday. Is that okay? Should you do something to plan your future? Or should you just let it take care of itself?

# Activities

INTERVIEW PEOPLE WHO DO interesting things. You might do this on the telephone, by letter, or by email.[3] Broaden your own interests by interviewing people who do things you don't know anything about. Write up your interviews in a notebook and share it with your class.

KEEP A SCRAPBOOK of newspaper articles about people who do unusual or interesting things. You might look for articles about people with unique jobs, unconventional hobbies, or anything else that catches your eye.

SEARCH THE INTERNET to learn more about your interests and hobbies. Use a search engine like Yahoo, Hotbot, Excite, or Altavista. (If you don't know how to use a particular search engine, read the tips or Help section.) Bookmark any sites you find that you want to visit again in the future.

## CHECK IT OUT

**Yahooligans! Hobbies Links**
*www.yahooligans.com/Sports_and_Recreation/Hobbies*
Links to sites about collecting, crafts, gardening, kites, magic, pets, puppetry, and more for kids.

EXPAND YOUR INTERESTS BY VOLUNTEERING.[4] This is a great way to learn new things, meet new people, and serve others. Check with your school, community center, place of worship, local United Way office, etc. to find out what opportunities are available to you.

GO MUSEUM HOPPING. Visit museums around your city. Look for different things you might be interested in. Do any of them relate to your purpose? Do any of them inspire you to do some goal-setting?

> *Variation:* Visit museums on the Internet. Many have their own Web sites with virtual exhibits. You might start by going to *http://www.yahoo.com* and doing a search for "museums."

TRY TO FIND AT LEAST THREE good reasons for studying math in school. Why learn math if you're interested in things that don't have anything to do with math? Does math do anything special for your mind? How might it help you to focus on problems and find solutions? Set goals? Find a purpose? Write your reasons and thoughts in your journal.[5]

> *Variation:* Try to find at least three good reasons for *everything* you're studying in school. Why learn about history? Science? Literature? Health? Geography? What else?

PLAN GOALS FOR THE FUTURE of your country. Suppose you're a member of the President's cabinet and you're able to plan goals for the future of the United States. Write at least five goals you think the U.S. should head towards in the future. Justify your goals. (If you live in a different country, plan goals for your own country.)

## CHECK IT OUT

**The White House**
1600 Pennsylvania Avenue
Washington, DC 20500
*www.whitehouse.gov*
When you finish writing your goals, consider sending them to the President. You can do this by mail, through the White House Web site (if your Web browser supports forms), or by email to:
*president@whitehouse.gov*

GO ON A SCAVENGER HUNT around your neighborhood or community. Look for interesting things around you. Does anything you see give you an idea of a direction you'd like to follow?

HAVE A CULTURAL EXPERIENCE. Encourage your family to accompany you to a symphony, ballet, opera or musical, or art exhibit to broaden your vision of things you might be interested in. Afterward, discuss your experience—and plan the next one. You might want to consider getting a family membership to an art museum, science museum, or children's museum in your area.

GO "MENTOR SHOPPING." If you have a strong interest in something, seek out a professor, a teacher, or community member who is involved with your interest.

---

[3] Get in touch with famous people with help from *The Kid's Address Book*. See "Choice and Accountability," page 32.
[4] See "Empathy," pages 81–82, for guidelines on how to volunteer.

[5] See "Empathy," pages 88, 89, and 92, for journaling resources.

Contact the person and ask if it might be possible to spend time together so you can learn from him or her.[6] IMPORTANT: Be sure to get permission from your parents or guardians. Ask them (or another responsible adult) to chaperon you when you meet with your mentor.

**START A CLUB FOR PEOPLE** who share your interest(s).[7] *Examples:* Computers Club, Dog Lovers Club, Dancers Club, Singers Club, Young Astronauts Club, Gardeners Club, Volleyball Club. Meet once a week or once a month.

**FIND A CLASS OR CAMP** that allows you to explore one of your interests. *Examples:* basketball camp, swimming class, water polo class, crafts class, science camp, etc. Develop a talent you've always wanted to develop. TIP: Ask about free classes at your community center.

**USE DAILY AFFIRMATIONS** to help you find your purpose and reach your goals. An affirmation is a simple statement you tell yourself often throughout the day. It might be about something you want to accomplish, feel, become, or be. When actor Jim Carrey was still a struggling comedian, he used to tell himself "I will earn ten million dollars a year by 1995!" You can use affirmations to form good habits ("Today I'll take a 20-minute walk"), strengthen a talent ("Today I'll really concentrate when I practice the piano"), explore a new interest or hobby ("Today I'll learn more about cars"), or develop a positive character trait ("Today I'll tell the truth"). You might want to start each day by reading or writing an affirmation.

## CHECK IT OUT

*Making the Most of Today: Daily Readings for Young People on Self-Awareness, Creativity, and Self-Esteem* by Pamela Espeland and Rosemary Wallner (Minneapolis: Free Spirit Publishing, 1998). A year's worth of quotations, readings, and affirmations to help all kids know themselves better, be more creative, and feel better about themselves.

---

[6] For a related activity, see "Establish a mentor file" on pages 131–132.
[7] See "Start a new club" on pages 160–161 for how-to tips and a resource.

**CREATE A BOARD GAME** in which players try to reach a goal. You might model your game after Monopoly, Life, Candyland, Chutes and Ladders, or any other game you enjoy playing (or used to enjoy playing when you were younger). Use these steps as guidelines:

**1.** Decide on a goal. This can be anything you choose—finishing high school or college; becoming a dancer, artist, computer programmer, chef, or forest ranger; learning to be a good speaker; developing friendships; getting married; raising children; etc.

**2.** Place "signposts" along the way from Start to Finish that relate to reaching the goal. *Examples:* "You get an A in math. Go forward two spaces." "You win first prize in an art contest. Go forward three spaces." "You get invited to a slumber party. Take an extra turn."

**3.** Place "traps" along the way that slow players' progress toward the goal. *Examples:* "You skip third period math class. Go back two spaces." "You miss the deadline for entering the art contest. Lose a turn." "You ignore someone who greets you in the cafeteria. Draw a penalty card."

Work with your class, club, or family to design and create a game board, playing pieces, bonus and penalty cards, etc. Decide on the rules. Then play your game and refine it if necessary. You might want to share your game with younger kids in your school.

**READ STORIES ABOUT PURPOSE,** direction, goals, focus, and vision. Look for these books:

*My Side of the Mountain* by Jean Craighead George (New York: Puffin Books, 1991). A young boy builds a treehouse in the Catskill Mountains and lives alone for a year, struggling to survive and ultimately realizing that he needs human companionship. Ages 11–14.

*Water Sky* by Jean Craighead George (New York: HarperCollins Children's Books, 1987). While living in Barrow, Alaska, with friends of his father, a boy learns the importance of whaling to the native Eskimo culture. Ages 11–14.

📖 *Wise Child* by Monica Furlong (New York: Random House, 1989). Abandoned by both of her parents, nine-year-old Wise Child goes to live with the witch woman Juniper, who begins to teach her the ways of herbs and magic. Ages 9–12.

📖 *Year of Impossible Goodbyes* by Sook Nyul Choi (New York: Dell, 1993). A young Korean girl survives the oppressive Japanese and Russian occupation of North Korea during the 1940s to later escape to freedom in South Korea. Ages 10–13.

# Character in *ACTION*

## Billy Green: A Sense of Purpose

Thirteen-year-old Billy Green hunkered over the computer at the National Science Teachers' Association (NSTA) Conference in St. Louis. He spoke to the 120 people who had sandwiched themselves into the meeting room—some at tables, some standing, some squatting on the floor. Another 100 had been turned away at the door. Billy and his younger brother, Kirk, were helping their dad, Tom Green, present a very popular session called "Using the Internet to Enhance Science Education." Before the conference, Billy had prepared a slide show demonstrating how to find resources on the Net.

As his audience watched, Billy demonstrated a search technique. "I'll use the Excite search engine to find out how dinosaurs became extinct," he explained. Billy brushed long strands of hair from his eyes and clicked on one icon after another. "It says here that once people thought dinosaurs died out because the mammals ate their food." A few teachers chuckled. "And here it says that one of the first theories was that dinosaurs died out because of the sniffles." Some teachers laughed out loud. "Here's a more recent theory," he said, scanning the computer screen. "It says that an asteroid threw up a cloud of dust, which blocked out the earth's rays and lowered the temperature. It was too cold for the dinosaurs, and that's why they died out."

Billy looked out at his audience. "It's fun to find all kinds of stuff on the Internet," he said. "But mostly I like using it to find answers to puzzles and games." He grinned, and the laughter grew even louder. Billy told the teachers how he had reached a dead end in the popular CD-ROM game *Myst*. He couldn't get the right combination to a safe he needed to continue

with the adventure. "So I went on the Net and found the solution." The teachers applauded.

This wasn't the first time Billy had helped science teachers. He had presented at an earlier NSTA conference and also at the Michigan Environmental Teachers' Conference. "I want to be a computer programmer when I'm older," Billy says. He knows it won't happen in one giant step, so he's doing it in small bits and bytes.

Billy sets goals for himself, and he has advice to offer others: "If someone skips school and gets bad grades, they have nothing. They can't get good jobs or anything else they want. When this happens, they don't like their lives. So it's important to work hard in school."

Billy first became interested in computers by way of Nintendo. That led him to real computers, computer games, searching the Internet, and programming. He spent two weeks at the University of Michigan learning "C," a computer language. This happened because he was selected as a high achiever by the Midwest Talent Search. His California Achievement Test (CAT) scores were above the 97th percentile in math and the 95th percentile in English. Billy had to write and rewrite an essay to convince the judges to choose him for the University of Michigan program. Writing isn't easy for him.

He wants to go to Michigan State University because his dad went there. Since a college education is expensive, he's already planning to work during the summers and save the money he earns. His mom, dad, and grandfather have agreed to help him, too. He'd like to win a scholarship but knows he can't count on that, so he's earning good grades now, taking special classes, and spending time on the Internet. On some days, his parents forbid him from going on the Net because he spends hours mucking around and surfing, monopolizing the family phone line.

"Billy likes to concentrate on one thing—like the Internet—to the exclusion of everything else," his father, Tom, explains. "He gets so intense. When he's trying to solve a problem on a computer game or the Net, he stops eating, ignores everyone, gets grouchy, and becomes so competitive that he's not always fun to play with. He's getting better now because he has a goal and he's determined to reach it."

"I want to make my own home page next," Billy says. "I think I'll have categories—movies, games, MUDs and MUSHes. MUDs and MUSHes are games you play on the Internet with other people. You can walk around virtual worlds, chat with other characters, explore dangerous areas with monsters, and solve puzzles.

"I'll practice what I learned at the University of Michigan this year, and next year I'll go back to learn graphics. Then I'll put it all together. You have to work to get your goals accomplished—work and go to special classes. You can't learn everything you need to know in school. But most of all, you have to practice."

## CHECK IT OUT

**Midwest Talent Search**
Northwestern University Center for Talent Development
Northwestern University
617 Dartmouth Place
Evanston, IL 60208
(847) 491-3782
*www.ctd.northwestern.edu*
Information about special programs, resources, and enrichment opportunities for all grades; information about other regional talent searches.

Billy Green at his computer

# Relationships

## With family, friends, self, and others

> "Personal relations are the important
> thing forever and ever."
> *E. M. Forster*

You may have heard or read about the three-year-old boy who fell into a gorilla exhibit at the Brookfield Zoo in Illinois in 1996. Binti Jua, an eight-year-old female gorilla who was carrying her own baby, Koola, on her back, hurried over to the unconscious boy, who had climbed a railing and fallen 18 feet. Binti gently picked him up, cradled him in her arms, and held him. Then she carried him over to the door where zookeepers could reach him, and carefully placed him on the floor. She continued to protect him from the advances of other gorillas until help came.

Onlookers were astounded at the seemingly understanding and sensitive behavior of the mother gorilla toward the human boy. Some animal behavior experts think that Binti might have acted differently if the boy had been running around in a threatening way, because gorillas, while not normally aggressive, will act to defend their territory and their babies. Nevertheless, Binti's behavior sparked a lot of discussion across the country.

It's difficult to know why Binti behaved the way she did, because she can't tell anyone how she felt at the time. Is it possible that Binti protected the boy because she had her own baby and had experienced the mothering instinct? What do you think?

You first learned about loving and caring in your relationship with your parents and family. When you are loved and nurtured, you can love and nurture in return. Babies who aren't loved and nurtured don't grow as well, and sometimes they die. If they live to be adults, they often have a difficult time developing relationships with other people.

You probably received tender loving care from your parents, and you're all set. But what if you think you didn't? What if your relationships with family members weren't as nurturing as you might have hoped or wanted them to be? Here's good news: You can *learn* to develop good relationships with your family, friends, yourself, and others. Following are some tips and suggestions you can try.[1]

# 12 Ways to Start and Strengthen Relationships

1. ***Be a person of good character.*** When you're positive, honest, loyal, and respectful, other people are naturally drawn to you. They recognize you as someone who's worth getting to know.

2. ***Be kind and caring.***[2] Notice and reach out to other people, especially when they're hurting. *Example:* Your friend is caught cheating on a test, and he's embarrassed and ashamed. You might write

---

[1] Sometimes people who haven't been loved and cared for need professional help learning how to love and care for others. If you think you might need professional help, talk to an adult you trust—a teacher, school counselor, religious leader, family member, or friend.
[2] See "Caring," pages 21–27.

a note telling him something you admire about him. By doing this, you're not condoning the cheating. Instead, you're letting him know that you still see his good qualities.

> "The greatest healing therapy is
> friendship and love."
> *Hubert Humphrey*

**3.  Be loving and supportive.** When you care for other people, you enjoy watching them succeed. You wish for good things to happen to them, and you support them when they're in need. *Example:* If you have a friend who's in trouble, try talking with her privately. Tell her how much you care about her and how worried you are that she might get hurt. This is the best way for you to influence your friend to think about her actions and make better choices.

True love is unconditional. You love your friend even when she makes poor choices. You love your little brother in spite of the fact that he constantly raids your hidden cache of candy. IMPORTANT: Unconditional love doesn't mean that you sacrifice your beliefs or values for another person. You can stay true to yourself *and* be a true friend.

> "If we would build on a sure foundation in
> friendship, we must love our friends for
> their sake rather than for our own."
> *Charlotte Brontë*

**4.  Be a good listener.** Show that you're interested in other people and their lives. Ask questions about their talents, passions, plans, goals, hopes, dreams, fears, and anxieties; find out what makes them happy or sad. *Example:* If your sister suddenly starts spending a lot of time alone in her room, try to find out why. She might not be willing to tell you when you first approach her. But if you're patient, persistent, and kind, you'll eventually gain her confidence and she may tell you what's bothering her.

> "You can make more friends in two
> months by becoming interested in other
> people than you can in two years by trying
> to get other people interested in you."
> *Dale Carnegie*

**5.  Spend time together and share experiences.** As much as you might like and appreciate another

person—a parent, sibling, close friend, or acquaintance—your relationship won't grow if you don't do things together and connect in other ways. You might plan special activities to share— or you might spend quiet time together reading, doing homework, studying, or watching the clouds go by.

**6.  Recognize when you have problems with others.** The first step in healing a wound is acknowledging that one exists. But don't just scratch it or put a Band-aid on it and hope it will go away. Try to find the cause of the wound. Was it something you said or did? How can you make up for it? Was it something another person said or did? How can you find out what's bothering him or her, and what, if anything, can you do to make things better? What might you do to improve the relationship?[3]

**7.  Be willing to compromise.** When you compromise with another person, you *both* get something you want. You might not get *everything* you want, but you reach an agreement that seems fair to everyone involved. *Example:* You're 15, and your dad still wants you to be home each night by 8:30 P.M. You'd like to be able to stay out later. You and your dad sit down together to talk about your curfew. You each express your point of view, and you listen carefully to each other. You agree to a compromise: 8:30 P.M. on school nights (unless there's a school activity), later on Fridays and Saturdays. Neither you nor your dad gets *everything* you want, but you both get *something* you want.

**8.  Talk about your feelings,** especially when problems arise. Be assertive.[4] Address the problem without blaming the person. *Example:* A friend borrows $10 from you and doesn't pay it back. You might say "I'm wondering how soon you'll be able to pay back the $10 I loaned to you. I have to buy some books tomorrow and I really need the cash. Could you have the money for me by tomorrow morning?" Or you might say "You're such a loser! You never pay me what you owe me. Don't ever ask me for a loan again!" Which approach is most likely to get your $10 back?

---

[3] See "Communication," pages 51–52.
[4] See "Respect," pages 217–218.

**9. *Don't play the blame game.*** If you think your parents, siblings, friends, and others have wronged you in any way, try to forgive them.[5] Let it go.

There's a story about an old man who gathered kindling for a living and sold it to others. He was an angry guy who held many grudges. Whenever someone did something mean to him, he wrote the person's name on a stick and put the stick in a sack on his back so he wouldn't forget the offense and could eventually get even. At night, he'd pull out all the sticks and plan strategies for revenge. Often just thinking about what he might do to get back at someone made him feel better. One day, as he was climbing a hill to collect dead branches from a tree, he lost his balance from the burden of sticks on his back and fell backwards to the bottom of the hill.

Holding grudges can weigh you down. When you let things go, you're free to move on and improve your relationships.

**10. *Try not to judge others.*** Not even when you're absolutely, positively sure that you're right and they're wrong. Nobody's perfect all of the time—not even you. It's your job to improve *yourself*, not everyone else you know.

> "Every man should have a fair sized cemetery in which to bury the faults of his friends."
> *Henry Brooks Adams*

**11. *Expand your circle of friends*** to include people who are different from you. Sometimes these friendships can bring the most rewards. You'll learn to see things from a new perspective. You'll become more tolerant and accepting.[6] Your world will grow in many positive ways.

**12. *Be friendly.*** You might say "But I'm too shy!" Or "Being friendly is too risky. I don't want to get hurt." Many people are shy or go through periods in their lives when they're shy. Being shy is okay. And most people are afraid of getting hurt—so you're not alone. But if you want to be friendlier, here are some tips you can try:

**F**riendliness starts with a simple "hello." Say "hello" (or "hi" or "how's it going?" or whatever feels comfortable to you) to people you see often, even if you don't know them well. Practice by standing in front of the mirror and watching yourself. Practice on your family. Tell your mom or brother that this is your goal. Try doing it once a day, then three times, and so on. The more you do it, the easier it gets, like learning to ride a bike.

**R**each out to others. Join groups, organizations, and clubs. Sit with someone you usually don't sit with at lunch. Get a pen pal.[7] Call someone on the phone.

**I**nclude others. Look for people who are left out of activities and groups and invite them to join you. The more people you're nice to, the more friends you'll have. I know a young man who once ran for president of his high school. He didn't hang out with the popular group, but he always talked to everyone and looked for people who were alone so he could include them. Some students laughed when he ran for school president, but they didn't laugh when he won.

**E**ye contact. If you look at people when you say "hi" or talk with them, they'll pay more attention to you. Practice on your family. Practice in the mirror. Try making eye contact with teachers, then with friends, and so on.

**N**ames. Learn and remember them. To most people, the most beautiful sound in the world is the sound of their own name. When you first meet someone new, repeat his or her name. To help you remember it in the future, make up a mnemonic or "hook." *Example:* You've just met someone named Justin Harmon. You might think "*Justin* is *just* and he *harmonizes* well." It's corny, but it works.

**D**on't focus only on yourself. Think of the person you're with. If you hang a picture of yourself in your window, you can't see through it to the world (and the people) on the other side. Ask questions and listen to the answers.

**S**mile. Your smile might warm up a person who doesn't know you exist. If you combine your smile with eye contact, you might start a fire of friendship. If you're not used to smiling very much, you may need practice!

---

[5] See "Forgiveness," pages 94–102.
[6] See "Justice," pages 144–145.

[7] See page 179 for pen-pal resources.

# Fun Ways to Strengthen Family Relationships

Does your family spend time together doing things everyone enjoys? If so, be thankful—and be willing to participate. If not, do something about it. Organize activities. Contribute ideas and suggestions. Let your parents and siblings know that you love them and want to be with them. Especially if your family hasn't formed the togetherness habit, you may need to be extra patient. Don't expect instant results, and don't assume that everyone will always want to go along with your plans. Even if your family activity turns into just you and your mom, or you and your big brother, or you and your grandpa, it still counts. Once other family members see how much fun you're having, they may decide to join in.

- ♡ Plan a once-a-week family activity for an evening when most family members are at home. *Examples:* Watch a video together. Take a walk. Have a picnic on the porch.

- ♡ Make cookies or other treats together, then divide them—half for your family to enjoy, and half to deliver to a neighbor.

- ♡ Play some of the old games stored in your basement or attic. Pull out Twister, Dominoes, Monopoly, or anything else that looks interesting. You might even play hide-and-seek or tag. The older you are, the sillier and more fun this can be.

- ♡ Have a pillow fight or a water fight (whatever your family and neighbors will tolerate).

- ♡ Take a hike, ride bikes, swim, play street hockey with brooms, or play family volleyball or tag football.

- ♡ Sing or perform together. Learn songs your parents used to sing. Play your violin, flute, drums (make your own), play rhythm sticks, or whatever you like to do.

- ♡ Teach each other dances. Show your parents the latest steps and moves; have them show you how to do the dances they enjoyed when they were younger (or the dances they like doing today).

- ♡ Tell stories. Ask your parents about the "good old days" (or the "bad old days"). Share your favorite story or experience. Or make a "chain story" together. The first person writes a sentence on a piece of paper, folds the paper over to hide the sentence, then passes it to the next person, who does the same . . . and so on. Read the story aloud after everyone has contributed.

- ♡ Make family rules. Decide together on your family "do's" and "don'ts." Agree on rewards for following the rules and consequences for breaking them. Write the rules on a chart and hang it in your home.

- ♡ Read together. Read books of quotations, favorite stories, magazines, and newspapers. You might even read scriptures, like the Bible or Koran, a prayer book, or another book important to your faith.

## CHECK IT OUT

*Bringing Up Parents: The Teenager's Handbook* by Alex J. Packer, Ph.D. (Minneapolis: Free Spirit Publishing, 1992). Straight talk and specific suggestions on how teens can take the initiative to resolve conflicts with parents, improve family communication, and help to create a happier, healthier home environment. Ages 13 & up.

*Dr. Ruth Talks About Grandparents: Advice for Kids on Making the Most of a Special Relationship* by Ruth K. Westheimer (New York: Farrar, Straus & Giroux, 1997). Dr. Ruth lost both her parents and her grandparents when she was just 10 years old. She has spent most of her life forging solid relationships and teaching others to do the same. In this warm, forthright book, she discusses the many ways in which grandparents can enrich children's lives and suggests how kids can help out in return and show appreciation. Ages 9–12.

*The Families Book: True Stories About Real Kids and the People They Live With and Love, Fun Things to Do with Your Family, Making and Keeping Family Traditions, Solving Family Problems, Staying Close to Faraway Relatives, and More!* by Arlene Erlbach (Minneapolis: Free Spirit Publishing, 1996). In the first part of this book, 35 kids ages 8–18 talk about their families and what makes them special. The second part is full of fun things to do with your family, suggestions for starting family traditions, and ways to solve family problems and strengthen family relationships. Ages 9–13.

# Fun Ways to Strengthen Friendships

> "Friendship is the hardest thing in the world to explain. It's not something you learn in school. But if you haven't learned the meaning of friendship, you really haven't learned anything."
> *Muhammad Ali*

❧ Make popcorn balls (or other treats) and bring them to someone new in your school.

❧ Have a water balloon toss (outside in the playground, please).

❧ Bring old baby pictures to class and share them.

❧ Take off your shoes and walk in the mud, go wading, or go puddle stomping.

❧ Cut each other's hair (but first ask parents if it's okay).

❧ Paint scenes on your windows with washable, removable paints (again, ask parents first).

❧ Fly kites.

❧ Read a play together. Assign different parts to different friends (or ask which parts they'd like to read).

❧ Learn to juggle, balance something on your nose, or share a magic trick.

❧ Have a "read-a-thon" or "music-a-thon." Share your favorite books or music.

❧ Volunteer together. Find out about opportunities available in your neighborhood or community, then choose one to try.[8] Or plan and do a service project together.[9]

❧ Start a club.[10]

❧ Choose any activity from this book and do it together. Help each other to develop positive character traits. Support each other's efforts to become strong, principled people.

## CHECK IT OUT

*The Best Friends Book: True Stories About Real Best Friends, Fun Things to Do with Your Best Friend, Solving Best Friends Problems, Long-Distance Best Friends, Finding New Friends, and More!* by Arlene Erlbach (Minneapolis: Free Spirit Publishing, 1995). In the first part of this book, 11 pairs and groups of best friends talk about what they love about each other, what drives them nuts, and what they do together. The second part is full of fun things to do with your friends, how to handle arguments and other bad times, and how to make new friends. Ages 9–13.

---

[8] See "Empathy," pages 81–82, for tips on how to volunteer.
[9] See "Caring," pages 23–24, for service project tips and resources.
[10] See "Start a new club" on pages 160–161 for how-to tips and a resource.

*Trust & Betrayal: Real Life Stories of Friends and Enemies* by Janet Bode (New York: Laureleaf, 1997). Teens talk about their best friends, worst enemies, and the importance of being accepted by their peers. Real-life stories help young adults learn to deal with the ups and downs of fitting in, getting out, and making the right choices about friendship. Ages 12 & up.

# Fun Things to Do When You're Alone

> "Friendship with oneself is all-important, because without it one cannot be friends with anyone else in the world."
> *Eleanor Roosevelt*

To *have* a good friend, you must *be* a good friend. And that means with yourself as well as others. Here are some ways to strengthen your relationship with Y-O-U:

* Find a quiet, private place where you can hang out with yourself and just think—an attic, basement, tree, under the porch, under your bed, or in your closet.

* Write in your journal about how you feel about things that happen to you each day or each week.[11] Or write poems, stories, or letters to yourself.

* Dress up in a friend's or parent's clothes, or go to a department store or sports shop and try on clothes you don't normally wear.

* Do something physical. Jog, practice throwing, shoot baskets, kick balls, skate, walk, lift weights, swim, dance, or whatever gets your heart beating and your blood circulating.

* Draw or paint. Copy characters from comic books or the comics section in your local newspaper. Check out books on drawing from your library and practice. Instead of *writing* in your journal, try *drawing* in your journal.

* Surprise your parents and wash the dishes, clean out a closet, or bake a treat.

* Practice a skill you'd like to learn, such as singing, dancing, playing a musical instrument, doing card tricks, or blowing bubbles.[12]

* Make something, such as jewelry, wood carvings, model cars or airplanes, or clothes.

* Read something. Read anything that interests you—books, comic books, encyclopedias, cookbooks, newspapers, magazines.

* Make a time capsule. Bury it in your backyard or hide it on a closet shelf. Plan to dig it up or take it out in five or ten years.

* If you haven't yet completed the inventories on pages 7–11, do them now (or plan to do them soon).

* Lie in your bed, under the clouds, or somewhere you're comfortable and just dream. Listen to soft, soothing music and let your mind wander.

# Character Dilemmas
*For journaling or writing essays, discussion, debate, role-playing, reflection*

**Suppose that . . .**

**1** You want to improve your relationship with your parents. Is it more important to be loving or obedient? Give examples to support your answer.

**2** A politician wants to get reelected. Is it more important for her to be truthful to her constituents or to establish warm relationships with them? Why?

**3** You can choose to have just one close friend or many friends who aren't as close. Which will you choose and why?

**4** Two of your friends recently stopped being friends. What do you think causes most friendships to break up?

**5** A married couple you know is getting divorced. Almost half of all American marriages today end in divorce. Why do you think the divorce rate is so high? How do you think divorce affects children?

[11] See "Endurance," pages 88, 89, and 92, for journaling resources.

[12] See "Problem Solving," page 188, for information about *Tricks of the Trade for Kids.*

What that might kids do to help themselves during a divorce? What could couples do to make marriages more successful or divorces more peaceful?

**6** A small country and a large, powerful country have an ongoing relationship. For many years, the large country has given the small country millions of dollars in aid including food, technology, and medical supplies. Now the leaders of the small country are asking the large country for help in stopping a revolution within its borders. The leaders want the large country to give them sophisticated weapons to use against the revolutionaries. What do you think the large country should do? Give reasons for your answer.

# Activities

**WRITE A SURPRISE LETTER** to your mother or father, guardian, brother, sister, grandparent, or another relative. In your letter, tell the person how much he or she means to you.

> *Variation:* Write Chain-of-Praise letters in your family, class, or club. You'll need one sheet of paper per person. Write the person's name at the top. Then pass each letter around, inviting everyone to write something they like or appreciate about the person. When you're through, everyone will have a letter of praise and support written by everyone else.

**EXPLORE THE INTERNET WITH YOUR FAMILY.** If you have Internet access from a home computer, arrange a time to sit down together and visit family-friendly sites. If you don't have access to the Internet at home, visit your local library and ask about free community Internet access.

---

## CHECK IT OUT

Here are three family-friendly sites kids and parents can visit together:

**American Museum of Natural History**
*www.amnh.org/kids*

**Bill Nye the Science Guy**
*www.nyelabs.com*

**Kids Connect @ the Library**
*www.ala.org/parentspage*

**HAVE A FAMILY DISCUSSION** about the "ideal family." Discuss each of the following questions. You might want to set some ground rules first, such as 1) Everyone answers as honestly as they can, and 2) Everyone listens respectfully to each other's answers without interrupting or criticizing. You might want to ask someone to volunteer as secretary/recorder to write down people's answers. Afterward, work together to create a chart or collage showing your family's view of the "ideal family."

**?** In the "ideal family," who's the breadwinner? The father, mother, both parents, or others?

**?** How many children does the "ideal family" have? How many boys? How many girls? Are children near the same age or farther apart?

**?** Where does the "ideal family" live? On a farm? In the city? On the moon? In a house? On a boat? On a mountaintop? In a small town? In an apartment building? In a cabin in the woods?

**?** Where do grandparents in the "ideal family" live? With their children and grandchildren? With other people? On their own?

**?** In the "ideal family," who's in charge of disciplining the children? The father, mother, grandfather, grandmother, or someone else?

**?** In the "ideal family," what is the role of each family member? Think about the father, mother, children, grandparents, aunts, uncles, etc.

**?** Is it possible for someone who never marries to have an "ideal family"? Why or why not? Can a person create an "ideal family" from friends and other relatives?

**?** Is divorce a solution to some marriage problems? Why or why not? If it is, when?

**PLAN A DANCE OR OTHER SOCIAL EVENT** for grandparents and grandkids at your school, club, or faith community. If you don't have a grandparent to bring along, invite another senior citizen you know and trust.

**WORK TOGETHER AS A FAMILY** to research your roots and create a family tree. Interview living relatives. Look through family records and family Bibles (if available) for information. Use the Internet to find long-lost family members. Make copies of your family tree to share with other relatives.

# CHECK IT OUT

*Ancestors Videos*

Produced for public television, this series of ten 30-minute programs goes on location to visit with family historians of various social, economic, and ethnic backgrounds. It explains how to search for your family's roots and describes many resources available to genealogists. Check to see if your school or library has a copy. To order, call 1-800-828-4727.

*Ancestors: A Beginner's Guide to Family History and Genealogy* by Jim Willard, Terry Willard, and Jane Wilson (Boston: Houghton Mifflin Company, 1997). The companion book to the television series provides additional information about family history research not included in the series and an extensive resource directory. Ages 13 & up.

**Ancestors**

*broadcasting.byu.edu/ancestors*

The Web site for the series includes tips and tricks, a Teacher's Guide, and the Ancestors Resource Guide, a state-by-state listing of genealogical resources.

**Branch Genealogical Libraries
of the Mormon Church**

The Genealogical Society
50 East North Temple Street
Salt Lake City, UT 84150
(801) 538-2978

The Mormon Church owns the largest collection of genealogical records in the world. You don't need to be a Mormon or have a Mormon in your family to use it. Contact the Genealogical Society to find out the location of the branch genealogical library nearest you.

---

**READ ABOUT FAMOUS PEOPLE OF THE PAST** to learn what kinds of relationships they developed with others. Did they marry, have close friends, have a family, or live alone? Did their relationships affect how successful they were? Why or why not? Was one particular person especially important in their lives?

> *Variation:* Write to famous people of the present and ask which of their relationships has been most important to them and why.[13]

**RESEARCH AN EXAMPLE** of communal living. Throughout history, many people have chosen to live in groups and share their possessions, property, and responsibilities. Choose one type of communal group and learn as much as you can about it. *Examples:*

- monastic communities (monks or nuns, such as the Benedictines, Franciscans, Carthusians, or Dominicans)
- Puritans
- the United Order
- Amish
- Shakers
- New Harmony
- Brook Farm
- Oneida Community
- Amana Society
- Twin Oaks
- kibbutzim
- the "hippie" communes of the 1960s

As you do your research, try to find answers to these questions:

**1.** Why did the people choose to live as they did?

**2.** What were the advantages of the communal relationship? The disadvantages?

**3.** If the commune is no longer in existence, what brought about its end?

**4.** How did people in the surrounding communities relate to those who lived in the commune?

**VISIT A LOCAL STORE THAT SELLS** greeting cards. Make a list of the different types of cards you see that are intended to strengthen relationships. *Examples:* birthday, anniversary, get well, congratulations, bon voyage (for people about to leave on a journey or vacation), Christmas, Easter, Valentine's Day, Mother's Day, Father's Day, sympathy, thank you, graduation, wedding, new baby, friendship, etc. Try to figure an average price for each type of card. Now imagine someone with a large family (grandparents, aunts, uncles, nieces, nephews, siblings, cousins, etc.) and many friends who always sends cards on special occasions and often sends them "just because." Calculate how much money that person might spend on cards during a typical year. TIP: Don't forget to include the price of postage!

---

[13] See "Choice and Accountability," page 32, for information about *The Kid's Address Book.*

*Variation:* If possible, find out who buys cards most often: men or women, younger or older. Show your results on a chart.

**DECIDE WHAT'S MOST IMPORTANT TO YOU** in a friend. Copy and complete the questionnaire on page 211. Afterward, consider these questions:

**?**   Did any of your rankings surprise you?

**?**   What do your rankings tell you about your friends? (Do your friends match your rankings? If not, why not?)

**?**   What do your rankings tell you about *yourself?*

**?**   Do you think that your rankings might change as you grow older? If so, which ones seem most likely to change? Why?

> *Variation:* Have everyone in your class or club complete the questionnaire. Afterward, discuss one or more of the questions listed above, or other questions your group wants to explore. Create a bar graph showing the results of the questionnaire labeled with percentages. *Example:* "55% of the group ranked 'fun' #1."

**WITH YOUR CLASS OR CLUB, DEBATE** the most important character trait for a friend to have. Give examples of why you think the trait you name is most important. After the debate, vote on which trait is the most important and who was the most persuasive debater.

**SURVEY YOUR CLASS OR SCHOOL** to find out how long friendships last when friends are the *same* gender, when friends are the *opposite* genders, when friends are the *same* age, and when friends are *different* ages. You can copy and use the survey on page 212 or write your own questions. Distribute the surveys and set up a collection box where people can return their completed surveys anonymously. Afterward, show the results of your survey on a bar graph and see if you can arrive at any conclusions. You might want to compare males to females and/or different age groups or grades. For question #6—"What do you think is the *most* important quality for a friend to have?"—you might want to make a poster listing the qualities and ranking them according to how often they were named on the surveys.

**ROLE-PLAY THINGS YOU CAN DO** in a new school to develop friendships. Role-play things other people can do to make a new person feel welcome.

**SWITCH SEATS IN YOUR CLASSROOM** once a week for 10 minutes so everyone can get better acquainted with each other.

**ARRANGE A PANEL DISCUSSION** with students from another school. Talk about ways to build or improve relationships between your schools. This might be a "rival" school or just another school in your community or city. You might also talk about ways to improve student-student and student-teacher relationships within your own school.

**CREATE A PHOTOGRAPHY BULLETIN BOARD** about friendship. Find people in your school or community from a wide variety of cultures. Ask each person "How can people from different cultures form good relationships?" Write down the response. With the person's permission, take his or her photograph. Display the pictures and responses on the bulletin board.

**LEARN ABOUT RELATIONSHIPS** among animals. *Example:* Did you know that blue whales will stay around an injured whale? Even when this puts them in danger of being wounded or caught? How can you explain this?

> *Variation:* Learn about relationships among people and animals.

## CHECK IT OUT

*The Dog Who Rescues Cats: The True Story of Ginny* by Philip Gonzales and Leonore Fleischer (New York: HarperPerennial, 1996). The heartwarming story of an adopted mixed-breed dog whose remarkable sixth sense leads her to rescue and nurture handicapped stray cats. If you enjoy this book, you might also want to read the sequel: *The Blessing of the Animals: True Stories of Ginny, the Dog Who Rescues Cats.* Ages 13 & up.

*Koko's Kitten* by Francine Patterson (New York: Scholastic, 1995). The true story of Koko, a famous sign-language-speaking gorilla, and her friendship with a kitten. For younger kids ages 6–9, but fun to read.

*Real Animal Heroes: True Stories of Courage, Devotion, and Sacrifice,* edited by Paul Drew Stevens (New York: Signet, 1997). These 53 true stories of life-saving animal bravery are examples of courage, commitment, and love. Ages 13 & up.

# What's Most Important in a Friend?

*Read the following list of qualities you might look for in a friend.*
*Rank them in order from 1 (most important to you) to 15 (least important to you).*

___ Family income level

___ High moral values/standards

___ Honesty

___ Intelligence/education

___ Interests/hobbies

___ Kindness toward others

___ Knows how to have fun/likes to have fun

___ Is law-abiding

___ Looks/personal appearance/clothes

___ Loyalty

___ Physical fitness/good health

___ Political beliefs

___ Popularity/social status

___ Race/ethnicity/cultural background

___ Religion/religious beliefs

See "Decide what's most important to you" on page 210.

# Friendship Survey

*This is an anonymous survey. Don't write your name anywhere on it! Please drop your completed survey in the collection box in* _____.
                                                          location

1.  Think of the *close* friendships you have with people of the *same* gender as you. (If you're a girl, think of your female friends. If you're a boy, think of your male friends.) How many of these friendships have lasted for:

    less than a year _____?      1–2 years _____?      more than 2 years _____?

2.  Think of the *close* friendships you have with people of the *opposite* gender. (If you're a girl, think of your male friends. If you're a boy, think of your female friends.) How many of these friendships have lasted for:

    less than a year _____?      1–2 years _____?      more than 2 years _____?

3.  Think of the *close* friendships you have with people the *same* age as you. (This includes both female and male friends.) How many of these friendships have lasted for:

    less than a year _____?      1–2 years _____?      more than 2 years _____?

4.  Think of the *close* friendships you have with people who are at least 3 years *older* than you. (This includes both female and male friends.) How many of these friendships have lasted for:

    less than a year _____?      1–2 years _____?      more than 2 years _____?

5.  Think of the *close* friendships you have with people who are at least 3 years *younger* than you. (This includes both female and male friends.) How many of these friendships have lasted for:

    less than a year _____?      1–2 years _____?      more than 2 years _____?

6.  What do you think is the *most* important quality for a friend to have?

    _____

*Please be sure to complete this information:*

You are a            ❑ male        ❑ female

What grade are you in?        _____

How old are you?        _____

## THANK YOU for taking this survey!

IMAGINE THAT ALIENS HAVE LANDED on Earth and you've been chosen to represent all of humanity in a first encounter with them. What will you say? What will you do? How will you act? How will you try to establish a peaceful and friendly relationship with them?[14]

> *Variation:* Research how aliens are usually depicted in science fiction books and movies. Are they friendly? Hostile? Appealing? Horrifying? Helpful? Threatening? Give examples. You might want to make a poster or comic book illustrating what you learn from your research.

ANALYZE U.S. FOREIGN RELATIONS with Japan, Great Britain, Germany, Russia, Canada, Mexico, or any other nation of your choosing. TIPS: Read newspapers and news magazines, search the Internet, or interview a Congressional representative or senator. Find out how the relationship between your country and the other country has changed over the past 5 or 10 years. What do you think would help to strengthen and maintain good relations with that country?

## CHECK IT OUT

To learn more about relations between the U.S. and other countries, contact:

### Committee on Foreign Relations
450 Dirksen Senate Office Building
Washington, DC 20510-6225
(202) 224-4651
*www.senate.gov/~foreign*
Learn which Republican and Democratic senators are currently serving on this senate standing committee. Contact one or more by mail, phone, or directly through the Web site.

### Foreign Affairs
58 East 68th Street
New York, NY 10021
1-800-829-5539
*www.foreignaffairs.org*
Published since 1922 by the nonprofit, nonpartisan Council on Foreign Relations, *Foreign Affairs* is the most widely read magazine on international affairs and U.S. foreign policy. Check your library for current and back issues; visit the Web site for current and past articles, a large archives, and extensive links to related sites.

---

[14] See "Communication," page 54, to learn how to contact the SETI (Search for Extraterrestrial Intelligence) Institute.

### Public Information
Bureau of Public Affairs
Department of State, Room 2206
Washington, DC 20520
(202) 647-6575
*www.state.gov*
Contact the State Department's Public Information office or visit the Web site for information about foreign affairs.

---

MAKE A TIMELINE showing how the relations between the U.S. and Russia have changed over the past 100 years. Keep in mind that for many years people used the name "Russia" to refer to the entire U.S.S.R. The Soviet Union was formed in 1917 and ceased to exist in 1991; today Russia is an independent republic and is officially called the Russian Federation.

RESEARCH THE RELATIONSHIPS among North Atlantic Treaty Organization (NATO) countries over the past 50 years. TIPS: Read newspapers and news magazines, search the Internet, or interview a Congressional representative or senator. Which countries have been dominant? How have the dominant countries influenced the other countries in keeping, restoring, or encouraging peaceful relationships? Report your findings verbally or in writing to your class, club, community group, or family.

## CHECK IT OUT

To learn more about the relations between NATO countries, contact:

### NATO
Office of Information and Press
1110 Brussels, Belgium
email: natodoc@hq.nato.int
*www.nato.int*

---

PLAY A "GETTING-TO-KNOW-YOU" GAME. Try this at the start of a school year or anytime you want to learn more about your classmates or friends. Start by randomly pairing off. The pairs have five minutes to discover three things they have in common that they *didn't* know about each other before now. *Examples:* Both wear the same size shoes; both get up early on Saturday mornings to watch the same cartoon show; both have the same birthday month; both like old Beatles records; both like pizza with anchovies.

READ STORIES ABOUT RELATIONSHIPS. Look for these books:

📖 *Anne of Green Gables* by Lucy Maude Montgomery (New York: Penguin, 1997). This is the classic story of Anne, an orphan, who is taken in by a middle-aged brother and sister. Anne's personality and mischief-making lighten their lives. Ages 11–14.

📖 *Belle Prater's Boy* by Ruth White (New York: Farrar, Straus & Giroux, Inc., 1996). Woodrow moves in with his grandparents after his mother mysteriously disappears. There he befriends his cousin, and together they learn to face the losses in their lives. Ages 12 & up.

📖 *The Blue Heron* by Avi (New York: Simon & Schuster, 1992). While spending the month of August on the Massachusetts shore with her father, stepmother, and their new baby, almost 13-year-old Maggie finds beauty in and draws strength from a great blue heron, even as the family around her unravels. Ages 11 & up.

📖 *Homecoming* by Cynthia Voigt (New York: Fawcett Book Co., 1987). Abandoned in a parking lot, Dicey, along with her little sister and two younger brothers, tries to find her aunt Cilla. After they walk the length of the Connecticut coastline, Cilla takes them in, but she considers it a duty, not a pleasure, and Dicey realizes that they can't stay there long. Ages 10–14.

📖 *Molly by Any Other Name* by Jean Davies Okimoto (New York: Scholastic Inc., 1993). A teenage Asian girl adopted by non-Asian parents decides to find out who her biological parents are. Ages 13–16.

# Character in *ACTION*

## Josh Lewis: Helping Friends in Need

Naturally friendly and confident, 17-year-old Josh Lewis always tried to be there when his friends needed him. He'd speak and joke with everyone and treated them all about the same. Friends constantly bummed rides off of him, and sometimes he piled eight people into his '88 Ford Thunderbird just because he didn't like to turn anyone down. He was a friend to anyone.

Josh was a big kid, standing 6'1" tall and weighing 225 pounds. On the football field, he was a friend to the younger guys when the older jocks gave them a hard time. Sensing hurt feelings, Josh would say "Cut it out. It isn't fun anymore." He also offered the freshman players advice, telling them who to block or what pass route to run when they were confused.

Once at a party a big kid began pushing around Josh's best friend, Patrick Avard. The guy was twice Patrick's size and about 50 pounds heavier than Josh. Josh jumped in and protected his friend. "If you've got a problem with Patrick," he warned, "you've got a problem with me, because he's my friend." And he took a few punches for Patrick.

Josh met his good friend Lesley Eddings when the two of them were in seventh grade. Josh had just moved into his grandparents' house. "Lesley was my first girlfriend," Josh remembers. "She was always a cheerleader, and I always played football. In high school I got her together with my friend, Ben. We all hung out together. We rented movies and swam together in Patrick's pool. Wherever the guys went, we dragged Lesley along."

On one fall evening, Josh's friendship for Lesley was tested to the fullest. Josh had picked up Lesley in his Thunderbird, and they were headed for Ben's house when the back right tire either blew out or came off. The car fishtailed, hit an embankment, flipped upside down, and slid backwards into a utility pole. The fuel tank ruptured, and within moments the car burst into flames.

Josh had blacked out when the car first flipped, and he became conscious just as he felt himself crawling out a side window. He searched frantically for Lesley, but she wasn't anywhere on the ground, so he knew she must still be inside the car. When he went to look, the car was filled with smoke and he could hardly see anything. Then he noticed her legs—not moving—and knew she must be unconscious. Josh tried to pull his friend through the window, but she was wearing her seat belt. He reached through the smoke and found it, pulling hard and panicking when it didn't release. He gritted his teeth and yanked with bull strength. The belt ripped loose and Josh dragged Lesley through the window.

Friends who were driving behind them called 911 and rushed them both to the hospital. Josh escaped with a cut to his head, and Leslie suffered burns on her upper right arm that required skin grafts. Josh remembers standing there at the accident, feeling numb as a zombie, watching his car burning in a big bonfire . . . but it was okay. His friend was safe.

Two months later, Josh was challenged again, and this time he became a friend to a stranger. He and Patrick had returned to Josh's house after a late-night movie, and it was raining hard. Since Josh's high-school football team had just won the state championship, he was tired. Patrick had driven and had come inside to call his folks when the two boys heard a loud *thud* outside the house. Josh thought the wind had blown a tree branch down onto Patrick's car, so he went out to investigate. He saw a light through the rain. A car had hit a ditch, gone airborne up a pine tree, and slid down the trunk into bushes.

Josh raced into the house shouting for his grandfather, who was the volunteer fire chief. "I've never run faster than that," Josh remembers. "Not even on the football field. I couldn't have taken more than fifteen seconds, but when I got back out, the car was in flames."

Without pausing to consider the danger, Josh jumped into the bushes and found the car door. There was a woman in the driver's seat, sitting in shock. Josh grabbed her and pulled her from the car to safety. She spoke incoherently, shouting that her children were inside the car. Josh charged back into the blazing car in a frenzied search for her kids. There were no kids in sight. Emerging from her

shock, the woman remembered that her children had not been with her after all.

Josh received a lot of attention after that, for saving both his friend Lesley and the stranger. He was awarded the U.S. Department of Justice's Young American Medal for Bravery and the Carnegie Medal, among others. But Josh insists that "it was no big deal." He was just doing what he'd do for any friend. The usual stuff—like sharing with them, sticking up for them, protecting them, and risking his life for them.

"Honestly and truly," Josh says, summing up his feelings about friendship, "if you have a handful of good friends you know you can trust and will always be there, you've been very well blessed."

Josh Lewis

# Respect

**Courtesy, manners, assertiveness, politeness, reverence**

> "Even if someone doesn't treat you with
> the respect you deserve, you can give
> them the respect they don't."
> *Sharon Martin*

I once taught a fifth-grade student by the name of Allen. He was a red-haired, freckle-faced boy who bounced around the class with the energy of a geyser. He was sometimes noisy, dressed sloppily, and often spoke out of turn. But he also did something that amazed me: Whenever he talked without first raising his hand, he would say "I'm sorry."

There's more: Whenever he wanted to get my attention, he would interrupt me at my desk with "Excuse me, please...." And if I gave him anything, even a compliment, he bubbled "Thanks a lot!"

He treated the other students the same way. There was a girl in our class with special needs who was two years older than any of the other kids and could hardly speak. One day at recess I watched from the school steps as Allen took out a large red ball, walked over to the girl, and slowly taught her to catch the ball from only a few feet away. Soon he threw the ball to another student and the three of them started playing catch. Any time the girl caught the ball, I heard Allen say "Great! Good job!" Then the other kids started saying it, too. Before long, it became a daily classroom activity for someone to spend time with our special girl. Allen's example spread to the others—in more ways than one. Soon other children were congratulating each other, saying "Excuse me," and so on. I could hardly believe it.

I learned a lot from Allen that year. One day I sneaked up to him and whispered in his ear "I have a secret for you." His eyes lit up as I whispered "You surely are polite and nice." He flashed his infectious grin that had become familiar to the whole class. Then he cocked his head and said "Thank you. But, Mrs. Lewis, that's no secret."

Do you remember learning about Sir Isaac Newton? The scientist who discovered gravity when an apple supposedly fell on his head? Sir Isaac also discovered and described some laws of motion. One of his laws says "For every action, there is an equal and opposite reaction." In other words, if you turn on a garden hose, the water will rush *out* (action) and the force of it will also push *backward* (reaction). If you don't hold tightly to the hose, it will jump out of your hand.

You might apply Sir Isaac's law to human behavior. If you push someone, you'll probably get pushed back. Similarly, if you treat people politely—with respect that is sincere—they'll treat *you* that way (most of the time). You'll be a better friend and leader. You'll impress your parents, teachers, and other adults, and they'll be more likely to choose you for special experiences and rewards. And you'll like *yourself* better. It feels good to be respectful, and it feels even better to be treated with respect.

Sincere respect means:

- 💜 using good manners; being courteous and polite; speaking to others in a kind voice; using polite body language

- 💜 showing consideration toward other people (including your elders, parents, guardians, teachers, peers, siblings, other family members, employers, and people in authority)

- 💜 honoring other people's wants, needs, ideas, differences, beliefs, customs, and heritage

- 💜 caring for other living things and the earth (animals, plants, the environment)

- 💜 obeying the rules, laws, and customs of your family, faith, community, and country.

Ralph Cantor, an author of the *Days of Respect* handbook,[1] defines respect as "mutual care and regard, dignity, and physical and emotional safety; a state in which everyone counts, and everyone counts upon everyone else. Respect is a quality that we can all define for ourselves—and we all know when we are receiving it, and when we aren't." In other words, respect is about *relationships:* with people we know and people we don't know; with our society, culture, government, and God or Higher Power; with the planet we live on and the living things we share it with; and even with ourselves.

When you treat all people with equal respect—especially those who can't do anything special for you—you accept what they are and appreciate what they *may become.* This type of respect is unselfish, sensitive, and a foundation for many other values and positive character traits.

Respect has a cornerstone, and it's called *self-respect.* It's easier to respect others if you first respect yourself. When you respect yourself, you don't belittle yourself out loud or in your private thoughts. You take care of your mind and body, and you don't use alcohol and drugs. You eat well, exercise regularly, and get enough sleep. You don't give in to sexual pressure. You do your best to stay physically, mentally, and emotionally healthy.[2]

[1] See page 221.
[2] See "Health," pages 103–114.

> "Self-respect has nothing to do with the approval of others."
> *Joan Didion*

Some people use rudeness, bullying, and force to try to win the respect of others. It doesn't work. People *fear* bullies, but they don't *respect* them. When you respect others, you admire them and like them. Nobody feels that way about a bully. If you think that you might be a bully, get help. Talk to your parents, a teacher, school counselor, or another adult you trust.

"You'd better respect me or I'll MAKE you respect me!"

# How to Disagree Respectfully

Being respectful toward other people doesn't mean that you always have to agree with them. You can still speak your mind and stick up for yourself. It's called *being assertive.*

Suppose that your teacher repeatedly calls you "Brain Child"—a name you don't like (even if it's said in fun). You can use the ASSERT Formula to deal with the problem respectfully. Here's how:

**A** stands for *"Attention."* Before you can work on a problem you've having with another person, you first have to get the person to listen to you. Wait until after class. Then go up to your teacher and say "Excuse me, but may I speak to you about something that's bothering me?" If the teacher is too busy to talk right then, ask if there's a better time. "If you can't talk now, how about tomorrow before school or after class?"

**S** stands for *"Soon, Simple, Short."* Don't put off talking to your teacher. Do it as soon as you can—unless you're too upset to talk. In that case, wait until you calm down. State the problem simply and briefly.

**S** stands for *"Specific Behavior."* Focus on the behavior of the person you're having trouble with, not how you feel about the person. Even if you're angry with your teacher, try to keep your angry feeling out of your voice and your body language. You might say "I really don't like being called 'Brain Child.'"

**E** stands for *"Effect on Me."* Help the person to understand the feelings and problems you're experiencing as a result of his or her behavior. You might say "I know you probably mean it as a compliment, but it embarrasses me in front of the class. And lately, when I walk down the hall, other kids are calling me 'Brain Child,' too."

**R** stands for *"Response."* Wait for a response from the other person. In this case, your teacher might say "I wasn't aware that being called 'Brain Child' bothered you" or "I'm sorry, I never meant to embarrass you."

**T** stands for *"Terms."* Suggest a solution to the problem. You might say "Would you be willing to stop calling me 'Brain Child'? Or at least stop calling me that in front of other people?" It's a reasonable request, and your teacher should agree to it. When that happens, say "Thanks. I appreciate being able to talk to you about this."

What if your teacher *doesn't* agree to your request? Talk to your parents and your school counselor. You have the right to be treated respectfully, too.

## CHECK IT OUT

*Stick Up for Yourself! Every Kid's Guide to Personal Power and Positive Self-Esteem* by Gershen Kaufman, Ph.D., Lev Raphael, Ph.D., and Pamela Espeland (Minneapolis: Free Spirit Publishing, 1999). Simple words and real-life examples show how you can stick up for yourself with other kids (including bullies and teasers), big sisters and brothers, even grownups. Ages 8–12.

# Character Dilemmas
*For journaling or writing essays, discussion, debate, role-playing, reflection*

**Suppose that . . .**

**1** Your mother stands in the doorway of your room and says "What a mess! I want you to clean this room *right now*." But you're doing your homework and an important assignment is due tomorrow. You don't have time to clean your room. What might you say to your mother that's both assertive and respectful?

**2** You're walking through a park with a group of friends. Some of them are carrying cans of soda. One friend finishes her soda and tosses the can on the ground. What might you say? What might you do? How might you teach your friend to be more respectful of the environment?

**3** You have an elderly neighbor who lives alone. You like to spend time in your backyard playing with friends or reading in the hammock. But whenever you're outside, your neighbor starts talking to you over the fence. You're not very interested in what she has to say, and sometimes you wish she'd just leave you alone. What are some respectful yet assertive things you might do and say?

**4** You've recently made friends with a new student in your class whose family immigrated from Tibet. Your friend has asked you to have dinner with her family tonight. You don't know anything about Tibetan customs. How can you be sure to behave respectfully at your friend's home?

**5** The leader of your youth group is getting married, and you're invited to the wedding. It's going to be a big Catholic wedding at a local basilica. You're Jewish, and you've never been to a Catholic service or church before. How can you show the proper reverence in a house of worship that's not of your faith?

**6** You're at a party at a friend's house when someone brings out a case of beer. Everyone at the party is under the legal drinking age. You could probably drink a beer without your parents finding out about it. Will you? Why or why not? Does it matter to you what the law says? Does self-respect play any part in your decision?

# Activities

**WRITE A POEM ABOUT RESPECT.** What does it mean to you? Or write a story about a time when you were treated with respect—or weren't treated with respect. You might turn your story into a skit and perform it for your class, club, or younger kids at your school.

## CHECK IT OUT

*All I Really Need to Know I Learned in Kindergarten* by Robert Fulghum (Boston: G.K. Hall, 1988). This entertaining book says a lot about respect, sharing, playing fair, not hitting people, and saying you're sorry when you hurt someone. All ages.

**MAKE A LIST OF DISRESPECTFUL WORDS** and phrases you say to yourself. Do you call yourself names? ("Idiot"? "Stupid"? "Zit-face"?). Do you put yourself down? ("I'm too dumb to do that . . ." "I'll never be able to do that . . ." "I might as well just give up. . . .") When you finish making your list, crumple it up, tear it up, shred it, stomp on it, and *throw it away*. Promise yourself that you'll never again use those words or phrases. Replace them with compliments, congratulations, and encouragement.

**LEARN ABOUT NETIQUETTE.** Millions of people are using the Internet for browsing, chatting, and email, and it's important for everyone to use good

online manners—called "netiquette." *Example:* USING ALL CAPITAL LETTERS LOOKS LIKE SHOUTING. Avoid doing this unless you mean to shout—then think first about how your reader might feel about being shouted at. Research what other people have written and said about respectful online behavior, then write a "Netiquette" brochure for your school.

## CHECK IT OUT

*Netiquette* by Virginia Shea (New York: Albion Publishing, 1994). The do's and don'ts of communicating online, recommended for everyone from "newbies" to wizards. Ages 13 & up.

### Netiquette Home Page
*www.albion.com/netiquette*
Take the "Netiquette Quiz," learn the "Core Rules of Netiquette," join a netiquette mailing list, and more at this site from the publishers of Virginia Shea's book.

### Yahoo's Netiquette Links
*www.yahoo.com*
Type "Netiquette" in the Search box for a list of links to sites with information about netiquette.

**DISCOVER HOW MATHEMATICIANS** have been respected (or not) throughout history. You might research one or more of the following:

- ▲ Pythagoras
- ▲ Euclid
- ▲ Archimedes
- ▲ Omar Khayyam
- ▲ Évariste Galois
- ▲ Descartes
- ▲ Sir Isaac Newton
- ▲ Carl Friedrich Gauss
- ▲ George Boole
- ▲ Bertrand Russell
- ▲ Kurt Gödel
- ▲ Blaise Pascal

Then discuss these questions with your class, club, or family:

**1.** Have mathematicians been revered as wise, treated like "nerds," or ignored?

**2.** What have mathematicians contributed to human life? How has their knowledge affected other fields?

**3.** Now that we have calculators and computers, is mathematics becoming obsolete?

**4.** Why should you learn math?

> *Variation:* Invite a mathematician to visit your class and talk about the meaning of math today. Why is it still important? What is it good for? Why do we need it? Why should we respect math and mathematicians?

**RESEARCH RESPECT AND COURTESY** in other cultures. Find out what rules of etiquette they have. How are they different from the rules of your culture? (TIP: Travel bureaus and embassies are great sources of information about cross-cultural etiquette.) Make a chart that shows and compares simple courtesies in several cultures. *Examples:* table manners; greetings; acceptable behavior in crowds; ways that children should show respect to adults; etc. You might want to compile a list of words and phrases that are considered polite in one culture and rude in other cultures. If you live in an ethnically diverse community, you might want to videotape interviews with people from various cultures.

## CHECK IT OUT

*Multicultural Manners: New Rules of Etiquette for a Changing Society* by Norine Dresser (New York: John Wiley & Sons, 1996). An informative, entertaining guide by the "Miss Manners" of multiculturalism for the *Los Angeles Times.* Ages 13 & up.

Visit your local library and look for books in these series:

- The "Culture Shock!" series (published by Graphic Arts Center Publishing Co.)

- The "Dos' and Don'ts Around the World" series (published by World Travel Institute Press)

- "The Simple Guide to Customs and Etiquette in . . ." series (published by Talman Co.).

**GUESS WHEN THIS WAS WRITTEN:**

> Our youth loves luxury. They have bad manners, contempt for authority, and disrespect for other people. Children nowadays are tyrants. They no longer rise when their elders enter the room. They contradict their parents, chatter before company, gobble their food, and tyrannize their teachers.

BONUS: Guess who wrote it. (The answers are printed upside down at the bottom of the page.) Afterward, answer these questions:

**?** Were you surprised to find out when this was written? Why or why not?

**?** What does it mean to you?

**FIND OUT HOW MANNERS HAVE CHANGED** for children. For example, is it still true that "children should be seen and not heard"? Visit your library and look for books by Emily Post, Amy Vanderbilt, Judith Martin ("Miss Manners"), Letitia Baldridge, and other writers who are experts on etiquette. Write an article about what you learn and submit it to your school or community newspaper.

## CHECK IT OUT

*How Rude! The Teenagers' Guide to Good Manners, Proper Behavior, and Not Grossing People Out* by Alex J. Packer, Ph.D. (Minneapolis: Free Spirit Publishing, 1997). Outrageous humor and sound advice guide teens through the mysterious world of manners from A ("Applause") to Z ("Zits"). Ages 13 & up.

*Social Smarts: Modern Manners for Today's Kids* by Elizabeth James (New York: Clarion Books, 1996). Advice on how to handle all kids of social situations and personal interactions. Ages 9–13.

**LEARN ABOUT AND PRACTICE** good table manners. Read one or more books about manners to learn the do's and don'ts of polite dining. Share what you learn with your class, club, or family. Then organize a dinner for a group of friends (boys and girls) where you can all practice your table manners. Give positive feedback and constructive criticism.

---

This criticism of young people's behavior was written (are you ready for this?) in the fifth century B.C.! The writer was Socrates, a famous philosopher.

**BRAINSTORM RULES OF RESPECT** for your family, class-room, club, or youth group to follow. Write down all brainstormed ideas without comment or criticism. Afterward, discuss the pros and cons of each idea. Vote to come up with a Top 10 list. Then brainstorm appropriate consequences for breaking the rules of respect. Write down and discuss those, too. Afterward, write the rules and consequences on a chart. Decorate your chart and display it where everyone can see it.

**WORK TO CREATE A CLIMATE OF RESPECT** and tolerance[3] in your school. You might start by surveying students, teachers, and staff about what they think are the biggest respect-related problems in your school. Does everyone in your school feel safe? If not, what feels unsafe to them? Do people feel as if their ideas and differences are respected? If not, why do they feel disrespected? Encourage student groups, teachers, and staff to work together to make your school more respectful.

# CHECK IT OUT

Tell your teacher about this book:

*Days of Respect: Organizing a School-Wide Violence Prevention Program* by Ralph Cantor with Paul Kivel, Allan Creighton, and The Oakland Men's Project (Alameda, CA: Hunter House Publishers, 1997). This handbook includes everything needed to plan and hold a multi-day, school-wide event on the theme of preventing violence and creating an atmosphere of respect in school. For grades 6–12.

**DRAW TWO-PANEL CARTOONS** showing different types of interactions between people. *Examples:* parent and child, teacher and student, two friends, two strangers, child and senior citizen, two neighbors, customer and store clerk, etc. In the first panel, show a situation in which one or both people are behaving disrespectfully. In the second panel, show the same situation, but this time both people are behaving respectfully.

**LISTEN TO POPULAR MUSIC.** You might listen to your favorite kind, or to many different kinds (pop,

rock, country, hip-hop, R&B, folk, bluegrass, etc.). Pay close attention to the lyrics. Consider these questions: Do the lyrics show respect for people, things, creatures, and the earth? Do you think that today's music has an influence on how respectful (or disrespectful) people are to each other? Do you think it affects how they respect (or disrespect) laws and rules? Find examples of positive and negative lyrics and play them for your class, family, or club.

**EXAMINE THE ROLE OF ETIQUETTE IN SPORTS.** What types of actions and behaviors make someone a "good sport"? What types of actions and behaviors make someone a "bad sport"? How do the rules of sports etiquette compare to the rules of family or community etiquette? Share your findings in a report.

**PLAY A "POLITICALLY CORRECT" NAME GAME.** You'll need two teams (Team A and Team B), a leader, and a stopwatch to play this game. First, the leader makes a list of *biased* words and phrases (words that discriminate or reflect a negative attitude) and *bias-free* alternatives. *Examples:*

| Biased | Bias-free |
| --- | --- |
| policeman | police officer |
| mailman | mail carrier |
| fireman | firefighter |
| waiter, waitress | server |
| blind person | person who is blind, person who is visually impaired |
| retard | person with a mental disability |
| mongoloid | person with Down syndrome |
| spastic | person with a seizure disorder |
| AIDS victim | person with AIDS |

Include biased and bias-free words and phrases for people of various ethnic groups, races, religions, ages, ideas, beliefs, jobs/professions, etc. *To play the game:* The leader says a biased word or phrase to Team A, who has 5–10 seconds to come up with the bias-free word or phrase. (Decide on the amount of time that seems reasonable for your group, then use the stopwatch.) If Team A comes up with the answer, they earn *one* point. If they don't, their turn passes to

---

[3] See "Justice," pages 142–154, for reasons to be tolerant, tips for being tolerant, and resources about tolerance.

Team B. If Team B comes up with the answer, they earn *two* points. Ask Team A the first three questions, Team B the next three questions, and so on for as long as people want to play (up to 24 questions). The team with the most points at the end of the game wins.

## CHECK IT OUT

*The Bias-Free Word Finder: A Dictionary of Nondiscriminatory Language* by Rosalie Maggio (Boston: Beacon Press, 1992). A comprehensive guide for everyone who wants to use language accurately, gracefully, and respectfully.

"Guidelines for Reporting and Writing about People with Disabilities" (The Research & Training Center on Independent Living, updated often). For a free copy of the current Guidelines, send a stamped, self-addressed envelope to RTC/IL Publications, University of Kansas, 4089 Dole Bldg., Lawrence, KS 66045. A partial list of the Guidelines is available online at: *www.lsi.ku.edu/lsi/internal/guidelines.html*

READ STORIES ABOUT RESPECT, courtesy, and manners. Look for these books:

*Altogether, One at a Time* by Elaine Lobl Konigsburg (New York: Aladdin Paperbacks, 1989). A collection of four short stories that describe kids learning to respect people with learning differences and also people of different ethnic groups, ages, and body types. Ages 9–13.

*The House of Wings* by Betsy Byars (New York: Puffin Books, 1982). Left with his grandfather until his parents are settled in Detroit, Sammy learns to respect and love the old man as they care for an injured crane together. Ages 9–13.

*Racing the Sun* by Paul Pitts (New York: Avon Books, 1988). Twelve-year-old Brandon has lived in the suburbs all his life. When his grandfather comes to live with the family, Brandon discovers the importance and difficulty of staying true to his Navajo heritage. Ages 11–13.

*Sixth-Grade Sleepover* by Eve Bunting (New York: Scholastic, Inc., 1987). Janey worries that her friends will learn of her fear of the dark when her sixth-grade reading group plans a sleepover. Ages 10–12.

*The Twelfth of June* by Marilyn Gould (Newport Beach, CA: Allied Crafts Press, 1994). Thirteen-year-old Janis wonders how her cerebral palsy will affect her future and her relationship with her friend Barney. Ages 10–14.

# Character in *ACTION*

## Helen Setuk: A Young Woman with Respect

"My Auntie Diane owns twenty dogs and many sleds, and she lets me take them dog mushing," explains Helen Setuk, a young South Central Alaskan woman from the Athabascan and Aleut tribes. "I train the dogs myself. I never use a whip or yell at them. I just tell them what to do. I reward them with food, and I love them. They know I respect them, and they respect me." Helen's dog team hasn't won any races (so far), but at the banquet at the end of one dog-mushing season, she received the Sportsmanship Award.

Because Helen also respects nature, her mother calls her "Miss Earth." Helen describes her feelings about the environment: "If I am walking in flowers, I will not step on them. I will go around them. I leave things growing where they are. And I never throw stuff on the ground. I collect cans so I can recycle them."

One day Helen's Auntie Diane asked her if she'd like to join a dance group that performs traditional native dances and songs. Both Helen and her little sister Laura wanted to join, and now they practice once a week at the Alaskan Native Medical Center. Helen and Laura have performed for the Museum of History and Fine Arts, at the 1996 Juneau Celebration, for elementary schools in Anchorage, and at other places throughout the city.

Helen especially enjoys doing the Raven Courtship dance. She dons her black pants and red tunic, throws a wool blanket over her shoulders, and dances as one of the Eagle Women. People of all ages dance together, and some of the women carry infants as they whirl around. The Raven, dressed in black, flirts with the Eagle Women, who pretend to ignore him. Sometimes Helen beats a drum as other dancers keep the rhythm with rattles.

Helen also dances at powwows. Sometimes she dances alone in the middle of the others, swaying to the drumbeats, her long, black hair swinging freely like a silk streamer. At the end of each performance, the elders step forward, and Helen applauds them. She moves out of their way when they pass to honor their wisdom and age. "I respect my elders because they give me my culture and heritage," she says. By connecting with her culture, Helen knows who she is. She knows her past and has reverence for her history. She understands that her culture will be important to her in the future, too.

Helen does her best to get along with others. "When my mother tells me to do something, I do it. I say 'please,' 'thank you,' and 'excuse me' to be polite. If my teacher tells me

Helen Setuk (left) and her sister Laura

that I did something wrong, I say 'I'm sorry. I'll try to do better next time.' I also respect myself. If I do something wrong, I tell myself 'It's okay. I just made a mistake.' I also respect and take care of my body."

Because Helen impressed adults with her dignity, courtesy, and reverence for all forms of life, she was selected to do a national TV commercial for Payless Drug Stores and was featured in advertisements in both *Time* and *Newsweek*. So watch for her in the future. If you're lucky, you might see her dance one day.

Helen (center) at the Juneau Celebration

# Responsibility

**Dependability, reliability, perseverance, being organized,
being punctual, honoring commitments, planning**

"You can't escape the responsibility
of tomorrow by evading it today."
*Abraham Lincoln*

When you're crouched at home plate with the bat cocked over your shoulder and the ball is whirling toward you, you can't suddenly step aside and ask someone else to hit it for you. It's too late, and if you refuse to swing at the ball, you'll be out and your team will suffer the loss. It's okay if you swing and miss the ball, because doing your best doesn't guarantee success. Making mistakes is an important part of learning and growing.

When you joined the baseball team, you accepted the *responsibility* of being a team member. You agreed to wear the uniform, go to practices, listen to your coaches, be on time for games, be a good sport, and do what you can to help your team win. Depending on your role on the team, you might have other responsibilities as well. If you're the captain, for example, you're not only responsible for your own behavior but also for the behavior and performance of the team as a whole.

Responsibility implies *dependability* and *reliability*. Your coaches and team members know they can count on you.[1] You might have bad days, you might make mistakes, but you won't purposefully or carelessly let the others down. You'll show up for practices even when you don't feel like it, or when you'd rather be doing something else. If you strike out or foul, you won't blame the pitcher, your bat, your coaches, other players, or bad luck. You'll resolve to do better next time, and meanwhile you'll practice to improve your skills. You'll have the *perseverance* to swing at the ball 10 times or 100 times or 1,000—whatever it takes to improve your chances of getting base hits or even home runs. (There's an old saying about perseverance that you might already know: "If at first you don't succeed, try, try again.")

As a human being, you have many types of responsibilities. They include:

✸ *Moral responsibility* to other people, animals, and the earth. This means caring, defending, helping, building, protecting, preserving, and sustaining. You're accountable for treating other people justly and fairly, for honoring other living things, and for being environmentally aware.

✸ *Legal responsibility* to the laws and ordinances of your community, state, and country. If there's a law you believe is outdated, unjust, discriminatory, or unfair, you can work to change, improve, or eliminate it. You can't simply decide to disobey it.[2]

✸ *Family responsibility.* This means treating your parents, siblings, and other relatives with love and respect, following your parents' rules, and doing chores and duties at home.

---

[1] See also "Honesty," pages 115–125; "Integrity," pages 135–141; and "Loyalty," pages 164–171, for related character traits.

[2] See "Loyalty," pages 164–171, for more about obedience.

☀ ***Community responsibility.*** Unless you're a hermit who lives in a cave, you're part of a community. As such, you're responsible for treating others as you want to be treated, for participating in community activities and decisions, and for being an active, contributing citizen.[3] If your neighborhood park is full of trash, don't wait for someone else to pick it up. You can read local and community newspapers to stay informed. When you're old enough, vote in elections. If you're feeling *really* responsible, you might even decide to run for office.

☀ ***Responsibility to customs, traditions, beliefs, and rules.*** These might come from your family, your community, your heritage, or your faith. Learn what they are and do your best to respect and follow them.

☀ ***Personal responsibility.*** It's up to you to become a person of good character. Your parents, teachers, religious leaders, scout leaders, and other caring adults will guide you, but only you can determine the kind of person you are and ultimately become.

> "Parents can only give good advice or put them on the right paths, but the final forming of a person's character lies in their own hands."
> *Anne Frank*

"But wait!" you might say. "This is a free country! Nobody can force me to accept all those responsibilities." In fact, freedom is meaningless without responsibility—and vice versa. Life is a balance between the two. Freedom without responsibility means that everyone does what they want, when they want, with no regard for anyone or anything but themselves. Responsibility without freedom means that everyone is forced to do the same things with no regard for individual wants and needs. You might think of freedom and responsibility as a matched pair of shoes. If you try to hop only on freedom's shoe, you'll be reckless and out of control. If you try to hop only on responsibility's shoe, you'll feel like a drone. You need both shoes to move through life with confidence, grace, and strength.

How can you become more responsible? You can start by ***getting organized.*** Buy or make a daily planner and learn to use it.[4] There are many student planners available, and they often come with instructions. Once you form the habit of using a daily planner effectively—jotting down important notes, marking due dates, keeping to-do lists, writing down goals[5]—you'll find that you no longer "forget" about upcoming tests or long-term assignments. When you note important appointments in your planner, you're less likely to miss them (or to show up late). Other people will appreciate you for ***being punctual*** and ***honoring your commitments.*** They will respect you more and your self-esteem will grow. It's a win-win situation all around.

And speaking of commitments: You can make a *personal commitment* to start being more responsible *today.* Tell yourself that this is the kind of person you want to be. Then be it.

> "The ultimate responsibility always lies within you, and opportunities are the ones you create."
> *Melissa Poe*

---

[3] See "Citizenship," pages 35–43.

[4] See page 231 for a related activity.
[5] See "Purpose," pages 195–197, for goal-setting steps.

## CHECK IT OUT

Visit your local office supplies store to find a daily planner. Or order a special student planner from:

**Day-Timers, Inc.**
One Day-Timer Plaza
Allentown, PA 18195-1551
1-800-805-2615
*www.daytimer.com*
The Day-Timers Student Planner is a loose-leaf binder with multiple features including monthly calendars, class schedule sheets, monthly planning sheets, project planning forms, inspiring monthly success messages, grade tracking sheets, and study tips.

**Franklin Covey**
2200 West Parkway Boulevard
Salt Lake City, UT 84119
1-800-819-1812
*www.franklincovey.com*
Franklin Covey offers all types of planners, calendars, and bags to help students organize, prioritize, keep track of assignments and goals, and take responsibility for their classwork and schedules.

# How to Plan

Whether you use a daily planner or not, you need to know *how to plan*. Planning is different from problem solving,[6] although you might use problem solving if you encounter obstacles while trying to make and carry out a plan. You can use planning in every area of your life, from deciding what to eat for breakfast to arranging a party for your friends, from tackling a chore around the house to approaching a science project. Simply put, planning means figuring out ahead of time how to do something so you can proceed efficiently. Planning is purposeful and deliberate.

Sometimes planning can be done in your head. ("Will I wear the blue sweater tomorrow or the red sweater? The blue one has spaghetti on it, so I'll wear the red one.") Sometimes you need to think through a plan and all of the steps involved. You might even want to write them down. The more detailed your plan is, the more likely it is to succeed.

Here's how to go about making a plan:

1.  ***Write a list of all the things you need to do this week.*** Then prioritize your list. Put a "1" by the most important task or job, a "2" by the next important one, and so on down your list.

2.  ***Write down when each task or job needs to be done.*** These "deadlines" might be imposed by other people (your mom wants you to clean your room by Sunday), or they might be self-imposed (you want to clean your room by Friday so you won't have to do it on the weekend).

3.  ***Write down what you'll need to accomplish each task or job.*** Any special materials, equipment, or resources? Tools? Books? Other people to help you? This way, you won't start something (like a homework assignment) and suddenly discover that you're missing an essential component (like your book, which you left at school).

4.  ***Always have a backup plan—a "plan B."*** Try to predict any problems that might arise and prevent you from carrying out your plan. Ask yourself some "What if. . . ?" questions: "What if it rains on the day I want to mow the lawn?" "What if I don't have time to finish a homework assignment on the night before it's due?" Then come up with answers.

You might want to write your plan on a chart. Then you can see at a glance how the parts fit together and whether there are any problems or conflicts. You can also use your chart to make notes and changes as the week progresses. You'll find an example of a planning chart at the top of page 228.

The more carefully you plan, the more organized you are. The more organized you are, the more responsible you become. The more responsible you become, the more your parents (and other people) trust you. Planning definitely has its rewards.

---

[6] See "Problem Solving," pages 184–193.

| JOB OR TASK (list, then prioritize) | WHAT I NEED TO DO IT | DONE BY WHEN? | BACKUP PLAN |
|---|---|---|---|
| 4. Mow lawn | Gas (ask Dad to buy some), trash bags | Saturday noon | If it rains on Saturday, do Sunday afternoon |
| 2. Read story for English class | English book (bring home Tuesday) | Wednesday morning by 10:30 class | Read in study hall before class on Wednesday |
| 1. Buy school supplies | Ask Mom to drive me to the store. Buy 1) notebook 2) paper 3) pencils | Monday night | Ask Dad or Megan to drive me, or walk there on my way home from school |
| 3. Clean my room | Pick up clothes, wash clothes, vacuum, dust, change sheets | Thursday night | If someone else is using the washing machine, wash clothes on Friday night |

# Character Dilemmas

*For journaling or writing essays, discussion, debate, role-playing, reflection*

**Suppose that . . .**

**1** You're a recent immigrant to the United States (or the country you now live in). Are you responsible for obeying the laws if you don't know what they are? If you unknowingly break a law, should you be held accountable?

**2** You have a real talent for gymnastics, but your parents can't afford to pay for lessons. Are they responsible for finding ways to support and encourage your talent? If they aren't responsible, who is?

**3** You're a parent whose child was caught painting graffiti on a school building. Are you responsible for the damage your child has done? If not, why not?

**4** Someone who lives in your neighborhood accidentally broke a water pipe while planting a tree on the boulevard. The boulevard is public property. Who should pay for repairing the damage? The person who broke the pipe? The city? The neighborhood organization? Would it make a difference if you knew that the person was a single parent with several children and a very limited income?

**5** Your school has a "closed campus" rule, meaning that students aren't allowed to leave the school grounds during school hours. A group of your friends regularly eats lunch at a nearby fast-food restaurant. Do you have any responsibility in this situation? If so, what is it? If not, why not?

**6** You read in the newspaper that many preschoolers in your town·haven't been immunized against childhood diseases. Their families don't believe in immunizing children. Should the children be immunized anyway? If so, who's responsible for seeing that it's done? Your town, state, or federal government? The police? Health officials? School officials? Other parents? You? No one? Would it make a difference if you knew that the families were objecting to the immunizations for religious reasons?

**7** You overhear your aunt and uncle telling your parents that they have no savings. They assume that after they retire, they'll be able to live on their Social Security. Meanwhile, they're spending the money they earn on travel, fancy cars, and other luxuries. You've been hearing on the news that the Social Security reserves might not be sufficient when "baby boomers" like your aunt and uncle reach retirement age. Who should be responsible for taking care of seniors who don't have enough money to live on? The government? The children of the "baby boomers"? All of society? Religious organizations? No one?

# Activities

**TELL ABOUT A TIME WHEN YOU** unknowingly broke a rule in your classroom or family, or a law in your community, and got caught. What happened to you? How did you feel?

> *Variation:* Write in your journal[7] about a time when you knowingly broke a rule and didn't get caught. What, if anything, happened? How did you feel? Would you do it again? Why or why not?

**THINK OF A NEW TALENT OR SKILL** you'd like to develop. Then:

**1.** Brainstorm all of the things you could do to develop that talent. *Examples:* Take classes at school or a community center; read books; watch videos.

**2.** Make a list of all the people you might ask for help. Write down their names and telephone numbers. Go down your list and contact people until you find someone who's willing to help you and has the time. (Check with your parents or guardians before contacting other adults.)

**3.** Create a schedule outlining the things you'll learn and do. Give yourself a deadline for each one.

**4.** Practice at least one-half hour each day, or an hour or two several times each week.

**5.** Perform your talent or share it with your family, class, or club.

**WRITE A POEM, JINGLE, PARAGRAPH,** or saying about responsibility. If you do this as a class (or even as a school), you might start each day by reading one over the PA system. Or create a Responsibility Bulletin Board to display students' thoughts and writings about responsibility.

**RESEARCH DISCOVERIES AND INVENTIONS** that have had both positive and negative consequences. *Examples:* In 1884, an anesthetic was developed that included cocaine as one of its ingredients. Cocaine has since been found to be highly addictive. In 1939, the pesticide DDT was developed to control insects that spread malaria. For years, it was used widely on farms and in homes; later it was discovered to be very harmful to the environment. If you make a discovery or create an invention, do you have a responsibility to share it with the world? Afterward, are you responsible for how your discovery or invention is used? Debate these questions with your friends, class, family, or club.

**CONSIDER WHETHER MATH** makes you more responsible. Does studying math have any effect on your organization or perseverance? Can the benefits of learning logic skills and analytical thinking spill over into other areas of your life? Draw a chart, graph, or mind map showing all of the connections you can think of between math and. . . ?

**RESEARCH RESPONSIBILITY IN ADVERTISING.** Suppose that an advertiser of a popular breakfast cereal claims that "Crunchie Critters" gives you more pep and energy than other breakfast foods. What if it isn't true? Are advertisers responsible for telling the truth? Watch a week's worth of television commercials and keep a record of any that seem to be exaggerations, unproved claims, or outright lies. Keep track of the TV stations that air the commercials. Afterward, write to your local stations and complain about any commercials that appear to be irresponsible.[8]

> *Variations:* Listen to radio commercials or clip advertisements out of magazines or newspapers. Or study advertisements you see on the World Wide Web.

**RESEARCH RESPONSIBILITY** toward indigenous peoples. Choose a country that was taken from an indigenous population by invaders, settlers, or foreign governments. *Examples:* Australia (its indigenous people are the Aborigines); the United States (the Native Americans); various countries in Africa. Did the "outsiders" behave responsibly or irresponsibly toward the indigenous peoples? Give examples to support your answer. Do you think that when one nation conquers another (as in a war), the conquering nation has a responsibility to treat the conquered peoples justly and fairly? Or is this a matter of "might makes right"? Give reasons

---

[7] See "Endurance," pages 88, 89, and 92, for journaling resources.

[8] See "Honesty," page 120, for resources on advertising.

for your answer. TIPS: If you decide to study the Native Americans, find out about the following:

- the false stereotypes of Native Americans that were spread by European settlers

- the Treaty of Greenville

- the Dawes Act (or General Allotment Act) of 1887

- the Indian Removal Act of 1830 (and the forced marches that resulted from it)

- the concepts of "reservations" and "assimilation"

- Wounded Knee

- the Indian Reorganization Act of 1934

- the Alaska Native Land Claims Settlement Act of 1971

**ORGANIZE A GRAFFITI REMOVAL PROGRAM.** Look around your neighborhood for graffiti. If you find some, contact your local police or city officials and ask whether there are any graffiti removal programs in place. If there aren't, start one. Ask for donations of paint and brushes, and invite the police to chaperon. Organize your friends, classmates, and families to wipe out graffiti.

**SURVEY YOUR NEIGHBORHOOD** and find out if there are any seniors who need help with such things as repairing fences, shopping for groceries, painting, doing minor repairs, lawn care, pet care, etc. Take responsibility and either do it yourself or get others to help you. Be sure to take an adult chaperon along (a parent or guardian) both when you survey your neighborhood and when you do your good deeds.

**WRITE A SKIT THAT DEMONSTRATES** your school's rules. Present it to the first all-school assembly in the fall. Don't forget to include humor in your skit; people remember things better when they can laugh. But don't make your skit *too* funny or people might miss the message.

**FIND A JOB OR START YOUR OWN BUSINESS.**[9] *Example:* Are you good at doing yard work? Collect names of neighborhood kids who do yard work. Make a one-page flyer describing the kinds of work you and the other kids can do. Decide how much you'll charge to do certain kinds of jobs, and include that information on your flyer. Distribute copies of your flyer around the neighborhood.

---

## CHECK IT OUT

*Better than a Lemonade Stand: Small Business Ideas for Kids* by Daryl Bernstein (Hillsboro, OR: Beyond Words Publishing, 1992). Describes dozens of money-making ventures including curb address painter, birthday party planner, dog walker, house checker, newsletter publisher, photographer, and sign maker. Daryl was 15 years old when he wrote and published this book. Ages 8–15.

*Kid Cash: Creative Money-Making Ideas* by Joe Lamancusa (New York: Tab Books, 1993). Dozens of concrete, creative suggestions for earning money, samples of advertising flyers, and tips on what to charge for your services, how to keep records, and how to handle your profits. Written by a 14-year-old with firsthand experience running his own business. Ages 9–13.

---

**MAKE A FAMILY JOBS CHART.** Your chart should have two columns: "Things to Do" and "Things Done." With your family, brainstorm a list of jobs that need to be done around the home every day or every week. Decide who's responsible for each job. Write each job on a strip of construction paper (you might choose a different color for each family member). Use removable tape to attach each job strip to the "Things to Do" column. Each person is responsible for moving his or her own job strips from the "Things to Do" column into the "Things Done" column. Try this chart for a week or two, then have a family meeting to discuss it. Does it seem to be working? Is everyone being responsible? Dependable? Reliable? Persevering? Organized? Make any necessary changes to the chart so it works well for everyone.

**CREATE A RESPONSIBILITY TREE.** Draw a large tree on poster paper. Find or make symbols that represent your responsibilities and hang them on your tree. *Examples:* a doll's shirt = taking care of your clothing; a small book = learning; a stop sign = obeying laws; a school house = taking care of your brother after school. If you have a small potted tree, you might hang your symbols from it like ornaments.

---

[9] See "Courage," pages 74–75, for information and resources on being an entrepreneur and starting your own business.

*Variation:* If everyone in your class makes Responsibility Trees, you can put them together in a Responsibility Forest.

**MAKE YOUR OWN DAILY PLANNER.** Buy a small binder and plenty of paper, or create your own binder using stiff cardboard, a hole punch, and yarn. Include:

✔ an identification page with your name and phone number

✔ 12 calendar pages, each one showing a full month (you might decorate each calendar page with symbols representing the month)

✔ a page for each day of the current month (so you can write down notes, ideas, assignment, appointments, etc.)

✔ a list of your classes, room numbers, class times, and teachers' names

✔ pages for friends' addresses and phone numbers

✔ pages describing upcoming projects or things you want to think about and plan

✔ a budget page (list things you want to save money for and how you plan to earn the money)

✔ a pocket (fold a piece of card stock or stiff paper and tape the sides) to hold notes, a pencil, and important reminders.

**FIND EXAMPLES OF POPULAR MUSIC** that promote responsibility, dependability, and perseverance. Bring them to school and share them with your class. (Clear them with your teacher first.) Do you think that music has the power to inspire people to be more responsible? Less responsible? Explain your answer.

**EXAMINE THE ROLE OF RESPONSIBILITY** in sports. Compare team sports to individual sports. Which sports seem to demand the most responsibility from the players? Which seem to promote responsibility? Which, if any, seem to promote irresponsible behavior?

*Variations:* Interview coaches and athletes in your school and community. Ask them to tell you their ideas about responsibility in sports. Or write to famous athletes.[10]

---

[10] Get in touch with famous athletes with help from *The Kid's Address Book*. See "Choice and Accountability," page 32.

**PLAY A "WHAT'S THEIR RESPONSIBILITY?" GAME.** Make a list of roles or careers in society. You can use the example below, add to it, or write your own list. Divide into two or more teams. Give each team the list of roles or careers. The object of the game is to list four different or unusual responsibilities for each role or career. Give a prize for 1) the most answers and 2) the most unusual answers.

| | |
|---|---|
| artist | mother |
| bank teller | musician |
| business executive | news reporter |
| cafeteria worker | nurse |
| child | nutritionist |
| city planner | pilot |
| club member | plumber |
| coach | police officer |
| computer programmer | principal |
| court justice | psychologist |
| directory assistance telephone operator | recreation/resort manager |
| doctor | religious leader |
| electrician | sales person |
| engineer | scientist |
| father | student |
| friend | teacher |
| governor | trash collector |
| grandparent | veterinarian |
| guardian | weather forecaster |
| landscape architect | writer |
| legislator | youth group |
| letter carrier | member |
| mayor | zoo owner |

**READ STORIES ABOUT RESPONSIBILITY,** dependability, reliability, perseverance, being organized, being punctual, and honoring commitments. Look for these books:

📖 *Dicey's Song* by Cynthia Voigt (New York: Atheneum, 1982). Dicey struggles with school, a job, and responsibility for her brothers and sisters as she adjusts to living with her grandmother. Ages 11–12.

📖 *Little House in the Big Woods* by Laura Ingalls Wilder (New York: HarperCollins, 1990). Young Laura Ingalls describes a year in the life of her pioneer family in the Midwest. Ages 8–12.

📖 *Malu's Wolf* by Ruth Craig (New York: Orchard Books, 1995). After Malu is permitted to raise a wolf pup, significant changes happen in the lives and traditions of the young girl's Stone Age clan. Ages 9–13.

📖 *Summer of the Swans* by Betsy Byars (New York: Puffin Books, 1981). A teenage girl gains new insight into herself and her family when her mentally retarded brother gets lost. Ages 10–14.

📖 *When the Road Ends* by Jean Thesman (New York: Avon Books, 1993). Sent to spend the summer in the country, three foster children and an older woman recovering from a serious accident are abandoned by a slovenly caretaker and must try to survive on their own. Ages 10–14.

# Character in *ACTION*

## Ellen Bigger: Taking Responsibility

**W**hen Ellen Bigger was in the fifth grade, her former Brownie leader was murdered by her husband, who was on drugs at the time. Ellen had spent many days at her leader's house and was a friend of her daughter. When she heard the news, she was deeply shocked. For a long time, she cried often and had trouble sleeping at night.

In sixth grade, Ellen heard a speech that changed the direction of her life. At the commissioning of the Coast Guard Cutter *Key Largo*, the speaker told the audience of the Coast Guard's efforts to keep drugs from coming into the United States. But the *real* challenge, the speaker emphasized, was for people *at home* to make the effort.

Ellen felt as if a fire had been lit under her. She felt responsible for helping to spread the anti-drugs message and was determined to find a way to do it. Her mom had just bought a computer, so Ellen planted herself in front of the screen that very weekend and designed a brochure. "Drugs can kill and destroy your life, tear apart your family, and break your heart," she wrote. "No matter what age you are, you can help fight the drug problem by pledging a drug-free life." She put a pledge form on the back and promised to send a decal if all the members of a family would take the pledge for a Drug-Free Home.

Ellen had $500 in savings that she had earned, and she spent all of it on the first printing of her brochure and postage to mail it out. Her family helped her to fold the brochures. The Girl Scout Council in Miami and the United Way printed additional copies and the decals. Ellen handed out brochures at shopping malls, festivals, churches, schools, and grocery stores. She received many responses in the mail from all over the country. Over the next few years, she would distribute more than 50,000 copies of

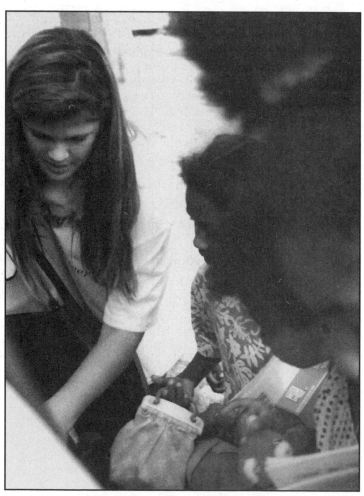

Ellen Bigger (left) working with kids

her brochure, finally hearing from places as far away as Brazil and Egypt.

One boy in a detention home wrote her a letter and asked her how he could get off drugs. Ellen worried and stewed over what to say. She finally wrote a message advising him to trust himself and pledge to stay off drugs one day at a time. She watched the mail, but he didn't write back.

She designed a T-shirt and buttons that said "I live in a Drug-Free Home, and I'm proud of it," decorated with a picture of a house tied with a red ribbon. When she was interviewed on television, her program spread across the U.S. She was invited to speak at conferences and workshops in Texas, Ohio, and Georgia.

Meanwhile, her parents still expected her to fulfill her family responsibilities. Ellen did chores, cooked some of the meals, and took care of the family dogs. She also volunteered at the local Red Cross, planted trees, and got involved in other volunteer projects with the Scouts. Her bedroom was a disaster area, piled high with papers, brochures, socks, and T-shirts tossed in corners and under her bed. (Nobody's perfect.)

During the summer after eighth grade, when Ellen was fourteen, she decided to organize another program. She had received many letters from kids who didn't know how to start their own projects. Ellen called her program "Youthwish." Through Youthwish, Ellen encouraged kids to volunteer, gave instructions for how to set up a volunteer fair, and explained how kids could share ideas for networking

with adults. She began a biweekly newsletter and asked a teacher to be her sponsor. The teacher helped Ellen to make Youthwish a nonprofit corporation so it wouldn't be taxed. Shortly after, Ellen won the Noxzema Extraordinary Teen Award for volunteering. She received $5,000 for her favorite charity. With that money, she set up $500 grants through Youthwish for kids who wanted to start their own programs.

The real prize came later, though. One day, Ellen was speaking and volunteering at a public event. A young man walked up to her and introduced himself. It was the boy who had written to her long ago from the detention home. He told Ellen that although he'd written to many people when he was imprisoned and alone, asking for help, she was the only one who had responded with a personal letter of encouragement. It had meant a lot to him. He was no longer using drugs, and he thanked her.

Ellen (center) and her friend Naomi delivering emergency supplies to Hurricane Andrew victims

## Awareness, prevention, caution, action

**D**id you know that teens are crime targets more often than any other age group? Every 19 seconds, a teen somewhere in the United States is a victim of a crime. Did you know that 50 percent of automobile deaths could be prevented if passengers wore seat belts? That it costs about $500 to replace a broken school window? That removing graffiti from school doors and walls can cost taxpayers (including your parents) $3,400 for each separate incident?[1]

Although some adults might dismiss you as "just a kid," there's a lot you can do to make the world a safer place by preventing crime in your neighborhood, community, and school. You shouldn't feel responsible for keeping everyone safe, but you shouldn't feel *excluded* from helping because of your age. When you work to make things safer for others, you make things safer for yourself, too.

Becoming more safety-conscious, promoting safety, and doing your part to work for safety are all good habits to develop. You can focus your efforts and energies on one (or many) safety-related areas, including:

**1.  Crime prevention.** You might decide to concentrate on:

- alcohol and drug abuse
- animal abuse
- arson
- child abuse and neglect
- curfew violations
- drunk driving
- environmental abuse
- graffiti
- kidnapping
- murder
- robbery/burglary/theft
- runaways
- sexual assault
- sexual harassment
- suicide
- truancy
- vandalism
- violence against people
- violence against property
- what else?

**2.  Accident prevention.** You could consider getting involved with:

- home safety (fire prevention, safe use of electricity, carbon monoxide, pesticides, poison prevention, etc.)

---

[1] *Sources:* National Crime Prevention Council and National Safety Council.

- neighborhood/community safety (sidewalks, playgrounds, traffic control, pedestrian walkways, public parks)
- preventing freak accidents
- sport/recreation safety (swimming, boating, biking, hunting, camping, climbing, walking, etc.)
- travel safety (automobile, bus, school bus, train, air travel, etc.)
- what else?

**3.  *Disease prevention.*** You might work to prevent disease by promoting:

- affordable health insurance
- anti-smoking efforts
- childhood immunizations
- clean water/air
- free or low-cost community clinics
- alleviating local or world hunger
- public awareness of alcohol and drug abuse
- public awareness of communicable diseases
- what else?

**4.  *Disaster prevention and preparation.*** You could help to educate people about:

- droughts
- earthquakes
- fires
- floods
- hurricanes
- landslides
- tornadoes
- volcanoes
- what else?

**5.  *National safety.*** On behalf of your own country and other countries around the world, you might speak out about and work against:

- germ warfare
- landmines
- nuclear attacks
- what else?

> "The world's children deserve
> to walk the earth in safety."
> *President Bill Clinton*

On the local level, you can encourage your family to develop safe habits. You can be watchful and careful about the things you do on your own and with friends. You can work to reduce crime in your school. You have the right to learn in a safe environment free from bullying, vandalism, violence, drugs and alcohol, and discipline problems. Unsafe and problem situations are created by only a small number of students. Imagine what might happen if the rest of you spoke out and took action to create a safe, supportive, nurturing school.

# Character Dilemmas

*For journaling or writing essays, discussion, debate, role-playing, reflection*

**Suppose that . . .**

**1** You're passing a frozen pond when you hear someone screaming for help who has fallen through the ice. The victim is too far from shore for you to reach out a hand, and if you walk onto the ice you'll probably fall through, too. The victim's head is bobbing in the water, and the temperature is below freezing. What might you do? How might you work to prevent such accidents in the future?

**2** You have a friend who's being pressured to join a gang. She has told you that this Friday after school, gang members will "jump" her—a form of initiation. You've warned your friend to take another way home, but she thinks it's too late to do anything about the gang. She doesn't feel she has any choice about joining, and she has warned you to mind your own business or else. What's your responsibility here? Do you have one? Should you consider your safety, too, if you decide to get involved?

**3** Following a highly competitive basketball game at another school (your team won), you and your friends are piling into a car to drive home. You notice that there are eight riders but only six seat belts. If you don't go with them, you'll be left alone, and you might be in danger of being bullied (or worse) by students from the other school. If you do go with them, someone—maybe you—will be riding without a seat belt. What might you do? What might you do in the future to prevent situations like this one from happening?

**4** You're baby-sitting late one night when you hear someone tampering with the lock on the back door. Then you hear a back window slide open. You reach for the phone line, but the phone is dead. You could slip out the front door and run to a neighbor's house, but there are four children sleeping upstairs. What might you do? What might you do in the future to prevent situations like this one from happening?

**5** Your best friend's father has a gun rack and keeps loaded guns in the house for protection. You know that your friend sometimes sneaks one of his father's guns and shoots birds. Should you say something to your friend? To your friend's father? To your parents? Or should you mind your own business? What other options might you have?

**6** You're hiking with some friends who start climbing in a slick, dangerous, rocky area. You get a "gut feeling" of uneasiness about it. If you refuse to go with them, they'll make fun of you and they might leave you behind. Besides, you've brought rock climbing equipment along, and you know how to use it. Your feeling of uneasiness is probably just your imagination . . . at least, that's what you tell yourself. Do you "trust your gut" or not? What might you do?

# Activities

**WRITE IN YOUR JOURNAL**[2] about safety issues that concern you. What worries you most at home, at school, in your neighborhood, in your community, in your nation, in the world?

> *Variation:* Choose one of your worries and turn it into a project. Set goals for yourself so you can turn your project into a reality.[3]

**WRITE A JINGLE ABOUT SAFETY** and set it to music. Make a recording of your jingle and ask a local radio station to play it as a public service announcement (PSA) for a day, week, or month. Or perform it over your school's PA system.

**CREATE A FLYER ABOUT POISON SAFETY** to educate others about the dangers.

*1. Contact your local poison control center* (look in the front of your phone book under Emergency Numbers). Or call information (411) and ask for the number. (If your town doesn't have a poison control center, getting one started would be a great project for your class, club, or school.) Ask for information (statistics) on poisonings in your town, city, or state. The poison control center might have a pamphlet or news release to send you.

*2. Write your flyer.* Include:

☠ the telephone number of the poison control center

☠ some of the statistics provided by the poison control center

☠ advice on what to say when reporting a possible poisoning (give your name, phone number, and address where you are; give the name of the substance—have the container in front of you when you call; the amount taken; the person's current condition or symptoms—vomiting? difficulty breathing? other symptoms?)

☠ safety tips on storing poisonous or potentially harmful substances (cleaning supplies, medications, solvents, etc.) in the home.

---

[2] See "Endurance," pages 88, 89, and 92, for journaling resources.
[3] See "Purpose," pages 195–197, for goal-setting steps and "Responsibility," page 227, for planning steps.

3. *Make copies of your flyer* to distribute to your neighbors, community centers, churches, schools, stores (ask permission first), and other places that are willing to take them and hand them out.

> *Variation:* Create a flyer about fire safety, swimming safety, bicycle safety, home safety, or any other topic that interests you.

PLAN AND CARRY OUT A CAMPAIGN to promote the use of seat belts. Visit your library or contact the National Safety Council and gather statistics on motor vehicle-related injuries and deaths related to *not* using seat belts. Make a poster showing how seat belts work; create a flyer or pamphlet about seat belt safety to hand out. Contact a local automobile dealership to see if there's a seat belt available that you can use for demonstrations.

## CHECK IT OUT

**National Safety Council**
1121 Spring Lake Drive
Itasca, IL 60143-3201
(630) 285-1121
1-800-621-7619
*www.nsc.org*
Contact the National Safety Council for information on motor vehicle-related injuries and deaths and seat belt use. If you visit the Web site, you can print out a copy of "The Safe-T Rangers on Vacation," a fun story about seat belt safety with activity pages. Go to: *www.nsc.org/traf/sbc/safet.htm*

PLAN AND CARRY OUT A CAMPAIGN to encourage kids to wear bicycle helmets. Visit your library or search the Internet for the latest statistics on bicycle injuries and deaths; learn how many school-age bikers use helmets. Graph the statistics you find. Learn if laws in your area require bikers to wear helmets. Create a brochure or flyer about bicycle helmet safety; see if local retailers will offer discounts on helmets.

> *Variation:* Perform a skit or puppet show for younger kids on bicycle safety in general.

## CHECK IT OUT

**The Bicycle Helmet Safety Institute**
4611 Seventh Street South
Arlington, VA 22204-1419
(703) 486-0100
*www.helmets.org*
Contact this nonprofit, consumer-funded advocacy program for tips on buying bicycle helmets, help for organizers of helmet programs, helmet-related statistics, and more.

PLAN AND CARRY OUT A CAMPAIGN to immunize children against childhood diseases.[4] Call your local health department and ask if you can make phone calls, set up a shuttle service, distribute brochures, or help out in other ways.

MAKE EMERGENCY PHONE NUMBER cards for your family, class, club, or youth group. Include local numbers for police emergency, fire, poison control, suicide prevention, etc. (TIP: You can find local emergency numbers at the front of your telephone book.) You might also list some national hotlines.[5] If possible, laminate the cards to make them more durable.

LEARN EMERGENCY FIRST AID. Invite someone from your local health department, fire department, or safety department to come to your class to train you in emergency first aid and CPR. Or take a course at your local community school, health department, Red Cross chapter, YMCA, or YWCA and learn to be a trainer. Then you can train other people at home, at school, and in your community.

HOLD A SAFETY FAIR at your school.[6] Invite representatives from the fire department, police department, safety council, recreation council, school district, and anyone else who is concerned with safety to put up displays. Invite other safety experts to make presentations.

> *Variation:* Work with your class or school to write a School Safety Proclamation. Put it on a poster, decorate it, and display it in the front hall of your school (or someplace else where students, teachers, and visitors will see it often). The proclamation could state your reasons for wanting a safe school.

---

[4] See "Health," page 107, for a related suggestion and resource.
[5] See "Endurance," pages 87–88, for national hotlines.
[6] See also the *Days of Respect* resource on page 221.

## CHECK IT OUT

**National School Safety Center**
4165 Thousand Oaks Boulevard, Suite 290
Westlake Village, CA 91362
(805) 373-9977
*www.nssc1.org*
The NSSC offers helpful booklets and videos addressing violence prevention, bullying, and conflict resolution for educators and parents. Call or write to request a free catalog.

---

START A CRIME CLUE BOX at your school. Here's how:[7]

**1.** Cover a large shoe box or other cardboard box with paper and write "Crime Clue Box" on the front, sides, and top. Cut a slit in the top. Place the box in your school office, media center, or classroom.

**2.** On or near the Crime Clue Box, post a sign about how the box should be used. Your sign might say something like this:

> The Crime Clue Box is for reporting crimes or other suspicious activities that you witness personally. Your clue will be taken seriously. Please do not misuse the Crime Clue Box.

**3.** Make copies of the Crime Clue Report form on page 239 and place them beside the Crime Clue Box.

**4.** Notify your local law enforcement agency or crime prevention council about your Crime Clue Box. They can collect the clues on a regular basis and follow up on the information.

**5.** If police or private citizens want to offer rewards for clues that lead to arrests, you might post a sign suggesting that witnesses write their birth dates (and/or other identifying number) in the upper right corner of the Crime Clue Report. This can be used to identify the witness who earns a reward.

> *Variation:* Start a Crime Clue Box at your community library, post office, clubhouse, local park building, or community center.

MEASURE OFF A DRUG-FREE School Zone. Most states now have laws requiring stiffer penalties for people who are caught using or selling drugs within 1,000 feet of a school. Find a tape measure and measure off 1,000 feet in all directions of your school. Contact your local police department or city offices and ask for support in placing warning signs to announce the Drug-Free School Zone.

SURVEY YOUR SCHOOL inside and out to look for unsafe conditions. You might do this with your class or make it a schoolwide activity, with each class or homeroom conducting its own survey. Take detailed notes about anything you have questions about; photograph any safety problems you see. Compile the results and present them to your principal. Give your principal time to review your findings, then ask him or her to let you know what repairs and safety improvements will be made. Find out how you can help. Repeat your survey at the end of the school year. Monitor what's been done and what still needs doing.

RESEARCH DRIVING SPEEDS and fatalities in several countries (including the United States, Western and Eastern European countries, Canada, and Mexico). Is there a connection between speed and the numbers of accidents and/or fatalities? Make a graph to show your results.

CALCULATE THE COSTS OF DRUNK DRIVING. According to The National Center on Addiction and Substance Abuse, accidents caused by drunk drivers cost every man, woman, and child in the United States over $400 each year. How much money might be saved in your town or city if drunk driving accidents could be cut by 25 percent? by 50 percent? by 75 percent? If they could be eliminated altogether? (TIP: Start by finding out the population of your town or city, then do the math.)

> *Variation:* Start a chapter of SADD (Students Against Driving Drunk) at your school.[8]

START A DRUNK DRIVING WATCH program in your community. Anyone who notices a suspicious car (one that is weaving, moving erratically, cutting corners or going too wide around corners, straddling lane markers, coming too close to other cars, driving without headlights at night, etc.) contacts the police

---

[7] This activity and the "Crime Clue Report" form on page 239 are adapted from *The Kid's Guide to Service Projects* by Barbara A. Lewis (Minneapolis: Free Spirit Publishing, 1995), pages 26–28. Used with permission of the publisher.

[8] See page 49 for information on how to contact SADD.

# Crime Clue Report

See "Start a Crime Clue Box" on page 238.

Today's Date: _____

**WHAT** happened? _____

_____

**WHO** did it? _____

Male or female? (Circle one)          M          F          Age? (Approximate) _____

Hair color and style: _____

Eye color: _____   Race or ethnic group: _____

Describe any scars or marks: _____

What language was the person speaking? _____

Describe the person's clothing, hat, shoes, glasses, etc.: _____

_____

**WHERE** did it happen? (If you don't know the address, describe houses, stores, and landmarks

nearby): _____

_____

**WHEN** did it happen? _____

Date: _____   Time: _____

If there was a car involved, give as much information as you can:

Color: _____   Make: _____

Year: _____   License plate #: _____

Dents or marks: _____

If the crime involved stolen goods, what was stolen? _____

_____

Do you know where the stolen goods are? _____

_____

Is there anything else you remember? _____

_____

_____

*What Do You Stand For?* copyright © 1998 by Barbara A. Lewis. Free Spirit Publishing Inc. This page may be photocopied.

239

immediately to report it. Be sure to include this information when you make your report:

∞ where you saw the suspicious car

∞ the direction the car was going

∞ the type and color of car

∞ the license plate number (if you could see it)

∞ what the car was doing (weaving, swerving, etc.).

**START A NEIGHBORHOOD WATCH** program in your community. Find out how by contacting your local police department or city offices. Some communities have special "Neighborhood Watch Program" signs that neighborhoods can post. These signs let strangers know that a neighborhood is organized and alert to suspicious activities and persons.

## CHECK IT OUT

**National Association of Town Watch**
7 Wynnewood Road, Suite 215
PO Box 303
Wynnewood, PA 19096
(610) 649-7055
*www.nationaltownwatch.org*
Call, write, or go online for help starting a neighborhood watch program.

**National Crime Prevention Council (NCPC)**
1000 Connecticut Avenue, NW, 13th Floor
Washington, DC 20036
(202) 466-6272
*www.ncpc.org*
Call or write to request a copy of the "Neighborhood Watch Organizers Guide" or go online to read it. NCPC is also the home of McGruff the Crime Dog. Visit this page on the Web site for activities, games, and tips from McGruff: *www.mcgruff.org*

**SURVEY YOUR NEIGHBORHOOD** to learn which neighbors don't have smoke alarms in their homes and/or deadbolts on their doors. Work with local police to find a sponsor to supply smoke alarms and deadbolts, or fundraise so you can purchase some and donate them to neighbors in need.

**PLAN A NEIGHBORHOOD CLEANUP DAY.** Create and distribute a flyer announcing the time and date and inviting your neighbors to participate. With your

family, survey your neighborhood and identify unsafe streets or sidewalks, unlighted alleys, abandoned lots or houses, or anything else that needs attention. Collect trash from streets, sidewalks, and parks. Contact your city council member and report the safety problems you found.

*Variation:* Plan a cleanup day at your home or school.

**ASK YOUR MAYOR TO PROCLAIM** a Safety Week for your town or city. Work with your city offices to choose safety activities and assign them to various companies, businesses, and service organizations. Contact your local TV and radio stations and ask them to advertise Safety Week.

**START A SAFE ESCORT** or walking service. Older kids might walk younger kids home from school. Or volunteers might escort elderly people to stores or other places.

**START A HOTLINE (RED)** or a warmline (yellow) for kids who need help to call. Find out if you can do this at your school or community center, or contact other community organizations that might be willing to donate desk space and one or more phone lines. Recruit volunteers and trainers. Gather names and numbers of people and organizations willing to serve as resources for referrals.

☏ *Hotline resources:* psychologists, doctors, police, suicide prevention experts, teen pregnancy experts, substance abuse experts, counselors, etc.

☏ *Warmline resources:* counselors, teachers, parents, and others available for tutoring and giving advice on friendship troubles, dating, getting along with family members, etc.

**VOLUNTEER TO WORK WITH LATCHKEY KIDS** in an after-school program that keeps them safe and off the streets.[9] You might teach a skill, play games, or read stories.

**MAKE A STREET SMART SAFETY TIPS** poster or mobile. Share it with your class, club, or siblings; younger kids (at your school or in latchkey programs); youth groups (Scouts, 4-H, Campfire); and anyone else who's interested. Here are some tips you might include:

---

[9] See "Caring," pages 26–27, for a story about Claudia Rodriguez, who started an after-school program for kids.

✔ Watch where you're going. Look and listen.

✔ Walk solidly and show that you're confident and assertive.

✔ Keep your head up and your eyes forward; don't stare at the ground.

✔ Don't walk or jog after dark. If you must, use busy, well-lighted sidewalks.

✔ Know what goes on in your neighborhood. Avoid dangerous spots.

✔ Don't carry large amounts of money or "show your dough." (But always carry enough coins to make a phone call.)

✔ Go with a buddy. Don't walk, jog, or ride subways alone.

✔ If you're taking a public bus or subway, make sure you know the route and your stop.

✔ Always let someone (your parents, brother, sister, a friend) know where you're going.

✔ If a stranger in a car tries to lure you over, ignore him or her. Go into the nearest store or walk toward a group of people.

✔ NEVER hitchhike.

✔ Follow your gut feelings. If you feel nervous about a place or a group of people, avoid them.

✔ If you drive a car, park in well-lighted areas.

✔ If someone follows or harasses you, don't worry about looking cool. Scream, yell, shout "STAY AWAY!" and run. Knock on someone's door or go into a store or business.

*Variation:* Make a safety coloring book for younger kids. Write a safety tip and draw a cartoon on each page. Contact your local safety council to see if there's a way to make multiple copies of your coloring book and distribute them to schools and clubs.

**LEARN HOW TO STAY "STREET SMART"** on the Web. The most basic, widely available, and easy-to-understand rules for online safety were written by Larry Magid, a syndicated columnist for the *Los Angeles Times.* You can read them at: *www.safekids.com/kidsrules.htm*

For a free printed copy of Larry Magid's complete brochure, "Child Safety on the Information Highway," call 1-800-843-5678.

## CHECK IT OUT

**CyberAngels**
*www.cyberangels.org*
This CyberAngels Internet Safety Organization is an excellent online source of thoughtful advice. Visit this site when you need information that goes beyond Larry Magid's basic rules.

**LEARN HOW TO PREPARE YOUR HOME** and family for any kind of disaster—from fires to earthquakes, floods to hurricanes. Contact your local Red Cross chapter and request copies of disaster education materials including "Your Family Disaster Plan" and "Your Family Disaster Supplies Kit." Study them with your family. Assign specific emergency preparedness chores to individual family members. Practice fire drills, tornado drills, and other drills so everyone will know exactly what to do and when if disaster should ever strike.

## CHECK IT OUT

**American Red Cross**
*www.redcross.org/services/disaster*
Visit the Disaster Services pages on the Red Cross Web site for disaster preparation tips. Learn how to prepare a Disaster Supplies Kit.

**MAKE A PIE CHART TO SHOW** where violent crimes against teens most often occur. Use these statistics from the National Crime Prevention Council:

▼ on the street, park, or playground: 36%

▼ at school: 24%

▼ at home: 14%

▼ in the office, at jobs: 6%

▼ in parking lots: 9%

▼ other/unknown: 11%

**START OR JOIN A CRIMEFIGHTING PROGRAM** for youth. Check with local law enforcement agencies and city agencies to see if any such programs are already in place in your area. If not, find out how you can start one, and seek support from city officials. Or join a national organization.

## CHECK IT OUT

**Teens, Crime, and the Community (TCC)**
Street Law, Inc.
1600 K Street, NW, Suite 602
Washington, DC 20006
(202) 293-0088
*www.nationaltcc.org*
Created by the National Crime Prevention Council (NCPC) and Street Law, funded by the Office of Juvenile Justice and Delinquency Prevention, TCC gets teens involved in crime prevention to make themselves safer and their communities stronger. If you call Street Law for information, ask for Teens, Crime, and the Community. You can also contact TCC through the NCPC (see page 240).

**Youth Crime Watch of America**
9200 South Dadeland Boulevard, Suite 417
Miami, FL 33156
(305) 670-2409
*www.ycwa.org*
This nonprofit organization assists youth in actively reducing crime and drug use in their schools and communities. It has been named a U.S. Department of Education Exemplary Program of Excellence.

CHOOSE A SPORT YOU ENJOY and make a list of safety tips for that sport. Share your ideas with a coach or faculty sponsor. If you notice unsafe conditions at games or practices, report them.

PLAY A "WHAT IF . . ." GAME. Brainstorm several unsafe situations and write them on index cards. *Examples:*

**?**   What if you have to stay late after school, and when you leave to walk home it's already getting dark?

**?**   What if you witness a bicycle accident?

**?**   What if you notice that your garage is full of paint cans, paint thinner, and old rags?

**?**   What if you visit a friend and notice a gun lying on a table?

**?**   What if you're hiking and you fall and twist your ankle?

**?**   What if you notice a stranger following you in a car?

**?**   What if you're home alone and a stranger comes to the door?

Divide into two teams (Team A and Team B). Pick a card and read the "What if. . .?" question aloud to Team A. They have one minute to think of a safety plan. If they do, they earn *one* point. If they don't, the question passes to Team B. If Team B comes up with a safety plan, they earn *two* points. Ask Team A the first three "What if. . .?" questions, Team B the next three, and so on for as long as people want to play (up to 12 questions). The team with the most points at the end of the game wins.

## CHECK IT OUT

*What Would You Do? A Kid's Guide to Tricky and Sticky Situations* by Linda Schwartz (Santa Barbara, CA: The Learning Works, 1990). This common-sense guide prepares kids to handle more than 70 unexpected, puzzling, and frightening situations at home, at school, or out on their own. Ages 8–12.

READ STORIES ABOUT SAFETY. Look for these books:

*The Boxcar Children* by Gertrude Warner (Cutchogue, NY: Buccaneer Books, 1992). Four orphans who have run away from the grandfather they have never met make their home in an abandoned boxcar. Ages 8–10.

*Call It Courage* by Armstrong Sperry (New York: MacMillan, 1940). Tired of being called a coward, a young Polynesian boy who is terrified of water sets out on a journey in a canoe in the South Pacific.

*Driver's Ed* by Caroline Cooney (New York: Dell, 1996). Three teenagers' lives are changed forever when they steal a stop sign from a dangerous intersection and a young mother is killed in an auto accident there. Ages 12 & up.

*Someone Is Hiding on Alcatraz Island* by Eve Bunting (Boston, MA: Berkley Publishing Group, 1986). When he gets in trouble with a gang at his San Francisco school, Danny flees to Alcatraz island, but the gang traps him and a Park Service employee in an old cell block. Ages 10–14.

*Trapped* by Roderic Jeffries (New York: HarperCollins, 1972). When Gerry and Bert are caught in a snowstorm during a hunting trip, the two boys must overcome their dislike for each other in order to survive.

# Character in *ACTION*

## Kempsville Middle School: The "Lifesavers"

**T**he soccer team from Kempsville Middle School in Virginia Beach, Virginia, was in the middle of a game when they noticed something unusual. The members of the other team were wearing a patch on their sleeves. When the Kempsville kids asked about it, they learned that the patch was in memory of a teammate who had died in a bicycle accident. He was hit by a car—and he wasn't wearing a helmet.

Back at school, seventh grader Chris Bagley charged into his classroom and told his teacher, Carolyn Stamm, and his classmates about it. "That hits home," said Chris's friend, T. Jack Bagby. "He was the same age as us, and he played soccer. That could happen to us, too."

Emily Mead spoke up. "It makes me mad, because a lot of kids get hurt or killed in bike accidents, and it wouldn't happen if they had been wearing helmets."

On the spot, Ms. Stamm's class decided to take on the problem as a project. They dubbed themselves the "Lifesavers" and started doing research.

They read books and newspapers and interviewed people in person and by telephone. The Kempsville kids learned that some 400,000 children in the United States are injured each year in bicycle-related accidents, about 300 are killed, and only five percent of all school-age bikers wear helmets.

With their research done, it was time to take action. The students phoned their city council and asked if they would pass a city ordinance requiring kids to wear bicycle helmets. The council said they'd have to get the idea approved by the state first. The kids called a state delegate and asked if he would help. The delegate said he'd have to be sure that the city council was in favor of it. What a runaround!

But the Kempsville middle schoolers weren't discouraged. They hunched over their desks, writing a flurry of letters to council members, other delegates to the state assembly, even the editor of the *Virginia Pilot*. Emily Mead's letter was printed in the newspaper, and that got the ball rolling. In her letter, Emily wrote: "More kids are killed and

The Kempsville Middle School "Lifesavers" at the International Future Problem Solving Conference in Providence, Rhode Island

injured each year on bicycles than on skateboards, roller skates, Big Wheels, and scooters combined. Ninety percent of the injuries are from collisions with cars. Eighty percent of fatal bicycle injuries and seventy-five percent of disabling injuries could have been prevented if the child had been wearing a bicycle helmet."

Meanwhile, the kids worked with the local police to write a grant for 500 bicycle helmets. They figured that they could save a few heads by passing out free helmets. The police helped them to sponsor a bike race, the "Champion Challenge," where they distributed the helmets and conducted bicycle safety inspections. To publicize the race, the Kempsville students visited several schools and put on homemade skits.

Hundreds of kids came to the race, and it was a huge success. At the race, student Lara McBride told a newspaper reporter that "Bicycles are more dangerous than motorcycles, because with motorcycles you can at least hear the engine, but with a bicycle you can't hear anything unless you have a bell or something."

After the race, the kids lobbied the city council, which passed a resolution in favor of the helmet ordinance. That satisfied the state governor, who in turn passed a law saying that other localities in Virginia could also institute bicycle safety ordinances. With everyone finally in agreement, the Kempsville kids got their ordinance, which requires bicyclists ages 14 years and under to wear protective helmets within the Virginia Beach city limits. The ordinance took effect on July 1, 1995.

"I'm proud of our work," Christie Padgett says. "Now adults know that we can make a difference in our community."

# Self-Discipline

## Self-control, self-restraint, self-reliance, independence

"Without discipline, there's no life at all."
*Katharine Hepburn*

**H**ave you ever been in a classroom when the teacher steps out for a few moments? The teacher is barely out the door when one student starts entertaining the others by telling jokes, drawing cartoons on the blackboard, or standing on a desk. In an instant, other students jump up, chase each other around the room, and wrestle on the floor. Missiles of wadded paper and erasers shoot across the desks. Then suddenly a spy shouts "The teacher is coming!" Instantly, the students rush for their seats. A desk is accidentally overturned. The teacher enters the room, hands on hips, and demands to know what's going on. Everyone sits quietly, pencils ready, with innocent smiles of conspiracy on their faces.

Sound familiar? Here's a contrasting story:

Unionville School in Indiana was a small school that housed students from first grade through high school. When I was teaching there, my students decided to have a real experience in democracy and wrote their own class constitution. One day there was a huge, unexpected snowstorm that dumped a two-foot layer of icing over Southern Indiana. Living 30 miles out of town, I was unable to make my way to school until two hours after it started. The principal greeted me with "Hey, you didn't even need to come in today. I sent someone down to your room to take care of your class, and the kids were already doing it for themselves. They were halfway through their English assignment."

What's the difference? In the first example, the students expected the teacher to control their behavior. Their discipline came from *without*. For the Unionville kids, their discipline came from *within*.

Discipline from *without*.     Discipline from *within*.

# Taking Charge of Your Life

When you were very young, your parents had to tell you what to do, and they had to do nearly everything for you. As you grew older, your parents (and other people) expected you to start making some of your own decisions and taking care of yourself in certain ways. You learned to do what you should ("will power") and stop yourself from doing what you shouldn't ("won't power"). You started using **self-discipline** and **self-control**. The more this happened, the more you freed your parents, your teachers, and even yourself, because you didn't have to keep making case-by-case decisions about your behavior. You *internalized* some of these decisions, and they became automatic and habitual.

When you depend on other people to determine your behavior and always be in charge of your "will power" and "won't power," you're like a pawn on a chessboard, waiting for someone to move you. You feel powerless—because you are. Self-discipline and self-control give you power over your life. It's only when you've developed these important traits that you can grow into the wonderful person you're meant to be.

> "I'm not afraid of storms, for I'm learning
> how to sail my ship."
> *Louisa May Alcott*

**Self-restraint** is what helps you in unpredictable or tempting situations. You hold your fists back when someone shoves you; you hold your tongue back when someone insults you. You can even put the brakes on your thoughts when a harmful idea or thought pops into your head. Using restraint doesn't mean that you let other people pick on you. You can still be assertive and stick up for yourself.[1] But you don't act impulsively in ways that hurt you or anyone else. You behave respectfully no matter what.

**Self-reliance** means that you always have someone you can count on—YOU. When you're home alone and feeling hungry, you don't wait for your parents to return and fix you something to eat. You make yourself a snack. If you want to learn how to play the guitar and your parents can't afford to pay for lessons, you get a part-time job and earn the money you need. If you know that you want to go to college someday, you do your best to earn good grades.

Chicago Bulls superstar Michael Jordan took cooking classes when he was an adolescent— "because girls weren't interested in me or whatever it was, and I thought, I may be alone for the rest of my life." He wanted to make sure he could take care of himself. (Of course, this assumes that women should do all of the cooking—a more common belief when Jordan was a teen than it is today.)

When you *demand* independence, the adults in your life usually pull tighter on your chain. When you *demonstrate* self-reliance—along with self-discipline, self-control, and self-restraint— adults often trust you more and *give* you more independence.

What can you do to develop and strengthen these character traits in yourself? Following are some strategies you can try.

# Eight Ways to Strengthen Your Self-Discipline

**1. Decide that you really** want *to be someone who's self-disciplined,* self-controlled, self-restrained, and self-reliant. Your desire will motivate you to make good choices. When there's something you want, you work to get it.

**2. Make a personal commitment** to develop and strengthen these traits. Write down specific things you'll do to fulfill your commitment. *Examples:* "I'm going to start washing my own clothes instead of expecting my parents to do it." "Starting tonight, I'm going to save half of the money I earn from babysitting." Tell someone you trust about your commitment. That person can encourage you to keep your promises to yourself. From time to time, tell him or her about the progress you're making.

**3. Learn the rules** that determine what you can and can't do. Family rules, school rules, society's rules, laws, the rules of your culture, heritage, traditions, and/or faith—find out what they are and follow them. Do this on your own, with your family, with your class, with your faith community.

---

[1] See "Respect," pages 217–218.

**4. Be accountable.** Accept responsibility for your behavior. Don't blame others for your actions and decisions.[2]

**5. Practice.** New character traits don't form on their own. If you wanted to learn to play hockey, you'd have to practice. At first your skates would refuse to stay beneath your body. With practice, however, you'd slowly gain the skills you need to stand, glide, and control the direction of the puck. Self-discipline is something you can teach yourself. If it's new to you, start slowly. *Example:*

☀ Do something you're supposed to do for one hour each day. Clean your room, do your homework without being told, stop yourself from speaking out in class without raising your hand, and so on.

☀ Increase the time to two hours, then three . . . and eventually most of the day.

**6. Do activities that enhance your self-discipline.** You might try yoga, walking, rock-climbing, practicing a musical instrument, or whatever else interests you.

**7. Eliminate harmful habits.** *Example:* If you spend several hours each week watching violent videos or TV programs, make a conscious decision to spend your time in healthier, more productive ways. You might start by watching different videos or TV programs, then gradually cut back on your TV-watching time.

**8. Start a self-discipline support group.** Tell a few close friends about your decision to develop and strengthen these character traits and ask if they'd like to join you. Talk together about your plans, dreams, mistakes, frustrations, and hopes for the future. Plan and do activities that strengthen your self-discipline.

> "There's only one corner of the universe you can be certain of improving, and that's your own self."
> *Aldous Huxley*

---

[2] See "Choice and Accountability," pages 28–34.

# Character Dilemmas

*For journaling or writing essays, discussion, debate, role-playing, reflection*

**Suppose that . . .**

**1** Someone you know has been calling you names on the way to school each morning. You've tried to ignore him and say nothing, but the verbal abuse keeps coming. How might you use self-restraint and stop the abuse at the same time? Is this even possible?

**2** You've just moved to a new town, and you'd really like to try out for the football team. To do this, you'll have to spend several hours each day practicing and working out. You'd also like to develop new friendships so you don't feel lonely. You sign up for football practice every night after school . . . and the next day, a group of popular kids invites you to play street hockey with them every night after school. What should you do? How could you handle this?

**3** You have strange and uncomfortable thoughts that keep squeezing their way into your brain. You want to do a little "brain housecleaning," but you aren't sure how to discipline your mind. What might you do?

**4** You bite your fingernails whenever you're under stress. You're sick of having ragged nails, but just thinking about stopping is enough to cause stress . . . and you start chomping your nails again. How can you discipline yourself to break this habit?

**5** You suspect that one of your friends has started smoking cigarettes. How might you help her develop the self-discipline to quit—without losing her friendship?

# Activities

**BRAINSTORM A LIST OF PROBLEMS** that might result from a lack of self-discipline. Consider how they might affect some or all of the following:

▼ personal appearance

▼ physical, mental, or emotional health

- school success
- life success
- friendships
- job performance
- talents
- participation in family, clubs, community, or faith
- marriage
- parenting
- anything else.

*Example:* What if a person didn't have the self-discipline to wash or comb her hair? Problems might include a sloppy appearance, poor self-esteem, disapproving teachers, disgusted friends (or no friends), inability to get a job, angry parents, and so on—plus an itchy head.

**DO SILLY EXERCISES** to strengthen your self-discipline. When you read these, you might laugh out loud or think they're *very* strange. Try them anyway. They really work!

1. Go to a fast-food place and buy the tastiest item on the menu. Keep it wrapped up and nearby while you study, practice, clean your room, etc. See how long you can go without eating it. Try it for five minutes the first time, then increase your resistance to ten minutes the next time, and so on.

2. The next time you get a mosquito bite, don't scratch it. This silly exercise has an added benefit: The less you scratch, the sooner the bite will stop itching.

Make up your own silly exercises—whatever works for you. Just keep in mind that your purpose is to become more self-disciplined. IMPORTANT: Don't carry this too far or hurt yourself in any way. If you've just had a long day and a hard soccer practice and you haven't eaten since lunch and you're dizzy with hunger, eat!

**ROLE-PLAY HOW YOU MIGHT TALK** with a younger brother or sister who's demonstrating a lack of self-discipline (*examples:* always late, doesn't complete chores or tasks, is doing poorly in school, etc.). How might you encourage or help your sibling to develop self-discipline?

**WRITE OR TELL A CHAIN STORY** about a make-believe prince or princess who has no self-discipline. You might do this with your family, class, club, or youth group. *Example:* The first person writes (or says) "Princess Miss-apline woke up every morning, stretched in her crisp white sheets and fluffy blankets, and simply couldn't force herself to get out of bed. . . ." The second person writes (or says) "This was a serious problem for the kingdom, because the Princess was the one who opened the palace gates each morning, and until the gates were open, the King's and Queen's advisors couldn't come inside. . . ." Decide in advance if your story will have a happy ending (the Princess learns self-discipline) or an unhappy ending (the Princess never learns self-discipline). Here are a few other characters you might want to write or tell about:

- Willy Won't-power (an athlete)
- Merva No-Nerva (a girl who's afraid of taking charge of her life)
- Ironless-Will Phil (a boy who watches TV 24 hours a day).

IMPORTANT: These and other make-believe names should only be used to stimulate creative thinking. They should not be used to make fun of real people.

**INTERVIEW SCIENTISTS, ENGINEERS,** and doctors to learn what role self-discipline has played in their lives. Compile your interviews into a booklet and donate it to your school library's biography section.

*Variation:* Interview any successful people of your choice.

**INVESTIGATE DIFFERENT ANIMAL** species to learn if they use discipline. Do gorillas, wolves, and lions discipline each other and themselves? Does one animal seem to be in charge of the others, or do they share this responsibility? Do they punish misbehavior? Write your findings in a log or in a chart, showing comparisons if you choose several animals or species. (What about birds? Fish? Insects?)

**VISIT WITH A PROFESSIONAL MATHEMATICIAN** (you might find one employed in an area industry or business, or teaching at a nearby college or university). Ask him or her to outline for you the self-discipline that's required to train the mind to think analytically. Write an article about what you learn and share it with your class, club, or family.

EXAMINE NATURE TO FIND EXAMPLES of discipline and order. Fibonacci numbers (named for the 12th-century European mathematician who discovered them) turn up everywhere in nature, from bees' family trees to petal arrangements on flowers, pine cones, groups of leaves, whirls on sunflower seeds, and more. The "Fibonacci sequence" of numbers goes like this: 0, 1, 1, 2, 3, 5, 8, 13 . . . and so on. Can you figure out the next two numbers in the sequence? (The answer is printed upside down at the bottom of the page.) Find as many Fibonacci numbers in nature as you can. List each object and its number.

## CHECK IT OUT

### Fibonacci Numbers and the Golden Section

*www.mcs.surrey.ac.uk/Personal/R.Knott/Fibonacci/fib.html*

Tons of fun and fascinating information about Fibonacci, the Fibonacci numbers, and where they appear in nature, plus puzzles where the answers all seem to involve Fibonacci numbers. This award-winning site is hosted by the Department of Computing of Surrey University in the United Kingdom.

EXPLORE TESSELATIONS. A tesselation is a repeating geometric pattern—forms that interlock without gaps or overlaps and can theoretically go on repeating forever. The Moors used tesselations in the palaces of the Alhambra in Spain; Japanese artists have made beautiful repeating patterns; Dutch artist M.C. Escher was a master of tesselations, creating them from lizards, fish, and birds. Create your own tesselation, using color and contrast to make each shape stand out.

## CHECK IT OUT

*M.C. Escher: His Life and Complete Graphic Work* by F.H. Bool et al. (New York: Harry N. Abrams, Inc., 1982). A big book with 606 Escher illustrations including 36 plates in full color. (NOTE: If your local library doesn't have this particular book, it's almost certain to have others about Escher, since his art is very popular.)

### The World of Escher

*www.worldofescher.com*

Visit this site to read Escher stories, essays, quotes, and a biographical chronology; view images in an online art museum; and more.

RESEARCH DISCIPLINE IN HISTORY. How have people of different times and cultures disciplined their children? What rewards and punishments have they used? Write an essay about your findings.

LEARN ABOUT TIMES IN HISTORY when the arts have been controlled. *Example:* In Nazi Germany, many painters were denounced as "degenerates" and forbidden to paint. When and where have the arts—painting, music, theater, literature—flourished? What kinds of circumstances—government, economic, political—seem to encourage the arts?

> *Variation:* Debate whether art should ever be controlled—or censored.

VISIT A JUVENILE DETENTION CENTER. Talk with the supervisor about the role self-discipline plays in the lives of the young people there. If possible, talk with some of the young people themselves. IMPORTANT: Get permission to visit, and go with chaperons. Afterward, talk about the experience with your family, class, or club.

DRAW CARTOONS SHOWING EXAMPLES of self-discipline vs. no discipline. *Examples:* Jenny gets out of bed on time; Ray sleeps through his alarm. Maurice does his homework; Keesha watches TV.

WRITE NEW LYRICS TO A POPULAR SONG—lyrics that encourage self-discipline, self-restraint, and self-reliance. You might choose a children's song, a rap, a rock song, a country music song, or anything else you like to listen to.

Here's the key to the Fibonacci Sequence: 1 + 1 = 2; 2 + 1 = 3; 3 + 2 = 5; 5 + 3 = 8; 8 + 5 = 13. So the next two numbers in the sequence are 21 (13 + 8) and 34 (21 + 13). Still don't get it? Each *new* Fibonacci number is added to the *preceding* Fibonacci number to get the *next* Fibonacci number.

**EXPLORE MUSICAL DYNAMICS AND CONTROL.** What happens when you alter the volume control on your stereo? You either increase the loudness *(crescendo)* or decrease it *(decrescendo)*. How does a change in volume make you feel? Do you think it's harder for a big choir to sing loudly or to sing softly? Which requires the most control? Listen to a choral recording and pay attention to the various dynamics you hear.

> *Variation:* Research musical symbols that control loudness, softness, speed, slowness, and so on. Ask a music teacher or look in a music dictionary. Make a poster illustrating the various symbols and telling what they mean.

**LEARN ABOUT SELF-DISCIPLINE IN SPORTS.** Which sport do you think requires the *most* self-discipline to play? Dodgeball? Football? Ping-pong? Tennis? What else? Does it take more self-control to play an individual sport or a team sport? Give reasons for your answer.

**PLAY A "STOP-WAIT-GO" GAME.** Make a list of situations for which people might choose to:

1.  *stop* and do nothing,

2.  *wait* to do anything, or

3.  *go* immediately and do something.

*Examples:*

**?**  You observe a student in your class cheating on a test. Do you *stop* (do nothing), *wait* (see if the teacher notices), or *go* (tell the teacher)?

**?**  You're trying to eat more healthfully when someone you like offers to buy you a chocolate malt. Do you *stop* (say "No, thanks"), *wait* (say "Let me take a rain check on that"), or *go* (say "Sure!")?

**?**  Your teacher publicly accuses you of stealing something from the classroom. Do you *stop* (say nothing), *wait* (think about what you might say or do), or *go* (defend yourself immediately)?

Make three colored cards for each player: red (for stop), yellow (for wait), and green (for go). As you read the situations aloud, each player holds up the card that represents his or her answer. Tally how people voted, then discuss the results. TIP: Not all situations have definite "right" or "wrong" answers. In many cases, the answers can be debated.

**READ STORIES ABOUT SELF-DISCIPLINE,** self-control, and self-reliance. Look for these books:

*From the Mixed-Up Files of Mrs. Basil E. Frankweiler* by E.L. Konigsburg (New York: Dell, 1997). After running away with her younger brother to live in the Metropolitan Museum of Art, 12-year-old Claudia strives to keep things in order in their new home and to become a changed person and a heroine to herself. Originally published in 1967. Ages 10–13.

*Island of the Blue Dolphins* by Scott O'Dell (New York: Bantam Doubleday Dell Books for Young Readers, 1997). Records the courage and self-reliance of a Native American girl who lived alone for 18 years on an isolated island off the coast of California. Originally published in 1960. Ages 10 & up.

*A Likely Place* by Paula Fox (New York: Simon & Schuster, 1975). A boy who can't spell or ever seem to please his parents spends a week with a kooky baby-sitter and makes a special friend. Originally published in 1967. Ages 9–12.

*My Side of the Mountain* by Jean Craighead George (New York: Puffin Books, 1991). A young boy builds a treehouse in the Catskill Mountains and lives alone for a year, struggling to survive and ultimately realizing that he needs human companionship. Ages 11–14.

*When the Phone Rang* by Harry Mazer (New York: Scholastic, 1989). When their parents are killed in an airplane crash, three siblings try to keep the family together in the face of overwhelming personal and financial problems. Ages 12–16.

# Character in *ACTION*

## Iris Zimmerman: Totally Disciplined

When 15-year-old Iris Zimmerman was in kindergarten, she tackled a boy around the neck and planted a kiss on his cheek. She also talked nonstop in class and spent a lot of time in the corner. As she grew older, she took her older sister Felicia's clothes without asking and messed them up.

Iris's dad enrolled Felicia in a fencing class. Iris ran around the Rochester Fencing Center for four years wishing she could fence, too. When Iris was six, she was accepted as a student, and she loved it. But while fencing helped Felicia learn assertiveness, it helped Iris learn self-discipline.

Iris began competing when she was nine years old. To develop her talent, she began going straight from school to lessons at the fencing center. She also learned to play the flute and the piano. Eventually she was accepted at the School of the Arts.

To maintain her mostly "A" average, Iris uses every hour of the day. She has made a strict schedule for herself, and she sticks to it. She studies in study hall at school and at home on weekends. She doesn't have much time to study in the evenings, because after fencing, she lifts weights to improve her strength and endurance. She falls in bed at night, feeling like a limp dishrag. But she thrives on the competition and self-discipline.

"I don't have time to do some of the normal girl things," Iris explains. "A lot of my friends go home from school and watch TV or just hang out. But I have to tell myself 'If I go with them, I'm not going to be ready to compete.' When I relax, I usually hang out with my sister and my fencing friends. This is what I want to do."

Her self-discipline and practice have already paid off. In 1995, Iris traveled to France and won the World Fencing Championship in the Under 17 category. In 1996, she went to Belgium and came in third place in the World Championship for the Under 20 category.

"I've learned that you have to be totally disciplined," Iris explains. "The greatest fear I have to overcome is the fear of losing. When you're on your way up, you have nothing to lose, but when you're at the top, you have a lot to lose.

"I've learned that I don't have any limitations. You can do anything you want to do . . . if you have the self-discipline."

Iris Zimmerman

# Wisdom

**Intelligence, learning, knowledge, understanding, intuition, common sense, being a lifelong learner**

"Dare to be wise!"
*Friedrich von Schiller*

Once, over a two-year period, I rode more 4,000 miles on a stationery bike. I know I traveled that far because there was an odometer attached to the handlebars. On the one hand, my body and mind benefited from the exercise. On the other, I had ridden a distance equivalent to the width of the United States . . . and had gone nowhere and learned nothing.

Wisdom goes beyond the distance you travel in life or the facts you accumulate along the way. It's possible to visit every country in the world and have an encyclopedia in your head and still not be wise. To be wise means to gather all of your experiences—everything you've done, seen, and heard, everywhere you've gone, everyone you've known—and build positive meaning from them to apply to your everyday life.

Wisdom is the responsible use of knowledge and experience. It's a journey, not a destination. If you're wise, you keep learning all your life. Wisdom is a beginning, not an end. If you're wise, your door is always open to new knowledge, new experiences, new roads to travel. Wisdom has no boundaries or fences. If you're wise, you're not afraid of new ideas, because you know that you can always decide to accept or reject them.

The Wright Brothers were determined to fly—in spite of the teasing, harassment, and skepticism they encountered along the way. People often told them "If God wanted people to fly, he would have given them wings." It may be hard for you to believe that people once thought this way, especially if you've ever ridden on an airplane. But if you watch the news and listen, you'll hear people saying similar things about the inventors, experimenters, and dreamers of today. Some people are afraid of the unknown; they aren't sure where great leaps in knowledge will lead. But knowledge should never be feared, because knowlege itself is seldom bad. It's the way people use (or misuse) knowledge that can sometimes be harmful. Having sound judgment is another part of being wise.

Many people throughout history have been called "wise" or credited with having wisdom—people like Albert Schweitzer, Mohandas Gandhi, Buddha, Jesus, Mohammed, Helen Keller, Mother Teresa, Eleanor Roosevelt, Thomas Jefferson, the Dalai Lama, and others. Even some fictional characters are considered wise—like Lisa Simpson of "The Simpsons." Being wise should *not* be confused with being a wisecracker, wiseacre, wisenheimer, or wise guy (Bart Simpson would head that list).

What might it mean to *you* to be wise? Your definition might be different from someone else's definition. You might want to ask various people you know—your parents, teachers, religious leaders, friends, and other people you trust and respect—what wisdom means to them.

252

# 16 Ways to Become Wise

**1.** ***Learn from experience.*** This includes positive *and* negative experiences. Let suffering and mistakes become your teachers; remember that mistakes teach you about things that *don't* work so you can discover what *does* work. Allow suffering to teach you patience, compassion, caring, and sharing with others. Reflect on the things that happen to you and the things you do. Accept responsibility for the choices you make—and the consequences.

**2.** ***Develop your mind.*** Learning doesn't end at 17 (or 18, or 21, or whatever age you stop going to school). Wise people are lifelong learners. Keep an open mind to new information and stay "teachable." Seek knowledge, ideas, cultures, and "to go boldly where no one has gone before" (to quote Captain Jean-Luc Picard of "Star Trek: The Next Generation"). Your mind has enormous power and potential; never be afraid to strengthen and stretch it even more.

**3.** ***Care for your body.*** You know that it's important to stay healthy. Eat well, get enough sleep and exercise, keep your body clean, and avoid harmful habits like smoking and drinking alcohol.

**4.** ***Care for your spirit.*** Your inner self needs TLC, too. Feed your spirit (or "mind," or "soul," or whatever you prefer to call it) with meditation or prayer. Exercise it with service to others; rest it with quiet contemplation . . . and time spent watching the clouds go by.

**5.** ***Know yourself and what you can become.*** Follow your interests and passions; explore and develop your talents. Knowing yourself also means acknowledging and accepting your limitations. If you don't enjoy hockey and you're not very good at it, you don't need to feel guilty about not trying out for the hockey team. On the other hand, if you *love* hockey and you're not very good at it, you know what to do: Learn. Get help. And practice, practice, practice.

**6.** ***Have confidence in your worth.*** Don't rely on others for approval and acceptance; your power comes from within. Don't count on others to get you going; be a self-starter.

**7.** ***Seek and build relationships with others.*** How you relate to others depends on how you relate to yourself. When you accept and appreciate yourself, it's easier to accept and appreciate others. Get to know other people and grow close to them—at home, at school, in your neighborhood and community. Be willing to learn from them. You may discover that people in your everyday life—your parents, grandparents, next-door neighbor, teachers, favorite aunt or uncle, best friend, youth group leader—are full of wisdom.

**8.  Seek and build relationships with the world.**
All of nature produces music together, like the members of an orchestra. Wise people are those who flow with nature's melody—with the forces of weather, animals, and the world's creatures. Learn to share, balance, and walk *with* nature. This means that you don't go out and wantonly shoot birds with your new BB gun. You respect the animals and other living things around you.

**9.  Develop your intuition.** When you're intuitive, you're able to feel or sense the feelings, beliefs, wants, and needs of others. Not everyone is naturally intuitive, but you can work to become more intuitive. One way to do this is by trying to imagine how other people feel. Put yourself in their place; walk in their moccasins.

**10. Use your common sense.** Often, common sense is simply a matter of thinking before you act—of drawing on what you already know without having to figure it out. Common sense is a kind of "folk wisdom." It's not sophisticated; it's not profound. Common sense tells you not to walk into the street in front of a moving car. It tells you to close the window when it's raining. It tells you that if you don't like being called names or bullied, other people don't like it either.

**11. Make plans and decisions based on fairness and truth.** Be tolerant of other people and ideas. Try not to judge them. Gather as much information as you can before forming an opinion.

**12. Try to see the "big picture."** When you can imagine what a puzzle might look like when it's put together, it's easier to see where individual pieces fit. *Example:* You understand that *all* people have a need to feel loved and accepted. You can't reach out to everyone in the world, but you can reach out to the individuals around you—people of all ages, races, religions, cultures, sizes, shapes, and so on. Seeing the "big picture" also means that you're better prepared for surprises and possible setbacks. You can see the tornado before the funnel cloud appears.

> "The most pathetic person in the world is
> someone who has sight, but has no vision."
> *Helen Keller*

**13. Be flexible and adaptable.** When your grandfather was young, he probably started a job or career that he stayed with for his entire working life. You might need to make three or four career changes over your lifetime. Today and increasingly in the future, the people who succeed are those who change, learn, and grow. Be open to new ideas.

> "In a time of drastic change it is
> the learners who inherit the future."
> *Eric Hoffer*

**14. Be willing to delay your wants.** You need to wait until you're old enough for certain things you want to have and do—buy a car, stay out past curfew, get your own apartment, and so on. Kids who can't wait to get what they want might steal, quit school, or run away. Adults who can't delay their wants might buy a home that's more than they can afford. If you're willing to work hard, build the skills you need, and wait for the right time, you can earn the good things you want, and that's part of wisdom.

**15. Dare to take risks or look foolish.** To become wise, you need the courage to look at things from different angles and challenge accepted ideas and usual ways of doing things. At times, people might make fun of you. Christopher Columbus looked silly to the rest of Europe when he challenged the idea that he'd drop off the edge of the earth if he sailed straight west.

> "Without risks, there is no chance of reward."
> *Richard Bangs*

**16. Give and take.** Wise people know to accept help from others—and to reach down and take another person's hand as they climb life's ladder.

> "Knowledge alone is not enough. It must
> be leavened with magnanimity before
> it becomes wisdom."
> *Adlai Stevenson*

You've probably noticed that this list includes many of the character traits discussed in earlier chapters of this book. You might want to create your own list of traits, qualities, and characteristics you believe are important to becoming wise. Carry your list with you and refer to it from time to time. Make changes and additions as you grow in wisdom.

# Character Dilemmas

*For journaling or writing essays, discussion, debate, role-playing, reflection*

### Suppose that . . .

**1** You're 16 years old and you really want to buy a car. Currently you're depending on your family and the bus for rides. You're already working three nights a week after school and every Saturday, and you're thinking about working even more hours—every night after school and Sundays, too. It would be hard to find time to do homework, and you'd have to drop your extracurricular activities, but you'd be able to buy your car a lot sooner. What would be the wise thing to do? Justify your answer.

**2** You're a parent whose 14-year-old son has been acting strangely lately. He's skipping classes, not doing his homework, coming home late at night, and spending all of his time at home in his room with the door closed. He's also moody and short-tempered. The whole family is worried about him. What would be the wise thing to do?

**3** Your best friend's father was injured on the job and can't work until he recovers. Your friend was planning to start college this fall, but her parents want her to work full-time to help the family until her father returns to work. Now your friend is asking for your advice. Should she go to college (she's on full scholarship) or delay starting until her father can work? She's worried about losing her scholarship . . . but she wants to help her family, too. What's the wisest advice you could give your friend?

**4** You think that your parents are too strict with you. They expect you to come home every day after school and do homework for at least two hours; they only let you watch certain TV shows; and they think your friends are "bad influences" and won't let you go to parties with them. Your friends are starting to ignore you because you're never available to hang out with them. One day they invite you to a party on Friday night. You know that the parents will be at home and there's no chance that anything bad might happen—but you also know that your parents won't let you go just because. Your friends encourage you to wait until they're asleep and sneak out your bedroom window. There's an excellent chance that your parents will never know. What's the wisest thing you can do? How might you respect your parents' wishes and also develop friendships? How might you get them to agree to be less strict with you?

**5** Your big sister picks on you all the time. One day, she scratches your parents' car when she takes it for a drive without their permission. She begs you to tell them that *you* accidentally scratched it with your bike as you rode into the carport. She promises that she'll never pick on you again if you'll cover for her. What are the wisest things you can do to help yourself, your sister, and your parents the most?

# Activities

**WRITE A SHORT STORY** about someone who demonstrates wisdom by delaying gratification—by waiting for the right time to do or get something he or she wants. *Example:* A teenager wants a new CD player but decides to save his money for college instead.

**WRITE A POEM OR LIMERICK** about age vs. wisdom. Are older people necessarily wiser than younger people? What does wisdom mean? You decide.

**DEBATE WHICH IS MORE IMPORTANT**—knowledge or wisdom. Which comes first? Can you have one without the other? Are there times when one should take precedence over the other? When? How? Why?

**EXPLORE ALBERT EINSTEIN'S BRAIN.** During the 1980s, Berkeley professor and brain researcher Marian Diamond acquired portions of Einstein's brain and studied them closely. She discovered that Einstein's brain had more glial cells per neuron than the average human brain. (Glial cells "glue" your brain together in synaptic connections; the more synaptic connections you have, the better.) Einstein was not only a mathematical genius, he was also a very wise man. Learn more about his brain and the scientist who studied it. Share your findings with your class, club, or family.

## CHECK IT OUT

*The Human Brain Coloring Book* by Marian C. Diamond (New York: Barnes & Noble, 1985). A fun way to learn about the brain, written by the California scientist who studied Einstein's brain.

**Neuroscience for Kids**
*faculty.washington.edu/chudler/neurok.html*
Do a search for "Marian Diamond" and find a link to a biography of this distinguished scientist (and beloved teacher).

**EXPLORE EINSTEIN'S THEORY** of time dilation. Stated simply, this theory proposes that the faster you travel, the slower time goes. Do you believe it? What might this theory mean to space travel? To colonizing other planets? Write your own version of this theory, using an example. Be sure to draw on your wisdom as well as your knowledge.

**MAKE A DRAWING, PAINTING,** or sculpture of Athena, the goddess of wisdom from Greek mythology. What did the Greeks believe about her? What was her role in Greek legend? You might research other examples of art (paintings, sculptures, mosaics, etc.) that feature Athena.

**CREATE A CHART SHOWING SYMBOLS** of wisdom used by various cultures around the world.[1] *Examples:* ant, crane, elephant, hedgehog, lotus, owl, pearl, scepter, tree. Include brief explanations of why each was believed to symbolize wisdom.

**RESEARCH THE LIFE OF A WISE PERSON** from the past. Try to discover if he or she lived by any particular "rules of wisdom." Find examples of wise things the person did or said. Share your findings on a chart or poster. You might title it "The Wisdom of. . . ." You might research one of the following people (or choose someone else who interests you):

- ✳ Jane Addams
- ✳ Susan B. Anthony
- ✳ Saint Augustine
- ✳ Marcus Aurelius
- ✳ Pearl S. Buck

- ✳ Buddha
- ✳ Confucius
- ✳ Albert Einstein
- ✳ Ralph Waldo Emerson
- ✳ Epictetus
- ✳ Anne Frank
- ✳ Benjamin Franklin
- ✳ Mohandas Gandhi
- ✳ Thomas Jefferson
- ✳ Jesus
- ✳ Learned Hand
- ✳ Thomas Hobbes
- ✳ Immanuel Kant
- ✳ Helen Keller
- ✳ Martin Luther King Jr.
- ✳ Lao Tzu
- ✳ Abraham Lincoln
- ✳ Anne Morrow Lindbergh
- ✳ Nelson Mandela
- ✳ Abraham Maslow
- ✳ Moses
- ✳ Satchel Paige
- ✳ Plato
- ✳ Eleanor Roosevelt
- ✳ Jean-Jacques Rousseau
- ✳ Albert Schweitzer
- ✳ Chief Seattle
- ✳ King Solomon
- ✳ Elizabeth Cady Stanton
- ✳ Mother Teresa
- ✳ Mark Twain
- ✳ Voltaire
- ✳ Malcolm X

*Variation:* Research the life of a wise person from the present. This can be anyone you admire or respect; it doesn't have to be a famous person.

**LEARN HOW WISE PEOPLE** have been treated throughout history. Have different countries and cultures traditionally revered wise people . . . or feared them? Can you see any relationship between how successful countries and cultures are and how much they respect wisdom and knowledge? You might look at ancient Egypt, classical Greece, the Middle Ages, the Renaissance, Nazi Germany, etc.

---

[1] See "Positive Attitudes," page 18, for a resource on symbols and symbolism.

**INTERVIEW A NATIVE AMERICAN** to learn how members of his or her tribe pass on their knowledge and wisdom to younger generations. Or interview someone from another culture.

**INTERVIEW ELDERS IN YOUR OWN FAMILY.** Sit down and talk with your grandparents, aunts and uncles, etc. Or, if you live too far away to do this in person, write letters. Ask them to share their wisdom with you. What advice would they like to give you? What's the most important life lesson they have learned?

**HAVE A FAMILY PLANNING SESSION.** Sit down together and brainstorm goals for your family's future—next week, next month, next year, next five years, and so on.[2] Share and respect each other's wisdom. Decide together on five or ten goals you'd like to actively pursue. You might also ask your family to help you plan your personal goals.

**COLLECT WORDS OF WISDOM.** Search books of quotations, books by writers you admire, and so on for quotations that inspire you with their wisdom. Make posters, collages, or clay tablets inscribed with your words of wisdom. Hang them around your school, club, classroom, or home.

> *Variation:* Illustrate your words of wisdom with colorful cartoons and share them with younger kids.

**LOOK FOR THE WISDOM IN POPULAR SONGS** of the past. TIP: You might research folk songs, spirituals, patriotic songs, protest songs, etc.

> *Variation:* Look for the wisdom in popular songs of the present. Is there a songwriter or group that you feel is especially wise? Give reasons why you feel that way.

**PLAY A "WHO'S THE WISER?" GAME.** Divide your class or club into two teams and three judges. A judge reads one of the dilemmas presented below. (Or your group can create its own original dilemmas.) Each team has two minutes to come up with a wise solution to the dilemma—or, if a solution isn't possible, at least a way to make things better. The teams present their solutions/ideas to the three judges, and they have two minutes to decide which solution/idea was the wiser. The team with the wiser solution/idea gets two points. If the judges can't agree, or if the solutions/ideas really

do seem equal, then both teams get two points. Play for 10–15 minutes or as long as people are interested in playing. IMPORTANT: Keep the game light. Avoid arguments. If necessary, stop the game to debrief and discuss.

1.  You're the parent of two children who both want to take piano lessons. Your children are very competitive and jealous of each other.

2.  You sense that your mother is deeply troubled about something, but when you ask "What's wrong?" she says "Nothing."

3.  A group of kids in your neighborhood are pestering you to hang out with them. You don't trust them, you're even a little afraid of them, and you certainly don't want to hang out with them.

4.  You're a bus driver on a city route. Two of your passengers start arguing with each other, and suddenly one pulls a knife.

5.  You're the only doctor present in a hospital emergency room when two patients come in at the same time. One is a small child with head injuries from a bicycle accident; another is a doctor who's bleeding from injuries sustained in an automobile accident. Both require your immediate attention.

6.  You have a friend who doesn't get along with her family, and she decides to run away from home. She confides in you and asks you not to tell anyone.

7.  You deliver newspapers to a senior citizen in your neighborhood, and you often stop to talk with him. One day he tells you that his children—all adults—want him to sell his house and move into an apartment. He wants to make them happy, but he loves his home.

8.  You're walking to school one morning when you notice smoke coming out of a window of a house in your neighborhood. You know the people who live there—a family with three small children. The smoke is coming from an upstairs bedroom window.

9.  Two of your friends are always fighting with each other. You like them both, but you don't want to be caught in the middle. Now they're saying that you have to choose between them.

---

[2] See "Purpose," pages 195–197, for goal-setting steps.

**10.** You're a government diplomat, and you've just been asked to negotiate peace talks between two nations that have traditionally fought and distrusted each other.

**READ STORIES ABOUT WISDOM.** Look for these books:

📖 *The Boy Who Lost His Face* by Louis Sachar (New York: Alfred Knopf, 1997). When David helps his schoolmates attack an elderly woman, she puts a curse on him. With the help of new friends and a very nice girl, he learns that popularity isn't everything. Ages 10–13.

📖 *The Giver* by Lois Lowry (Boston: Houghton Mifflin, 1993). Given his lifetime assignment at the Ceremony of Twelve, Jonas becomes the receiver of memories shared by only one other in his community and discovers the terrible truth about the society in which he lives. Ages 12 & up.

📖 *The Midwife's Apprentice* by Karen Cushman (New York: Clarion, 1995). A nameless, homeless girl is taken in by a sharp-tempered midwife, and in spite of obstacles and hardship, she eventually gains the three things she wants most and learns just how wise she really is. Ages 12 & up.

📖 *Siddhartha* by Herman Hesse (New York: Fine Communications, 1994). This book tells the story of Siddhartha, the young Buddha, and his determination to reach nirvana, the ultimate state of enlightenment. Originally published in 1951. Ages 13 & up.

📖 *Winter Camp* by Kirkpatrick Hill (New York: Margaret McElderry Books, 1993). After the death of both their parents, a brother and sister move in with their neighbor Natasha, an old Athabascan Indian woman who believes that learning to work and live in the woods is as important as reading books and going to school. When winter comes and their skills are put to the test, they realize the wisdom of the "old ways." Ages 10 & up.

# Character in *ACTION*

## Elisha Williams: Young but Wise

Sixteen-year-old Elisha Williams clung to the tree trunk with shaking knees. He *would not* give up. He *would* climb this 50-foot tree, walk the thin line, and rappel down. "I have this thing about heights," Elisha explains, recalling the experience. "I used to be afraid of diving boards until I practiced and got over it. So I knew I could do this, too."

And he did. But there was another girl in his group who was terrified by the ropes course. Crying loudly, she backed down after climbing halfway up the tree. Elisha walked over to her and said "It's okay. There are some things we're so afraid to do that it might take someone else to help us through it. It doesn't make a difference how far you go, if you just try." She wiped her eyes and smiled at him gratefully.

Elisha believes that without struggle, progress isn't possible. And he knows what he's talking about, because his own life has been a struggle. When he was very young, he "grew up on the road" because his mother was a traveling preacher. It wasn't easy sleeping in a different bed almost every night. Then, when Elisha was in grade school, he and his mom finally settled in Columbia, Missouri. They had little money, but they refused to accept welfare. Elisha did his part to make sure that they could support themselves. He sold subscription cards for *Boys' Life*, shoveled snow, and did chores for people. When he was old enough to get a job, he bussed dishes at a restaurant and bagged groceries at a store. He shared his earnings with his mother.

Although Elisha's friends were kids who rode bikes, went fishing, and stayed out of trouble, there was violence elsewhere in their neighborhood. One day, Elisha was outside playing with his LEGOs when a man carrying a gun rushed past. He came so close that Elisha could have reached out and touched him. "Another kid got killed when he crossed an alley nearby," Elisha says. "I heard the shot."

Often, street fights happened outside his apartment building, and once a gang member was shot.

The next morning, Elisha found a bullet on the ground. He picked it up and kept it as a reminder.

"I've never tasted a drug or alcohol," he says, "and I've never been in a gang. I've never smoked and never had a moral problem. But I still try to be nice to other people who have. Maybe my example will rub off on them."

Elisha believes "You should accept yourself for who you are and never make excuses. Reading was hard for me when I was in first grade, so my mother pulled me out of school and taught me herself. I don't try to hide that. Instead, I tell people about it. Now I'm about to graduate from high school with a B average. I've accomplished something, and I want to keep doing my best in everything I can."

His nephew used to poke fun at him for being overweight, so Elisha confronted that problem, too. "I took better care of myself, watched what I ate, and started lifting weights." Today Elisha stands 6'2" tall and weighs 180 pounds. He tries to succeed at everything he does, but he's not afraid of failure. "If you give your best and it doesn't work out, you know that you tried, and you can learn from that."

He spends his free time speaking to young people at churches, and he encourages them to take risks and be themselves. "I tell them they don't have to play basketball to be great," he explains. "They can help other people, serve them, and teach them." He leads by example. He shovels snow for older neighbors in the winter, tutors younger kids, and plants trees for his community. During one summer, he volunteered at a day-care center every day.

"When I need encouragement, I talk to my mom or write in my diary," Elisha says. "I've been keeping a diary since I was fourteen. I write about how I feel about teen pregnancy, drugs, child abuse—things you see on TV and in the streets. I write about my plans for the next day. I like to be organized." He has a clear sense of what he wants from life and the future. "Happiness doesn't have to be money," he explains. "Struggling through problems, helping others deal with things, serving them, accepting yourself, leading others—that's happiness."

Elisha Williams

# Resources for Teachers and Parents

## Organizations, Programs, and Curricular Materials

**American Association of School Administrators**
801 North Quincy Street, Suite 700
Arlington, VA 22203-1730
(703) 528-0700
*www.aasa.org*
AASA published *Teaching Values and Ethics, Problems and Solutions: A Critical Issues Report* by Kristen J. Amundson, a major compilation of information. Also publishes a newsletter and journal.

**American Bar Association**
Division for Public Education
541 North Fairbanks Court, Fifteenth Floor
Chicago, IL 60611-3314
(312) 988-5735
*www.abanet.org/publiced*
Materials available from the ABA include articles, teaching strategies, and a student forum on character education.

**American Federation of Teachers**
555 New Jersey Avenue, NW
Washington, DC 20001
(202) 879-4400
*www.aft.org*
Provides strong leadership in support of character education; produces newspaper articles and other publications that support character education and include implemention suggestions.

**American Youth Foundation**
2331 Hampton Avenue
St. Louis, MO 63139
(314) 646-6000
*www.ayf.com*
Develops leadership capacities of young people; hosts camps, conferences, and "I Dare You" Leadership Awards; encourages positive character traits in youth.

**Association for Moral Education**
Department of Curriculum and Instruction
125 Peik Hall
159 Pillsbury Drive, SE
Minneapolis, MN 55455
(612) 625-6372
Conducts scholarly research into moral development and implementation of school programs; holds an annual conference.

**Association for Supervision and Curriculum Development (ASCD)**
1703 North Beauregard Street
Alexandria, VA 22311-1714
1-800-933-2723
*www.ascd.org*
Has publications available on moral education and character development; has established a Character Education Network. For information about the Network, contact Karen Bohlin at (617) 353-3262.

**Center for Civic Education**
5146 Douglas Fir Road
Calabasas, CA 91302-1467
(818) 591-9231
*www.civiced.org*
Fosters participation in civic life; offers programs in civic education for schools, materials, and leadership training. Publishes *CIVITAS: A Framework for Civic Education.*

**Center for the 4th and 5th Rs**
SUNY Cortland
PO Box 2000
Education Department
Cortland, NY 13045
(607) 753-2455
*www.cortland.edu/www/c4n5rs*
Encourages practicing and teaching respect and responsibility; serves as a resource in character education; publishes a newsletter; has a browsing library.

**Center for Learning**
21590 Center Ridge Road
Rocky River, OH 44116
1-800-767-9090
*www.centerforlearning.org*
Publishes values-based curriculum units authored by teachers; administers ASCD's Character Education Network.

**Character Counts Coalition**
Josephson Institute of Ethics
4640 Admiralty Way, Suite 1001
Marina del Rey, CA 90292-6601
(310) 306-1868
*www.charactercounts.org*
An alliance of over 100 nonprofit organizations dedicated to fortifying the character of America's youth with "Six Pillars of Character": trustworthiness, respect, responsibility, fairness, caring, and citizenship. Supplies educational materials for different age groups for use by teachers, parents, civic leaders, and youth leaders.

**Character Development Foundation**
PO Box 4782
Manchester, NH 03108-4782
(603) 472-3063
*www.charactered.org*
Promotes character development of children at home, in schools, and in communities with workshops and a speakers' bureau.

**Character Education Institute at California University**
250 University Avenue
California, PA 15419
(724) 938-1561
*www.cup.edu/education/charactered*
A resource center with books, periodicals, articles, character education teaching materials, and newsletters.

**Character Education Partnership**
1025 Connecticut Avenue, NW, Suite 1011
Washington, DC 20036
1-800-988-8081
*www.character.org*
A nonprofit partnership of approximately 500 groups. Maintains an excellent database of character education resources, provides an informative newsletter, and hosts an annual conference on character education.

**CHARACTERplus™**
Cooperating School Districts of Greater St. Louis
8225 Florissant Road
St. Louis, MO 63121
1-800-835-8282
*csd.org/staffdev/chared/characterplus.html*
CHARACTERplus is a school-business-community partnership that works to reduce "at-risk" behaviors (gang violence, absenteeism, teen pregnancy, etc.) and strengthen students' character, responsibility, and achievement. Schools provide a caring, supportive climate.

**The Communitarian Network**
2130 H Street, NW, Suite 703
Washington, DC 20052
(202) 994-7997
*www.gwu.edu/~ccps*
Advocates good citizenship and social responsibility. Publishes an online newsletter and frequent articles on character education.

**Community of Caring, Inc.**
1325 G Street, NW, Suite 500
Washington, DC 20005
(202) 393-1250
Provides well-developed educational materials for grades K–12 and excellent consulting. Endorsed by the National Association of Secondary School Principals. A project of the Joseph P. Kennedy, Jr. Foundation.

**Council of the Great City Schools**
1301 Pennsylvania Avenue, NW, Suite 702
Washington, DC 20004
*www.cgcs.org*
(202) 393-2427
Conducts studies of problems shared by urban schools and uses recommendations to improve education.

**Developmental Studies Center**
2000 Embarcadero, Suite 305
Oakland, CA 94606
(510) 533-0213
*www.devstu.org*
Established the Child Development Project to foster ethical, social, and intellectual development of children. Provides curricular materials and much more.

**Educators for Social Responsibility**
23 Garden Street
Cambridge, MA 02138
1-800-370-2515
*www.esrnational.org*
This professional association of educators who encourage civic involvement offers workshops, materials, research, and a library; publishes a journal.

**ERIC Clearinghouse on Reading, English and Communication**
Indiana University
Smith Research Center
2805 East 10th Street, Suite 140
Bloomington, IN 47408-2698
1-800-759-4723
*www.indiana.edu/~eric_rec*
One of 16 federally administered ERIC (Education Resource Information Center) clearinghouses. Provides a wide variety of free information (online resources, some printed materials, book lists, question-and-answer services, lesson plans) related to character education. Produces its own education materials which are available to teachers and parents.

**Ethics Resource Center**
1747 Pennsylvania Avenue, NW, Suite 400
Washington, DC 20006
(202) 737-2258
*www.ethics.org*
Provides a variety of character educational materials; has videos on developing character for different age groups; does consulting. (NOTE: As of this writing, ERC's Web site is maintained by Lockheed Martin.)

**The Giraffe Project**
PO Box 759
Langley, WA 98260
(360) 221-7989
*www.giraffe.org*
Finds, commends, and publicizes students and adults who "stick their necks out" for the common good; inspires citizens to make a difference. Has educational materials for grades K–12.

**Heartwood Institute**
425 North Craig Street, Suite 302
Pittsburgh, PA 15213
1-800-432-7810
*www.heartwoodethics.org*
Produces educational materials to support children's books about courage, loyalty, justice, respect, hope, honesty, and love. Mainly for elementary grades.

**The Institute for Global Ethics**
PO Box 563
Camden, ME 04843
(207) 236-6658
*www.globalethics.org*
Dedicated to elevating public awareness and promoting discussion of ethics in a global context. Provides ethics training, publications, consulting, and curricular materials for middle and high schools and other organizations.

**Jefferson Center for Character Education**
PO Box 4137
Mission Viejo, CA 92690-4137
(949) 770-7602
*www.jeffersoncenter.org*
Develops and provides curricula, programs, and publications that teach core values and ethical decision-making skills which foster good conduct, personal and civic responsibility, academic achievement, and workforce readiness; provides training for teachers and parents.

**Josephson Institute of Ethics**
4640 Admiralty Way, Suite 1001
Marina del Rey, CA 90292-6610
(310) 306-1868
*www.josephsoninstitute.org*
A membership organization that advocates ethical decision making by focusing on action and behavior. Provides training, seminars, publications, and educational materials on ethics and values. Established the Character Counts Coalition.

**Lions-Quest**
32 South Street, Suite 500
Baltimore, MD 21202
1-800-446-2700
*www.lions-quest.org*
Encourages family-school-community partnerships for youth development. Programs and materials focus on needs of elementary through high school to develop character, confidence competency, and cooperation. Works with Lions Club International.

**Live Wire Media**
273 Ninth Street
San Francisco, CA 94103
1-800-359-5437
*www.livewiremedia.com*
Produce videos on the *Power of Choice* for grades 1–12.

**National Association of Secondary School Principals**
1904 Association Drive
Reston, VA 22091-1537
(703) 860-0200
*www.nassp.org*
Developed an ethics program, *Ethical Decision-Making,* through partnership with community. Cooperates with the Joseph Kennedy, Jr. Foundation in supporting the Community of Caring model character education program.

**National Council for the Social Studies**
8555 Sixteenth Street
Silver Springs, MD 20910
1-800-683-0812
*www.ncss.org*
Offers resources for teachers on a variety of topics including civic ideals and practices.

**National Education Association**
1201 Sixteenth Street, NW
Washington, DC 20036
(202) 833-4000
*www.nea.org*
Provides a strong voice and encouragement for character education.

**National School Boards Association**
1680 Duke Street
Alexandria, VA 22314
(703) 838-6722
*www.nsba.org*
Has made character education a high priority in educational plans of their school districts; *The School Board Journal* has given prominent coverage to those that are implementing character education.

**National Youth Leadership Council**
1667 Snelling Avenue, N.
St. Paul, MN 55108
(651) 631-2955
*www.nylc.org*
Works to encourage youth leadership and service into schools; sponsors conferences, a magazine, books, videos, and a clearinghouse for service.

**People Wise Publications**
PO Box 80208
Rancho Santa Margarita, CA 92688
1-800-229-3455
Publishes Gene Bedley's *Values in Action,* a school-wide program for ages 4–13 encouraging Respect, Compassion, Integrity, Positive Mental Attitude, Cooperation, Initiative, and Perseverance.

**Phi Delta Kappa**
408 North Union
PO Box 789
Bloomington, IN 47402
1-800-766-1156
*www.pdkintl.org*
Publishes *Phi Delta Kappan,* including many articles on values; has character education titles in its "Fastback Series" of publications.

**Positive Action Company**
264 4th Avenue South
Twin Falls, ID 83301
1-800-345-2974
*www.positiveaction.net*
Produces the *Positive Action Family Kit* with lesson manual and activities that encourage positive character traits in youth. Also produces the Positive Action curriculum for schools.

**Search Institute**
Banks Building
615 First Avenue, NE, Suite 125
Minneapolis, MN 55413
1-800-888-7828
*www.search-institute.org*
Provides innovative educational materials, consulting, and connecting.

**Southern Poverty Law Center**
400 Washington Avenue
Montgomery, AL 36104
(334) 956-8200
*www.splcenter.org*
A national education project dedicated to helping teachers foster equity, respect, and understanding in the classroom and beyond. Its *Teaching Tolerance* magazine is available free to teachers; write on school letterhead.

**U.S. Department of Education**
400 Maryland Avenue, SW
Washington, DC 20202
*www.ed.gov*
1-800-872-5327
Offers listing of educational materials.

**WiseSkills Resources**
PO Box 491
Santa Cruz, CA 95061
1-888-947-3754
*www.wiseskills.com*
Publishes the *WISE SKILLS* multicultural character education materials for grades K–8; includes "wise skills, "wise quotes," "wise lives."

# Recommended Reading

Aristotle. *Nicomachean Ethics*, M. Oswald, trans. (Indianapolis: Liberal Arts Press, 1962).

Bennett, William J., *The Children's Book of Virtues* (New York: Simon & Schuster, 1995).

Benninga, Jacques. *Moral, Character and Civic Education in the Elementary School* (New York: Teachers College Press, 1991).

Borysenko, Joan, Ph.D., *Guilt Is the Teacher, Love Is the Lesson* (New York: Warner Books, 1990).

Carter, Stephen L., *Integrity* (New York: Basic Books, 1996).

Chopra, Deepak, *The Seven Spiritual Laws of Success* (San Rafael, CA: Amber-Allen Publishing, 1993).

Coles, Robert, *The Moral Life of Children* (Boston: Houghton Mifflin Company, 1986).

Damon, William, *The Moral Child: Nurturing Children's Natural Moral Growth* (New York: The Free Press, 1988).

Eyre, Linda, and Richard Eyre, *Teaching Your Children Values* (New York: Simon & Schuster, 1993).

Kilpatrick, William, *Why Johnny Can't Tell Right from Wrong* (New York: Simon & Schuster, 1992).

Lickona, Thomas, *Educating for Character: How Our Schools Can Teach Respect and Responsibility* (New York: Bantam Books, 1991).
_____ *Raising Good Children* (New York: Bantam Books, 1991).

Loren, Michael L., M.D., *The Road to Virtue: Resolutions for Daily Living* (New York: Avon, 1996).

Moorman, Chick, *Where the Heart Is: Stories of Home and Family* (Saginaw, MI: Personal Power Press, 1995).

Reimer, Joseph, Diana P. Paolitto, and Richard H. Hersh, *Promoting Moral Growth: From Piaget to Kohlberg* (3rd ed.) (Prospect Heights, IL: Waveland, 1983).

Reuben, Steven Carr, Ph.D., *Children of Character: A Parent's Guide* (Santa Monica, CA: Canter & Associates, Inc., 1997).

# Index

# Index to Web Sites

# About the Author

**B**arbara Lewis is a national award-winning author and educator who teaches kids how to think and solve real problems. Her students at Jackson Elementary School in Salt Lake City, Utah, have worked to clean up hazardous waste, improve sidewalks, plant thousands of trees, and fight crime. They have instigated and pushed through several laws in their state legislature and an amendment to a national law, garnering 10 national awards including two President's Environmental Youth Awards, the Arbor Day Award, the Renew America Award, and A Pledge and a Promise Environmental Award. They have also been recognized in the *Congressional Record* three times.

Barbara has been featured in many national newspapers, magazines, and news programs including *Newsweek, The Wall Street Journal, Family Circle,* "CBS This Morning," "CBS World News," and CNN. She has also written many articles and short stories for national magazines. Her other books for Free Spirit Publishing—*The Kid's Guide to Social Action, Kids with Courage,* and *The Kid's Guide to Service Projects*—have won *Parenting*'s Reading-Magic Award and been named "Best of the Best for Children" by the American Library Association, among other honors.

Barbara has lived in Indiana, New Jersey, Switzerland, and Belgium. She and her husband, Larry, are currently doing mission work in Poland. Their primary residence is in Park City, Utah. They have four children: Mike, Andrea, Chris, and Sam.

# Other Great Books from Free Spirit

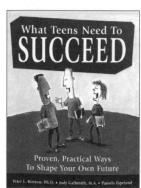